D0055572

FOR REFERENCE

Do Not Take From This Room

My Fellow Citizens

The Inaugural Addresses of the Presidents of the United States

1789–2009

MY FELLOW CITIZENS

THE INAUGURAL ADDRESSES OF THE PRESIDENTS OF THE UNITED STATES

1789–2009

WITH AN INTRODUCTION BY

ARTHUR M. SCHLESINGER, JR.

AND COMMENTARY BY

FRED L. ISRAEL

Facts On File
An imprint of Infobase Publishing

My Fellow Citizens:
The Inaugural Addresses of the Presidents of the United States
1789–2009

Originally published by Crown Publishers, Inc. © 1965
Copyright © 2010, 2007 Infobase Publishing

Facts On File, Inc.
An imprint of Infobase Publishing
132 West 31st Street
New York NY 10001

Library of Congress Cataloging-in-Publication Data

My fellow citizens : the inaugural addresses of the presidents of the United States, 1789–2009 / with an introduction by Arthur M. Schlesinger, Jr. and commentary by Fred L. Israel.
p. cm.
ISBN 978-0-8160-8253-7
1. Presidents—United States—Inaugural addresses
J81.4.M94 2010
352.23'860973—dc22   2009032184

Text design by Lina Farinella
Cover printed by Art Print, Taylor, PA
Book printed and bound by Dunn & Company, Clinton, MA
Date printed: January 2010
Printed in the United States of America

10 9 8 7 6 5 4 3 2 1

This book is printed on acid-free paper.

TABLE OF CONTENTS

INTRODUCTION

BY ARTHUR M. SCHLESINGER JR.

I do solemnly swear (or affirm) that I will faithfully execute the Office of President of the United States, and will, to the best of my Ability, preserve, protect, and defend the Constitution of the United States

—OATH AS PRESCRIBED IN THE CONSTITUTION,
ARTICLE II, SECTION 1

AMERICA HAS NO MORE solemn rite than the inauguration of a president. Every four years since 1789 the austere ceremony has suspended the passions of politics to permit an interlude of national reunion. "We have called by different names brethren of the same principle," said Jefferson after one of the angriest elections of our history. "We are all Republicans, we are all Federalists." Putting doubts and disagreements aside, the nation listens for a moment as one people to the words of the man they have chosen for the highest office in the land. And every president, as he takes the oath, has his opportunity to confide to his countrymen his philosophy of government, his conception of the presidency, and his vision of the future "to recall what our place in history has been," as Franklin Roosevelt said at his third inauguration (1941), "and to rediscover what we are and what we may be." Some have done this more arrestingly than others; but together the inaugural addresses offer an unusual panorama of American history.

George Washington delivered the first inaugural address from a balcony at Federal Hall on New York City's Wall Street; he gave the second indoors at Congress Hall in Philadelphia. The first inauguration to be held in Washington was Thomas Jefferson's in the Senate Chamber of the Capitol in 1801. Not until James Monroe's inauguration in 1817 did the ceremony in Washington take place outdoors. Thereafter, inaugurations were open to the public. Until recently, most presidents were inaugurated at the Capitol's East Portico; since Ronald Reagan in 1981, the ceremony has moved over to the West Portico.

James Madison, urged on by his vivacious wife, Dolley, held the first official inaugural ball in 1809. John Quincy Adams in 1825 was the first president to reject traditional breeches at his inauguration and wear long trousers. Martin Van Buren in 1837 was the first president actually born in the United States. James K. Polk's inauguration (1845) was the first to be reported by telegraph; James Buchanan's (1857), the first to be photographed; William McKinley's (1897), the first to be filmed; Calvin Coolidge's (1925), the first to be carried live on radio; Harry Truman's (1949), the first to be televised; Bill Clinton's (1997), the first to be put on the Internet. The long parade of inaugural addresses records the growth of the United States from the predominantly rural nation of 1789, made up of 4 million people in 13 states straggling along the Atlantic seaboard, into the mighty computerized society of today, with more than 300 million in 50 states stretching from sea to sea and thrusting into the Pacific and toward the Arctic Circle. The addresses record too the parallel transformation of a weak nation isolated on the periphery of world politics into the most powerful nation known to history, with interests and obligations everywhere on earth.

At the same time, these addresses reflect the tragic problems that growth and change have brought to the American community. The idyllic days when John Adams talked of our "national innocence," when Monroe spoke of "the happy Government under which we live," when Polk asked, "Who shall assign limits to the achievements of free minds and free hands under the protection of this glorious Union?" have given way to the somber apprehensions that have shadowed the inaugural pronouncements of the last generation. "Dark pictures and gloomy forebodings are worse than useless," said McKinley as late as 1901; but his successor, Theodore Roosevelt, could not escape the troubling proposition: "Never before have men tried so vast and formidable an experiment as that of administering the affairs of a continent under the form of a democratic republic." Power gave new perplexity to both domestic and foreign affairs. So the rise of industrialism throughout the nineteenth century brought grave problems in its wake. As early as 1889, Benjamin Harrison began to worry about "our great corporations," and four years later Cleveland described them as too often "conspiracies against the interest of the people." At the same time, Cleveland, warning against the "evils of paternalism," added, "While the people should patriotically and cheerfully support their Government, its functions do not include support of the people." But the new social questions could not be ignored. "Modern life," said Theodore Roosevelt, "is both complex and intense, and the tremendous changes wrought by the extraordinary industrial development of the last half century are felt in every fiber of our social and political being." By 1913, Wilson asked the nation to count the human cost of industrial growth, "the cost of lives snuffed out, of energies overtaxed and broken, the fearful physical and spiritual cost to the men and women and children upon whom the dead weight and burden of it all has fallen pitilessly the years through." Answering his question, Wilson demanded that government "be put at the service of humanity" in order to shield ordinary people "from the consequences of great industrial and social processes which they cannot alter, control, or singly cope with."

Our domestic policy has also confronted with rising intensity the problem of the absorption of ethnic minorities. The early presidents frequently recommended, in the ornate language of Madison, that the nation "carry on the benevolent plans which have so meritoriously applied to the conversion of our aboriginal neighbors from the degradation and wretchedness of savage life to a participation in the improvements of which the human mind and manners are susceptible in a civilized state"—a recommendation which, alas, had small effect on his countrymen's treatment of the Indians. After the Civil War, presidents betrayed concern about the mounting flow of immigrants. "There are men of all races," said Benjamin Harrison, "even the best, whose coming is necessarily a burden upon our public revenues or a threat to social order. These should be identified and excluded." Taft displayed special anxiety over "the admission of Asiatic immigrants who cannot be amalgamated with our population." But the idea of exclusion on ethnic grounds came into increasing conflict with the American conscience. Nor can modern America accept Taft's complacent message to Negro Americans that "it is not the disposition or within the province of the Federal Government to interfere with regulation by Southern States of their domestic affairs." Better the blunt language of Grant: The ex-slave "is not possessed of the civil rights which citizenship should carry with it. This is wrong, and should be corrected. To this correction I stand committed, so far as Executive influence can avail."

In foreign affairs our presidents can no longer, with Jefferson, reject "entangling alliances" or, with Monroe, congratulate the nation on the "peculiar felicity" that preserves us from the upheavals of the world outside. As the United States has grown, the planet has shrunk. "We have become a great nation," said Theodore Roosevelt, "forced by the fact of its greatness into relations with the other nations of the earth." "We are provincials no longer," said Wilson in 1917. "There can be no turning back." Even Calvin Coolidge, while hoping to resurrect the old isolationism, had to concede that "we cannot live to ourselves alone." Franklin Roosevelt proclaimed in 1945, after three testing years of war, "We have learned that we must live as men, not as ostriches, nor as dogs in the manger. We have learned to be citizens of the world, members of the human community." It was a bitter education. John F. Kennedy, reminding his fellow countrymen that "the graves of young Americans who answered the call to service surround the globe," spoke the hard wisdom of history in summoning the nation "to bear the burden of a long twilight struggle . . . against the common enemies of man: tyranny, poverty, disease and war itself."

These addresses, as they illuminate the national experience, also illuminate the presidency itself. No president ever took his accession to power lightly. Many followed Washington in remarking that "no event could have filled me with greater anxieties" (though none has been so querulous as Grant in complaining that he had been "the subject of abuse and slander scarcely ever equaled in political history"). The inaugural series displays the growing understanding that the presidency itself had to be the center of action in the American system. In 1841, William Henry Harrison could speak of "the impropriety of Executive interference in the legislation of Congress" and even regret that the Constitution had not made the secretary for the Treasury "entirely independent of the Executive." But the addresses of the twentieth century, except for the decade of the 1920s, nearly all assume, without bothering to argue the point, that active and purposeful leadership is the essence of the presidency.

It must be conceded that, even in the field of political oratory, the inaugural address is an inferior art form. It is rarely an occasion for original thought or stimulating reflection. The platitude quotient tends to be high, the rhetoric stately, the surprises few. It is astonishing to note how few truly memorable inaugural addesses there have been: certainly Washington's first, Jefferson's first, Lincoln's second, Franklin Roosevelt's first and Kennedy's; perhaps also Lincoln's first, Theodore Roosevelt's, Wilson's first, Franklin Roosevelt's second. The 2001 inaugural delivered by George W. Bush got a favorable review from a former Jimmy Carter speechwriter (Hendrik Hertzberg) who called it, persuasively, "by far the best Inaugural Address in forty years." Inagural addresses vary considerably among themselves. They differ in length—from 135 words of Washington's second to the 8,445 words of William Henry Harrison's (ironically the president who served the shortest term made the longest address). They differ in concept—from Taft's heavily programmatic discourse to the unimpeachable banalities of Eisenhower. They differ in policy—from FDR's second ("We have begun to bring private autocratic powers into their proper subordination to the public's government") to Ronald Reagan's first ("Government is not the solution to our problem; government is the problem").

Yet a great strand binds them together. Washington declared at the beginning of the republic, "The preservation of the sacred fire of liberty and the destiny of the republican model of government are justly considered, perhaps, as deeply, as finally, staked on the experiment entrusted to the hands of the American people." This is the recurrent theme. "Great is the stake placed in our hands," said Jackson, for the American experience "will be decisive in the opinion of mankind of the practicability of our federal system of government." Van Buren, having taken office at the end of the first half-century of the Constitution, reviewed the record of "our great experiment" and concluded that "America will present to every friend of mankind the cheering proof that a popular government, wisely formed, is wanting in no element of endurance or strength." "Upon the success of our experiment," said Theodore Roosevelt, "much depends, not only as regards our own welfare, but as regards the welfare of mankind. If we fail, the cause of free self-government throughout the world will rock to its foundations." "If we lose that sacred fire," said Franklin Roosevelt, ". . . then we shall reject the destiny which Washington strove so valiantly and so triumphantly to establish." The sacred fire has sometimes flickered and sputtered through more than two centuries of American independence. But it burns steadily on today, and "the glow from that fire," in the words of John F. Kennedy, "can truly light the world." The addresses in this volume suggest the resources of faith and of hope that will strengthen American presidents in the years to come as they confront the perils and possibilities of an uncertain future. And every president, in his most anxious hour, must respond to the magnanimity and resolve of Abraham Lincoln: "With malice toward none, with charity for all, with firmness in the right as God gives us to see the right, let us strive on to finish the work we are in . . . to do all which may achieve and cherish a just and lasting peace among ourselves and with all nations."

GEORGE WASHINGTON

FIRST INAUGURAL ADDRESS
IN THE CITY OF NEW YORK

APRIL 30, 1789

COMMENTARY

In 1789, a new era dawned for America. The inauguration of George Washington as first president of the United States also inaugurated a national republican government. Stretching from the Atlantic Ocean to the Mississippi River and from the Great Lakes to Spanish-held Florida, America possessed a territorial domain equal to all of western Europe plus the British Isles. The census of 1790 listed the population as just short of 4 million, which included some 700,000 slaves. Nine-tenths of these overwhelmingly rural people lived east of the Appalachians. Philadelphia, the largest city, had slightly more than 42,000 inhabitants, followed by New York with 33,000, and Boston's 18,000. Communications were poor and most Americans lived comparatively isolated lives. An express rider could cover the distance between New York and Boston in 96 hours, but it took from 8 to 10 days to do the trip by regular stagecoach. Traveling inland was even more difficult. Commercial supplies from Richmond took approximately one month to reach the western part of Virginia. Spread over a vast land mass, this heterogeneous, mobile population faced the major test of welding the individualistic states into an enduring federal republic. Many European observers doubted it could be done. Washington faced the tremendous task of launching the new government. Enormously moved by the warm confidence placed in him by the people, the modest president wrote the he foresaw only "an ocean of difficulties, without that competency of political skill, abilities, and inclination which are necessary to manage the helm . . . Integrity and firmness are all I can promise." On April 30, 1789, a festive crowd assembled before Federal Hall in New York to witness the inauguration. The chancellor of

1

New York State, Robert Livingston, administered the oath of office toward the people. He proclaimed in a loud voice, "Long live George Washington, the President of the United States." The crowd took up the cry and roared its approval as cannons boomed. Washington then entered the small Senate chamber, where, embarrassed, but solemn, he delivered the first inaugural address.

Fellow citizens of the Senate and of the House of Representatives:

Among the vicissitudes incident to life no event could have filled me with greater anxieties than that of which the notification was transmitted by your order, and received on the 14th day of the present month. On the one hand, I was summoned by my Country, whose voice I can never hear but with veneration and love, from a retreat which I had chosen with the fondest predilection, and, in my flattering hopes, with an immutable decision, as the asylum of my declining years; a retreat which was rendered every day more necessary as well as more dear to me by the addition of habit to inclination, and of frequent interruptions in my health to the gradual waste committed on it by time. On the other hand, the magnitude and difficulty of the trust to which the voice of my country called me, being sufficient to awaken in the wisest and most experienced of her citizens a distrustful scrutiny into his qualifications, could not but overwhelm with despondence one who, inheriting inferior endowments from nature and unpracticed in the duties of civil administration, ought to be peculiarly conscious of his own deficiencies. In this conflict of emotions all I dare aver is that it has been my faithful study to collect my duty from a just appreciation of every circumstance by which it might be affected. All I dare hope is that if, in executing this task, I have been too much swayed by a grateful remembrance of former instances, or by an affectionate sensibility to this transcendent proof of the confidence of my fellow citizens, and have thence too little consulted my incapacity as well as disinclination for the weighty and untried cares before me, my error will be palliated by the motives which mislead me, and its consequences be judged by my country with some share of the partiality in which they originated.

Such being the impressions under which I have, in obedience to the public summons, repaired to the present station, it would be peculiarly improper to omit in this first official act my fervent supplications to that Almighty Being who rules over the universe, who presides in the councils of nations, and whose providential aids can supply every human defect, that His benediction may consecrate to the liberties and happiness of the people of the United

States a Government instituted by themselves for these essential purposes, and may enable every instrument employed in its administration to execute with success the functions allotted to his charge. In tendering this homage to the Great Author of every public and private good, I assure myself that it expresses your sentiments not less than my own, nor those of my fellow citizens at large less than either. No people can be bound to acknowledge and adore the Invisible Hand which conducts the affairs of men more than those of the United States. Every step by which they have advanced to the character of an independent nation seems to have been distinguished by some token of providential agency; and in the important revolution just accomplished in the system of their united government the tranquil deliberations and voluntary consent of so many distinct communities from which the event has resulted can not be compared with the means by which most governments have been established without some return of pious gratitude, along with an humble anticipation of the future blessings which the past seem to presage. These reflections, arising out of the present crisis, have forced themselves too strongly on my mind to be suppressed. You will join with me, I trust, in thinking that there are none under the influence of which the proceedings of a new and free government can more auspiciously commence.

By the article establishing the executive department it is made the duty of the President, to recommend to your consideration such measures as he shall judge necessary and expedient. The circumstances under which I now meet you will acquit me from entering into that subject further than to refer to the great constitutional charter under which you are assembled, and which, in defining your powers, designates the objects to which your attention is to be given. It will be more consistent with those circumstances, and far more congenial with the feelings which actuate me, to substitute, in place of a recommendation of particular measures, the tribute that is due to the talents, the rectitude, and the patriotism which adorn the characters selected to devise and adopt them. In these honorable qualifications I behold the surest pledges that as on one side no local prejudices or attachments, no separate views nor party animosities, will misdirect the comprehensive and equal eye which ought to watch over this great assemblage of communities and interests, so, on another, that the foundation of our national policy will be laid in the pure and immutable principles of private morality, and the preeminence of free government be exemplified by all the attributes which can win the affections of its citizens and command the respect of the world. I dwell on this prospect with every satisfaction which an ardent love for my country can inspire, since there is no truth more thoroughly established than that there exists in the economy and course of nature an indissoluble union between virtue and happiness; between duty and advantage; between the genuine maxims of an honest and magnanimous policy and the solid rewards of public prosperity and felicity; since we ought to be no less persuaded that the propitious smiles of Heaven can never be expected on a nation that disregards the eternal rules of order and right which Heaven itself has ordained; and since the preservation of the sacred fire of liberty and the destiny of the republican model of government are justly considered, perhaps, as deeply, as finally, staked on the experiment entrusted to the hands of the American people. Besides the ordinary objects submitted to your care, it will remain with your judgment to decide how far an exercise of the occasional power delegated by the Fifth Article of the Constitution is rendered expedient at the present juncture by the nature of objections which have been urged against the system, or by the degree of inquietude which has given birth to them. Instead of undertaking particular recommendations on this subject, in which I could be guided by no lights derived from official opportunities, I shall again give way to my entire confidence in your discernment and pursuit of the public good; for I assure myself that whilst you carefully avoid every alteration which might endanger the benefits of an united and effective government, or which ought to await the future lessons of experience, a reverence for the characteristic rights of freemen and a regard for the public harmony will sufficiently influence your deliberations on the question how far the former can be impregnably fortified or the latter be safely and advantageously promoted.

To the foregoing observations I have one to add, which will be most properly addressed to the House of Representatives. It concerns myself, and will therefore be as brief as possible. When I was first honored with a call into the service of my country, then on the eve of an arduous struggle for its liberties, the light in which I contemplated my duty required that I should renounce every pecuniary compensation. From this resolution I have in no instance departed; and being still under the impressions which produced it, I must decline as inapplicable to myself any share in the personal emoluments which may be indispensably included in a permanent provision for the executive department, and must accordingly pray that the pecuniary estimates for the station in which I am placed may during my continuance in it be limited to such actual expenditures as the public good may be thought to require.

Having thus imparted to you my sentiments as they have been awakened by the occasion which brings us together, I shall take my present leave; but not without resorting once more to the benign Parent of the Human Race in humble supplication that, since He has been pleased to favor the American people with opportunities for deliberating in perfect tranquillity, and dispositions for deciding with unparalleled unanimity on a form of government for the security of their union and the advancement of their happiness, so His divine blessing may be equally conspicuous in the enlarged views, the temperate consultations, and the wise measures on which the success of this Government must depend.

—— SECOND INAUGURAL ADDRESS ——

MARCH 4, 1793

COMMENTARY

In 1792, Washington again received every electoral vote. There were no primaries, no conventions, no formal nominations, no national committees to manage a campaign. The Constitution merely states that "each State shall appoint, in such Manner as the Legislature thereof may direct, a Number of Electors, equal to the whole Number of Senators and Representatives to which that State may be entitled in Congress." In most states, the people did not vote, but instead the legislatures selected the electors. Everyone knew, though, that on the first Wednesday in December, the date prescribed by law, each elector would write the name of George Washington. On March 4, 1793, Washington delivered the shortest inaugural address in history—135 words.

Fellow citizens:

I am again called upon by the voice of my country to execute the functions of its Chief Magistrate. When the occasion proper for it shall arrive, I shall endeavor to express the high sense I entertain of this distinguished honor, and of the confidence which has been reposed in me by the people of united America. Previous to the execution of any official act of the President the Constitution requires an oath of office. This oath I am now about to take, and in your presence: That if it shall be found during my administration of the Government I have in any instance violated willingly or knowingly the injunctions thereof; I may, besides incurring constitutional punishment, be subject to the upbraidings of all who are now witnesses of the present solemn ceremony.

JOHN ADAMS

INAUGURAL ADDRESS
IN THE CITY OF PHILADELPHIA

MARCH 4, 1797

COMMENTARY

Washington limited himself to two presidential terms. After 20 years of almost continuous service to his country, climaxed by the successful launching of the new government, he eagerly sought retirement at Mount Vernon. The Constitution made no provision for political parties, and, in his Farewell Address, Washington warned against the "baneful effects of the Spirit of Party." Inevitably, though, public differences over foreign and domestic policies, as well as strong and ambitious leaders, caused political polarity to take shape and grow. By the early 1790s, supporters of Secretary of the Treasury Alexander Hamilton's national fiscal system, based upon a liberal interpretation of the Constitution, referred to themselves as Federalists. On the other hand, Thomas Jefferson's followers, Democratic Republicans or Republicans, opposed a strong centralized government, envisioning a nation of small farmers on constant guard against exploitation by urban capitalism. To Jefferson, the Constitution enumerated all jurisdiction belonging to the federal government and reserved all other authority to the states. Hamilton argued that a vast body of power had to be implied from the Constitution's general clauses. Washington accepted Hamilton's position, supporting his financial measures to strengthen the national government. In foreign affairs, the Federalists looked at the French Revolution with distrust while the Republicans thought the French had followed America's example. These combined differences reflected sectional and economic diversities prevalent in the Union, which was not yet firmly bound together. Fortunately, Washington, with his enormous prestige and national popularity, had led the nation for its first eight years.

The election of 1796 developed into a contested battle between the Feder-
alist and the Republicans. At this time, party machinery as we understand it
today had not evolved. Federalist members of Congress informally caucused and
nominated John Adams for the presidency and Thomas Pinckney for the vice
presidency. Jefferson led the Republicans, with Aaron Burr of New York named
for second place. But the Constitution was still construed according to the let-
ter, and the electoral college made the final decision. In 10 of the 16 states, the
legislature chose electors; the method varied in the other six. In Rhode Island, for
example, town meetings selected the state's four electors, while in Kentucky, four
special districts were created, each naming one elector. On the first Wednesday
in February 1797, the 138 ballots were counted in the presence of Congress. Each
elector had written two names; at this time, before the adoption of the Twelfth
Amendment, the name with the highest number of votes became president and
the runner-up vice president. John Adams received 71 votes and Thomas Jeffer-
son 68. These two, therefore, became president and vice president, respectively.

The simple inaugural ceremony occurred in the Senate chamber in Phila-
delphia, the temporary capital, on March 4, 1797. At the close of his address,
Adams started to leave the hall, but stepped back to give his predecessor the
honor of walking first. Washington declined, and went down the aisle following
the new chief executive.

When it was first perceived, in early times, that no middle course for America remained between unlimited submission to a foreign legislature and a
total independence of its claims, men of reflection were less apprehensive
of danger from the formidable power of fleets and armies they must determine to resist than from those contests and dissensions which would
certainly arise concerning the forms of government to be instituted over
the whole and over the parts of this extensive country. Relying, however,
on the purity of their intentions, the justice of their cause, and the integrity and intelligence of the people, under an overruling Providence which
had so signally protected this country from the first, the representatives of
this nation, then consisting of little more than half its present number, not
only broke to pieces the chains which were forging and the rod of iron that
was lifted up, but frankly cut asunder the ties which had bound them, and
launched into an ocean of uncertainty.

The zeal and ardor of the people during the Revolutionary war, supplying the place of government, commanded a degree of order sufficient at

least for the temporary preservation of society. The Confederation which was early felt to be necessary was prepared from the models of the Batavian and Helvetic confederacies, the only examples which remain with any detail and precision in history, and certainly the only ones which the people at large had ever considered. But reflecting on the striking difference in so many particulars between this country and those where a courier may go from the seat of government to the frontier in a single day, it was then certainly foreseen by some who assisted in Congress at the formation of it that it could not be durable.

Negligence of its regulations, inattention to its recommendations, if not disobedience to its authority, not only in individuals but in States, soon appeared with their melancholy consequences; universal languor, jealousies and rivalries of States, decline of navigation and commerce, discouragement of necessary manufactures, universal fall in the value of lands and their produce, contempt of public and private faith, loss of consideration and credit with foreign nations, and at length in discontents, animosities, combinations, partial conventions, and insurrection, threatening some great national calamity.

In this dangerous crisis the people of America were not abandoned by their usual good sense, presence of mind, resolution, or integrity. Measures were pursued to concert a plan to form a more perfect union, establish justice, insure domestic tranquillity, provide for the common defense, promote the general welfare, and secure the blessings of liberty. The public disquisitions, discussions, and deliberations issued in the present happy Constitution of Government.

Employed in the service of my country abroad during the whole course of these transactions, I first saw the Constitution of the United States in a foreign country. Irritated by no literary altercation, animated by no public debate, heated by no party animosity, I read it with great satisfaction, as the result of good heads prompted by good hearts, as an experiment better adapted to the genius, character, situation, and relations of this nation and country than any which had ever been proposed or suggested. In its general principles and great outlines it was conformable to such a system of government as I had ever most esteemed, and in some States, my own native State in particular, had contributed to establish. Claiming a right of suffrage, in common with my fellow-citizens, in the adoption or rejection of a constitution which was to rule me and my posterity, as well as them and theirs, I did not hesitate to express my approbation of it on all occasions, in public and in private. It was not then, nor has been since, any objection to it in my mind that the Executive and Senate were not more permanent. Nor have I ever entertained a thought of promoting any alteration in it but such as the people themselves, in the course of their experience, should see and feel to be necessary or expedient, and by their representatives in Congress and the State legislatures, according to the Constitution itself, adopt and ordain.

Returning to the bosom of my country after a painful separation from it for ten years, I had the honor to be elected to a station under the new order of things, and I have repeatedly laid myself under the most serious obligations to support the Constitution. The operation of it has equaled the most sanguine expectations of its friends, and from an habitual attention to it, satisfaction in its administration, and delight in its effects upon the peace, order, prosperity, and happiness of the nation I have acquired an habitual attachment to it and veneration for it.

What other form of government, indeed, can so well deserve our esteem and love?

There may be little solidity in an ancient idea that congregations of men into cities and nations are the most pleasing objects in the sight of superior intelligences, but this is very certain, that to a benevolent human mind there can be no spectacle presented by any nation more pleasing, more noble, majestic, or august, than an assembly like that which has so often been seen in this and the other Chamber of Congress, of a Government in which the Executive authority, as well as that of all the branches of the Legislature, are exercised by citizens selected at regular periods by their neighbors to make and execute laws for the general good. Can anything essential, anything more than mere ornament and decoration, be added to this by robes and diamonds? Can authority be more amiable and respectable when it descends from accidents or institutions established in remote antiquity than when it springs fresh from the hearts and judgments of an honest and enlightened people? For it is the people only that are represented. It is their power and majesty that is reflected, and only for their good, in every legitimate government, under whatever form it may appear. The existence of such a government as ours for any length of time is a full proof of a general dissemination of knowledge and virtue throughout the whole body of the people. And what object or consideration more pleasing than this can be presented to the human mind? If national pride is ever justifiable or excusable it is when it springs, not from power or riches, grandeur or glory, but from conviction of national innocence, information, and benevolence.

In the midst of these pleasing ideas we should be unfaithful to ourselves if we should ever lose sight of the danger to our liberties if anything partial or extraneous should infect the purity of our free, fair, virtuous, and independent elections. If an election is to be determined by a majority of a single vote, and that can be procured by a party through artifice or corruption, the Government may be the choice of a party for its own ends, not of the nation for the national good. If that solitary suffrage can be obtained by foreign nations by flattery or menaces, by fraud or violence, by terror, intrigue, or venality, the Government may not be the choice of the American people, but of foreign nations. It may be foreign nations who govern us, and not we, the people, who govern ourselves; and candid men will acknowledge that in such cases choice would have little advantage to boast of over lot or chance.

Such is the amiable and interesting system of government (and such are some of the abuses to which it may be exposed) which the people of America have exhibited to the admiration and anxiety of the wise and virtuous of all nations for eight years under the administration of a citizen who, by a long course of great actions, regulated by prudence, justice, temperance, and fortitude, conducting a people inspired with the same virtues and animated with the same ardent patriotism and love of liberty to independence and peace, to increasing wealth and unexampled prosperity, has merited the gratitude of his fellow-citizens, commanded the highest praises of foreign nations, and secured immortal glory with posterity.

In that retirement which is his voluntary choice may he long live to enjoy the delicious recollection of his services, the gratitude of mankind, the happy fruits of them to himself and the world, which are daily increasing, and that splendid prospect of the future fortunes of this country which is opening from year to year. His name may be still a rampart, and the knowledge that he lives a bulwark, against all open or secret enemies of his country's peace. This example has been recommended to the imitation of his successors by both Houses of Congress and by the voice of the legislatures and the people throughout the nation.

On this subject it might become me better to be silent or to speak with diffidence; but as something may be expected, the occasion, I hope, will be admitted as an apology if I venture to say that if a preference, upon principle, of a free republican government, formed upon long and serious reflection, after a diligent and impartial inquiry after truth; if an attachment to the Constitution of the United States, and a conscientious determination to support it until it shall be altered by the judgments and wishes of the

people, expressed in the mode prescribed in it; if a respectful attention to
the constitutions of the individual States and a constant caution and delicacy toward the State governments; if an equal and impartial regard to the
rights, interest, honor, and happiness of all the States in the Union, without
preference or regard to a northern or southern, an eastern or western, position, their various political opinions on unessential points or their personal
attachments; if a love of virtuous men of all parties and denominations; if
a love of science and letters and a wish to patronize every rational effort to
encourage schools, colleges, universities, academies, and every institution
for propagating knowledge, virtue, and religion among all classes of the
people, not only for their benign influence on the happiness of life in all its
stages and classes, and of society in all its forms, but as the only means of
preserving our Constitution from its natural enemies, the spirit of soph-
istry, the spirit of party, the spirit of intrigue, the profligacy of corruption,
and the pestilence of foreign influence, which is the angel of destruction
to elective governments; if a love of equal laws, of justice, and humanity
in the interior administration; if an inclination to improve agriculture,
commerce, and manufacturers for necessity, convenience, and defense; if
a spirit of equity and humanity toward the aboriginal nations of America,
and a disposition to meliorate their condition by inclining them to be more
friendly to us, and our citizens to be more friendly to them; if an inflexible
determination to maintain peace and inviolable faith with all nations, and
that system of neutrality and impartiality among the belligerent powers of
Europe which has been adopted by this Government and so solemnly sanctioned by both Houses of Congress and applauded by the legislatures of the
States and the public opinion, until it shall be otherwise ordained by Congress; if a personal esteem for the French nation, formed in a residence of
seven years chiefly among them, and a sincere desire to preserve the friendship which has been so much for the honor and interest of both nations; if,
while the conscious honor and integrity of the people of America and the
internal sentiment of their own power and energies must be preserved, an
earnest endeavor to investigate every just cause and remove every colorable
pretense of complaint; if an intention to pursue by amicable negotiation a
reparation for the injuries that have been committed on the commerce of
our fellow-citizens by whatever nation, and if success can not be obtained,
to lay the facts before the Legislature, that they may consider what further
measures the honor and interest of the Government and its constituents
demand; if a resolution to do justice as far as may depend upon me, at all

times and to all nations, and maintain peace, friendship, and benevolence with all the world; if an unshaken confidence in the honor, spirit, and resources of the American people, on which I have so often hazarded my all and never been deceived; if elevated ideas of the high destinies of this country and of my own duties toward it, founded on a knowledge of the moral principles and intellectual improvements of the people deeply engraven on my mind in early life, and not obscured but exalted by experience and age; and, with humble reverence, I feel it to be my duty to add, if a veneration for the religion of a people who profess and call themselves Christians, and a fixed resolution to consider a decent respect for Christianity among the best recommendations for the public service, can enable me in any degree to comply with your wishes, it shall be my strenuous endeavor that this sagacious injunction of the two Houses shall not be without effect.

With this great example before me, with the sense and spirit, the faith and honor, the duty and interest, of the same American people pledged to support the Constitution of the United States, I entertain no doubt of its continuance in all its energy, and my mind is prepared without hesitation to lay myself under the most solemn obligations to support it to the utmost of my power.

And may that Being who is supreme over all, the Patron of Order, the Fountain of Justice, and the Protector in all ages of the world of virtuous liberty, continue His blessing upon this nation and its Government and give it all possible success and duration consistent with the ends of His providence.

THOMAS JEFFERSON

FIRST INAUGURAL ADDRESS

MARCH 4, 1801

COMMENTARY

By 1800, the Federalists found themselves handicapped by factional strife. Many Southerners disliked the New England Adams, and intraparty rivalry had become intensely bitter. In foreign affairs, the Federalists divided over Adams's conciliatory French policy, which narrowly avoided war in spite of French seizures of American merchant ships. In this crisis, Adams thrust aside the advice of Hamilton, who favored war, and followed an independent course that promoted peace. The war scare, however, gave the Federalists an opportunity to strike against their Republican adversaries. In 1798, Congress passed a series of acts directed against the French and other foreigners allegedly influential in Jefferson's party. The most objectionable of these alien and sedition laws made it a crime to "write, print, utter or publish" any "false, scandalous and malicious" statements against the government. This clause, aimed at sniping Republican editors, was strictly enforced by Federalist judges. This was further evidence to Jefferson and his followers of a dangerous concentration of power by the national government. The alien and sedition laws, plus the Federalist handling of foreign affairs, became the main issues in the 1800 campaign.

Congressional party caucuses selected candidates for president and vice president—the Republicans chose Jefferson and Aaron Burr, and the Federalist chose Adams and Charles C. Pinckney. The bitter campaign that followed was waged through letter writing and newspaper articles. Each side masterfully mobilized its forces, marking the beginning of modern political elections. When the electoral ballots were counted, Jefferson and Burr each had 73 votes to Adams's 65 and Pinckney's 64. (One Rhode Island elector had declined to support Pinckney, but Republican discipline led to an embarrassing tie. The Twelfth Amendment, passed in 1804, eliminated comparable situations by providing that each elector must cast a separate ballot for president and vice president.) According to the Constitution, the House of Representatives, voting by state, now had to choose the president—either Jefferson or Burr. On the thirty-sixth ballot, Jefferson received the needed majority and was declared elected. Hamilton, who disliked Jefferson but feared Burr, had caused Federalist representatives from two equally divided states to cast blank ballots, thus allowing Jefferson's supporters to carry these states and the presidency.

It had long been popularly believed that at noon, March 4, 1801, Thomas Jefferson, unattended by a living soul, rode up the Capitol hill, tied his horse to the picket fence, entered the Senate chamber, and took the oath of office as the third president of the United States. Although this story is not true, it served for many generations to illustrate the inauguration of the "Man of the People." In reality, Jefferson, surrounded by a crowd and some militiamen, left his boarding-house and walked across the open space between it and the unfinished Capitol—the first president to take the oath in the new city of Washington. The ceremony was held in the small Senate chamber. Afterward, the president read his address in a low, almost inaudible, voice.

Friends and fellow citizens:

Called upon to undertake the duties of the first executive office of our country, I avail myself of the presence of that portion of my fellow citizens which is here assembled to express my grateful thanks for the favor with which they have been pleased to look toward me, to declare a sincere consciousness that the task is above my talents, and that I approach it with those anxious and awful presentiments which the greatness of the charge and the weakness of my powers so justly inspire. A rising nation, spread over a wide and fruitful land, traversing all the seas with the rich productions of their industry, engaged in commerce with nations who feel power and forget right, advancing rapidly to destinies beyond the reach of mortal eye; when I contemplate these transcendent objects, and see the honor, the happiness, and the hopes of this beloved country committed to the issue and the auspices of this day, I shrink from the contemplation, and humble myself before the magnitude of the undertaking. Utterly, indeed, should I despair did not the presence of many whom I here see remind me that in the other high authorities provided by our Constitution I shall find resources of wisdom, of virtue, and of zeal on which to rely under all difficulties. To you, then, gentlemen, who are charged with the sovereign functions of legislation, and to those associated with you, I look with encouragement for that guidance and support which may enable us to steer with safety the vessel in which we are all embarked amidst the conflicting elements of a troubled world.

During the contest of opinion through which we have passed the animation of discussions and of exertions has sometimes worn an aspect which might impose on strangers unused to think freely and to speak and to write what they think; but this being now decided by the voice of the nation, announced according to the rules of the Constitution, all will, of course, arrange themselves under the will of the law, and unite in common efforts for the common good. All, too, will bear in mind this sacred principle, that though the will of the majority is in all cases to prevail, that will to be rightful must be reasonable; that the minority possess their equal rights, which equal law must protect, and to violate would be oppression. Let us, then, fellow citizens, unite with one heart and one mind. Let us restore to social intercourse that harmony and affection without which liberty and even life itself are but dreary things. And let us reflect that, having banished from our land that religious intolerance under which mankind so long bled and suffered, we have yet gained little if we countenance a political intolerance as despotic, as wicked, and capable of as bitter and bloody persecutions. During the throes and convulsions of the ancient world, during the agonizing spasms of infuriated man, seeking through blood and slaughter his long-lost liberty, it was not wonderful that the agitation of the billows should reach even this distant and peaceful shore; that this should be more felt and feared by some and less by others, and should divide opinions as to measures of safety. But every difference of opinion is not a difference of principle. We have called by different names brethren of the same principle. We are all Republicans, we are all Federalists. If there be any among us who would wish to dissolve this Union or to change its republican form, let them stand undisturbed as monuments of the safety with which error of opinion may be tolerated where reason is left free to combat it. I know, indeed, that some honest men fear that a republican government can not be strong, that this Government is not strong enough; but would the honest patriot, in the full tide of successful experiment, abandon a government which has so far kept us free and firm on the theoretic and visionary fear that this Government, the world's best hope, may by possibility want energy to preserve itself? I trust not. I believe this, on the contrary, the strongest Government on earth. I believe it the only one where every man, at the call of the law, would fly to the standard of the law, and would meet invasions of the public order as his own personal concern. Sometimes it is said that man can not be trusted with the government of himself. Can he, then, be trusted with the government of others? Or have we found angels in the forms of kings to govern him? Let history answer this question.

Let us, then, with courage and confidence pursue our own Federal and Republican principles, our attachment to union and representative government. Kindly separated by nature and a wide ocean from the exterminating havoc of one quarter of the globe; too high-minded to endure the degradations of the others; possessing a chosen country, with room enough for our descendants to the thousandth and thousandth generation; entertaining a due sense of our equal right to the use of our own faculties, to the acquisitions of our own industry, to honor and confidence from our fellow citizens, resulting not from birth, but from our actions and their sense of them; enlightened by a benign religion, professed, indeed, and practiced in various forms, yet all of them inculcating honesty, truth, temperance, gratitude, and the love of man; acknowledging and adoring an overruling Providence, which by all its dispensations proves that it delights in the happiness of man here and his greater happiness hereafter; with all these blessings, what more is necessary to make us a happy and a prosperous people? Still one thing more, fellow citizens; a wise and frugal Government, which shall restrain men from injuring one another, shall leave them otherwise free to regulate their own pursuits of industry and improvement, and shall not take from the mouth of labor the bread it has earned. This is the sum of good government, and this is necessary to close the circle of our felicities.

About to enter, fellow citizens, on the exercise of duties which comprehend everything dear and valuable to you, it is proper you should understand what I deem the essential principles of our Government, and consequently those which ought to shape its Administration. I will compress them within the narrowest compass they will bear, stating the general principle, but not all its limitations. Equal and exact justice to all men, of whatever state or persuasion, religious or political; peace, commerce, and honest friendship with all nations, entangling alliances with none; the support of the State governments in all their rights, as the most competent administrations for our domestic concerns and the surest bulwarks against antirepublican tendencies; the preservation of the General Government in its whole constitutional vigor, as the sheet anchor of our peace at home and safety abroad; a jealous care of the right of election by the people; a mild and safe corrective of abuses which are lopped by the sword of revolution where peaceable remedies are unprovided; absolute acquiescence in the decisions of the majority, the vital principle of republics, from which is no appeal but to force, the vital principle and immediate parent of despotism; a well-disciplined militia, our best reliance in peace and for the first moments of war till regulars may relieve them; the supremacy of the civil over the military authority; economy in the public expense, that labor may be lightly burthened; the honest payment of our debts and sacred preservation of the public faith; encouragement of agriculture, and of commerce as its handmaid; the diffusion of information and arraignment of all abuses at the bar of the public reason; freedom of religion; freedom of the press, and freedom of person under the protection of the habeas corpus, and trial by juries impartially selected. These principles form the bright constellation which has gone before us and guided our steps through an age of revolution and reformation. The wisdom of our sages and blood of our heroes have been devoted to their attainment. They should be the creed of our political faith, the text of civic instruction, the touchstone by which to try the services of those we trust; and should we wander from them in moments of error or of alarm, let us hasten to retrace our steps and to regain the road which alone leads to peace, liberty, and safety.

I repair, then, fellow citizens, to the post you have assigned me. With experience enough in subordinate offices to have seen the difficulties of this the greatest of all, I have learnt to expect that it will rarely fall to the lot of imperfect man to retire from this station with the reputation and the favor which bring him into it. Without pretensions to that high confidence you reposed in our first and greatest revolutionary character, whose preeminent services had entitled him to the first place in his country's love and destined for him the fairest page in the volume of faithful history, I ask so much confidence only as may give firmness and effect to the legal administration of your affairs. I shall often go wrong through defect of judgment. When right, I shall often be thought wrong by those whose positions will not command a view of the whole ground. I ask your indulgence for my own errors, which will never be intentional, and your support against the errors of others, who may condemn what they would not if seen in all its parts. The approbation implied by your suffrage is a great consolation to me for the past, and my future solicitude will be to retain the good opinion of those who have bestowed it in advance, to conciliate that of others by doing them all the good in my power, and to be instrumental to the happiness and freedom of all.

Relying, then, on the patronage of your good will, I advance with obedience to the work, ready to retire from it whenever you become sensible how much better choice it is in your power to make. And may that Infinite Power which rules the destinies of the universe lead our councils to what is best, and give them a favorable issue for your peace and prosperity.

——— SECOND INAUGURAL ADDRESS ———

MARCH 4, 1805

COMMENTARY

Jefferson's first administration won the approval of the nation and brought him to the height of his popularity. The major policies of Washington and Adams had not been upset; a social revolution had not occurred. In the election of 1804, the Federalist candidate, C.C. Pinckney, hard-pressed for a suitable issue, received 14 electoral votes to Jefferson's 162. Only Connecticut and Delaware remained solid in their opposition. With the exception of Washington and Monroe, no president ever received a more decisive electoral endorsement.

In his second inaugural address, Jefferson modestly devoted only one paragraph to the Louisiana Purchase. Without a doubt, though, this acquisition was his greatest triumph and one of the most fortunate events in American history. Napoleon had acquired the vast territory from France's ally Spain, and here he planned to establish a new empire in the Western Hemisphere. Americans shuddered with apprehension. New Orleans was an indispensable port for the shipment of products grown in the Ohio Valley. If a strong power occupied the city, would the mouth of the Mississippi River forever be closed to American commerce? "There is on the globe one single spot, the possessor of which is our natural and habitual enemy," wrote Jefferson to Robert Livingston, the American minister to France. "It is New Orleans, through which the produce of three-eighths of our territory must pass to market." Jefferson's fears seemed confirmed when the Spanish in 1802, still in authority, suspended the "right of deposit." The president now sent James Monroe to Paris; together with Livingston, he had instructions to purchase the city of New Orleans. To their complete surprise, Napoleon offered the whole province. For 80 million francs, *or about $15 million, the United States obtained some 828,000 square miles lying between the Mississippi River and the Rocky Mountains, certainly the greatest real estate bargain in history. An exuberant Livingston announced: "We have lived long, but this is the noblest work of our whole lives.... From this day the United States take their place among the powers of the first rank.... The instruments which we have just signed will cause no tears to be shed: they prepare ages of happiness for innumerable generations of human creatures."*

The news of the great purchase came as a shock to the perplexed Jefferson since Livingston and Monroe had exceeded their instructions. For years, Jefferson and his supporters had repeatedly denounced the Federalists for their broad interpretation of the Constitution. Yet here was an opportunity to double the size of the nation. Did the president have the authority to purchase foreign territory? The flexible Jefferson now broadly construed his treaty-making power and approved the sale. "If our friends think differently, certainly I shall acquiesce with satisfaction." On December 20, 1803, the United States formally took possession of Louisiana.

On March 4, 1805, Jefferson, accompanied by several militia units and scores of admiring citizens, walked to the Capitol and took his second oath. The president read his inaugural address "in so low a voice," recorded John Quincy Adams, "that not half of it was heard by any part of the crowded auditory." In comparing his first inaugural dddress with the second, Jefferson commented in his draft notes: "The former one was an exposition of the principles on which I thought it my duty to administer the government. The second then should naturally be a conte rendue, or a statement of facts, showing that I have conformed to those principles. The former was promise: this is performance."

Proceeding, fellow citizens, to that qualification which the Constitution requires, before my entrance on the charge again conferred upon me, it is my duty to express the deep sense I entertain of this new proof of confidence from my fellow citizens at large, and the zeal with which it inspires me, so to conduct myself as may best satisfy their just expectations.

On taking this station on a former occasion, I declared the principles on which I believed it my duty to administer the affairs of our commonwealth. My conscience tells me that I have, on every occasion, acted up to that declaration, according to its obvious import, and to the understanding of every candid mind.

In the transaction of your foreign affairs, we have endeavored to cultivate the friendship of all nations, and especially of those with which we have the most important relations. We have done them justice on all occasions, favored where favor was lawful, and cherished mutual interests and intercourse on fair and equal terms. We are firmly convinced, and we act on that conviction, that with nations, as with individuals, our interests soundly calculated, will ever be found inseparable from our moral duties; and history bears witness to the fact, that a just nation is taken on its word, when recourse is had to armaments and wars to bridle others.

At home, fellow citizens, you best know whether we have done well or ill. The suppression of unnecessary offices, of useless establishments and expenses, enabled us to discontinue our internal taxes. These covering our land with officers, and opening our doors to their intrusions, had already begun that process of domiciliary vexation which, once entered, is scarcely to be restrained from reaching successively every article of produce and property. If among these taxes some minor ones fell which had not been inconvenient, it was because their amount would not have paid the officers who collected them, and because, if they had any merit, the state authorities might adopt them, instead of others less approved.

The remaining revenue on the consumption of foreign articles, is paid cheerfully by those who can afford to add foreign luxuries to domestic comforts, being collected on our seaboards and frontiers only, and incorporated with the transactions of our mercantile citizens, it may be the pleasure and pride of an American to ask, what farmer, what mechanic, what laborer, ever sees a tax-gatherer of the United States? These contributions enable us to support the current expenses of the government, to fulfil contracts with foreign nations, to extinguish the native right of soil within our limits, to extend those limits, and to apply such a surplus to our public debts, as places at a short day their final redemption, and that redemption once effected, the revenue thereby liberated may, by a just repartition among the states, and a corresponding amendment of the constitution, be applied, in time of peace, to rivers, canals, roads, arts, manufactures, education, and other great objects within each state. In time of war, if injustice, by ourselves or others, must sometimes produce war, increased as the same revenue will be increased by population and consumption, and aided by other resources reserved for that crisis, it may meet within the year all the expenses of the year, without encroaching on the rights of future generations, by burdening them with the debts of the past. War will then be but a suspension of useful works, and a return to a state of peace, a return to the progress of improvement.

I have said, fellow citizens, that the income reserved had enabled us to extend our limits; but that extension may possibly pay for itself before we are called on, and in the meantime, may keep down the accruing interest; in all events, it will repay the advances we have made. I know that the acquisition of Louisiana has been disapproved by some, from a candid apprehension that the enlargement of our territory would endanger its union. But who can limit the extent to which the federative principle may operate effectively? The larger our association, the less will it be shaken by local passions; and in any view, is it not better that the opposite bank of the Mississippi should be settled by our own brethren and children, than by strangers of another family? With which shall we be most likely to live in harmony and friendly intercourse?

In matters of religion, I have considered that its free exercise is placed by the constitution independent of the powers of the general government. I have therefore undertaken, on no occasion, to prescribe the religious exercises suited to it; but have left them, as the constitution found them, under the direction and discipline of state or church authorities acknowledged by the several religious societies.

The aboriginal inhabitants of these countries I have regarded with the commiseration their history inspires. Endowed with the faculties and the rights of men, breathing an ardent love of liberty and independence, and occupying a country which left them no desire but to be undisturbed, the stream of overflowing population from other regions directed itself on these shores; without power to divert, or habits to contend against, they have been overwhelmed by the current, or driven before it; now reduced within limits too narrow for the hunter's state, humanity enjoins us to teach them agriculture and the domestic arts; to encourage them to that industry which alone can enable them to maintain their place in existence, and to prepare them in time for that state of society, which to bodily comforts adds the improvement of the mind and morals. We have therefore liberally furnished them with the implements of husbandry and household use; we have placed among them instructors in the arts of first necessity; and they are covered with the aegis of the law against aggressors from among ourselves.

But the endeavors to enlighten them on the fate which awaits their present course of life, to induce them to exercise their reason, follow its dictates, and change their pursuits with the change of circumstances, have powerful obstacles to encounter; they are combated by the habits of their bodies, prejudice of their minds, ignorance, pride, and the influence of interested and crafty individuals among them, who feel themselves something in the present order of things, and fear to become nothing in any other. These persons inculcate a sanctimonious reverence for the customs of their ancestors; that whatsoever they did, must be done through all time; that reason is a false guide, and to advance under its counsel, in their physical, moral, or political condition, is perilous innovation; that their duty is to remain as their Creator made them, ignorance being safety, and knowledge full of danger; in short, my friends, among them is seen the action and counteraction of good sense and bigotry; they, too, have their anti-philosophers, who find an interest in keeping things in their present state, who dread reformation, and exert all their faculties to maintain the ascendency of habit over the duty of improving our reason, and obeying its mandates.

In giving these outlines, I do not mean, fellow citizens, to arrogate to myself the merit of the measures; that is due, in the first place, to the reflecting character of our citizens at large, who, by the weight of public opinion, influence and strengthen the public measures; it is due to the sound discretion with which they select from among themselves those to whom they confide the legislative duties; it is due to the zeal and wisdom of the characters thus selected, who lay the foundations of public happiness in wholesome laws, the execution of which alone remains for others; and it is due to the able and faithful auxiliaries, whose patriotism has associated with me in the executive functions.

During this course of administration, and in order to disturb it, the artillery of the press has been levelled against us, charged with whatsoever its licentiousness could devise or dare. These abuses of an institution so important to freedom and science, are deeply to be regretted, inasmuch as they tend to lessen its usefulness, and to sap its safety; they might, indeed, have been corrected by the wholesome punishments reserved and provided by the laws of the several States against falsehood and defamation; but public duties more urgent press on the time of public servants, and the offenders have therefore been left to find their punishment in the public indignation.

Nor was it uninteresting to the world, that an experiment should be fairly and fully made, whether freedom of discussion, unaided by power, is not sufficient for the propagation and protection of truth; whether a government, conducting itself in the true spirit of its constitution, with zeal and purity, and doing no act which it would be unwilling the whole world should witness, can be written down by falsehood and defamation. The experiment has been tried; you have witnessed the scene; our fellow citizens have looked on, cool and collected; they saw the latent source from which these outrages proceeded; they gathered around their public functionaries, and when the constitution called them to the decision by suffrage, they pronounced their verdict, honorable to those who had served them, and consolatory to the friend of man, who believes he may be intrusted with his own affairs.

No inference is here intended, that the laws, provided by the State against false and defamatory publications, should not be enforced; he who has time, renders a service to public morals and public tranquillity, in reforming these abuses by the salutary coercions of the law; but the experiment is noted, to prove that, since truth and reason have maintained their ground against false opinions in league with false facts, the press, confined to truth, needs no other legal restraint; the public judgment will correct false reasonings and opinions, on a full hearing of all parties; and no other definite line can be drawn between the inestimable liberty of the press and its demoralizing licentiousness. If there be still improprieties which this rule would not restrain, its supplement must be sought in the censorship of public opinion.

Contemplating the union of sentiment now manifested so generally, as auguring harmony and happiness to our future course, I offer to our country sincere congratulations. With those, too, not yet rallied to the same point, the disposition to do so is gaining strength; facts are piercing through the veil drawn over them; and our doubting brethren will at length see, that the mass of their fellow citizens, with whom they cannot yet resolve to act, as to principles and measures, think as they think, and desire what they desire; that our wish, as well as theirs, is, that the public efforts may be directed honestly to the public good, that peace be cultivated, civil and religious liberty unassailed, law and order preserved; equality of rights maintained, and that state of property, equal or unequal, which results to every man from his own industry, or that of his fathers. When satisfied of these views, it is not in human nature that they should not approve and support them; in the meantime, let us cherish them with patient affection; let us do them justice, and more than justice, in all competitions of interest; and we need not doubt that truth, reason, and their own interests, will at length prevail, will gather them into the fold of their country, and will complete their entire union of opinion, which gives to a nation the blessing of harmony, and the benefit of all its strength.

I shall now enter on the duties to which my fellow citizens have again called me, and shall proceed in the spirit of those principles which they have approved. I fear not that any motives of interest may lead me astray; I am sensible of no passion which could seduce me knowingly from the path of justice; but the weakness of human nature, and the limits of my own understanding, will produce errors of judgment sometimes injurious to your interests. I shall need, therefore, all the indulgence I have heretofore experienced; the want of it will certainly not lessen with increasing years. I shall need, too, the favor of that Being in whose hands we are, who led our forefathers, as Israel of old, from their native land, and planted them in a country flowing with all the necessaries and comforts of life; who has covered our infancy with his providence, and our riper years with his wisdom and power; and to whose goodness I ask you to join with me in supplications, that he will so enlighten the minds of your servants, guide their councils, and prosper their measures, that whatsoever they do, shall result in your good, and shall secure to you the peace, friendship, and approbation of all nations.

JAMES MADISON

FIRST INAUGURAL ADDRESS

MARCH 4, 1809

COMMENTARY

The renewed Napoleonic Wars became the most serious problem for Jefferson's second administration. Although the young nation followed Washington's advice to avoid entanglement with foreign countries, British and French seizures of American merchant ships and the impressment of sailors threatened to disrupt the peace. The war in Europe caught the United States in the middle—the British blockaded Napoleon's empire and he retaliated with the Berlin and Milan decrees prohibiting neutrals from trading with England. Each combatant determined to use power to prevent its opponent from benefiting from American trade. Diplomatic attempts to ease these commercial restrictions failed.

Confronted with a drastic sailor shortage, arrogant British commanders boarded American ships and removed numbers of men, whom they arbitrarily accused of desertion. An English officer, refusing to recognize a naturalized American, regarded as British, for example, any sailor who said "paise" for "peas." This abominable practice caused citizens by the hundreds to be impressed into British service, from which there was no release except by death or the cessation of the conflict. The most humiliating outrage occurred on June 22, 1807, when the British warship Leopard *stopped the U.S. frigate* Chesapeake *off the Virginia coast and demanded the surrender of alleged deserters. When Captain James Barrow refused to muster his crew for inspection, the* Leopard *fired at point-blank range, killing three and wounding 18 American seamen.*

An incensed nation clamored for war. Jefferson wrote in August 1807 that he never envisioned helping Napoleon but "the English being equally tyrannical at sea as he is on land and that tyranny bearing on us in every point of either *honor or interest, I say 'Down with England' and as for what Bonaparte is then to do with us, let us trust to the chapter of accidents." Before going to war, however, the president decided to try commercial pressure. On December 22, 1807, Congress passed the Embargo Act, prohibiting foreign commerce. Jefferson calculated that war-causing incidents would stop and, in addition, hundreds of thousands of British laborers would be thrown out of work as foreign importation halted. This, he felt, would cause England to reevaluate the policies of seizure and impressment. But within one year, this unilateral attempt to secure a peaceful redress of grievances created an economic depression in the United States. The commercial counties of New England talked of secession, damning Jefferson and his embargo. Annual exports fell from $108 million to $22 million. Business failed. Shipbuilding stopped. Wheat plunged from $2.00 per bushel to seventy-five cents. Tobacco glutted the idle wharves. On March 1, 1809, three days before the end of his term, Jefferson signed the congressional resolution repealing his attempt at economic coercion. "The embargo act," admitted the president, "is certainly the most embarrassing we ever had to execute."*

The election of 1808 occurred while the embargo remained in force. Jefferson, determined to retire, selected Secretary of State James Madison as his successor. Charles C. Pickney again received the nomination of the Federalist congressional caucus. Hoping to win back many supporters who had left the party four years earlier, the revived Federalists emphasized the unpleasant features of the embargo, accusing Jefferson of truckling to Napoleon. Most of the state legislatures still chose presidential electors, but by the terms of the Twelfth Amendment, now in effect, each elector cast a separate ballot for president and vice president. Pinckney received only 47 votes to Madison's 122. Despite the growing dissatisfaction with the embargo, Jefferson's Republicans again triumphed.

Chief Justice John Marshall administered the oath of office to Madison on March 4, 1809, in the new House chambers. In delivering his inaugural, one observer noted Madison appeared "extremely pale and trembled excessively when he first began to speak but soon gained confidence and spoke audibly." After the ceremonies, the president returned to his home on F Street, near the Treasury, and lived there until Jefferson left for Monticello the following week.

Unwilling to depart from examples of the most revered authority, I avail myself of the occasion now presented to express the profound impression made on me by the call of my country to the station to the duties of which I am about to pledge myself by the most solemn of sanctions. So distinguished a mark of confidence, proceeding from the deliberate and tranquil suffrage of a free and virtuous nation, would under any circumstances have commanded my gratitude and devotion, as well as filled me with an awful sense of the trust to be assumed. Under the various circumstances which give peculiar solemnity to the existing period, I feel that both the honor and the responsibility allotted to me are inexpressibly enhanced.

The present situation of the world is indeed without a parallel and that of our own country full of difficulties. The pressure of these, too, is the more severely felt because they have fallen upon us at a moment when the national prosperity being at a height not before attained, the contrast resulting from the change has been rendered the more striking. Under the benign influence of our republican institutions, and the maintenance of peace with all nations whilst so many of them were engaged in bloody and wasteful wars, the fruits of a just policy were enjoyed in an unrivaled growth of our faculties and resources. Proofs of this were seen in the improvements of agriculture, in the successful enterprises of commerce, in the progress of manufacturers and useful arts, in the increase of the public revenue and the use made of it in reducing the public debt, and in the valuable works and establishments everywhere multiplying over the face of our land.

It is a precious reflection that the transition from this prosperous condition of our country to the scene which has for some time been distressing us is not chargeable on any unwarrantable views, nor, as I trust, on any involuntary errors in the public councils. Indulging no passions which trespass on the rights or the repose of other nations, it has been the true glory of the United States to cultivate peace by observing justice, and to entitle themselves to the respect of the nations at war by fulfilling their neutral obligations with the most scrupulous impartiality. If there be candor in the world, the truth of these assertions will not be questioned; posterity at least will do justice to them.

This unexceptionable course could not avail against the injustice and violence of the belligerent powers. In their rage against each other, or impelled by more direct motives, principles of retaliation have been introduced equally contrary to universal reason and acknowledged law. How long their arbitrary edicts will be continued in spite of the demonstrations that not even a pretext for them has been given by the United States, and of the fair and liberal attempt to induce a revocation of them, can not be anticipated. Assuring myself that under every vicissitude the determined spirit and united councils of the nation will be safeguards to its honor and its essential interests, I repair to the post assigned me with no other discouragement than what springs from my own inadequacy to its high duties. If I do not sink under the weight of this deep conviction it is because I find some support in a consciousness of the purposes and a confidence in the principles which I bring with me into this arduous service.

To cherish peace and friendly intercourse with all nations having correspondent dispositions; to maintain sincere neutrality toward belligerent nations; to prefer in all cases amicable discussion and reasonable accommodation of differences to a decision of them by an appeal to arms; to exclude foreign intrigues and foreign partialities, so degrading to all countries and so baneful to free ones; to foster a spirit of independence too just to invade the rights of others, too proud to surrender our own, too liberal to indulge unworthy prejudices ourselves and too elevated not to look down upon them in others; to hold the union of the States as the basis of their peace and happiness; to support the Constitution, which is the cement of the Union, as well in its limitations as in its authorities; to respect the rights and authorities reserved to the States and to the people as equally incorporated with and essential to the success of the general system; to avoid the slightest interference with the right of conscience or the functions of religion, so wisely exempted from civil jurisdiction; to preserve in their full energy the other salutary provisions in behalf of private and personal rights, and of the freedom of the press; to observe economy in public expenditures; to liberate the public resources by an honorable discharge of the public debts; to keep within the requisite limits a standing military force, always remembering that an armed and trained militia is the firmest bulwark of republics; that without standing armies their liberty can never be in danger, nor with large ones safe; to promote by authorized means improvements friendly to agriculture, to manufactures, and to external as well as internal commerce; to favor in like manner the advancement of science and the diffusion of information as the best aliment to true liberty; to carry on the benevolent plans which have been so meritoriously applied to the conversion of our aboriginal neighbors from the degradation and wretchedness of savage life to a participation of the improvements of which the human mind and manners are susceptible in a civilized state as far as sentiments and intentions such as these can aid the fulfillment of my duty, they will be a resource which can not fail me.

It is my good fortune, moreover, to have the path in which I am to tread lighted by examples of illustrious services successfully rendered in the most trying difficulties by those who have marched before me. Of those of my immediate predecessor it might least become me here to speak. I may, however, be pardoned for not suppressing the sympathy with which my heart is full in the rich reward he enjoys in the benedictions of a beloved country, gratefully bestowed or exalted talents zealously devoted through a long career to the advancement of its highest interest and happiness.

But the source to which I look or the aids which alone can supply my deficiencies is in the well-tried intelligence and virtue of my fellow-citizens, and in the counsels of those representing them in the other departments associated in the care of the national interests. In these my confidence will under every difficulty be best placed, next to that which we have all been encouraged to feel in the guardianship and guidance of that Almighty Being whose power regulates the destiny of nations, whose blessings have been so conspicuously dispensed to this rising Republic, and to whom we are bound to address our devout gratitude for the past, as well as our fervent supplications and best hopes for the future.

———— SECOND INAUGURAL ADDRESS ————

MARCH 4, 1813

COMMENTARY

On June 1, 1812, Madison recommended a declaration of war against Great Britain. The causes of the War of 1812, like those of most wars, appear varied and complex. In his message to Congress, the president cited the impressment of seamen and the repeated violation of neutral rights as major causes. In addition, spokesmen for the West held England responsible for encouraging Indian attacks by supplying them with powder and guns. "They will no longer have an opportunity of intriguing with our Indian neighbors, and setting on the ruthless savage to tomahawk our women and children," claimed Congressman Felix Grundy of Tennessee, an early proponent of war. Also, land-hungry Westerners coveted the fertile plains of Canada. Henry Clay, the young Speaker of the House of Representatives, boasted that the Kentucky militia alone could capture Montreal and Quebec. Even Jefferson thought that the taking of Canada was only a matter of marching. In the South, hostile Indians and runaway slaves took refuge in Spanish Florida. The frontiersmen of Georgia and Louisiana fought for Canada on the assumption that Northwesterners would assist in capturing Florida from England's ally. Ironically, the greatest opposition to war came from the maritime sections of New England that suffered the most from impressment and seizures. The General Assembly of Connecticut, for example, condemned the war, and the governor of Massachusetts refused to furnish militiamen to the federal government. In New Hampshire, the legislature protested against "hasty...rash, and ruinous measures," and made veiled hints at secession. These Federalist strongholds had suffered from arbitrary British acts, but the profits of successful voyages made confiscations endurable. As Federalist leader Timothy Pickering put it, the United States had chosen to fight against "the world's last hope, Britain's fast-anchored isle."

The start of the war also found the United States on the eve of a presidential election. The Federalists held a meeting attended by leaders from 11 states, usually regarded as the first national nominating convention, and chose as their candidate DeWitt Clinton, the lieutenant governor of New York. Leading Republicans caucused and endorsed Madison's reelection. Clinton opposed the war with England and promised peace, while Madison sought a mandate for his policies. But there was no vigorous campaigning. Instead, most state legislatures still chose electors who then cast their ballots. The results closely followed the sectional pattern evidenced by the vote on the war resolution: Madison carried every southern and western state, receiving 128 votes, while Clinton received 89—New York, New Jersey, Delaware, and Maryland, plus all of New England, with the exception of the frontier state of Vermont. Although the war faction won, the election demonstrated that a powerful opposition existed.

No invitations were sent out for the second inauguration, as Madison wished to have the ceremonies as informal as possible. Accompanied by cavalry, marine, and artillery units, the president rode to the Capitol on March 4, 1813. To the large audience present, he justified the war and his attempts to avoid it.

About to add the solemnity of an oath to the obligations imposed by a second call to the station in which my country heretofore placed me, I find in the presence of this respectable assembly an opportunity of publicly repeating my profound sense of so distinguished a confidence and of the responsibility united with it. The impressions on me are strengthened by such an evidence that my faithful endeavors to discharge my arduous duties have been favorably estimated, and by a consideration of the momentous period at which the trust has been renewed. From the weight and magnitude now belonging to it I should be compelled to shrink if I had less reliance on the support of an enlightened and generous people, and felt less deeply a conviction that the war with a powerful nation, which forms so prominent a feature in our situation, is stamped with that justice which invites the smiles of Heaven on the means of conducting it to a successful termination.

May we not cherish this sentiment without presumption when we reflect on the characters by which this war is distinguished?

It was not declared on the part of the United States until it had been long made on them, in reality though not in name; until arguments and postulations had been exhausted; until a positive declaration had been received that the wrongs provoking it would not be discontinued; nor until this last appeal could no longer be delayed without breaking down the spirit of the nation, destroying all confidence in itself and in its political institutions, and either perpetuating a state of disgraceful suffering or regaining by more costly sacrifices and more severe struggles our lost rank and respect among independent powers.

On the issue of the war are staked our national sovereignty on the high seas and the security of an important class of citizens whose occupations give the proper value to those of every other class. Not to contend for such a stake is to surrender our equality with other powers on the element common to all and to violate the sacred title which every member of the society has to its protection. I need not call into view the unlawfulness of the practice by which our mariners are forced at the will of every cruising officer from their own vessels into foreign ones, nor paint the outrages inseparable from it. The proofs are in the records of each successive Administration of our Government, and the cruel sufferings of that portion of the American people have found their way to every bosom not dead to the sympathies of human nature.

As the war was just in its origin and necessary and noble in its objects, we can reflect with a proud satisfaction that in carrying it on no principle of justice or honor, no usage of civilized nations, no precept of courtesy or humanity, have been infringed. The war has been waged on our part with scrupulous regard to all these obligations, and in a spirit of liberality which was never surpassed. How little has been the effect of this example on the conduct of the enemy?

They have retained as prisoners of war citizens of the United States not liable to be so considered under the usages of war.

They have refused to consider as prisoners of war, and threatened to punish as traitors and deserters, persons emigrating without restraint to the

United States, incorporated by naturalization into our political family, and fighting under the authority of their adopted country in open and honorable war for the maintenance of its rights and safety. Such is the avowed purpose of a Government which is in the practice of naturalizing by thousands citizens of other countries, and not only of permitting but compelling them to fight its battles against their native country.

They have not, it is true, taken into their own hands the hatchet and the knife, devoted to indiscriminate massacre, but they have let loose the savages armed with these cruel instruments; have allured them into their service, and carried them to battle by their sides, eager to glut their savage thirst with the blood of the vanquished and to finish the work of torture and death on maimed and defenseless captives. And, what was never before seen, British commanders have extorted victory over the unconquerable valor of our troops by presenting to the sympathy of their chief captives awaiting massacre from their savage associates. And now we find them, in further contempt of the modes of honorable warfare, supplying the place of a conquering force by attempts to disorganize our political society, to dismember our confederated Republic. Happily, like others, these will recoil on the authors; but they mark the degenerate counsels from which they emanate, and if they did not belong to a sense of unexampled inconsistencies might excite the greater wonder as proceeding from a Government which founded the very war in which it has been so long engaged on a charge against the disorganizing and insurrectional policy of its adversary.

To render the justice of the war on our part the more conspicuous, the reluctance to commence it was followed by the earliest and strongest manifestations of a disposition to arrest its progress. The sword was scarcely out of the scabbard before the enemy was apprised of the reasonable terms on which it would be resheathed. Still more precise advances were repeated, and have been received in a spirit forbidding every reliance not placed on the military resources of the nation.

These resources are amply sufficient to bring the war to an honorable issue. Our nation is in number more than half that of the British Isles. It is composed of a brave, a free, a virtuous, and an intelligent people. Our country abounds in the necessaries, the arts, and the comforts of life. A general prosperity is visible in the public countenance. The means employed by the British cabinet to undermine it have recoiled on themselves; have given to our national faculties a more rapid development, and, draining or diverting the precious metals from British circulation and British vaults, have poured them into those of the United States. It is a propitious consideration that an unavoidable war should have found this seasonable facility for the contributions required to support it. When the public voice called for war, all knew, and still know, that without them it could not be carried on through the period which it might last, and the patriotism, the good sense, and the manly spirit of our fellow citizens are pledges for the cheerfulness with which they will bear each his share of the common burden. To render the war short and its success sure, animated and systematic exertions alone are necessary, and the success of our arms now may long preserve our country from the necessity of another resort to them. Already have the gallant exploits of our naval heroes proved to the world our inherent capacity to maintain our rights on one element. If the reputation of our arms has been thrown under clouds on the other, presaging flashes of heroic enterprise assure us that nothing is wanting to correspondent triumphs there also but the discipline and habits which are in daily progress.

James Monroe

First Inaugural Address

M A R C H   4 ,   1 8 1 7

Commentary

On Christmas Eve, 1814, representatives of the United States and England signed the Treaty of Ghent, ending almost three years of war. The treaty avoided most major disagreements, such as impressment and ship seizures, and simply restored peace on the basis of the status quo antebellum. Disputed questions were referred to adjudication commissions or left to settle themselves. For the next decade, purely American issues dominated politics. In fact, these years witnessed such an unusual political calm on a national level that they are often labeled "the era of good feelings." But major sectional forces also crystallized during this period—sectional forces that would determine the cause of the country's history through the end of the Civil War.

A spirit of American nationalism, nevertheless, did take concrete form in a variety of cultural, diplomatic, judicial, and political activities. "The war," wrote Secretary of the Treasury Albert Gallatin, "has renewed and reinstated the national feeling and character which the Revolution had given, and which were daily lessening. . . . The people are more American; they feel and act more as a nation." Perhaps the greatest national occurrence was the westward movement that accelerated after 1815 with large-scale settlements in the Mississippi Valley and the Southwest. Between Monroe's election and the end of his administration, six new states, with a total area of almost 300,000 square miles, entered the Union. This ever-continuing westward migration swelled as public roads and canals eased the journey. Robert Fulton's steamboat revolutionized water travel, and, before the end of 1819, 60 had been launched on the Mississippi River. Each new improvement in transportation reduced travel time.

In 1817, travel from Boston to New York took 40 hours compared with 80 hours a decade earlier. The exuberant spirit of the period is captured by Monroe in his first inaugural address. "If we look to the history of other nations, ancient or modern," boasted the president, "we find no example of a growth so rapid, so gigantic, of a people so prosperous and happy . . . the heart of every citizen must expand with joy when he reflects how near our Government has approached to perfection."

In the election of 1816, the warning Federalists, discredited by their opposition to the War of 1812, did not formally nominate a presidential candidate. The Republican caucus selected Secretary James Monroe, who received 183 electoral votes to 34 cast for Rufus King of New York. On March 4, 1817, the inaugural ceremonies took place outdoors for the first time since 1789. Monroe had informed the president of the Senate that, according to custom, he would take the oath in the chamber of the House of Representatives. A dispute arose, though, between the Senate committee appointed to oversee the arrangement of details and Speaker of the House Henry Clay. To settle the matter, "an elevated portico" was constructed in front of the Capitol. From here, Monroe repeated the oath of office and delivered his inaugural address to "an immense concourse of officers, of the Government, foreign officers, strangers, and citizens." When Monroe concluded, "a single gun announced the fact; salutes followed at the navy yard . . . after which the President was escorted to his house by a long cavalcade of militia and citizens on horseback and in carriages."

I should be destitute of feeling if I was not deeply affected by the strong proof which my fellow citizens have given me of their confidence in calling me to the high office whose functions I am about to assume. As the expression of their good opinion of my conduct in the public service, I derive from it a gratification which those who are conscious of having done all that they could to merit it can alone feel. My sensibility is increased by a just estimate of the importance of the trust and of the nature and extent of its duties, with the proper discharge of which the highest interests of a great and free people are intimately connected. Conscious of my own deficiency, I cannot enter on these duties without great anxiety for the result. From a just responsibility I will never shrink, calculating with confidence that in my best efforts to promote the public welfare my motives will always be duly appreciated and my conduct be viewed with that candor and indulgence which I have experienced in other stations.

In commencing the duties of the chief executive office it has been the practice of the distinguished men who have gone before me to explain the principles which would govern them in their respective Administrations. In following their venerated example my attention is naturally drawn to the great causes which have contributed in a principal degree to produce the present happy condition of the United States. They will best explain the nature of our duties and shed much light on the policy which ought to be pursued in future.

From the commencement of our Revolution to the present day almost forty years have elapsed, and from the establishment of this Constitution twenty-eight. Through this whole term the Government has been what may emphatically be called self-government. And what has been the effect? To whatever object we turn our attention, whether it relates to our foreign or domestic concerns, we find abundant cause to felicitate ourselves in the excellence of our institutions. During a period fraught with difficulties and marked by very extraordinary events the United States have flourished beyond example. Their citizens individually have been happy and the nation prosperous.

Under this Constitution our commerce has been wisely regulated with foreign nations and between the States; new States have been admitted into our Union; our territory has been enlarged by fair and honorable treaty, and with great advantage to the original States; the States, respectively protected by the National Government under a mild, parental system against foreign dangers, and enjoying within their separate spheres, by a wise partition of power, a just proportion of the sovereignty, have improved their police, extended their settlements, and attained a strength and maturity which are the best proofs of wholesome laws well administered. And if we look to the condition of individuals what a proud spectacle does it exhibit! On whom has oppression fallen in any quarter of our Union? Who has been deprived of any right of person or property? Who restrained from offering his vows in the mode which he prefers to the Divine Author of his being? It is well known that all these blessings have been enjoyed in their fullest extent; and I add with peculiar satisfaction that there has been no example of a capital punishment being inflicted on anyone for the crime of high treason.

Some who might admit the competency of our Government to these beneficent duties might doubt it in trials which put to the test its strength and efficiency as a member of the great community of nations. Here too experience has afforded us the most satisfactory proof in its favor. Just as this Constitution was put into action several of the principal States of Europe had become much agitated and some of them seriously convulsed. Destructive wars ensued, which have of late only been terminated. In the course of these conflicts the United States received great injury from several of the parties. It was their interest to stand aloof from the contest, to demand justice from the party committing the injury, and to cultivate by a fair and honorable conduct the friendship of all. War became at length inevitable, and the result has shown that our Government is equal to that, the greatest of trials, under the most unfavorable circumstances. Of the virtue of the people and of the heroic exploits of the Army, the Navy, and the militia I need not speak.

Such, then, is the happy Government under which we live—a Government adequate to every purpose for which the social compact is formed; a Government elective in all its branches, under which every citizen may by his merit obtain the highest trust recognized by the Constitution; which contains within it no cause of discord, none to put at variance one portion of the community with another; a Government which protects every citizen in the full enjoyment of his rights, and is able to protect the nation against injustice from foreign powers.

Other considerations of the highest importance admonish us to cherish our Union and to cling to the Government which supports it. Fortunate as we are in our political institutions, we have not been less so in other circumstances on which our prosperity and happiness essentially depend. Situated within the temperate zone, and extending through many degrees of latitude along the Atlantic, the United States enjoy all the varieties of climate, and every production incident to that portion of the globe. Penetrating internally to the Great Lakes and beyond the sources of the great rivers which communicate through our whole interior, no country was ever happier with respect to its domain. Blessed, too, with a fertile soil, our produce has always been very abundant, leaving, even in years the least favorable, a surplus for the wants of our fellow men in other countries. Such is our peculiar felicity that there is not a part of our Union that is not particularly interested in preserving it. The great agricultural interest of the nation prospers under its protection. Local interests are not less fostered by it. Our fellow-citizens of the North engaged in navigation find great encouragement in being made the favored carriers of the vast productions of the other portions of the United States, while the inhabitants of these are amply recompensed, in their turn, by the nursery for seamen and naval force thus formed and reared up for the support of our common rights. Our manufactures find a generous encouragement by the policy which patronizes domestic industry, and the surplus of our produce a steady and profitable market by local wants in less-favored parts at home.

Such, then, being the highly favored condition of our country, it is the interest of every citizen to maintain it. What are the dangers which menace us? If any exist they ought to be ascertained and guarded against.

In explaining my sentiments on this subject it may be asked, What raised us to the present happy state? How did we accomplish the Revolution? How remedy the defects of the first instrument of our Union, by infusing into the National Government sufficient power for national purposes, without impairing the just rights of the States or affecting those of individuals? How sustain and pass with glory through the late war? The Government has been in the hands of the people. To the people, therefore, and to the faithful and able depositaries of their trust is the credit due. Had the people of the United States been educated in different principles, had they been less intelligent, less independent, or less virtuous can it be believed that we should have maintained the same steady and consistent career or been blessed with the same success? While, then, the constituent body retains its present sound and healthful state everything will be safe. They will choose competent and faithful representatives for every department. It is only when the people become ignorant and corrupt, when they degenerate into a populace, that they are incapable of exercising the sovereignty. Usurpation is then an easy attainment, and an usurper soon found. The people themselves become the willing instruments of their own debasement and ruin. Let us, then, look to the great cause, and endeavor to preserve it in full force. Let us by all wise and constitutional measures promote intelligence among the people as the best means of preserving our liberties.

Dangers from abroad are not less deserving of attention. Experiencing the fortune of other nations, the United States may be again involved in war, and it may in that event be the object of the adverse party to overset our Government, to break our Union, and demolish us as a nation. Our distance from Europe and the just, moderate, and pacific policy of our Government may form some security against these dangers, but they ought to be anticipated and guarded against. Many of our citizens are engaged in commerce and navigation, and all of them are in a certain degree dependent on their prosperous state. Many are engaged in the fisheries. These interests are exposed to invasion in the wars between other powers, and we should disregard the faithful admonition of experience if we did not expect it. We must support our rights or lose our character, and with it, perhaps, our liberties. A people who fail to do it can scarcely be said to hold a place among independent nations. National honor is national property of the highest value. The sentiment in the mind of every citizen is national strength. It ought therefore to be cherished.

To secure us against these dangers our coast and inland frontiers should be fortified, our Army and Navy, regulated upon just principles as to the force of each, be kept in perfect order, and our militia be placed on the best practicable footing. To put our extensive coast in such a state of defense as to secure our cities and interior from invasion will be attended with expense, but the work when finished will be permanent, and it is fair to presume that a single campaign of invasion by a naval force superior to our own, aided by a few thousand land troops, would expose us to greater expense, without taking into the estimate the loss of property and distress of our citizens, than would be sufficient for this great work. Our land and naval forces should be moderate, but adequate to the necessary purposes; the former to garrison and preserve our fortifications and to meet the first invasions of a foreign foe, and, while constituting the elements of a greater force, to preserve the science as well as all the necessary implements of war in a state to be brought into activity in the event of war; the latter, retained within the limits proper in a state of peace, might aid in maintaining the neutrality of the United States with dignity in the wars of other powers and in saving the property of their citizens from spoliation. In time of war, with the enlargement of which the great naval resources of the country render it susceptible, and which should be duly fostered in time of peace, it would contribute essentially, both as an auxiliary of defense and as a powerful engine of annoyance, to diminish the calamities of war and to bring the war to a speedy and honorable conclusion.

But it ought always to be held prominently in view that the safety of these States and of everything dear to a free people must depend in an eminent degree on the militia. Invasions may be made too formidable to be resisted by any land and naval force which it would comport either with the principles of our Government or the circumstances of the United States to maintain. In such cases recourse must be had to the great body of the people, and in a manner to produce the best effect. It is of the highest importance, therefore, that they be so organized and trained as to be prepared for any emergency. The arrangement should be such as to put at the command of the Government the ardent patriotism and youthful vigor of the country. If formed on equal and just principles, it can not be oppressive. It is the crisis which makes the pressure, and not the laws which provide a remedy for it. This arrangement should be formed, too, in time of peace, to be the better prepared for war. With such an organization of such a people the United States have nothing to dread from foreign invasion. At its approach an overwhelming force of gallant men might always be put in motion.

Other interests of high importance will claim attention, among which the improvement of our country by roads and canals, proceeding always with a constitutional sanction, holds a distinguished place. By thus facilitating the intercourse between the States we shall add much to the convenience and comfort of our fellow citizens, much to the ornament of the country, and, what is of greater importance, we shall shorten distances, and, by making each part more accessible to and dependent on the other, we shall bind the Union more closely together. Nature has done so much for us by intersecting the country with so many great rivers, bays, and lakes, approaching from distant points so near to each other, that the inducement to complete the work seems to be peculiarly strong. A more interesting spectacle was perhaps never seen than is exhibited within the limits of the United States; a territory so vast and advantageously situated, containing objects so grand, so useful, so happily connected in all their parts.

Our manufacturers will likewise require the systematic and fostering care of the Government. Possessing as we do all the raw materials, the fruit of our own soil and industry, we ought not to depend in the degree we have done on supplies from other countries. While we are thus dependent the sudden event of war, unsought and unexpected, can not fail to plunge us into the most serious difficulties. It is important, too, that the capital which nourishes our manufacturers should be domestic, as its influence in that case instead of exhausting, as it may do in foreign hands, would be felt advantageously on agriculture and every other branch of industry. Equally important is it to provide at home a market for our raw materials, as by extending the competition it will enhance the price and protect the cultivator against the casualties incident to foreign markets.

With the Indian tribes it is our duty to cultivate friendly relations and to act with kindness and liberality in all our transactions. Equally proper is it to persevere in our efforts to extend to them the advantages of civilization.

The great amount of our revenue and the flourishing state of the Treasury are a full proof of the competency of the national resources for any emergency, as they are of the willingness of our fellow citizens to bear the burdens which the public necessities require. The vast amount of vacant lands, the value of which daily augments, forms an additional resource of great extent and duration. These resources, besides accomplishing every other necessary purpose, put it completely in the power of the United States to discharge the national debt at an early period. Peace is the best time for improvement and preparation of every kind; it is in peace that our commerce flourishes most, that taxes are most easily paid, and that the revenue is most productive.

The Executive is charged officially in the Departments under it with the disbursement of the public money, and is responsible for the faithful application of it to the purposes for which it is raised. The Legislature is the watchful guardian over the public purse. It is its duty to see that the disbursement has been honestly made. To meet the requisite responsibility every facility should be afforded to the Executive to enable it to bring the public agents intrusted with the public money strictly and promptly to account. Nothing should be presumed against them; but if, with the requisite facilities, the public money is suffered to lie long and uselessly in their hands, they will not be the only defaulters, nor will the demoralizing effect be confined to them. It will evince a relaxation and want of tone in the Administration which will be felt by the whole community. I shall do all I can to secure economy and fidelity in this important branch of the Administration, and I doubt not that the Legislature will perform its duty with equal zeal. A thorough examination should be regularly made, and I will promote it.

It is particularly gratifying to me to enter on the discharge of these duties at a time when the United States are blessed with peace. It is a state most consistent with their prosperity and happiness. It will be my sincere desire to preserve it, so far as depends on the Executive, on just principles with all nations, claiming nothing unreasonable of any and rendering to each what is due.

Equally gratifying is it to witness the increased harmony of opinion which pervades our Union. Discord does not belong to our system. Union is recommended as well by the free and benign principles of our Government, extending its blessings to every individual, as by the other eminent advantages attending it. The American people have encountered together great dangers and sustained severe trials with success. They constitute one great family with a common interest. Experience has enlightened us on some questions of essential importance to the country. The progress has been slow, dictated by a just reflection and a faithful regard to every interest connected with it. To promote this harmony in accord with the principles of our republican Government and in a manner to give them the most complete effect, and to advance in all other respects the best interests of our Union, will be the object of my constant and zealous exertions.

Never did a government commence under auspices so favorable, nor ever was success so complete. If we look to the history of other nations, ancient or modern, we find no example of a growth so rapid, so gigantic, of a people so prosperous and happy. In contemplating what we have still to perform, the heart of every citizen must expand with joy when he reflects how near our Government has approached to perfection; that in respect to it we have no essential improvement to make; that the great object is to preserve it in the essential principles and features which characterize it, and that is to be done by preserving the virtue and enlightening the minds of the people; and as a security against foreign dangers to adopt such arrangements as are indispensable to the support of our independence, our rights and liberties. If we persevere in the career in which we have advanced so far and in the path already traced, we can not fail, under the favor of a gracious Providence, to attain the high destiny which seems to await us.

In the Administrations of the illustrious men who have preceded me in this high station, with some of whom I have been connected by the closest ties from early life, examples are presented which will always be found highly instructive and useful to their successors. From these I shall endeavor to derive all the advantages which they may afford. Of my immediate predecessor, under whom so important a portion of this great and successful experiment has been made, I shall be pardoned for earnest wishes that he may long enjoy in his retirement the affections of a grateful country, the best reward of exalted talents and the most faithful and meritorious service. Relying on the aid to be derived from the other departments of the Government, I enter on the trust to which I have been called by the suffrages of my fellow citizens with my fervent prayers to the Almighty that He will be graciously pleased to continue to us that protection which He has already so conspicuously displayed in our favor.

──────── SECOND INAUGURAL ADDRESS ────────

MARCH 5, 1821

COMMENTARY

In 1820, the Federalists did not nominate a presidential candidate and Monroe received all but one of the electoral votes. William Plummer of New Hampshire cast his ballot for John Quincy Adams because he thought that Monroe had shown "a want of foresight and economy" and also, he explained, no man should share with Washington "the honor of a unanimous election to the Presidency."

In his second inaugural address, Monroe proudly proclaimed that "no serious conflict has arisen" to divide the nation. "By steadily pursuing this course in this spirit," he said, "there is every reason to believe that our system will soon attain the highest degree of perfection of which human institutions are capable." In retrospect, though, Monroe's first administration saw the start of the struggle over slavery that would ultimately disrupt the Union. A serious conflict had begun during the so-called era of good feelings, a conflict that shattered Monroe's optimistic prediction for America.

In February, 1819, Representative James Tallmadge of New York proposed an amendment to the territory of Missouri's statehood petition prohibiting the future importation of slaves into the prospective state and the eventual freeing of those children of slaves born after Missouri's admission. An acrimonious debate deadlocked the issue. Did Congress have the right to regulate slavery in the territories? Would the current North-South balance—11 slave states and 11 free—be disrupted? Hundreds of resolutions adopted by mass meetings and state legislatures for and against the amendment flooded Congress. Thomas Cobb of Georgia predicted that passage would mean dissolution of the Union. From Monticello, Jefferson described the debates as "a fire bell in the night— I considered it at once as the knell of the Union." While the bitter controversy raged, the area of Maine petitioned Congress for admission as a state. Finally, in February, 1820, Congress voted to admit Missouri as a slave state with Maine entering free. In addition, no slavery would be allowed in the remainder of the Louisiana Purchase north of the 36° 30' parallel, Missouri's southern boundary. Compromise settled this question but sectional feelings had been aroused that would continue to divide the North and the South. "I take it for granted," said John Quincy Adams, "that the present question is a mere preamble—a title page to a great, tragic volume."

Inaugural Day, 1821, fell on a Sunday and Monroe, after consulting with Chief Justice Marshall, deferred the ceremonies to the following day. On March 5, the president, escorted by members of his cabinet, rode to the Capitol in a driving sleet storm that churned Washington's streets into almost impassable quagmires. The rather pompous English minister to America described the scene: "Monday, when we all attended the president's inauguration, in lace coats and silk stockings, was a most wretched day of snow and mud and cold: and though we had acquired an invitation in from from the Secretary of State, we had a tremendous crowd of sturdy and ragged citizens to squeeze through on our way into the House of Representatives. . . . We stuck about ten paces from the door and were utterly unable to get in until the arrival of the president, who to our great concern and satisfaction was squeezed as handsomely and detained as long as ourselves. . . . In addition to the squeezing and shoving which the poor Prezzy experienced at the door, his speech, which was indeed rather long, was occasionally interrupted by queer sounds from the gallery." Monroe's second inaugural address mainly summarized his first term in office. He made no mention of the growing sectional tensions but instead stressed how "the whole Union is knit together by the sentiments of mutual respect."

Fellow citizens:

I shall not attempt to describe the grateful emotions which the new and very distinguished proof of the confidence of my fellow citizens, evinced by my reelection to this high trust, has excited in my bosom. The approbation which it announces of my conduct in the preceding term affords me a consolation which I shall profoundly feel through life. The general accord with which it has been expressed adds to the great and never-ceasing obligations which it imposes. To merit the continuance of this good opinion, and to carry it with me into my retirement as the solace of advancing years, will be the object of my most zealous and unceasing efforts.

Having no pretensions to the high and commanding claims of my predecessors, whose names are so much more conspicuously identified with our Revolution, and who contributed so preeminently to promote its success, I consider myself rather as the instrument than the cause of the union which has prevailed in the late election. In surmounting, in favor of my humble pretensions, the difficulties which so often produce division in like occurrences, it is obvious that other powerful causes, indicating the great strength and stability of our Union, have essentially contributed to draw you together. That these powerful causes exist, and that they are permanent, is my fixed opinion; that they may produce a like accord in all questions touching, however remotely, the liberty, prosperity and happiness of our country will always be the object of my most fervent prayers to the Supreme Author of All Good.

In a government which is founded by the people, who possess exclusively the sovereignty, it seems proper that the person who may be placed by their suffrages in this high trust should declare on commencing its duties the principles on which he intends to conduct the Administration. If the person thus elected has served the preceding term, an opportunity is afforded him to review its principal occurrences and to give such further explanation respecting them as in his judgment may be useful to his constituents. The events of one year have influence on those of another, and, in like manner, of a preceding on the succeeding Administration. The movements of a great nation are connected in all their parts. If errors have been committed they ought to be corrected; if the policy is sound it ought to be supported. It is by a thorough knowledge of the whole subject that our fellow citizens are enabled to judge correctly of the past and to give a proper direction to the future.

Just before the commencement of the last term the United States had concluded a war with a very powerful nation on conditions equal and honorable to both parties. The events of that war are too recent and too deeply impressed on the memory of all to require a development from me. Our commerce had been in a great measure driven from the sea, our Atlantic and inland frontiers were invaded in almost every part; the waste of life along our coast and on some parts of our inland frontiers, to the defense of which our gallant and patriotic citizens were called, was immense, in addition to which not less than $120,000,000 were added at its end to the public debt.

As soon as the war had terminated, the nation, admonished by its events, resolved to place itself in a situation which should be better calculated to prevent the recurrence of a like evil, and, in case it should recur, to mitigate its calamities. With this view, after reducing our land force to the basis of a peace establishment, which has been further modified since, provision was made for the construction of fortifications at proper points through the whole extent of our coast and such an augmentation of our naval force as should be well adapted to both purposes. The laws making this provision were passed in 1815 and 1816, and it has been since the constant effort of the Executive to carry them into effect.

The advantage of these fortifications and of an augmented naval force in the extent contemplated, in a point of economy, has been fully illustrated by a report of the Board of Engineers and Naval Commissioners lately communicated to Congress, by which it appears that in an invasion by 20,000 men, with a correspondent naval force, in a campaign of six months only, the whole expense of the construction of the works would be defrayed by the difference in the sum necessary to maintain the force which would be adequate to our defense with the aid of those works and that which would be incurred without them. The reason of this difference is obvious. If fortifications are judiciously placed on our great inlets, as distant from our cities as circumstances will permit, they will form the only points of attack, and the enemy will be detained there by a small regular force a sufficient time to enable our militia to collect and repair to that on which the attack is made.

A force adequate to the enemy, collected at that single point, with suitable preparation for such others as might be menaced, is all that would be requisite. But if there were no fortifications, then the enemy might go where he pleased, and, changing his position and sailing from place to place, our force must be called out and spread in vast numbers along the whole coast and on both sides of every bay and river as high up in each as it might be navigable for ships of war. By these fortifications, supported by our Navy, to which they would afford like support, we should present to other powers an armed front from St. Croix to the Sabine, which would protect in the event of war our whole coast and interior from invasion; and even in the wars of other powers, in which we were neutral, they would be found eminently useful, as, by keeping their public ships at a distance from our cities, peace and order in them would be preserved and the Government be protected from insult.

It need scarcely be remarked that these measures have not been resorted to in a spirit of hostility to other powers. Such a disposition does not exist toward any power. Peace and good will have been, and will hereafter be, cultivated with all, and by the most faithful regard to justice. They have been dictated by a love of peace, of economy, and an earnest desire to save the lives of our fellow-citizens from that destruction and our country from that devastation which are inseparable from war when it finds us unprepared for it. It is believed, and experience has shown, that such a preparation is the best expedient that can be resorted to prevent war. I add with much pleasure that considerable progress has already been made in these measures of defense, and that they will be completed in a few years, considering the great extent and importance of the object, if the plan be zealously and steadily persevered in.

The conduct of the Government in what relates to foreign powers is always an object of the highest importance to the nation. Its agriculture, commerce, manufactures, fisheries, revenue, in short, its peace, may all be affected by it. Attention is therefore due to this subject.

At the period adverted to the powers of Europe, after having been engaged in long and destructive wars with each other, had concluded a peace, which happily still exists. Our peace with the power with whom we had been engaged had also been concluded. The war between Spain and the colonies in South America, which had commenced many years before, was then the only conflict that remained unsettled. This being a contest between different parts of the same community, in which other powers had not interfered, was not affected by their accommodations.

This contest was considered at an early stage by my predecessor a civil war in which the parties were entitled to equal rights in our ports. This decision, the first made by any power, being formed on great consideration of the comparative strength and resources of the parties, the length of time, and successful opposition made by the colonies, and of all other circumstances on which it ought to depend, was in strict accord with the law of nations. Congress has invariably acted on this principle, having made no change in our relations with either party. Our attitude has therefore been that of neutrality between them, which has been maintained by the Government with the strictest impartiality. No aid has been afforded to either, nor has any privilege been enjoyed by the one which has not been equally open to the other party, and every exertion has been made in its power to enforce the execution of the laws prohibiting illegal equipments with equal rigor against both.

By this equality between the parties their public vessels have been received in our ports on the same footing; they have enjoyed an equal right to purchase and export arms, munitions of war, and every other supply, the exportation of all articles whatever being permitted under laws which were passed long before the commencement of the contest; our citizens have traded equally with both, and their commerce with each has been alike protected by the Government.

Respecting the attitude which it may be proper for the United States to maintain hereafter between the parties, I have no hesitation in stating it as my opinion that the neutrality heretofore observed should still be adhered to. From the change in the Government of Spain and the negotiation now depending, invited by the Cortes and accepted by the colonies, it may be presumed, that their differences will be settled on the terms proposed by the colonies. Should the war be continued, the United States, regarding its occurrences, will always have it in their power to adopt such measures respecting it as their honor and interest may require.

Shortly after the general peace a band of adventurers took advantage of this conflict and of the facility which it afforded to establish a system of buccaneering in the neighboring seas, to the great annoyance of the commerce of the United States, and, as was represented, of that of other powers. Of this spirit and of its injurious bearing on the United States strong proofs were afforded by the establishment at Amelia Island, and the purposes to which it was made instrumental by this band in 1817, and by the occurrences which took place in other parts of Florida in 1818, the details of which in both instances are too well known to require to be now recited. I am satisfied had a less decisive course been adopted that the worst consequences would have resulted from it. We have seen that these checks, decisive as they were, were not sufficient to crush that piratical spirit. Many culprits brought within our limits have been condemned to suffer death, the punishment due to that atrocious crime. The decisions of upright and enlightened tribunals fall equally on all whose crimes subject them, by a fair interpretation of the law, to its censure. It belongs to the Executive not to suffer the executions under these decisions to transcend the great purpose for which punishment is necessary. The full benefit of example being secured, policy as well as humanity equally forbids that they should be carried further. I have acted on this principle, pardoning those who appear to have been led astray by ignorance of the criminality of the acts they had committed, and suffering the law to take effect on those only in whose favor no extenuating circumstances could be urged.

Great confidence is entertained that the late treaty with Spain, which has been ratified by both the parties, and the ratifications whereof have been exchanged, has placed the relations of the two countries on a basis of permanent friendship. The provision made by it for such of our citizens as have claims on Spain of the character described will, it is presumed, be very satisfactory to them, and the boundary which is established between the territories of the parties westward of the Mississippi, heretofore in dispute, has, it is thought, been settled on conditions just and advantageous to both. But to the acquisition of Florida too much importance can not be attached. It secures to the United States a territory important in itself, and whose importance is much increased by its bearing on many of the highest interests of the Union. It opens to several of the neighboring States a free passage to the ocean, through the Province ceded, by several rivers, having their sources high up within their limits. It secures us against all future annoyance from powerful Indian tribes. It gives us several excellent harbors in the Gulf of Mexico for ships of war of the largest size. It covers by its position in the Gulf the Mississippi and other great waters within our extended limits, and thereby enables the United States to afford complete protection to the vast and very valuable productions of our whole Western country, which find a market through those streams.

By a treaty with the British Government, bearing date on the 20th of October, 1818, the convention regulating the commerce between the United States and Great Britain, concluded on the 3d of July, 1815, which was about expiring, was revived and continued for the term of ten years from the time of its expiration. By that treaty, also, the differences which had arisen under the treaty of Ghent respecting the right claimed by the United States for their citizens to take and cure fish on the coast of His Britannic Majesty's dominions in America, with other differences on important interests, were adjusted to the satisfaction of both parties. No agreement has yet been entered into respecting the commerce between the United States and the British dominions in the West Indies and on this continent. The restraints imposed on that commerce by Great Britain, and reciprocated by the United States on a principle of defense, continue still in force.

The negotiation with France for the regulation of the commercial relations between the two countries, which in the course of the last summer had been commenced at Paris, has since been transferred to this city, and will be pursued on the part of the United States in the spirit of conciliation, and with an earnest desire that it may terminate in an arrangement satisfactory to both parties.

Our relations with the Barbary Powers are preserved in the same state and by the same means that were employed when I came into this office. As early as 1801 it was found necessary to send a squadron into the Mediterranean for the protection of our commerce and no period has intervened, a short term excepted, when it was thought advisable to withdraw it. The great interests which the United States have in the Pacific, in commerce and in the fisheries, have also made it necessary to maintain a naval force there. In disposing of this force in both instances the most effectual measures in our power have been taken, without interfering with its other duties, for the suppression of the slave trade and of piracy in the neighboring seas.

The situation of the United States in regard to their resources, the extent of their revenue, and the facility with which it is raised affords a most gratifying spectacle. The payment of nearly $67,000,000 of the public debt, with the great progress made in measures of defense and in other improvements of various kinds since the late war, are conclusive proofs of this extraordinary prosperity, especially when it is recollected that these expenditures have been defrayed without a burthen on the people, the direct tax and excise having been repealed soon after the conclusion of the late war, and the revenue applied to these great objects having been raised in a manner not to be felt. Our great resources therefore remain untouched for any purpose which may affect the vital interests of the nation. For all such purposes they are inexhaustible. They are more especially to be found in the virtue, patriotism, and intelligence of our fellow citizens, and in the devotion with which they would yield up by any just measure of taxation all their property in support of the rights and honor of their country.

Under the present depression of prices, affecting all the productions of the country and every branch of industry, proceeding from causes explained on a former occasion, the revenue has considerably diminished, the effect of which has been to compel Congress either to abandon these great measures of defense or to resort to loans or internal taxes to supply the deficiency. On the presumption that this depression and the deficiency in the revenue arising from it would be temporary, loans were authorized for the demands of the last and present year. Anxious to relieve my fellow-citizens in 1817 from every burthen which could be dispensed with and the state of the Treasury permitting it, I recommended the repeal of the internal taxes, knowing that such relief was then peculiarly necessary in consequence of the great exertions made in the late war. I made that recommendation under a pledge that should the public exigencies require a recurrence to them at any time while I remained in this trust, I would with equal promptitude perform the duty which would then be alike incumbent on me. By the experiment now making it will be seen by the next session of Congress whether the revenue shall have been so augmented as to be adequate to all these necessary purposes. Should the deficiency still continue, and especially should it be probable that it would be permanent, the course to be pursued appears to me to be obvious. I am satisfied that under certain circumstances loans may be resorted to with great advantage. I am equally well satisfied, as a general rule, that the demands of the current year, especially in time of peace, should be provided for by the revenue of that year.

I have never dreaded, nor have I ever shunned, in any situation in which I have been placed making appeals to the virtue and patriotism of my fellow citizens, well knowing that they could never be made in vain, especially in times of great emergency or for purposes of high national importance. Independently of the exigency of the case, many considerations of great weight urge a policy having in view a provision of revenue to meet to a certain extent the demands of the nation, without relying altogether on the precarious resource of foreign commerce. I am satisfied that internal duties and excises, with corresponding imposts on foreign articles of the same kind, would, without imposing any serious burdens on the people, enhance the price of produce, promote our manufactures, and augment the revenue, at the same time that they made it more secure and permanent.

The care of the Indian tribes within our limits has long been an essential part of our system, but, unfortunately, it has not been executed in a manner to accomplish all the objects intended by it. We have treated them as independent nations, without their having any substantial pretensions to that rank. The distinction has flattered their pride, retarded their improvement, and in many instances paved the way to their destruction. The progress of our settlements westward, supported as they are by a dense population, has constantly driven them back, with almost the total sacrifice of the lands which they have been compelled to abandon. They have claims on the magnanimity and, I may add, on the justice of this nation which we must all feel. We should become their real benefactors; we should perform the office of their Great Father, the endearing title which they emphatically give to the Chief Magistrate of our Union. Their sovereignty over vast territories should cease, in lieu of which the right of soil should be secured to each individual and his posterity in competent portions; and for the territory thus ceded by each tribe some reasonable equivalent should be granted, to be vested in permanent funds for the support of civil government over them and for the education of their children, for their instruction in the arts of husbandry, and to provide sustenance for them until they could provide it for themselves. My earnest hope is that Congress will digest some plan, founded on these principles, with such improvements as their wisdom may suggest, and carry it into effect as soon as it may be practicable.

Europe is again unsettled and the prospect of war increasing. Should the flame light up in any quarter, how far it may extend it is impossible to foresee. It is our peculiar felicity to be altogether unconnected with the causes which produce this menacing aspect elsewhere. With every power we are in perfect amity, and it is our interest to remain so if it be practicable on just conditions. I see no reasonable cause to apprehend variance with any power, unless it proceed from a violation of our maritime rights. In these contests, should they occur, and to whatever extent they may be carried, we shall be neutral; but as a neutral power we have rights which it is our duty to maintain. For like injuries it will be incumbent on us to seek redress in a spirit of amity, in full confidence that, injuring none, none would knowingly injure us. For more imminent dangers we should be prepared, and it should always be recollected that such preparation adapted to the circumstances and sanctioned by the judgment and wishes of our constituents can not fail to have a good effect in averting dangers of every kind. We should recollect also that the season of peace is best adapted to these preparations.

If we turn our attention, fellow citizens, more immediately to the internal concerns of our country, and more especially to those on which its future welfare depends, we have every reason to anticipate the happiest results. It is now rather more than forty-four years since we declared our independence, and thirty-seven since it was acknowledged. The talents and virtues which were displayed in that great struggle were a sure presage of all that has since followed. A people who were able to surmount in their infant state such great perils would be more competent as they rose into manhood to repel any which they might meet in their progress. Their physical strength would be more adequate to foreign danger, and the practice of self-government, aided by the light of experience, could not fail to produce an effect equally salutary on all those questions connected with the internal organization. These favorable anticipations have been realized.

In our whole system, national and State, we have shunned all the defects which unceasingly preyed on the vitals and destroyed the ancient Republics. In them there were distinct orders, a nobility and a people, or the people governed in one assembly. Thus, in the one instance there was a perpetual conflict between the orders in society for the ascendency, in which the victory of either terminated in the overthrow of the government and the ruin of the state; in the other, in which the people governed in a body, and whose dominions seldom exceeded the dimensions of a county in one of our States, a tumultuous and disorderly movement permitted only a transitory existence. In this great nation there is but one order, that of the people, whose power, by a peculiarly happy improvement of the representative principle, is transferred from them, without impairing in the slightest degree their sovereignty, to bodies of their own creation, and to persons elected by themselves, in the full extent necessary for all the purposes of free, enlightened and efficient government. The whole system is elective, the complete sovereignty being in the people, and every officer in every department deriving his authority from and being responsible to them for his conduct.

Our career has corresponded with this great outline. Perfection in our organization could not have been expected in the outset either in the National or State Governments or in tracing the line between their respective powers. But no serious conflict has arisen, nor any contest but such as are managed by argument and by a fair appeal to the good sense of the people, and many of the defects which experience had clearly demonstrated in both Governments have been remedied. By steadily pursuing this course in this spirit there is every reason to believe that our system will soon attain the highest degree of perfection of which human institutions are capable, and that the movement in all its branches will exhibit such a degree of order and harmony as to command the admiration and respect of the civilized world.

Our physical attainments have not been less eminent. Twenty-five years ago the river Mississippi was shut up and our Western brethren had no outlet for their commerce. What has been the progress since that time? The river has not only become the property of the United States from its source to the ocean, with all its tributary streams, with the exception of the upper part of the Red River only, but Louisiana, with a fair and liberal boundary on the western side and the Floridas on the eastern, have been ceded to us. The United States now enjoy the complete and uninterrupted sovereignty over the whole territory from St. Croix to the Sabine. New States, settled from among ourselves in this and in other parts, have been admitted into our Union in equal participation in the national sovereignty with the original States. Our population has augmented in an astonishing degree and extended in every direction. We now, fellow citizens, comprise within our limits the dimensions and faculties of a great power under a Government possessing all the energies of any government ever known to the Old World, with an utter incapacity to oppress the people.

Entering with these views the office which I have just solemnly sworn to execute with fidelity and to the utmost of my ability, I derive great satisfaction from a knowledge that I shall be assisted in the several Departments by the very enlightened and upright citizens from whom I have received so much aid in the preceding term. With full confidence in the continuance of that candor and generous indulgence from my fellow citizens at large which I have heretofore experienced, and with a firm reliance on the protection of Almighty God, I shall forthwith commence the duties of the high trust to which you have called me.

John Quincy Adams

Inaugural Address

MARCH 4, 1825

Commentary

An event in Monroe's second administration had made his name important. In this annual message to Congress in December 1823, the president enunciated the so-called Monroe Doctrine, which has become a sacrosanct part of American foreign policy. Europe, declared the chief executive, would be forbidden to establish any new dependencies in the Western Hemisphere and could no longer interfere in the affairs of New World nations in such a way as to threaten their independence. In future years, corollaries and interpretations would be added to Monroe's statements, making them cardinal principles of the nation's unwritten constitution. "I look upon the message," said Daniel Webster, "as forming a bright page in our history.... It elevated the hopes and gratified the patriotism of the people."

The election of 1824 shattered the once harmonious Republican party and paved the way for new political coalitions. Monroe represented the last of the Revolutionary statesmen—the generation that had controlled America's affairs since Bunker Hill and Yorktown was now practically extinct. New issues, new questions, and new leaders had grown to maturity. Unfortunately, though, these new issues stressed the growing sectionalism, and the new leaders reflected this development.

By the early 1820s, congressional nominating caucuses had come under increasing criticism. Even a poll of representatives taken in January 1824 revealed that 181 of the 261 members thought a presidential caucus inexpedient. The minority met, however, and selected Secretary of the Treasury William Crawford. Most state legislatures disregarded Crawford's nomination, held their own caucuses, and expressed preference for several other members of Monroe's cabinet—Secretary of State John Quincy Adams, Secretary of War John Calhoun, and Attorney General William Wirt. In addition, Speaker of the House Henry Clay and General Andrew Jackson, hero of the Battle of New Orleans, had formidable supporters. All of these candidates were nominally Republicans, but they represented particular interests and had little appeal outside of their own sections. As was the custom, each state chose electors on different days and even in different months; therefore, the 1824 election was a long and drawn-out process. By the middle of December, the last of the electors voted but the ballots showed that no candidate had obtained a majority, as required by the Constitution. Jackson received 99 votes, Adams 84, Crawford 41, and Clay 37. For the first time, a majority of the states held popular elections to choose electors. Here, Jackson led with 153,544, while Adams was second with 108,740. Clay obtained 47,136 and Crawford trailed with 46,618. The actual choice of the president now lay with the House of Representatives, voting by states and limited to the three highest on the electoral list. Clay, eliminated, advised his friends to vote for Adams. Amid frenzied political excitement in the House, the final tally gave Adams 13 states to 7 for Jackson and 4 for Crawford. John Quincy Adams became the sixth president of the United States. Two days after his election, Adams appointed Clay to head the State Department. Jackson and his supporters immediately raised the cry of "corrupt bargain," deliberate thwarting of the people's choice. Castigating Clay as the "Judas of the West," Jackson vowed political revenge. Before 1825 ended, the Tennessee legislature nominated Jackson for the presidency and he resigned his Senate seat to begin a three-year campaign.

John Quincy Adams recorded in his diary the events that surrounded his inauguration:

> *Washington, March 4, 1825. —After two successive sleepless nights, I entered upon this day with a supplication to Heaven, first for my country; secondly, for myself and for those connected with my good name and fortunes, that the last results of its events may be auspicious and blessed. About half-past eleven o'clock I left my house with an escort of several companies of militia and a cavalcade of citizens.... I repaired to the hall of the House of Representatives, and after delivering from the Speaker's chair my inaugural address to a crowded auditory, I pronounced from a volume of the laws held up to me by John Marshall, the oath faithfully to execute the*

office of President of the United States... I retired from the hall,
passed in review the military companies drawn up in front of the
Capitol, and returned to my house.

Adams devoted most of his inaugural address to summarizing the nation's
achievements. In a striking departure, though, he endorsed federally sponsored
internal improvements, which, he said, would be blessed by the "unborn mil-
lions of our posterity."

In compliance with an usage coeval with the existence of our Federal Constitution, and sanctioned by the example of my predecessors in the career
upon which I am about to enter, I appear, my fellow citizens, in your presence and in that of Heaven to bind myself by the solemnities of religious
obligation to the faithful performance of the duties allotted to me in the
station to which I have been called.

In unfolding to my countrymen the principles by which I shall be governed in the fulfillment of those duties my first resort will be to that Constitution which I shall swear to the best of my ability to preserve, protect, and
defend. That revered instrument enumerates the powers and prescribes the
duties of the Executive Magistrate, and in its first words declares the purposes to which these and the whole action of the Government instituted by
it should be invariably and sacredly devoted to form a more perfect union,
establish justice, insure domestic tranquillity, provide for the common defense, promote the general welfare, and secure the blessings of liberty to the
people of this Union in their successive generations. Since the adoption of
this social compact one of these generations has passed away. It is the work
of our forefathers. Administered by some of the most eminent men who
contributed to its formation, through a most eventful period in the annals
of the world, and through all the vicissitudes of peace and war incidental
to the condition of associated man, it has not disappointed the hopes and
aspirations of those illustrious benefactors of their age and nation. It has
promoted the lasting welfare of that country so dear to us all; it has to an
extent far beyond the ordinary lot of humanity secured the freedom and
happiness of this people. We now receive it as a precious inheritance from
those to whom we are indebted for its establishment, doubly bound by the
examples which they have left us and by the blessings which we have enjoyed as the fruits of their labors to transmit the same unimpaired to the
succeeding generation.

In the compass of thirty-six years since this great national covenant was instituted a body of laws enacted under its authority and in conformity with its provisions has unfolded its powers and carried into practical operation its effective energies. Subordinate departments have distributed the executive functions in their various relations to foreign affairs, to the revenue and expenditures, and to the military force of the Union by land and sea. A coordinate department of the judiciary has expounded the Constitution and the laws, settling in harmonious coincidence with the legislative will numerous weighty questions of construction which the imperfection of human language had rendered unavoidable. The year of jubilee since the first formation of our Union has just elapsed; that of the declaration of our independence is at hand. The consummation of both was effected by this Constitution.

Since that period a population of four million has multiplied to twelve. A territory bounded by the Mississippi has been extended from sea to sea. New States have been admitted to the Union in numbers nearly equal to those of the first Confederation. Treaties of peace, amity, and commerce have been concluded with the principal dominions of the earth. The people of other nations, inhabitants of regions acquired not by conquest, but by compact, have been united with us in the participation of our rights and duties, of our burdens and blessings. The forest has fallen by the ax of our woodsmen; the soil has been made to teem by the tillage of our farmers; our commerce has whitened every ocean. The dominion of man over physical nature has been extended by the invention of our artists. Liberty and law have marched hand in hand. All the purposes of human association have been accomplished as effectively as under any other government on the globe, and at a cost little exceeding in a whole generation the expenditure of other nations in a single year.

Such is the unexaggerated picture of our condition under a Constitution founded upon the republican principle of equal rights. To admit that this picture has its shades is but to say that it is still the condition of men upon earth. From evil, physical, moral, and political, it is not our claim to be exempt. We have suffered sometimes by the visitation of Heaven through disease; often by the wrongs and injustice of other nations, even to the extremities of war; and, lastly, by dissensions among ourselves; dissensions perhaps inseparable from the enjoyment of freedom, but which have more than once appeared to threaten the dissolution of the Union, and with it the overthrow of all the enjoyments of our present lot and all our earthly hopes of the future. The causes of these dissensions have been various, founded upon differences of speculation in the theory of republican government;

upon conflicting views of policy in our relations with foreign nations; upon jealousies of partial and sectional interests, aggravated by prejudices and prepossessions which strangers to each other are ever apt to entertain.

It is a source of gratification and of encouragement to me to observe that the great result of this experiment upon the theory of human rights has at the close of that generation by which it was formed been crowned with success equal to the most sanguine expectations of its founders. Union, justice, tranquillity, the common defense, the general welfare, and the blessings of liberty; all have been promoted by the Government under which we have lived. Standing at this point of time, looking back to that generation which has gone by and forward to that which is advancing, we may at once indulge in grateful exultation and in cheering hope. From the experience of the past we derive instructive lessons for the future. Of the two great political parties which have divided the opinions and feelings of our country, the candid and the just will now admit that both have contributed splendid talents, spotless integrity, ardent patriotism, and disinterested sacrifices to the formation and administration of this Government, and that both have required a liberal indulgence for a portion of human infirmity and error. The revolutionary wars of Europe, commencing precisely at the moment when the Government of the United States first went into operation under this Constitution, excited a collision of sentiments and of sympathies which kindled all the passions and imbittered the conflict of parties till the nation was involved in war and the Union was shaken to its center. This time of trial embraced a period of five and twenty years, during which the policy of the Union in its relations with Europe constituted the principal basis of our political divisions and the most arduous part of the action of our Federal Government. With the catastrophe in which the wars of the French Revolution terminated, and our own subsequent peace with Great Britain, this baneful weed of party strife was uprooted. From that time no difference of principle, connected either with the theory of government or with our intercourse with foreign nations, has existed or been called forth in force sufficient to sustain a continued combination of parties or to give more than wholesome animation to public sentiment or legislative debate. Our political creed is, without a dissenting voice that can be heard, that the will of the people is the source and the happiness of the people the end of all legitimate government upon earth; that the best security for the beneficence and the best guaranty against the abuse of power consists in the freedom, the purity, and the frequency of popular elections; that the General Government of the Union and the separate governments of the States are all sovereignties of limited powers, fellow servants of the same masters, uncontrolled within their respective spheres, uncontrollable by encroachments upon each other; that the firmest security of peace is the preparation during peace of the defenses of war; that a rigorous economy and accountability of public expenditures should guard against the aggravation and alleviate when possible the burden of taxation; that the military should be kept in strict subordination to the civil power; that the freedom of the press and of religious opinion should be inviolate; that the policy of our country is peace and the ark of our salvation union are articles of faith upon which we are all now agreed. If there have been those who doubted whether a confederated representative democracy were a government competent to the wise and orderly management of the common concerns of a mighty nation, those doubts have been dispelled; if there have been projects of partial confederacies to be erected upon the ruins of the Union, they have been scattered to the winds; if there have been dangerous attachments to one foreign nation and antipathies against another, they have been extinguished. Ten years of peace, at home and abroad, have assuaged the animosities of political contention and blended into harmony the most discordant elements of public opinion. There still remains one effort of magnanimity, one sacrifice of prejudice and passion, to be made by the individuals throughout the nation who have heretofore followed the standards of political party. It is that of discarding every remnant of rancor against each other, of embracing as countrymen and friends, and of yielding to talents and virtue alone that confidence which in times of contention for principle was bestowed only upon those who bore the badge of party communion.

The collisions of party spirit which originate in speculative opinions or in different views of administrative policy are in their nature transitory. Those which are founded on geographical divisions, adverse interests of soil, climate, and modes of domestic life are more permanent, and therefore, perhaps, more dangerous. It is this which gives inestimable value to the character of our Government, at once federal and national. It holds out to us a perpetual admonition to preserve alike and with equal anxiety the rights of each individual State in its own government and the rights of the whole nation in that of the Union. Whatsoever is of domestic concernment, unconnected with the other members of the Union or with foreign lands, belongs exclusively to the administration of the State governments. Whatsoever directly involves the rights and interests of the federative fraternity or of foreign powers is of the resort of this General Government. The duties of both are obvious in the general principle, though sometimes perplexed with difficulties in the detail. To respect the rights of the State governments is the inviolable duty of that of the Union; the government of every State will feel its own obligation to respect and preserve the rights of the whole. The prejudices everywhere too commonly entertained against distant strangers are worn away, and the jealousies of jarring interests are allayed by the composition and functions of the great national councils annually assembled from all quarters of the Union at this place. Here the distinguished men from every section of our country, while meeting to deliberate upon the great interests of those by whom they are deputed, learn to estimate the talents and do justice to the virtues of each other. The harmony of the nation is promoted and the whole Union is knit together by the sentiments of mutual respect, the habits of social intercourse, and the ties of personal friendship formed between the representatives of its several parts in the performance of their service at this metropolis.

Passing from this general review of the purposes and injunctions of the Federal Constitution and their results as indicating the first traces of the path of duty in the discharge of my public trust, I turn to the Administration of my immediate predecessor as the second. It has passed away in a period of profound peace, how much to the satisfaction of our country and to the honor of our country's name is known to you all. The great features of its policy, in general concurrence with the will of the Legislature, have been to cherish peace while preparing for defensive war; to yield exact justice to other nations and maintain the rights of our own; to cherish the principles of freedom and of equal rights wherever they were proclaimed; to discharge with all possible promptitude the national debt; to reduce within the narrowest limits of efficiency the military force; to improve the organization and discipline of the Army; to provide and sustain a school of military science; to extend equal protection to all the great interests of the nation; to promote the civilization of the Indian tribes, and to proceed in the great system of internal improvements within the limits of the constitutional power of the Union. Under the pledge of these promises, made by that eminent citizen at the time of his first induction to this office, in his career of eight years the internal taxes have been repealed; sixty millions of the public debt have been discharged; provision has been made for the comfort and relief of the aged and indigent among the surviving warriors of the Revolution; the regular armed force has been reduced and its constitution revised and perfected; the accountability for the expenditure of public moneys has been made more effective; the Floridas have been peaceably acquired, and our boundary has been extended to the Pacific Ocean; the independence of the southern nations of this hemisphere has been recognized, and recommended by example and by counsel to the potentates of Europe; progress has been made in the defense of the country by fortifications and the increase of the Navy, toward the effectual suppression of the African traffic in slaves; in alluring the aboriginal hunters of our land to the cultivation of the soil and of the mind, in exploring the interior regions of the Union, and in preparing by scientific researches and surveys for the further application of our national resources to the internal improvement of our country.

In this brief outline of the promise and performance of my immediate predecessor the line of duty for his successor is clearly delineated. To pursue to their consummation those purposes of improvement in our common condition instituted or recommended by him will embrace the whole sphere of my obligations. To the topic of internal improvement, emphatically urged by him at his inauguration, I recur with peculiar satisfaction. It is that from which I am convinced that the unborn millions of our posterity who are in future ages to people this continent will derive their most fervent gratitude to the founders of the Union; that in which the beneficent action of its Government will be most deeply felt and acknowledged. The magnificence and splendor of their public works are among the imperishable glories of the ancient republics. The roads and aqueducts of Rome have been the admiration of all after ages, and have survived thousands of years after all her conquests have been swallowed up in despotism or become the spoil of barbarians. Some diversity of opinion has prevailed with regard to the powers of Congress for legislation upon objects of this nature. The most respectful deference is due to doubts originating in pure patriotism and sustained by venerated authority. But nearly twenty years have passed since the construction of the first national road was commenced. The authority for its construction was then unquestioned. To how many thousands of our countrymen has it proved a benefit? To what single individual has it ever proved an injury? Repeated, liberal, and candid discussions in the Legislature have conciliated the sentiments and approximated the opinions of enlightened minds upon the question of constitutional power. I can not but hope that by the same process of friendly, patient, and persevering deliberation all constitutional objections will ultimately be removed. The extent and limitation of the powers of the General Government in relation to this transcendently important interest will be settled and acknowledged to the common satisfaction of all, and every speculative scruple will be solved by a practical public blessing.

Fellow citizens, you are acquainted with the peculiar circumstances of the recent election, which have resulted in affording me the opportunity of addressing you at this time. You have heard the exposition of the principles which will direct me in the fulfillment of the high and solemn trust imposed upon me in this station. Less possessed of your confidence in advance than any of my predecessors, I am deeply conscious of the prospect that I shall stand more and oftener in need of your indulgence. Intentions upright and pure, a heart devoted to the welfare of our country, and the unceasing application of all the faculties allotted to me to her service are all the pledges that I can give for the faithful performance of the arduous duties I am to undertake. To the guidance of the legislative councils, to the assistance of the executive and subordinate departments, to the friendly cooperation of the respective State governments, to the candid and liberal support of the people so far as it may be deserved by honest industry and zeal, I shall look for whatever success may attend my public service; and knowing that "except the Lord keep the city the watchman waketh but in vain," with fervent supplications for His favor, to His overruling providence I commit with humble but fearless confidence my own fate and the future destinies of my country.

ANDREW JACKSON

FIRST INAUGURAL ADDRESS

MARCH 4, 1829

COMMENTARY

*For four years, President Adams's programs were bitterly assailed by his po-
litical opponents, who promptly seized every opportunity to discredit him.
Once Adams, so provoked by this virulent hostility, penned in his diary: "The
skunks of party slander have been squirting around the House of Representatives, thence to issue and perfume the atmosphere of the Union." Gradually the
supporters of John Calhoun, William Crawford, and Jackson drew together to
form a new political coalition pledged to return to original principles of the
Republican Party. After winning a majority of House seats in 1826, the group,
first called the Opposition, assumed the name Democratic-Republicans, or,
more simply, the Democratic Party.*

*In 1828, all but two states sanctioned popular voting for the electors, forc-
ing politics to take on a new tone as the campaign was fought in newspapers,
journals, and before mass meetings. Caucuses of several state legislatures put
forth only two candidates—Adams and Jackson. Very little mention was made
of the problems of the day as advocates of each man shunted aside the tariff, internal improvements, and foreign policy, concentrating instead on slanderous
statements to arouse partisan hate. In a disgraceful exhibition of unfair tactics,
both sides engaged in publishing vituperative pamphlets containing unsubstantiated character assaults. An alliance of the West, the South, and the lower
classes of the Middle Atlantic states, however, won the election for Jackson, who
was portrayed as the champion of the plain people. The indomitable Indian
fighter and military hero received 171 ballots to 83 for Adams—Jackson polled
647,231 votes to Adams's 509,097. In addition, the Democrats controlled both*

houses of Congress. For the first time since the founding of the republic, a president hailed from an inland state.

As Inauguration Day drew closer, towns and cities along the way from Tennessee to Washington planned elaborate welcoming ceremonies. But the death of Mrs. Jackson on January 8 changed the joy to mourning. Jackson arrived in the capital after a quiet and uneventful trip. On March 4, 1829, surrounded by "gigs, wood wagons, vehicles of every sort crowded with women eager to be near the chief, and followed by the officers of his suite, worthies of the Revolution, and hundred of strangers without distinction of rank," Jackson walked to the Capitol, and at noon, on the East Portico, took the oath of office. "The scene," recorded one observer, "was a most beautiful and inspiring spectacle. The building, noble in its size, with its richly sculptured capitals and cornices: the massive columns; the far-spreading wings and terraces; the grounds and gates, with the crowd of carriages without; the line of soldiers in the park; the towering flight of steps, covered with members of Congress, officers of the army, foreign ministers, ladies dressed in all the varying hues of fashion; the President; the crowd of heads and the innumerable eyes bent on one spot, all taken together presented to the outward eye an assemblage of images never to be forgotten." After Jackson's short inaugural address, the crowd surged forward to grasp his hand. With the greatest of difficulty, the president mounted his horse and started for the White House.

Fellow citizens:

About to undertake the arduous duties that I have been appointed to perform by the choice of a free people, I avail myself of this customary and solemn occasion to express the gratitude which their confidence inspires and to acknowledge the accountability which my situation enjoins. While the magnitude of their interests convinces me that no thanks can be adequate to the honor they have conferred, it admonishes me that the best return I can make is the zealous dedication of my humble abilities to their service and their good.

As the instrument of the Federal Constitution it will devolve on me for a stated period to execute the laws of the United States, to superintend their foreign and their confederate relations, to manage their revenue, to command their forces, and, by communications to the Legislature, to watch over and to promote their interests generally. And the principles of action by which I shall endeavor to accomplish this circle of duties it is now proper for me briefly to explain.

In administering the laws of Congress I shall keep steadily in view the limitations as well as the extent of the Executive power trusting thereby to discharge the functions of my office without transcending its authority. With foreign nations it will be my study to preserve peace and to cultivate friendship on fair and honorable terms, and in the adjustment of any differences that may exist or arise to exhibit the forbearance becoming a powerful nation rather than the sensibility belonging to a gallant people.

In such measures as I may be called on to pursue in regard to the rights of the separate States I hope to be animated by a proper respect for those sovereign members of our Union, taking care not to confound the powers they have reserved to themselves with those they have granted to the Confederacy.

The management of the public revenue; that searching operation in all governments; is among the most delicate and important trusts in ours, and it will, of course, demand no inconsiderable share of my official solicitude. Under every aspect in which it can be considered it would appear that advantage must result from the observance of a strict and faithful economy. This I shall aim at the more anxiously both because it will facilitate the extinguishment of the national debt, the unnecessary duration of which is incompatible with real independence, and because it will counteract that tendency to public and private profligacy which a profuse expenditure of money by the Government is but too apt to engender. Powerful auxiliaries to the attainment of this desirable end are to be found in the regulations provided by the wisdom of Congress for the specific appropriation of public money and the prompt accountability of public officers.

With regard to a proper selection of the subjects of impost with a view to revenue, it would seem to me that the spirit of equity, caution and compromise in which the Constitution was formed requires that the great interests of agriculture, commerce, and manufactures should be equally favored, and that perhaps the only exception to this rule should consist in the peculiar encouragement of any products of either of them that may be found essential to our national independence.

Internal improvement and the diffusion of knowledge, so far as they can be promoted by the constitutional acts of the Federal Government, are of high importance.

Considering standing armies as dangerous to free governments in time of peace, I shall not seek to enlarge our present establishment, nor disregard that salutary lesson of political experience which teaches that the military should be held subordinate to the civil power. The gradual increase of our

Navy, whose flag has displayed in distant climes our skill in navigation and our fame in arms; the preservation of our forts, arsenals, and dockyards, and the introduction of progressive improvements in the discipline and science of both branches of our military service are so plainly prescribed by prudence that I should be excused for omitting their mention sooner than for enlarging on their importance. But the bulwark of our defense is the national militia, which in the present state of our intelligence and population must render us invincible. As long as our Government is administered for the good of the people, and is regulated by their will; as long as it secures to us the rights of person and of property, liberty of conscience and of the press, it will be worth defending; and so long as it is worth defending a patriotic militia will cover it with an impenetrable aegis. Partial injuries and occasional mortifications we may be subjected to, but a million of armed freemen, possessed of the means of war, can never be conquered by a foreign foe. To any just system, therefore, calculated to strengthen this natural safeguard of the country I shall cheerfully lend all the aid in my power.

It will be my sincere and constant desire to observe toward the Indian tribes within our limits a just and liberal policy, and to give that humane and considerate attention to their rights and their wants which is consistent with the habits of our Government and the feelings of our people.

The recent demonstration of public sentiment inscribes on the list of Executive duties, in characters too legible to be overlooked, the task of reform, which will require particularly the correction of those abuses that have brought the patronage of the Federal Government into conflict with the freedom of elections, and the counteraction of those causes which have disturbed the rightful course of appointment and have placed or continued power in unfaithful or incompetent hands.

In the performance of a task thus generally delineated I shall endeavor to select men whose diligence and talents will insure in their respective stations able and faithful cooperation, depending for the advancement of the public service more on the integrity and zeal of the public officers than on their numbers.

A diffidence, perhaps too just, in my own qualifications will teach me to look with reverence to the examples of public virtue left by my illustrious predecessors, and with veneration to the lights that flow from the mind that founded and the mind that reformed our system. The same diffidence induces me to hope for instruction and aid from the coordinate branches of the Government, and for the indulgence and support of my fellow citizens generally. And a firm reliance on the goodness of that Power whose

providence mercifully protected our national infancy, and has since upheld
our liberties in various vicissitudes, encourages me to offer up my ardent
supplications that He will continue to make our beloved country the object
of His divine care and gracious benediction.

——— SECOND INAUGURAL ADDRESS ———

MARCH 4, 1833

COMMENTARY

*With the victory of Andrew Jackson in 1828, something of a new democratic era
began as the frontier creed, allied with the rise of the common man to political
importance, won a national election. In his first inaugural address, Jackson spoke
about the important duties of the presidency, proceeding to outline his general
philosophy of government. He dealt with the need for a judicious tariff, lowering
of the national debt, administrative efficiency, "a just and liberal policy" toward
the Indians, and internal improvements "so far as they can be promoted by the
constitutional acts of the Federal Government." In general, his administration
followed the prescription of the inaugural. The major issue not mentioned,
though, and the one destined to be the most controversial and emotional during
his tenure in the White House, was the Bank of the United States.*

*The second Bank of the United States had been granted a 20-year fed-
eral charter in 1816. A private corporation with immense financial powers, the
Bank, originally part of Hamilton's financial program, served as the depository
for U.S. funds without paying interest for their use. In return, the Bank and its
several branches paid out government drafts and transferred public money free
of charge. Its notes were exempt from taxation. But for these privileges, the Bank
gave the government a sizable bonus. Through sound programs, the Bank established a reliable and more uniform currency. Notes of state and private banks
depreciated as the directors of the Bank carried out deflationary policies with
an iron hand. To those farmers and merchants who favored liberal borrowing policies combined with inflationary programs, the unwarrantable actions
of the "monster bank" seemed to resemble a gigantic octopus "sucking the blood
from the arteries of the toilers on the farm and in the shop." As the Bank grew,
its branches vigorously competed with local banks for business. When several
states taxed the branch office, as they did every other commercial concern, the*

Supreme Court intervened. In McCulloch vs. Maryland (1819), the Court ruled that a state could not tax a corporation charted by the United States as Chief Justice John Marshall said, "the power to tax involves the power to destroy." Thus, the Bank and its branches had still another advantage in their competition with local financial institutions—another reason why animosity increased against the "monster."

In his lengthy first message to Congress in 1829, Jackson attacked the Bank as being monopolistic and unconstitutional. Proposing a national bank founded upon "the credit of the Government and its revenues . . . which would avoid all constitutional difficulties and at the same time secure all the advantages to the Government and country that were expected to result from the present bank," the president served notice to the directors and shareholders that he would not recommend renewal of the charter. Attorney General Roger B. Taney summarized the Jacksonian feeling when he described the "power concentrated in the hands of a few individuals—exercised in secret and unseen although felt—irresponsible and above the control of the people or the government for the 20 years of its charter."

Backed by Henry Clay, Daniel Webster, and other opponents of Jackson, Nicholas Biddle, the director of the Bank of the United States, applied for a recharter in 1832, although the old charter had four years to run. Clay envisioned that a Bank veto would damage Jackson's chances for reelection, especially in the key state of Pennsylvania. Jackson vetoed the bill on July 10, 1832. In a stinging message, the president repudiated Marshall and Hamilton and lashed out at the rich men who "have besought us to make them richer by act of Congress. By attempting to gratify their desires we have in the results of our legislation arrayed section against section, interest against interest, and man against man, in a fearful commotion which threatens to shake the foundations of our Union." The veto delighted Clay and the National Republicans. Nicholas Biddle described the message as "a manifesto of anarchy, such as Marat or Robespierre might have issued." Beyond any doubt, the Bank now would be the major issue in the 1832 campaign.

The National Republicans held a nominating convention at Baltimore and selected Henry Clay to oppose Jackson. A bitter campaign followed, intensified by an unusual third entry, the Anti-Masonic party, which pledged itself to a national program but one tinged with prejudice against Catholic immigration. The Bank, though, remained the central topic. Torchlight parades, campaign songs, cartoons, and huge barbecues attended by thousands who swarmed to "camp grounds" to see and hear the speakers illustrated the further democratization of presidential elections. The electoral college still met;

but from this election on, they would be guided by the will of the people. When the polls closed and the votes were counted, it was evident that the people had soundly endorsed Jackson and his policies. The well-liked president carried 16 of the 24 states with 219 electoral votes. Clay received 49 electoral votes and William Wirt, the Anti-Masonic candidate, carried Vermont's 7. In the popular column, Jackson obtained 687,502 votes, or just under 150,000 more than his combined opposition. "My opinion is," wrote Wirt, "that he may be President for life if he chooses." It was indeed a great triumph for "Old Hickory."

On March 4, 1833, Jackson began his second term with a simple inaugural ceremony in the House chamber. He took part in no festivities, returned to the White House, and retired early.

Fellow citizens:

The will of the American people, expressed through their unsolicited suffrages, calls me before you to pass through the solemnities preparatory to taking upon myself the duties of President of the United States for another term. For their approbation of my public conduct through a period which has not been without its difficulties, and for this renewed expression of their confidence in my good intentions, I am at a loss for terms adequate to the expression of my gratitude. It shall be displayed to the extent of my humble abilities in continued efforts so to administer the Government as to preserve their liberty and promote their happiness.

So many events have occurred within the last four years which have necessarily called forth, sometimes under circumstances the most delicate and painful, my views of the principles and policy which ought to be pursued by the General Government that I need on this occasion but allude to a few leading considerations connected with some of them.

The foreign policy adopted by our Government soon after the formation of our present Constitution, and very generally pursued by successive Administrations, has been crowned with almost complete success, and has elevated our character among the nations of the earth. To do justice to all and to submit to wrong from none has been during my Administration its governing maxim, and so happy have been its results that we are not only at peace with all the world, but have few causes of controversy, and those of minor importance, remaining unadjusted.

In the domestic policy of this Government there are two objects which especially deserve the attention of the people and their representatives, and which have been and will continue to be the subjects of my increasing solicitude. They are the preservation of the rights of the several States and the integrity of the Union.

These great objects are necessarily connected, and can only be attained by an enlightened exercise of the powers of each within its appropriate sphere in conformity with the public will constitutionally expressed. To this end it becomes the duty of all to yield a ready and patriotic submission to the laws constitutionally enacted and thereby promote and strengthen a proper confidence in those institutions of the several States and of the United States which the people themselves have ordained for their own government.

My experience in public concerns and the observation of a life somewhat advanced confirm the opinions long since imbibed by me, that the destruction of our State governments or the annihilation of their control over the local concerns of the people would lead directly to revolution and anarchy, and finally to despotism and military domination. In proportion, therefore, as the General Government encroaches upon the rights of the States, in the same proportion does it impair its own power and detract from its ability to fulfill the purposes of its creation. Solemnly impressed with these considerations, my countrymen will ever find me ready to exercise my constitutional powers in arresting measures which may directly or indirectly encroach upon the rights of the States or tend to consolidate all political power in the General Government. But of equal and, indeed of incalculable, importance is the union of these States, and the sacred duty of all to contribute to its preservation by a liberal support of the General Government in the exercise of its just powers. You have been wisely admonished to "accustom yourselves to think and speak of the Union as of the palladium of your political safety and prosperity, watching for its preservation with jealous anxiety, discountenancing whatever may suggest even a suspicion that it can in any event be abandoned, and indignantly frowning upon the first dawning of any attempt to alienate any portion of our country from the rest or to enfeeble the sacred ties which now link together the various parts." Without union our independence and liberty would never have been achieved; without union they never can be maintained. Divided into twenty-four, or even a smaller number, of separate communities, we shall see our internal trade burdened with numberless restraints and exactions; communication between distant points and sections obstructed or cut off; our sons made soldiers to deluge with blood the fields they now till in peace; the mass of our people borne down and impoverished by taxes to support armies and navies, and military leaders at the head of their victorious legions becoming our lawgivers and judges. The loss of liberty, of all good government, of peace, plenty, and happiness, must inevitably follow a dissolution of the Union. In supporting it, therefore, we support all that is dear to the freeman and the philanthropist.

The time at which I stand before you is full of interest. The eyes of all nations are fixed on our Republic. The event of the existing crisis will be decisive in the opinion of mankind of the practicability of our federal system of government. Great is the stake placed in our hands; great is the responsibility which must rest upon the people of the United States. Let us realize the importance of the attitude in which we stand before the world. Let us exercise forbearance and firmness. Let us extricate our country from the dangers which surround it and learn wisdom from the lessons they inculcate.

Deeply impressed with the truth of these observations, and under the obligation of that solemn oath which I am about to take, I shall continue to exert all my faculties to maintain the just powers of the Constitution and to transmit unimpaired to posterity the blessings of our Federal Union. At the same time, it will be my aim to inculcate by my official acts the necessity of exercising by the General Government those powers only that are clearly delegated; to encourage simplicity and economy in the expenditures of the Government; to raise no more money from the people than may be requisite for these objects, and in a manner that will best promote the interests of all classes of the community and of all portions of the Union. Constantly bearing in mind that in entering into society "individuals must give up a share of liberty to preserve the rest," it will be my desire so to discharge my duties as to foster with our brethren in all parts of the country a spirit of liberal concession and compromise, and, by reconciling our fellow-citizens to those partial sacrifices which they must unavoidably make for the preservation of a greater good, to recommend our invaluable Government and Union to the confidence and affections of the American people.

Finally, it is my most fervent prayer to that Almighty Being before whom I now stand, and who has kept us in His hands from the infancy of our Republic to the present day, that He will so overrule all my intentions and actions and inspire the hearts of my fellow citizens that we may be preserved from dangers of all kinds and continue forever a united and happy people.

MARTIN VAN BUREN

INAUGURAL ADDRESS

MARCH 4, 1837

COMMENTARY

In 1836, after Andrew Jackson had served his two terms, he chose the mercurial politician Martin Van Buren as his successor, and the Democratic convention promptly and unanimously nominated him. Two years earlier, the national Republicans, at Clay's urging, changed their name to the Whig Party, symbolizing their opposition to "the reign of King Andrew." The Whigs shunned a national convention in 1836 because of the many disparate factions within their ranks. Adopting the strategy of nominating several candidates with strong local appeal, they hoped to throw the election into the House of Representatives for a final decision. Van Buren, lacking a large national following, pledged himself to "tread generally in the footsteps of President Jackson." Jackson's enormous popularity immeasurably assisted Van Buren. He carried 15 of the 26 states, receiving 170 electoral ballots to the combined total of 64 for his four opponents. In the popular vote, Van Buren polled 761,500 to 736,250 for the Whig candidates.

On March 4, 1837, Andrew Jackson, now nearing his seventieth birthday, witnessed the inauguration of his heir. Seated beside Van Buren, he rode to the Capitol as the thousands who lined Pennsylvania Avenue wildly cheered. "For once," wrote Thomas Hart Benton, "the rising was eclipsed by the setting sun. It was gratitude and admiration . . . the acclaim of posterity breaking from the bosoms of contemporaries." As the new president delivered his long, sanctimonious address, one astute observer noted that most eyes were turned on "Old Hickory." In fact, while Van Buren spoke, copies of Jackson's affectionate Farewell Address circulated among the crowd. For eight years Jackson had

condemned sectionalism when it impugned loyalty to the Union and, holding
the vision of an egalitarian society before the masses, had repeatedly displayed
his faith in the common man. The great democratic society of which Jefferson
had spoken almost reached fulfillment during the administration of Andrew
Jackson. It remained to be seen if his disciples could carry forward his political
philosophy.

Fellow citizens:

The practice of all my predecessors imposes on me an obligation I cheerfully fulfill; to accompany the first and solemn act of my public trust with an avowal of the principles that will guide me in performing it and an expression of my feelings on assuming a charge so responsible and vast. In imitating their example I tread in the footsteps of illustrious men, whose superiors it is our happiness to believe are not found on the executive calendar of any country. Among them we recognize the earliest and firmest pillars of the Republic; those by whom our national independence was first declared, him who above all others contributed to establish it on the field of battle, and those whose expanded intellect and patriotism constructed, improved, and perfected the inestimable institutions under which we live. If such men in the position I now occupy felt themselves overwhelmed by a sense of gratitude for this the highest of all marks of their country's confidence, and by a consciousness of their inability adequately to discharge the duties of an office so difficult and exalted, how much more must these considerations affect one who can rely on no such claims for favor or forbearance. Unlike all who have preceded me, the Revolution that gave us existence as one people was achieved at the period of my birth; and whilst I contemplate with grateful reverence that memorable event, I feel that I belong to a later age and that I may not expect my countrymen to weigh my actions with the same kind and partial hand.

So sensibly, fellow citizens, do these circumstances press themselves upon me that I should not dare to enter upon my path of duty did I not look for the generous aid of those who will be associated with me in the various and coordinate branches of the Government; did I not repose with unwavering reliance on the patriotism, the intelligence, and the kindness of a people who never yet deserted a public servant honestly laboring their cause; and, above all, did I not permit myself humbly to hope for the sustaining support of an ever watchful and beneficent Providence.

To the confidence and consolation derived from these sources it would be ungrateful not to add those which spring from our present fortunate condition. Though not altogether exempt from embarrassments that disturb our tranquillity at home and threaten it abroad, yet in all the attributes of a great, happy, and flourishing people we stand without a parallel in the world. Abroad we enjoy the respect and, with scarcely an exception, the friendship of every nation; at home, while our Government quietly but efficiently performs the sole legitimate end of political institutions, in doing the greatest good to the greatest number, we present an aggregate of human prosperity surely not elsewhere to be found.

How imperious, then, is the obligation imposed upon every citizen, in his own sphere of action, whether limited or extended, to exert himself in perpetuating a condition of things so singularly happy. All the lessons of history and experience must be lost upon us if we are content to trust alone to the peculiar advantages we happen to possess. Position and climate and the bounteous resources that nature has scattered with so liberal a hand, even the diffused intelligence and elevated character of our people, will avail us nothing if we fail sacredly to uphold those political institutions that were wisely and deliberately formed with reference to every circumstance that could preserve or might endanger the blessings we enjoy. The thoughtful framers of our Constitution legislated for our country as they found it. Looking upon it with the eyes of statesmen and patriots, they saw all the sources of rapid and wonderful prosperity; but they saw also that various habits, opinions and institutions peculiar to the various portions of so vast a region were deeply fixed. Distinct sovereignties were in actual existence, whose cordial union was essential to the welfare and happiness of all. Between many of them there was, at least to some extent, a real diversity of interests, liable to be exaggerated through sinister designs; they differed in size, in population, in wealth, and in actual and prospective resources and power; they varied in the character of their industry and staple productions, and [in some] existed domestic institutions which, unwisely disturbed, might endanger the harmony of the whole. Most carefully were all these circumstances weighed, and the foundations of the new Government laid upon principles of reciprocal concession and equitable compromise. The jealousies which the smaller States might entertain of the power of the rest were allayed by a rule of representation confessedly unequal at the time, and designed forever to remain so. A natural fear that the broad scope of general legislation might bear upon and unwisely control particular interests was counteracted by limits strictly drawn around the action of the Federal authority, and to the people and the States was left unimpaired their sovereign power over the innumerable subjects embraced in the internal government of a just republic, excepting such only as necessarily appertain to the concerns of the whole confederacy or its intercourse as a united community with the other nations of the world.

This provident forecast has been verified by time. Half a century, teeming with extraordinary events, and elsewhere producing astonishing results, has passed along, but on our institutions it has left no injurious mark. From a small community we have risen to a people powerful in numbers and in strength; but with our increase has gone hand in hand the progress of just principles. The privileges, civil and religious, of the humblest individual are still sacredly protected at home, and while the valor and fortitude of our people have removed far from us the slightest apprehension of foreign power, they have not yet induced us in a single instance to forget what is right. Our commerce has been extended to the remotest nations; the value and even nature of our productions have been greatly changed; a wide difference has arisen in the relative wealth and resources of every portion of our country; yet the spirit of mutual regard and of faithful adherence to existing compacts has continued to prevail in our councils and never long been absent from our conduct. We have learned by experience a fruitful lesson; that an implicit and undeviating adherence to the principles on which we set out can carry us prosperously onward through all the conflicts of circumstances and vicissitudes inseparable from the lapse of years.

The success that has thus attended our great experiment is in itself a sufficient cause for gratitude, on account of the happiness it has actually conferred and the example it has unanswerably given. But to me, my fellow citizens, looking forward to the far distant future with ardent prayers and confiding hopes, this retrospect presents a ground for still deeper delight. It impresses on my mind a firm belief that the perpetuity of our institutions depends upon ourselves; that if we maintain the principles on which they were established they are destined to confer their benefits on countless generations yet to come, and that America will present to every friend of mankind the cheering proof that a popular government, wisely formed, is wanting in no element of endurance or strength. Fifty years ago its rapid failure was boldly predicted. Latent and uncontrollable causes of dissolution were supposed to exist even by the wise and good, and not only did unfriendly or speculative theorists anticipate for us the fate of past republics, but the fears of many an honest patriot overbalanced his sanguine hopes. Look back on these forebodings, not hastily but reluctantly made, and see how in every instance they have completely failed.

An imperfect experience during the struggles of the Revolution was supposed to warrant the belief that the people would not bear the taxation requisite to discharge an immense public debt already incurred and to pay the necessary expenses of the Government. The cost of two wars has been paid, not only without a murmur; but with unequaled alacrity. No one is now left to doubt that every burden will be cheerfully borne that may be necessary to sustain our civil institutions or guard our honor or welfare. Indeed, all experience has shown that the willingness of the people to contribute to these ends in cases of emergency has uniformly outrun the confidence of their representatives.

In the early stages of the new Government, when all felt the imposing influence as they recognized the unequaled services of the first President, it was a common sentiment that the great weight of his character could alone bind the discordant materials of our Government together and save us from the violence of contending factions. Since his death nearly forty years are gone. Party exasperation has been often carried to its highest point; the virtue and fortitude of the people have sometimes been greatly tried; yet our system, purified and enhanced in value by all it has encountered, still preserves its spirit of free and fearless discussion, blended with unimpaired fraternal feeling.

The capacity of the people for self-government, and their willingness, from a high sense of duty and without those exhibitions of coercive power so generally employed in other countries, to submit to all needful restraints and exactions of municipal law, have also been favorably exemplified in the history of the American States. Occasionally, it is true, the ardor of public sentiment, outrunning the regular progress of the judicial tribunals or seeking to reach cases not denounced as criminal by the existing law, has displayed itself in a manner calculated to give pain to the friends of free government and to encourage the hopes of those who wish for its overthrow. These occurrences, however, have been far less frequent in our country than in any other of equal population on the globe, and with the diffusion of intelligence it may well be hoped that they will constantly diminish in frequency and violence. The generous patriotism and sound common sense of the great mass of our fellow citizens will assuredly in time produce this result; for as every assumption of illegal power not only wounds the majesty of the law, but furnishes a pretext for abridging the liberties of the people, the latter have the most direct and permanent interest in preserving the landmarks of social order and maintaining on all occasions the inviolability of those constitutional and legal provisions which they themselves have made.

In a supposed unfitness of our institutions for those hostile emergencies which no country can always avoid their friends found a fruitful source of apprehension, their enemies of hope. While they foresaw less promptness of action than in governments differently formed, they overlooked the far more important consideration that with us war could never be the result of individual or irresponsible will, but must be a measure of redress for injuries sustained voluntarily resorted to by those who were to bear the necessary sacrifice, who would consequently feel an individual interest in the contest, and whose energy would be commensurate with the difficulties to be encountered. Actual events have proved their error; the last war, far from impairing, gave new confidence to our Government, and amid recent apprehensions of a similar conflict we saw that the energies of our country would not be wanting in ample season to vindicate its rights. We may not possess, as we should not desire to possess, the extended and ever ready military organization of other nations; we may occasionally suffer in the outset for the want of it; but among ourselves all doubt upon this great point has ceased, while a salutary experience will prevent a contrary opinion from inviting aggression from abroad.

Certain danger was foretold from the extension of our territory, the multiplication of States, and the increase of population. Our system was supposed to be adapted only to boundaries comparatively narrow. These have been widened beyond conjecture; the members of our Confederacy are already doubled, and the numbers of our people are incredibly augmented. The alleged causes of danger have long surpassed anticipation, but none of the consequences have followed. The power and influence of the Republic have arisen to a height obvious to all mankind; respect for its authority was not more apparent at its ancient than it is at its present limits; new and inexhaustible sources of general prosperity have been opened; the effects of distance have been averted by the inventive genius of our people, developed and fostered by the spirit of our institutions; and the enlarged variety and amount of interests, productions, and pursuits have strengthened the chain of mutual dependence and formed a circle of mutual benefits too apparent ever to be overlooked.

In justly balancing the powers of the Federal and State authorities difficulties nearly insurmountable arose at the outset and subsequent collisions were deemed inevitable. Amid these it was scarcely believed possible that a scheme of government so complex in construction could remain uninjured.

From time to time embarrassments have certainly occurred; but how just is the confidence of future safety imparted by the knowledge that each in succession has been happily removed. Overlooking partial and temporary evils as inseparable from the practical operation of all human institutions, and looking only to the general result, every patriot has reason to be satisfied. While the Federal Government has successfully performed its appropriate functions in relation to foreign affairs and concerns evidently national, that of every State has remarkably improved in protecting and developing local interests and individual welfare; and if the vibrations of authority have occasionally tended too much toward one or the other, it is unquestionably certain that the ultimate operation of the entire system has been to strengthen all the existing institutions and to elevate our whole country in prosperity and renown.

The last, perhaps the greatest, of the prominent sources of discord and disaster supposed to lurk in our political condition was the institution of domestic slavery. Our forefathers were deeply impressed with the delicacy of this subject, and they treated it with a forbearance so evidently wise that in spite of every sinister foreboding it never until the present period disturbed the tranquillity of our common country. Such a result is sufficient evidence of the justice and the patriotism of their course; it is evidence not to be mistaken that an adherence to it can prevent all embarrassment from this as well as from every other anticipated cause of difficulty or danger. Have not recent events made it obvious to the slightest reflection that the least deviation from this spirit of forbearance is injurious to every interest, that of humanity included? Amidst the violence of excited passions this generous and fraternal feeling has been sometimes disregarded; and standing as I now do before my countrymen, in this high place of honor and of trust, I can not refrain from anxiously invoking my fellow citizens never to be deaf to its dictates. Perceiving before my election the deep interest this subject was beginning to excite, I believed it a solemn duty fully to make known my sentiments in regard to it, and now, when every motive for misrepresentation has passed away, I trust that they will be candidly weighed and understood. At least they will be my standard of conduct in the path before me. I then declared that if the desire of those of my countrymen who were favorable to my election was gratified, I must go into the Presidential chair the inflexible and uncompromising opponent of every attempt on the part of Congress to abolish slavery in the District of Columbia against the wishes of the slaveholding States, and also with a determination equally decided to resist the slightest interference with it in the States where it exists. I submitted also to my fellow citizens, with fullness and frankness, the reasons which led me to this determination. The result authorizes me to believe that they have been approved and are confided in by a majority of the people of the United States, including those whom they most immediately affect. It now only remains to add that no bill conflicting with these views can ever receive my constitutional sanction. These opinions have been adopted in the firm belief that they are in accordance with the spirit that actuated the venerated fathers of the Republic, and that succeeding experience has proved them to be humane, patriotic, expedient, honorable, and just. If the agitation of this subject was intended to reach the stability of our institutions, enough has occurred to show that it has signally failed, and that in this as in every other instance the apprehensions of the timid and the hopes of the wicked for the destruction of our Government are again destined to be disappointed. Here and there, indeed, scenes of dangerous excitement have occurred, terrifying instances of local violence have been witnessed, and a reckless disregard of the consequences of their conduct has exposed individuals to popular indignation; but neither masses of the people nor sections of the country have been swerved from their devotion to the bond of union and the principles it has made sacred. It will be ever thus. Such attempts at dangerous agitation may periodically return, but with each the object will be better understood. That predominating affection for our political system which prevails throughout our territorial limits, that calm and enlightened judgment which ultimately governs our people as one vast body, will always be at hand to resist and control every effort, foreign or domestic, which aims or would lead to overthrow our institutions.

What can be more gratifying than such a retrospect as this? We look back on obstacles avoided and dangers overcome, on expectations more than realized and prosperity perfectly secured. To the hopes of the hostile, the fears of the timid, and the doubts of the anxious actual experience has given the conclusive reply. We have seen time gradually dispel every unfavorable foreboding and our Constitution surmount every adverse circumstance dreaded at the outset as beyond control. Present excitement will at all times magnify present dangers, but true philosophy must teach us that none more threatening than the past can remain to be overcome; and we ought, for we have just reason, to entertain an abiding confidence in the stability of our institutions and an entire conviction that if administered in the true form, character, and spirit in which they were established they are abundantly adequate to preserve to us and our children the rich blessings already derived from them, to make our beloved land for a thousand generations that chosen spot where happiness springs from a perfect equality of political rights.

For myself, therefore, I desire to declare that the principle that will govern me in the high duty to which my country calls me is a strict adherence to the letter and spirit of the Constitution as it was designed by those who framed it. Looking back to it as a sacred instrument carefully and not easily framed; remembering that it was throughout a work of concession and compromise; viewing it as limited to national objects; regarding it as leaving to the people and the States all power not explicitly parted with, I shall endeavor to preserve, protect, and defend it by anxiously referring to its provision for direction in every action. To matters of domestic concernment which it has intrusted to the Federal Government and to such as relate to our intercourse with foreign nations I shall zealously devote myself; beyond those limits I shall never pass.

To enter on this occasion into a further or more minute exposition of my views on the various questions of domestic policy would be as obtrusive as it is probably unexpected. Before the suffrages of my countrymen were conferred upon me I submitted to them, with great precision, my opinions on all the most prominent of these subjects. Those opinions I shall endeavor to carry out with my utmost ability.

Our course of foreign policy has been so uniform and intelligible as to constitute a rule of Executive conduct which leaves little to my discretion, unless, indeed, I were willing to run counter to the lights of experience and the known opinions of my constituents. We sedulously cultivate the friendship of all nations as the conditions most compatible with our welfare and the principles of our Government. We decline alliances as adverse to our peace. We desire commercial relations on equal terms, being ever willing to give a fair equivalent for advantages received. We endeavor to conduct our intercourse with openness and sincerity, promptly avowing our objects and seeking to establish that mutual frankness which is as beneficial in the dealings of nations as of men. We have no disposition and we disclaim all right to meddle in disputes, whether internal or foreign, that may molest other countries, regarding them in their actual state as social communities, and preserving a strict neutrality in all their controversies. Well knowing the tried valor of our people and our exhaustless resources, we neither anticipate nor fear any designed aggression; and in the consciousness of our own just conduct we feel a security that we shall never be called upon to exert our determination never to permit an invasion of our rights without punishment or redress.

In approaching, then, in the presence of my assembled countrymen, to make the solemn promise that yet remains, and to pledge myself that I will faithfully execute the office I am about to fill, I bring with me a settled purpose to maintain the institutions of my country, which I trust will atone for the errors I commit.

In receiving from the people the sacred trust twice confided to my illustrious predecessor, and which he has discharged so faithfully and so well, I know that I can not expect to perform the arduous task with equal ability and success. But united as I have been in his counsels, a daily witness of his exclusive and unsurpassed devotion to his country's welfare, agreeing with him in sentiments which his countrymen have warmly supported, and permitted to partake largely of his confidence, I may hope that somewhat of the same cheering approbation will be found to attend upon my path. For him I but express with my own the wishes of all, that he may yet long live to enjoy the brilliant evening of his well-spent life; and for myself, conscious of but one desire, faithfully to serve my country, I throw myself without fear on its justice and its kindness. Beyond that I only look to the gracious protection of the Divine Being whose strengthening support I humbly solicit, and whom I fervently pray to look down upon us all. May it be among the dispensations of His providence to bless our beloved country with honors and with length of days. May her ways be ways of pleasantness and all her paths be peace.

WILLIAM HENRY HARRISON

INAUGURAL ADDRESS

MARCH 4, 1841

COMMENTARY

Van Buren planned to follow in Jackson's footsteps by endorsing programs acceptable to both southern and western farmers and to the growing working class of the North. But within two months of the inauguration, a general financial and business collapse caused by overspeculative investments in land and industry confronted the president. Stock prices tumbled. Imports fell and customs revenue dwindled. In New York City, unemployed workers demonstrated against high rents and inflated food costs. In the South, cotton prices halved. Writing in 1897, the noted historian John Burgess commented that "Van Buren and his advisors decided very properly not to involve the Government, but to let the people work themselves through the disaster by the natural course of business." Likewise, the distinguished scholar Edward Channing observed in his History of the United States, *published in 1921, that nothing could be done as the causes "may possibly be found in the workings of nature . . . synchronized with a maxima of sun spots." Although contemporary cartoons vividly depicted depression conditions—shylock pawnbrokers, hungry women begging, and undernourished children—Van Buren's concept of democracy, sanctioned by these later historians, did not include any sort of government assistance. Pressed by the opponents of banks, the administrations did propose an independent Treasury bill that divorced the government from all national and state banks. As could be expected, the depression, which persisted until 1843, turned many Van Buren supporters into opponents.*

The Whigs lost no chance to discredit the Democrats, comparing the independent Treasury system to "the captain of a ship at sea who seizes the lifeboats to save himself and his crew, but permits the passengers to drown." Meeting in December 1839, the Whig convention, in an attempt to conciliate factional differences, bypassed Clay and nominated General William Henry Harrison, the 67-year-old hero of the Battle of Tippecanoe (1811). The Whig strategy stressed songs, parades, gigantic balls and, as Nicholas Biddle advised, "not one single word about [Harrison's] principles, or his creed—let him say nothing—promise nothing." Log cabins, in which the general's birth allegedly occurred, were pulled through the streets as people sang:

> *"Tippecanoe and Tyler too,*
> *Tippecanoe and Tyler too,*
> *And with them we'll beat little Van, Van, Van,*
> *And with them we'll beat little Van, Van, Van—*
> *Oh! Van is a used-up man!"*

On Election Day, Van Buren and the Democrats suffered a humiliating defeat, receiving only 60 electoral votes to Harrison's 234.

Harrison's inauguration took place on a beautiful day. Mounted on a white charger, the president-elect led the procession to the Capitol. Escorted to the East Portico, Harrison delivered a platitudinous speech of 8,466 words—the longest inaugural address. One month after his accession, the president succumbed to pneumonia.

Called from a retirement which I had supposed was to continue for the residue of my life to fill the chief executive office of this great and free nation, I appear before you, fellow citizens, to take the oaths which the Constitution prescribes as a necessary qualification for the performance of its duties; and in obedience to a custom coeval with our Government and what I believe to be your expectations I proceed to present to you a summary of the principles which will govern me in the discharge of the duties which I shall be called upon to perform.

It was the remark of a Roman consul in an early period of that celebrated Republic that a most striking contrast was observable in the conduct of candidates for offices of power and trust before and after obtaining them, they seldom carrying out in the latter case the pledges and promises made in the former. However much the world may have improved in many respects in the lapse of upward of two thousand years since the remark was made by the virtuous and indignant Roman, I fear that a strict examination of the annals of some of the modern elective governments would develop similar instances of violated confidence.

Although the fiat of the people has gone forth proclaiming me the Chief Magistrate of this glorious Union, nothing upon their part remaining to be done, it may be thought that a motive may exist to keep up the delusion under which they may be supposed to have acted in relation to my principles and opinions; and perhaps there may be some in this assembly who have come here either prepared to condemn those I shall now deliver, or, approving them, to doubt the sincerity with which they are now uttered. But the lapse of a few months will confirm or dispel their fears. The outline of principles to govern and measures to be adopted by an Administration not yet begun will soon be exchanged for immutable history, and I shall stand either exonerated by my countrymen or classed with the mass of those who promised that they might deceive and flattered with the intention to betray. However strong may be my present purpose to realize the expectations of a magnanimous and confiding people, I too well understand the dangerous temptations to which I shall be exposed from the magnitude of the power which it has been the pleasure of the people to commit to my hands not to place my chief confidence upon the aid of that Almighty Power which has hitherto protected me and enabled me to bring to favorable issues other important but still greatly inferior trusts heretofore confided to me by my country.

The broad foundation upon which our Constitution rests being the people; a breath of theirs having made, as a breath can unmake, change, or modify it; it can be assigned to none of the great divisions of government but to that of democracy. If such is its theory, those who are called upon to administer it must recognize as its leading principle the duty of shaping their measures so as to produce the greatest good to the greatest number. But with these broad admissions, if we would compare the sovereignty acknowledged to exist in the mass of our people with the power claimed by other sovereignties, even by those which have been considered most purely democratic, we shall find a most essential difference. All others lay claim to power limited only by their own will. The majority of our citizens, on the contrary, possess a sovereignty with an amount of power precisely equal to that which has been granted to them by the parties to the national compact, and nothing beyond. We admit of no government by divine right, believing that so far as power is concerned the Beneficent Creator has made no distinction amongst men; that all are upon an equality, and that the only legitimate right to govern is an express grant of power from the governed. The Constitution of the United States is the instrument containing this grant of power to the several departments composing the Government. On an examination of that instrument it will be found to contain declarations of power granted and of power withheld. The latter is also susceptible of division into power which the majority had the right to grant, but which they do not think proper to intrust to their agents, and that which they could not have granted, not being possessed by themselves. In other words, there are certain rights possessed by each individual American citizen which in his compact with the others he has never surrendered. Some of them, indeed, he is unable to surrender, being, in the language of our system, unalienable. The boasted privilege of a Roman citizen was to him a shield only against a petty provincial ruler, whilst the proud democrat of Athens would console himself under a sentence of death for a supposed violation of the national faith, which no one understood and which at times was the subject of the mockery of all, or the banishment from his home, his family, and his country with or without an alleged cause, that it was the act not of a single tyrant or hated aristocracy, but of his assembled countrymen. Far different is the power of our sovereignty. It can interfere with no one's faith, prescribe forms of worship for no one's observance, inflict no punishment but after well-ascertained guilt, the result of investigation under rules prescribed by the Constitution itself. These precious privileges, and those scarcely less important of giving expression to his thoughts and opinions, either by writing or speaking, unrestrained but by the liability for injury to others, and that of a full participation in all the advantages which flow from the Government, the acknowledged property of all, the American citizen derives from no charter granted by his fellow-man. He claims them because he is himself a man, fashioned by the same Almighty hand as the rest of his species and entitled to a full share of the blessings with which He has endowed them. Notwithstanding the limited sovereignty possessed by the people of the United States and the restricted grant of power to the Government which they have adopted, enough has been given to accomplish all the objects for which it was created. It has been found powerful in war, and hitherto justice has been administered, and intimate union effected, domestic tranquillity preserved, and personal liberty secured to the citizen. As was to be expected, however, from the defect of language and the necessarily sententious manner in which the Constitution is written, disputes have arisen as to the amount of power which it has actually granted or was intended to grant.

This is more particularly the case in relation to that part of the instrument which treats of the legislative branch, and not only as regards the exercise of powers claimed under a general clause giving that body the authority to pass all laws necessary to carry into effect the specified pow-ers, but in relation to the latter also. It is, however, consolatory to reflect that most of the instances of alleged departure from the letter or spirit of the Constitution have ultimately received the sanction of a majority of the people. And the fact that many of our statesmen most distinguished for talent and patriotism have been at one time or other of their political career on both sides of each of the most warmly disputed questions forces upon us the inference that the errors, if errors there were, are attributable to the intrinsic difficulty in many instances of ascertaining the intentions of the framers of the Constitution rather than the influence of any sinister or unpatriotic motive. But the great danger to our institutions does not ap-pear to me to be in a usurpation by the Government of power not granted by the people, but by the accumulation in one of the departments of that which was assigned to others. Limited as are the powers which have been granted, still enough have been granted to constitute a despotism if con-centrated in one of the departments. This danger is greatly heightened, as it has been always observable that men are less jealous of encroachments of one department upon another than upon their own reserved rights. When the Constitution of the United States first came from the hands of the Con-vention which formed it, many of the sternest republicans of the day were alarmed at the extent of the power which had been granted to the Federal Government, and more particularly of that portion which had been as-signed to the executive branch. There were in it features which appeared not to be in harmony with their ideas of a simple representative democracy or republic, and knowing the tendency of power to increase itself, particu-larly when exercised by a single individual, predictions were made that at no very remote period the Government would terminate in virtual mon-archy. It would not become me to say that the fears of these patriots have been already realized; but as I sincerely believe that the tendency of mea-sures and of men's opinions for some years past has been in that direction, it is, I conceive, strictly proper that I should take this occasion to repeat the assurances I have heretofore given of my determination to arrest the progress of that tendency if it really exists and restore the Government to its pristine health and vigor, as far as this can be effected by any legitimate exercise of the power placed in my hands.

I proceed to state in as summary a manner as I can my opinion of the sources of the evils which have been so extensively complained of and the correctives which may be applied. Some of the former are unquestionably to be found in the defects of the Constitution; others, in my judgment, are attributable to a misconstruction of some of its provisions. Of the former is the eligibility of the same individual to a second term of the Presidency. The sagacious mind of Mr. Jefferson early saw and lamented this error, and attempts have been made, hitherto without success, to apply the amendatory power of the States to its correction. As, however, one mode of correction is in the power of every President, and consequently in mine, it would be useless, and perhaps invidious, to enumerate the evils of which, in the opinion of many of our fellow citizens, this error of the sages who framed the Constitution may have been the source and the bitter fruits which we are still to gather from it if it continues to disfigure our system. It may be observed, however, as a general remark, that republics can commit no greater error than to adopt or continue any feature in their systems of government which may be calculated to create or increase the lover of power in the bosoms of those to whom necessity obliges them to commit the management of their affairs; and surely nothing is more likely to produce such a state of mind than the long continuance of an office of high trust. Nothing can be more corrupting, nothing more destructive of all those noble feelings which belong to the character of a devoted republican patriot. When this corrupting passion once takes possession of the human mind, like the love of gold it becomes insatiable. It is the never dying worm in his bosom, grows with his growth and strengthens with the declining years of its victim. If this is true, it is the part of wisdom for a republic to limit the service of that officer at least to whom she has intrusted the management of her foreign relations, the execution of her laws, and the command of her armies and navies to a period so short as to prevent his forgetting that he is the accountable agent, not the principal; the servant, not the master. Until an amendment of the Constitution can be effected public opinion may secure the desired object. I give my aid to it by renewing the pledge heretofore given that under no circumstances will I consent to serve a second term.

But if there is danger to public liberty from the acknowledged defects of the Constitution in the want of limit to the continuance of the Executive power in the same hands, there is, I apprehend, not much less from a misconstruction of that instrument as it regards the powers actually given. I can not conceive that by a fair construction any or either of its provisions would be found to constitute the President a part of the legislative power. It can not be claimed from the power to recommend, since, although enjoined as a duty upon him, it is a privilege which he holds in common with every other citizen; and although there may be something more of confidence in the propriety of the measures recommended in the one case than in the other, in the obligations of ultimate decision there can be no difference. In the language of the Constitution, all the legislative powers, which it grants, are vested in the Congress of the United States. It would be a solecism in language to say that any portion of these is not included in the whole.

It may be said, indeed, that the Constitution has given to the Executive the power to annul the acts of the legislative body by refusing to them his assent. So a similar power has necessarily resulted from that instrument to the judiciary, and yet the judiciary forms no part of the Legislature. There is, it is true, this difference between these grants of power: The Executive can put his negative upon the acts of the Legislature for other cause than that of want of conformity to the Constitution, whilst the judiciary can only declare void those which violate that instrument. But the decision of the judiciary is final in such a case, whereas in every instance where the veto of the Executive is applied it may be overcome by a vote of two-thirds of both Houses of Congress. The negative upon the acts of the legislative by the executive authority, and that in the hands of one individual, would seem to be an incongruity in our system. Like some others of a similar character, however, it appears to be highly expedient, and if used only with the forbearance and in the spirit which was intended by its authors it may be productive of great good and be found one of the best safeguards to the Union. At the period of the formation of the Constitution the principle does not appear to have enjoyed much favor in the State governments. It existed but in two, and in one of these there was a plural executive. If we would search for the motives which operated upon the purely patriotic and enlightened assembly which framed the Constitution for the adoption of a provision so apparently repugnant to the leading democratic principle that the majority should govern, we must reject the idea that they anticipated from it any benefit to the ordinary course of legislation. They knew too well the high degree of intelligence which existed among the people and the enlightened character of the State legislatures not to have the fullest confidence that the two bodies elected by them would be worthy representatives of such constituents, and, of course, that they would require no aid in conceiving and maturing the measures which the circumstances of the country might require. And it is preposterous to suppose that a thought could for a moment have been entertained that the President, placed at the capital, in the center of the country, could better understand the wants and wishes of the people than their own immediate representatives, who spend a part of every year among them, living with them, often laboring with them, and bound to them by the triple tie of interest, duty, and affection. To assist or control Congress, then, in its ordinary legislation could not, I conceive, have been the motive for conferring the veto power on the President. This argument acquires additional force from the fact of its never having been thus used by the first six Presidents—and two of them were members of the Convention, one presiding over its deliberations and the other bearing a larger share in consummating the labors of that august body than any other person. But if bills were never returned to Congress by either of the Presidents above referred to upon the ground of their being inexpedient or not as well adapted as they might be to the wants of the people, the veto was applied upon that of want of conformity to the Constitution or because errors had been committed from a too hasty enactment.

There is another ground for the adoption of the veto principle, which had probably more influence in recommending it to the Convention than any other. I refer to the security which it gives to the just and equitable action of the Legislature upon all parts of the Union. It could not but have occurred to the Convention that in a country so extensive, embracing so great a variety of soil and climate, and consequently of products, and which from the same causes must ever exhibit a great difference in the amount of the population of its various sections, calling for a great diversity in the employments of the people, that the legislation of the majority might not always justly regard the rights and interests of the minority, and that acts of this character might be passed under an express grant by the words of the Constitution, and therefore not within the competency of the judiciary to declare void; that however enlightened and patriotic they might suppose from past experience the members of Congress might be, and however largely partaking, in the general, of the liberal feelings of the people, it was impossible to expect that bodies so constituted should not sometimes be controlled by local interests and sectional feelings. It was proper, therefore, to provide some umpire from whose situation and mode of appointment more independence and freedom from such influences might be expected. Such a one was afforded by the executive department constituted by the Constitution. A person elected to that high office, having his constituents in every section, State, and subdivision of the Union, must consider himself bound by the most solemn sanctions to guard, protect, and defend the rights of all and of every portion, great or small, from the injustice and oppression of the rest.

I consider the veto power, therefore given by the Constitution to the Executive of the United States solely as a conservative power, to be used only first, to protect the Constitution from violation; secondly, the people from the effects of hasty legislation where their will has been probably disregarded or not well understood; and, thirdly, to prevent the effects of combinations violative of the rights of minorities. In reference to the second of these objects I may observe that I consider it the right and privilege of the people to decide disputed points of the Constitution arising from the general grant of power to Congress to carry into effect the powers expressly given; and I believe with Mr. Madison that repeated recognitions under varied circumstances in acts of the legislative, executive, and judicial branches of the Government, accompanied by indications in different modes of the concurrence of the general will of the nation, as affording to the President sufficient authority for his considering such disputed points as settled.

Upward of half a century has elapsed since the adoption of the present form of government. It would be an object more highly desirable than the gratification of the curiosity of speculative statesmen if its precise situation could be ascertained, a fair exhibit made of the operations of each of its departments, of the powers which they respectively claim and exercise, of the collisions which have occurred between them or between the whole Government and those of the States or either of them. We could then compare our actual condition after fifty years' trial of our system with what it was in the commencement of its operations and ascertain whether the predictions of the patriots who opposed its adoption or the confident hopes of its advocates have been best realized. The great dread of the former seems to have been that the reserved powers of the States would be absorbed by those of the Federal Government and a consolidated power established, leaving to the States the shadow only of that independent action for which they had so zealously contended and on the preservation of which they relied as the last hope of liberty. Without denying that the result to which they looked with so much apprehension is in the way of being realized, it is obvious that they did not clearly see the mode of its accomplishment. The General Government has seized upon none of the reserved rights of the States. As far as any open warfare may have gone, the State authorities have amply maintained their rights. To a casual observer our system presents no appearance of discord between the different members which compose it. Even the addition of many new ones has produced no jarring. They move in their respective orbits in perfect harmony with the central head and with each other. But there is still an undercurrent at work by which, if not seasonably checked, the worst apprehensions of our antifederal patriots will be realized, and not only will the State authorities be overshadowed by the great increase of power in the executive department of the General Government, but the character of that Government, if not its designation, be essentially and radically changed. This state of things has been in part effected by causes inherent in the Constitution and in part by the never failing tendency of political power to increase itself. By making the President the sole distributer of all the patronage of the Government the framers of the Constitution do not appear to have anticipated at how short a period it would become a formidable instrument to control the free operations of the State governments. Of trifling importance at first, it had early in Mr. Jefferson's Administration become so powerful as to create great alarm in the mind of that patriot from the potent influence it might exert in controlling the freedom of the elective franchise. If such could have then been the effects of its influence, how much greater must be the danger at this time, quadrupled in amount as it certainly is and more completely under the control of the Executive will than their construction of their powers allowed or the forbearing characters of all the early Presidents permitted them to make. But it is not by the extent of its patronage alone that the executive department has become dangerous, but by the use which it appears may be made of the appointing power to bring under its control the whole revenues of the country. The Constitution has declared it to be the duty of the President to see that the laws are executed, and it makes him the Commander in Chief of the Armies and Navy of the United States. If the opinion of the most approved writers upon that species of mixed government which in modern Europe is termed monarchy in contradistinction to despotism is correct, there was wanting no other addition to the powers of our Chief Magistrate to stamp a monarchical character on our Government but the control of the public finances; and to me it appears strange indeed that anyone should doubt that the entire control which the President possesses over the officers who have the custody of the public money, by the power of removal with or without cause, does, for all mischievous purposes at least, virtually subject the treasure also to his disposal. The first Roman Emperor, in his attempt to seize the sacred treasure, silenced the opposition of the officer to whose charge it had been committed by a significant allusion to his sword. By a selection of political instruments for the care of the public money a reference to their commissions by a President would be quite as effectual an argument as that of

Caesar to the Roman knight. I am not insensible of the great difficulty that exists in drawing a proper plan for the safe keeping and disbursement of the public revenues, and I know the importance which has been attached by men of great abilities and patriotism to the divorce, as it is called, of the Treasury from the banking institutions. It is not the divorce which is complained of, but the unhallowed union of the Treasury with the executive department, which has created such extensive alarm. To this danger to our republican institutions and that created by the influence given to the Executive through the instrumentality of the Federal officers I propose to apply all the remedies which may be at my command. It was certainly a great error in the framers of the Constitution not to have made the officer at the head of the Treasury Department entirely independent of the Executive. He should at least have been removable only upon the demand of the popular branch of the Legislature. I have determined never to remove a Secretary of the Treasury without communicating all the circumstances attending such removal to both Houses of Congress.

The influence of the Executive in controlling the freedom of the elective franchise through the medium of the public officers can be effectually checked by renewing the prohibition published by Mr. Jefferson forbidding their interference in elections further than giving their own votes, and their own independence secured by an assurance of perfect immunity in exercising this sacred privilege of freemen under the dictates of their own unbiased judgments. Never with my consent shall an officer of the people, compensated for his services out of their pockets, become the pliant instrument of Executive will.

There is no part of the means placed in the hands of the Executive which might be used with greater effect for unhallowed purposes than the control of the public press. The maxim which our ancestors derived from the mother country that, the freedom of the press is the great bulwark of civil and religious liberty, is one of the most precious legacies which they have left us. We have learned, too, from our own as well as the experience of other countries, that golden shackles, by whomsoever or by whatever pretense imposed, are as fatal to it as the iron bonds of despotism. The presses in the necessary employment of the Government should never be used, to clear the guilty or to varnish crime. A decent and manly examination of the acts of the Government should be not only tolerated, but encouraged.

Upon another occasion I have given my opinion at some length upon the impropriety of Executive interference in the legislation of Congress, that the article in the Constitution making it the duty of the President to communicate information and authorizing him to recommend measures was not intended to make him the source in legislation, and, in particular, that he should never be looked to for schemes of finance. It would be very strange, indeed, that the Constitution should have strictly forbidden one branch of the Legislature from interfering in the origination of such bills and that it should be considered proper that an altogether different department of the Government should be permitted to do so. Some of our best political maxims and opinions have been drawn from our parent isle. There are others, however, which can not be introduced in our system without singular incongruity and the production of much mischief, and this I conceive to be one. No matter in which of the houses of Parliament a bill may originate nor by whom introduced, a minister or a member of the opposition, by the fiction of law, or rather of Constitutional principle, the sovereign is supposed to have prepared it agreeably to his will and then submitted it to Parliament for their advice and consent. Now the very reverse is the case here, not only with regard to the principle, but the forms prescribed by the Constitution. The principle certainly assigns to the only body constituted by the Constitution, the legislative body, the power to make laws, and the forms even direct that the enactment should be ascribed to them. The Senate, in relation to revenue bills, have the right to propose amendments, and so has the Executive by the power given him to return them to the House of Representatives with his objections. It is in his power also to propose amendments in the existing revenue laws, suggested by his observations upon their defective or injurious operation. But the delicate duty of devising schemes of revenue should be left where the Constitution has placed it, with the immediate representatives of the people. For similar reasons the mode of keeping the public treasure should be prescribed by them, and the further removed it may be from the control of the Executive the more wholesome the arrangement and the more in accordance with republican principle.

Connected with this subject is the character of the currency. The idea of making it exclusively metallic, however well intended, appears to me to be fraught with more fatal consequences than any other scheme having no relation to the personal rights of the citizens that has ever been devised. If any single scheme could produce the effect of arresting at once that mutation of condition by which thousands of our most indigent fellow citizens by their industry and enterprise are raised to the possession of wealth, that is the one. If there is one measure better calculated than another to produce that state of things so much deprecated by all true republicans, by which the rich are daily adding to their hoards and the poor sinking deeper into penury, it is an exclusive metallic currency. Or if there is a process by which the character of the country for generosity and nobleness of feeling may be destroyed by the great increase and neck toleration of usury, it is an exclusive metallic currency.

Amongst the other duties of a delicate character which the President is called upon to perform is the supervision of the government of the Territories of the United States. Those of them which are destined to become members of our great political family are compensated by their rapid progress from infancy to manhood for the partial and temporary deprivation of their political rights. It is in this District only where American citizens are to be found who under a settled policy are deprived of many important political privileges without any inspiring hope as to the future. Their only consolation under circumstances of such deprivation is that of the devoted exterior guards of a camp, that their sufferings secure tranquillity and safety within. Are there any of their countrymen, who would subject them to greater sacrifices, to any other humiliations than those essentially necessary to the security of the object for which they were thus separated from their fellow citizens? Are their rights alone not to be guaranteed by the application of those great principles upon which all our Constitutions are founded? We are told by the greatest of British orators and statesmen that at the commencement of the War of the Revolution the most stupid men in England spoke of their American subjects. Are there, indeed, citizens of any of our States who have dreamed of their subjects in the District of Columbia? Such dreams can never be realized by any agency of mine. The people of the District of Columbia are not the subjects of the people of the States, but free American citizens. Being in the latter condition when the Constitution was formed, no words used in that instrument could have been intended to deprive them of that character. If there is anything in the great principle of unalienable rights so emphatically insisted upon in our Declaration of Independence, they could neither make nor the United States accept a surrender of their liberties and become the subjects, in other words, the slaves, of their former fellow-citizens. If this be true, and it will scarcely be denied by anyone who has a correct idea of his own rights as an American citizen, the grant to Congress of exclusive jurisdiction in the District of Columbia can be interpreted, so far as respects the aggregate people of the United States, as meaning nothing more than to allow to Congress the controlling power necessary to afford a free and safe exercise of the functions assigned to the General Government by the Constitution. In all other respects the legislation of Congress should be adapted to their peculiar position and wants and be conformable with their deliberate opinions of their own interests.

I have spoken of the necessity of keeping the respective departments of the Government, as well as all the other authorities of our country, within their appropriate orbits. This is a matter of difficulty in some cases, as the powers which they respectively claim are often not defined by any distinct lines. Mischievous, however, in their tendencies as collisions of this kind may be, those which arise between the respective communities which for certain purposes compose one nation are much more so, for no such nation can long exist without the careful culture of those feelings of confidence and affection which are the effective bonds to union between free and confederated states. Strong as is the tie of interest, it has been often found ineffectual. Men blinded by their passions have been known to adopt measures for their country in direct opposition to all the suggestions of policy. The alternative, then, is to destroy or keep down a bad passion by creating and fostering a good one, and this seems to be the corner stone upon which our American political architects have reared the fabric of our Government. The cement which was to bind it and perpetuate its existence was the affectionate attachment between all its members. To insure the continuance of this feeling, produced at first by a community of dangers, of sufferings, and of interests, the advantages of each were made accessible to all. No participation in any good possessed by any member of our extensive Confederacy, except in domestic government, was withheld from the citizen of any other member. By a process attended with no difficulty, no delay, no expense but that of removal, the citizen of one might become the citizen of any other, and successively of the whole. The lines, too, separating powers to be exercised by the citizens of one State from those of another seem to be so distinctly drawn as to leave no room for misunderstanding. The citizens of each State unite in their persons all the privileges which that character confers and all that they may claim as citizens of the United States, but in no case can the same persons at the same time act as the citizen of two separate States, and he is therefore positively precluded from any interference with the reserved powers of any State but that of which he is for the time being a citizen. He may, indeed, offer to the citizens of other States his advice as to their management, and the form in which it is tendered is left to his own discretion and sense of propriety. It may be observed, however, that organized associations of citizens requiring compliance with their wishes too much resemble the recommendations of Athens to her allies, supported by an armed and powerful fleet. It was, indeed, to the ambition of the leading States of Greece to control the domestic concerns of the others that the destruction of that celebrated Confederacy, and subsequently of all its members, is mainly to be attributed, and it is owing to the absence of that spirit that the Helvetic Confederacy has for so many years been preserved. Never has there been seen in the institutions of the separate members of any confederacy more elements of discord. In the principles and forms of government and religion, as well as in the circumstances of the several Cantons, so marked a discrepancy was observable as to promise anything but harmony in their intercourse or permanency in their alliance, and yet for ages neither has been interrupted. Content with the positive benefits which their union produced, with the independence and safety from foreign aggression which it secured, these sagacious people respected the institutions of each other, however repugnant to their own principles and prejudices.

Our Confederacy, fellow citizens, can only be preserved by the same forbearance. Our citizens must be content with the exercise of the powers with which the Constitution clothes them. The attempt of those of one State to control the domestic institutions of another can only result in feelings of distrust and jealousy, the certain harbingers of disunion, violence, and civil war, and the ultimate destruction of our free institutions. Our Confederacy is perfectly illustrated by the terms and principles governing a common copartnership. There is a fund of power to be exercised under the direction of the joint councils of the allied members, but that which has been reserved by the individual members is intangible by the common Government or the individual members composing it. To attempt it finds no support in the principles of our Constitution.

It should be our constant and earnest endeavor mutually to cultivate a spirit of concord and harmony among the various parts of our Confederacy. Experience has abundantly taught us that the agitation by citizens of one part of the Union of a subject not confided to the General Government, but exclusively under the guardianship of the local authorities, is productive of no other consequences than bitterness, alienation, discord, and injury to the very cause which is intended to be advanced. Of all the great interests which appertain to our country, that of union, cordial, confiding, fraternal union, is by far the most important, since it is the only true and sure guaranty of all others.

In consequence of the embarrassed state of business and the currency, some of the States may meet with difficulty in their financial concerns. However deeply we may regret anything imprudent or excessive in the engagements into which States have entered for purposes of their own, it does not become us to disparage the States governments, nor to discourage them from making proper efforts for their own relief. On the contrary, it is our duty to encourage them to the extent of our Constitutional authority to apply their best means and cheerfully to make all necessary sacrifices and submit to all necessary burdens to fulfill their engagements and maintain their credit, for the character and credit of the several States form a part of the character and credit of the whole country. The resources of the country are abundant, the enterprise and activity of our people proverbial, and we may well hope that wise legislation and prudent administration by the respective governments, each acting within its own sphere, will restore former prosperity.

Unpleasant and even dangerous as collisions may sometimes be between the constituted authorities of the citizens of our country in relation to the lines which separate their respective jurisdictions, the results can be of no vital injury to our institutions if that ardent patriotism, that devoted attachment to liberty, that spirit of moderation and forbearance for which our countrymen were once distinguished, continue to be cherished. If this continues to be the ruling passion of our souls, the weaker feeling of the mistaken enthusiast will be corrected, the Utopian dreams of the scheming politician dissipated, and the complicated intrigues of the demagogue rendered harmless. The spirit of liberty is the sovereign balm for every injury which our institutions may receive. On the contrary, no care that can be used in the construction of our Government, no division of powers, no distribution of checks in its several departments, will prove effectual to keep us a free people if this spirit is suffered to decay; and decay it will without constant nurture. To the neglect of this duty the best historians agree in attributing the ruin of all the republics with whose existence and fall their writings have made us acquainted. The same causes will ever produce the same effects, and as long as the love of power is a dominant passion of the human bosom, and as long as the understandings of men can be warped and their affections changed by operations upon their passions and prejudices, so long will the liberties of a people depend on their own constant attention to its preservation. The danger to all well established free governments arises from the unwillingness of the people to believe in its existence or from the influence of designing men diverting their attention from the quarter whence it approaches to a source from which it can never come. This is the old trick of those who would usurp the government of their country. In the name of democracy they speak, warning the people against the influence of wealth and the danger of aristocracy. History, ancient and modern, is full of such examples. Caesar became the master of the Roman people and the senate under the pretense of supporting the democratic claims of the former against the aristocracy of the latter; Cromwell, in the character of protector of the liberties of the people, became the dictator of England, and Bolivar possessed himself of unlimited power with the title of his country's liberator. There is, on the contrary, no instance on record of an extensive and well established republic being changed into an aristocracy. The tendencies of all such governments in their decline is to monarchy, and the antagonist principle to liberty there is the spirit of faction, a spirit which assumes the character and in times of great excitement imposes itself upon the people as the genuine spirit of freedom, and, like the false Christs whose coming was foretold by the Savior, seeks to, and were it possible would, impose upon the true and most faithful disciples of liberty. It is in periods like this that it behooves the people to be most watchful of those to whom they have intrusted power. And although there is at times much difficulty in distinguishing the false from the true spirit, a calm and dispassionate investigation will detect the counterfeit, as well by the character of its operations as the results that are produced. The true spirit of liberty, although devoted, persevering, bold, and uncompromising in principle, that secured is mild and tolerant and scrupulous as to the means it employs, whilst the spirit of party, assuming to be that of liberty, is harsh, vindictive, and intolerant, and totally reckless as to the character of the allies which it brings to the aid of its cause. When the genuine spirit of liberty animates the body of a people to a thorough examination of their affairs, it leads to the excision of every excrescence which may have fastened itself upon any of the departments of the government, and restores the system to its pristine health and beauty. But the reign of an intolerant spirit of party amongst a free people seldom fails to result in a dangerous accession to the executive power introduced and established amidst unusual professions of devotion to democracy.

The foregoing remarks relate almost exclusively to matters connected with our domestic concerns. It may be proper, however, that I should give some indications to my fellow citizens of my proposed course of conduct in the management of our foreign relations. I assure them, therefore, that it is my intention to use every means in my power to preserve the friendly intercourse which now so happily subsists with every foreign nation, and that although, of course, not well informed as to the state of pending negotiations with any of them, I see in the personal characters of the sovereigns, as well as in the mutual interests of our own and of the governments with which our relations are most intimate, a pleasing guaranty that the harmony so important to the interests of their subjects as well as of our citizens will not be interrupted by the advancement of any claim or pretension upon their part to which our honor would not permit us to yield. Long the defender of my country's rights in the field, I trust that my fellow citizens will not see in my earnest desire to preserve peace with foreign powers any indication that their rights will ever be sacrificed or the honor of the nation tarnished by any admission on the part of their Chief Magistrate unworthy of their former glory. In our intercourse with our aboriginal neighbors the same liberality and justice which marked the course prescribed to me by two of my illustrious predecessors when acting under their direction in the discharge of the duties of superintendent and commissioner shall be strictly observed. I can conceive of no more sublime spectacle, none more likely to propitiate an impartial and common Creator, than a rigid adherence to the principles of justice on the part of a powerful nation in its transactions with a weaker and uncivilized people whom circumstances have placed at its disposal.

Before concluding, fellow citizens, I must say something to you on the subject of the parties at this time existing in our country. To me it appears perfectly clear that the interest of that country requires that the violence of the spirit by which those parties are at this time governed must be greatly mitigated, if not entirely extinguished, or consequences will ensue which are appalling to be thought of.

If parties in a republic are necessary to secure a degree of vigilance sufficient to keep the public functionaries within the bounds of law and duty, at that point their usefulness ends. Beyond that they become destructive of public virtue, the parent of a spirit antagonist to that of liberty, and eventually its inevitable conqueror. We have examples of republics where the love of country and of liberty at one time were the dominant passions of the whole mass of citizens, and yet, with the continuance of the name and forms of free government, not a vestige of these qualities remaining in the bosoms of any one of its citizens. It was the beautiful remark of a distinguished English writer that, in the Roman senate Octavius had a party and Anthony a party, but the Commonwealth had none. Yet the senate continued to meet in the temple of liberty to talk of the sacredness and beauty of the Commonwealth and gaze at the statues of the elder Brutus and of the Curtii and Decii, and the people assembled in the forum, not, as in the days of Camillus and the Scipios, to cast their free votes for annual magistrates or pass upon the acts of the senate, but to receive from the hands of the leaders of the respective parties their share of the spoils and to shout for one or the other, as those collected in Gaul or Egypt and the lesser Asia would furnish the larger dividend. The spirit of liberty had fled, and, avoiding the abodes of civilized man, had sought protection in the wilds of Scythia or Scandinavia; and so under the operation of the same causes and influences it will fly from our Capitol and our forums. A calamity so awful, not only to our country, but to the world, must be deprecated by every patriot and every tendency to a state of things likely to produce it immediately checked. Such a tendency has existed, and does exist. Always the friend of my countrymen, never their flatterer, it becomes my duty to say to them from this high place to which their partiality has exalted me that there exists in the land a spirit hostile to their best interests, hostile to liberty itself. It is a spirit contracted in its views, selfish in its objects. It looks to the aggrandizement of a few even to the destruction of the interests of the whole. The entire remedy is with the people. Something, however, may be effected by the means which they have placed in my hands. It is union that we want, not of a party for the sake of that party, but a union of the whole country for the sake of the whole country, for the defense of its interests and its honor against foreign aggression, for the defense of those principles for which our ancestors so gloriously contended. As far as it depends upon me it shall be accomplished. All the influence that I possess shall be exerted to prevent the formation at least of an Executive party in the halls of the legislative body. I wish for the support of no member of that body to any measure of mine that does not satisfy his judgment and his sense of duty to those from whom he holds his appointment, nor any confidence in advance from the people but that asked for by Mr. Jefferson, to give firmness and effect to the legal administration of their affairs.

I deem the present occasion sufficiently important and solemn to justify me in expressing to my fellow citizens a profound reverence for the Christian religion and a thorough conviction that sound morals, religious liberty, and a just sense of religious responsibility are essentially connected with all true and lasting happiness; and to that good Being who has blessed us by the gifts of civil and religious freedom, who watched over and prospered the labors of our fathers and has hitherto preserved to us institutions far exceeding in excellence those of any other people, let us unite in fervently commending every interest of our beloved country in all future time.

Fellow citizens, being fully invested with that high office to which the partiality of my countrymen has called me, I now take an affectionate leave of you. You will bear with you to your homes the remembrance of the pledge I have this day given to discharge all the high duties of my exalted station according to the best of my ability, and I shall enter upon their performance with entire confidence in the support of a just and generous people.

James K. Polk

Inaugural Address

MARCH 4, 1845

Commentary

The westward advancement from the Appalachians to the Mississippi River and to the Far West brought major repercussions in politics, economics, and thought. When Jefferson became president in 1801, the population of the United States stood at 5.3 million. Forty years later it hovered around 17 million. Jefferson presided over 17 states comprising 460,537 square miles, compared with 28 states in 1845 and a land area of 1,239,060 square miles. Some 250,000 immigrants landed between 1783 and 1820. In 1847 alone, more than that number arrived. Without pause, the frontier moved ever westward. Missouri's population increased 550 percent in 30 years. In 1820, 14,000 Americans lived in Arkansas; in 1840, 97,500; and more than 209,000 in 1850. On the Pacific Coast, California, when admitted to the Union in 1850, boasted almost 100,000 settlers, a tenfold increase in two years. "What the Mediterranean Sea was to the Greeks," wrote Frederick Jackson Turner, "breaking the bond of custom, offering new experiences, calling out new institutions and activities, that, and more, the ever retreating frontier has been to the United States." By the end of Polk's administration, the United States had annexed Texas, the Oregon territory, and the Mexican Cession (the future states of Nevada, Utah, Colorado, New Mexico, Arizona, and California). But as the nation expanded, the problems encountered would tax the very foundations of the republic.

The further extension of America's boundaries dominated the 1844 presidential campaign. Texas had sough admission to the Union since gaining independence from Mexico in 1836. But many Northerners feared that several additional slave states would be carved from this huge area equal in size to France. The South coveted Texas, said James Russell Lowell, to have "bigger pens to cram slaves in." "Texas," echoed Daniel Webster, "is likely to be a slave-holding country, and I frankly avow my entire unwillingness to do anything that shall extend the slavery of the African race on this continent." Both Presidents Jackson and Van Buren deferred action. Rebuffed, the Lone Star Republic, under the shrewd guidance of Sam Houston, spoke about diplomatic and economic ties with England. By 1841, these overtures had aroused many Americans, now concerned at the thought of British intervention in Texas. Would such an alliance abolish slavery and make the territory a haven for runaways? Would Yankee mills be denied cheap Texas cotton? Was American security endangered? On April 22, 1844, President John Tyler, taking the initiative, submitted an annexation treaty to the Senate, which promptly defeated it along almost straight party lines. The election campaign already had begun and the ballot box would decide the annexation question.

A deadlocked Democratic convention finally chose the first "dark horse" presidential candidate, Congressman James K. Polk of Tennessee. An ardent expansionist, Polk committed himself unreservedly to the annexation of Texas plus the reoccupation of the disputed Oregon territory to 54° 40'. Undoubtedly, Van Buren's stand against Texas statehood cost him Southern Democratic support and the nomination. The Whigs again turned to Henry Clay, long an opponent of immediate annexation. "I consider the annexation of Texas at this time," explained Clay, "as a measure compromising the national character, involving us certainly in war with Mexico, probably with other foreign nations . . . and not called for by any general expression of public opinion." During the campaign, the Great Compromiser, thinking he had misjudged American sentiment, attempted to straddle the Texas issue. He now lost his abolitionist supporters—and the election. Polk triumphed, receiving 170 electoral votes to Clay's 105. The popular vote, though, gave Polk a very narrow victory—1,337,243 to 1,299,068.

The Texas story has a sequel. Regarding the election as a plebiscite, the outgoing Congress passed a joint resolution of annexation, which President Tyler signed three days before the end of his term.

On March 4, 1845, Polk was duly inaugurated. The crowd gathered before the Capitol stood in a pouring rain and heard the president reaffirm the Democratic platform declaration on Texas. Polk slowly read these statements, emphasizing each word: "I regard the question of annexation as belonging exclusively to the United States and Texas. They are independent powers competent to contract, and foreign nations have no right to interfere with them or to take exceptions to their reunion." Two days later, though, Mexico formally protested against the annexation of Texas, calling it the "most unjust act of aggression in the annals of modern history." At the end of March, the Mexican government broke diplomatic relations with the United States and took steps to augment its armed forces.

～◦～

Fellow citizens:

Without solicitation on my part, I have been chosen by the free and voluntary suffrages of my countrymen to the most honorable and most responsible office on earth. I am deeply impressed with gratitude for the confidence reposed in me. Honored with this distinguished consideration at an earlier period of life than any of my predecessors, I can not disguise the diffidence with which I am about to enter on the discharge of my official duties.

If the more aged and experienced men who have filled the office of President of the United States even in the infancy of the Republic distrusted their ability to discharge the duties of that exalted station, what ought not to be the apprehensions of one so much younger and less endowed now that our domain extends from ocean to ocean, that our people have so greatly increased in numbers, and at a time when so great diversity of opinion prevails in regard to the principles and policy which should characterize the administration of our Government? Well may the boldest fear and the wisest tremble when incurring responsibilities on which may depend our country's peace and prosperity, and in some degree the hopes and happiness of the whole human family.

In assuming responsibilities so vast I fervently invoke the aid of that Almighty Ruler of the Universe in whose hands are the destinies of nations and of men to guard this Heaven favored land against the mischiefs which without His guidance might arise from an unwise public policy. With a firm reliance upon the wisdom of Omnipotence to sustain and direct me in the path of duty which I am appointed to pursue, I stand in the presence of this assembled multitude of my countrymen to take upon myself the solemn obligation to the best of my ability to preserve, protect, and defend the Constitution of the United States.

A concise enumeration of the principles which will guide me in the administrative policy of the Government is not only in accordance with the examples set me by all my predecessors, but is eminently befitting the occasion.

The Constitution itself, plainly written as it is, the safeguard of our federative compact, the offspring of concession and compromise, binding together in the bonds of peace and union this great and increasing family of free and independent States, will be the chart by which I shall be directed.

It will be my first care to administer the Government in the true spirit of that instrument, and to assume no powers not expressly granted or clearly implied in its terms. The Government of the United States is one of delegated and limited powers, and it is by a strict adherence to the clearly granted powers and by abstaining from the exercise of doubtful or unauthorized implied powers that we have the only sure guaranty against the recurrence of those unfortunate collisions between the Federal and State authorities which have occasionally so much disturbed the harmony of our system and even threatened the perpetuity of our glorious Union.

To the States, respectively, or to the people have been reserved the powers not delegated to the United States by the Constitution nor prohibited by it to the States. Each State is a complete sovereignty within the sphere of its reserved powers. The Government of the Union, acting within the sphere of its delegated authority, is also a complete sovereignty. While the General Government should abstain from the exercise of authority not clearly delegated to it, the States should be equally careful that in the maintenance of their rights they do not overstep the limits of powers reserved to them. One of the most distinguished of my predecessors attached deserved importance to "the support of the State governments in all their rights, as the most competent administration for our domestic concerns and the surest bulwark against antirepublican tendencies," and to the preservation of the General Government in its whole constitutional vigor, as the sheet anchor of our peace at home and safety abroad.

To the Government of the United States has been intrusted the exclusive management of our foreign affairs. Beyond that it wields a few general enumerated powers. It does not force reform on the States. It leaves individuals, over whom it casts its protecting influence, entirely free to improve their own condition by the legitimate exercise of all their mental and physical powers. It is a common protector of each and all the States; of every man who lives upon our soil, whether of native or foreign birth; of every religious sect, in their worship of the Almighty according to the dictates of their own conscience; of every shade of opinion, and the most free inquiry; of every art, trade, and occupation consistent with the laws of the States.

And we rejoice in the general happiness, prosperity, and advancement of our country, which have been the offspring of freedom, and not of power.

This most admirable and wisest system of well regulated self-government among men ever devised by human minds has been tested by its successful operation for more than half a century, and if preserved from the usurpations of the Federal Government on the one hand and the exercise by the States of powers not reserved to them on the other, will, I fervently hope and believe, endure for ages to come and dispense the blessings of civil and religious liberty to distant generations. To effect objects so dear to every patriot I shall devote myself with anxious solicitude. It will be my desire to guard against that most fruitful source of danger to the harmonious action of our system which consists in substituting the mere discretion and caprice of the Executive or of majorities in the legislative department of the Government for powers which have been withheld from the Federal Government by the Constitution. By the theory of our Government majorities rule, but this right is not an arbitrary or unlimited one. It is a right to be exercised in subordination to the Constitution and in conformity to it. One great object of the Constitution was to restrain majorities from oppressing minorities or encroaching upon their just rights. Minorities have a right to appeal to the Constitution as a shield against such oppression.

That the blessings of liberty which our Constitution secures may be enjoyed alike by minorities and majorities, the Executive has been wisely invested with a qualified veto upon the acts of the Legislature. It is a negative power, and is conservative in its character. It arrests for the time hasty, inconsiderate, or unconstitutional legislation, invites reconsideration, and transfers questions at issue between the legislative and executive departments to the tribunal of the people. Like all other powers, it is subject to be abused. When judiciously and properly exercised, the Constitution itself may be saved from infraction and the rights of all preserved and protected.

The inestimable value of our Federal Union is felt and acknowledged by all. By this system of united and confederated States our people are permitted collectively and individually to seek their own happiness in their own way, and the consequences have been most auspicious. Since the Union was formed the number of the States has increased from thirteen to twenty-eight; two of these have taken their position as members of the Confederacy within the last week. Our population has increased from three to twenty millions. New communities and States are seeking protection under its aegis, and multitudes from the Old World are flocking to our shores to participate in its blessings. Beneath its benign sway peace and prosperity

prevail. Freed from the burdens and miseries of war, our trade and intercourse have extended throughout the world. Mind, no longer tasked in
devising means to accomplish or resist schemes of ambition, usurpation,
or conquest, is devoting itself to man's true interests in developing his faculties and powers and the capacity of nature to minister to his enjoyments.
Genius is free to announce its inventions and discoveries, and the hand
is free to accomplish whatever the head conceives not incompatible with
the rights of a fellow being. All distinctions of birth or of rank have been
abolished. All citizens, whether native or adopted, are placed upon terms
of precise equality. All are entitled to equal rights and equal protection. No
union exists between church and state, and perfect freedom of opinion is
guaranteed to all sects and creeds.

These are some of the blessings secured to our happy land by our Federal Union. To perpetuate them it is our sacred duty to preserve it. Who
shall assign limits to the achievements of free minds and free hands under the protection of this glorious Union? No treason to mankind since
the organization of society would be equal in atrocity to that of him who
would lift his hand to destroy it. He would overthrow the noblest structure
of human wisdom, which protects himself and his fellow-man. He would
stop the progress of free government and involve his country either in anarchy or despotism. He would extinguish the fire of liberty, which warms
and animates the hearts of happy millions and invites all the nations of
the earth to imitate our example. If he say that error and wrong are committed in the administration of the Government, let him remember that
nothing human can be perfect, and that under no other system of government revealed by Heaven or devised by man has reason been allowed so
free and broad a scope to combat error. Has the sword of despots proved to
be a safer or surer instrument of reform in government than enlightened
reason? Does he expect to find among the ruins of this Union a happier
abode for our swarming millions than they now have under it? Every lover
of his country must shudder at the thought of the possibility of its dissolution, and will be ready to adopt the patriotic sentiment; Our Federal
Union, it must be preserved. To preserve it the compromises which alone
enabled our fathers to form a common Constitution for the government
and protection of so many States and distinct communities, of such diversified habits, interests, and domestic institutions, must be sacredly and re-
ligiously observed. Any attempt to disturb or destroy these compromises,
being terms of the compact of union, can lead to none other than the most
ruinous and disastrous consequences.

It is a source of deep regret that in some sections of our country misguided persons have occasionally indulged in schemes and agitations whose object is the destruction of domestic institutions existing in other sections; institutions which existed at the adoption of the Constitution and were recognized and protected by it. All must see that if it were possible for them to be successful in attaining their object the dissolution of the Union and the consequent destruction of our happy form of government must speedily follow.

I am happy to believe that at every period of our existence as a nation there has existed, and continues to exist, among the great mass of our people a devotion to the Union of the States which will shield and protect it against the moral treason of any who would seriously contemplate its destruction. To secure a continuance of that devotion the compromises of the Constitution must not only be preserved, but sectional jealousies and heartburnings must be discountenanced, and all should remember that they are members of the same political family, having a common destiny. To increase the attachment of our people to the Union, our laws should be just. Any policy which shall tend to favor monopolies or the peculiar interests of sections or classes must operate to the prejudice of the interest of their fellow-citizens, and should be avoided. If the compromises of the Constitution be preserved, if sectional jealousies and heartburnings be discountenanced, if our laws be just and the Government be practically administered strictly within the limits of power prescribed to it, we may discard all apprehensions for the safety of the Union.

With these views of the nature, character, and objects of the Government and the value of the Union, I shall steadily oppose the creation of those institutions and systems which in their nature tend to pervert it from its legitimate purposes and make it the instrument of sections, classes, and individuals. We need no national banks or other extraneous institutions planted around the Government to control or strengthen it in opposition to the will of its authors. Experience has taught us how unnecessary they are as auxiliaries of the public authorities; how impotent for good and how powerful for mischief.

Ours was intended to be a plain and frugal government, and I shall regard it to be my duty to recommend to Congress and, as far as the Executive is concerned, to enforce by all the means within my power the strictest economy in the expenditure of the public money which may be compatible with the public interests.

A national debt has become almost an institution of European monarchies. It is viewed in some of them as an essential prop to existing governments. Melancholy is the condition of that people whose government can be sustained only by a system which periodically transfers large amounts from the labor of the many to the coffers of the few. Such a system is incompatible with the ends for which our republican Government was instituted. Under a wise policy the debts contracted in our Revolution and during the War of 1812 have been happily extinguished. By a judicious application of the revenues not required for other necessary purposes, it is not doubted that the debt which has grown out of the circumstances of the last few years may be speedily paid off.

I congratulate my fellow-citizens on the entire restoration of the credit of the General Government of the Union and that of many of the States. Happy would it be for the indebted States if they were freed from their liabilities, many of which were incautiously contracted. Although the Government of the Union is neither in a legal nor a moral sense bound for the debts of the States, and it would be a violation of our compact of union to assume them, yet we can not but feel a deep interest in seeing all the States meet their public liabilities and pay off their just debts at the earliest practicable period. That they will do so as soon as it can be done without imposing too heavy burdens on their citizens there is no reason to doubt. The sound moral and honorable feeling of the people of the indebted States can not be questioned, and we are happy to perceive a settled disposition on their part, as their ability returns after a season of unexampled pecuniary embarrassment, to pay off all just demands and to acquiesce in any reasonable measures to accomplish that object.

One of the difficulties which we have had to encounter in the practical administration of the Government consists in the adjustment of our revenue laws and the levy of the taxes necessary for the support of Government. In the general proposition that no more money shall be collected than the necessities of an economical administration shall require all parties seem to acquiesce. Nor does there seem to be any material difference of opinion as to the absence of right in the Government to tax one section of country, or one class of citizens, or one occupation, for the mere profit of another. Justice and sound policy forbid the Federal Government to foster one branch of industry to the detriment of another, or to cherish the interests of one portion to the injury of another portion of our common country. I have heretofore declared to my fellow citizens that, in my judgment it is the duty of the Government to extend, as far as it may be practicable to do so, by its revenue laws and all other means within its power, fair and just protection to all of the great interests of the whole Union, embracing agriculture, manufactures, the mechanic arts, commerce, and navigation. I have also declared my opinion to be, in favor of a tariff for revenue; and that, in adjusting the details of such a tariff I have sanctioned such moderate discriminating duties as would produce the amount of revenue needed and at the same time afford reasonable incidental protection to our home industry, and that I was, opposed to a tariff for protection merely, and not for revenue.

The power, to lay and collect taxes, duties, imposts, and excises, was an indispensable one to be conferred on the Federal Government, which without it would possess no means of providing for its own support. In executing this power by levying a tariff of duties for the support of Government, the raising of revenue should be the object and protection the incident. To reverse this principle and make protection the object and revenue the incident would be to inflict manifest injustice upon all other than the protected interests. In levying duties for revenue it is doubtless proper to make such discriminations within the revenue principle as will afford incidental protection to our home interests. Within the revenue limit there is a discretion to discriminate; beyond that limit the rightful exercise of the power is not conceded. The incidental protection afforded to our home interests by discriminations within the revenue range it is believed will be ample. In making discriminations all our home interests should as far as practicable be equally protected. The largest portion of our people are agriculturists. Others are employed in manufactures, commerce, navigation, and the mechanic arts. They are all engaged in their respective pursuits and their joint labors constitute the national or home industry. To tax one branch of this home industry for the benefit of another would be unjust. No one of these interests can rightfully claim an advantage over the others, or to be enriched by impoverishing the others. All are equally entitled to the fostering care and protection of the Government. In exercising a sound discretion in levying discriminating duties within the limit prescribed, care should be taken that it be done in a manner not to benefit the wealthy few at the expense of the toiling millions by taxing lowest the luxuries of life, or articles of superior quality and high price, which can only be consumed by the wealthy, and highest the necessaries of life, or articles of coarse quality and low price, which the poor and great mass of our people must consume. The burdens of government should as far as practicable be distributed justly and equally among all classes of our population. These general views, long entertained on this subject, I have deemed it proper to reiterate. It is a subject upon which conflicting interests of sections and occupations are supposed to exist, and a spirit of mutual concession and compromise in adjusting its details should be cherished by every part of our widespread country as the only means of preserving harmony and a cheerful acquiescence of all in the operation of our revenue laws. Our patriotic citizens in every part of the Union will readily submit to the payment of such taxes as shall be needed for the support of their Government, whether in peace or in war, if they are so levied as to distribute the burdens as equally as possible among them.

The Republic of Texas has made known her desire to come into our Union, to form a part of our Confederacy and enjoy with us the blessings of liberty secured and guaranteed by our Constitution. Texas was once a part of our country, was unwisely ceded away to a foreign power, is now independent, and possesses an undoubted right to dispose of a part or the whole of her territory and to merge her sovereignty as a separate and independent state in ours. I congratulate my country that by an act of the late Congress of the United States the assent of this Government has been given to the reunion, and it only remains for the two countries to agree upon the terms to consummate an object so important to both.

I regard the question of annexation as belonging exclusively to the United States and Texas. They are independent powers competent to contract, and foreign nations have no right to interfere with them or to take exceptions to their reunion. Foreign powers do not seem to appreciate the true character of our Government. Our Union is a confederation of independent States, whose policy is peace with each other and all the world. To enlarge its limits is to extend the dominions of peace over additional territories and increasing millions. The world has nothing to fear from military ambition in our Government. While the Chief Magistrate and the popular branch of Congress are elected for short terms by the suffrages of those millions who must in their own persons bear all the burdens and miseries of war, our Government can not be otherwise than pacific. Foreign powers should therefore look on the annexation of Texas to the United States not as the conquest of a nation seeking to extend her dominions by arms and violence, but as the peaceful acquisition of a territory once her own, by adding another member to our confederation, with the consent of that member, thereby diminishing the chances of war and opening to them new and ever-increasing markets for their products.

To Texas the reunion is important, because the strong protecting arm of our Government would be extended over her, and the vast resources of her fertile soil and genial climate would be speedily developed, while the safety of New Orleans and of our whole southwestern frontier against hostile aggression, as well as the interests of the whole Union, would be promoted by it.

In the earlier stages of our national existence the opinion prevailed with some that our system of confederated States could not operate successfully over an extended territory, and serious objections have at different times been made to the enlargement of our boundaries. These objections were earnestly urged when we acquired Louisiana. Experience has shown that they were not well founded. The title of numerous Indian tribes to vast tracts of country has been extinguished; new States have been admitted into the Union; new Territories have been created and our jurisdiction and laws extended over them. As our population has expanded, the Union has been cemented and strengthened. As our boundaries have been enlarged and our agricultural population has been spread over a large surface, our federative system has acquired additional strength and security. It may well be doubted whether it would not be in greater danger of overthrow if our present population were confined to the comparatively narrow limits of the original thirteen States than it is now that they are sparsely settled over a more expanded territory. It is confidently believed that our system may be safely extended to the utmost bounds of our territorial limits, and that as it shall be extended the bonds of our Union, so far from being weakened, will become stronger.

None can fail to see the danger to our safety and future peace if Texas remains an independent state or becomes an ally or dependency of some foreign nation more powerful than herself. Is there one among our citizens who would not prefer perpetual peace with Texas to occasional wars, which so often occur between bordering independent nations? Is there one who would not prefer free intercourse with her to high duties on all our products and manufactures which enter her ports or cross her frontiers? Is there one who would not prefer an unrestricted communication with her citizens to the frontier obstructions which must occur if she remains out of the Union? Whatever is good or evil in the local institutions of Texas will remain her own whether annexed to the United States or not. None of the present States will be responsible for them any more than they are for the local institutions of each other. They have confederated together for certain specified objects. Upon the same principle that they would refuse to form a perpetual union with Texas because of her local institutions our forefathers would have been prevented from forming our present Union. Perceiving no valid objection to the measure and many reasons for its adoption vitally affecting the peace, the safety, and the prosperity of both countries, I shall on the broad principle which formed the basis and produced the adoption of our Constitution, and not in any narrow spirit of sectional policy, endeavor by all Constitutional, honorable, and appropriate means to consummate the expressed will of the people and Government of the United States by the reannexation of Texas to our Union at the earliest practicable period.

Nor will it become in a less degree my duty to assert and maintain by all Constitutional means the right of the United States to that portion of our territory which lies beyond the Rocky Mountains. Our title to the country of the Oregon is clear and unquestionable, and already are our people preparing to perfect that title by occupying it with their wives and children. But eighty years ago our population was confined on the west by the ridge of the Alleghanies. Within that period, within the lifetime, I might say of some of my hearers, our people, increasing to many millions, have filled the eastern valley of the Mississippi, adventurously ascended the Missouri to its headsprings, and are already engaged in establishing the blessings of self-government in valleys of which the rivers flow to the Pacific. The world beholds the peaceful triumphs of the industry of our emigrants. To us belongs the duty of protecting them adequately wherever they may be upon our soil. The jurisdiction of our laws and the benefits of our republican institutions should be extended over them in the distant regions which they have selected for their homes. The increasing facilities of intercourse will easily bring the States, of which the formation in that part of our territory can not be long delayed, within the sphere of our federative Union. In the meantime every obligation imposed by treaty or conventional stipulations should be sacredly respected.

In the management of our foreign relations it will be my aim to observe a careful respect for the rights of other nations, while our own will be the subject of constant watchfulness. Equal and exact justice should characterize all our intercourse with foreign countries. All alliances having a tendency to jeopard the welfare and honor of our country or sacrifice any one of the national interests will be studiously avoided, and yet no opportunity will be lost to cultivate a favorable understanding with foreign governments by which our navigation and commerce may be extended and the ample products of our fertile soil, as well as the manufactures of our skillful artisans, find a ready market and remunerating prices in foreign countries.

In taking care that the laws be faithfully executed, a strict performance of duty will be exacted from all public officers. From those officers, especially, who are charged with the collection and disbursement of the public revenue will prompt and rigid accountability be required.

Any culpable failure or delay on their part to account for the moneys intrusted to them at the times and in the manner required by law will in every instance terminate the official connection of such defaulting officer with the Government.

Although in our country the Chief Magistrate must almost of necessity be chosen by a party and stand pledged to its principles and measures, yet in his official action he should not be the President of a part only, but of the whole people of the United States. While he executes the laws with an impartial hand, shrinks from no proper responsibility, and faithfully carries out in the executive department of the Government the principles and policy of those who have chosen him, he should not be unmindful that our fellow-citizens who have differed with him in opinion are entitled to the full and free exercise of their opinions and judgments, and that the rights of all are entitled to respect and regard.

Confidently relying upon the aid and assistance of the coordinate departments of the Government in conducting our public affairs, I enter upon the discharge of the high duties which have been assigned me by the people, again humbly supplicating that Divine Being who has watched over and protected our beloved country from its infancy to the present hour to continue His gracious benedictions upon us, that we may continue to be a prosperous and happy people.

ZACHARY TAYLOR

INAUGURAL ADDRESS

MARCH 5, 1849

COMMENTARY

Polk's administration presided over the acquisition of vast new western lands. The brief but decisive Mexican war settled the Texas boundary issues, and the defeated nation ceded the enormous New Mexico and California territory to America—adding 1,193,061 square miles to the national domain. Discovery of gold in the Sacramento Valley shortly after the war accelerated the settlement of California, which was admitted to the Union in 1850. In 1846, the long-contested Oregon territory dispute with Great Britain was finally settled by extending the existing continental line along the forty-ninth parallel. Thus, the nation's boundaries now stretched from the Atlantic to the Pacific, encompassing more than 1.4 billion acres, an area about five times larger than the combined lands of Germany, France, and Italy. Unfortunately, though, this broad expansion precipitated further sectional and party divisions.

The pressing question of slavery in the newly acquired territories disrupted both the Whigs and Democrats at their 1848 nominating conventions. A divided Democratic party chose the moderate Senator Lewis Cass of Michigan, who believed in "popular sovereignty"—that is, slavery should be decided by the people in each territory. The Whigs again bypassed Clay and turned to General Zachary Taylor, the popular military hero of the Mexican war. Taylor gave no pledges except "honesty, truthfulness, [and] integrity," causing the Whigs to avoid adopting either a policy statement or a platform. Die-hard opponents of slavery assembled around Martin Van Buren on a Free Soil ticket pledged to "free soil, free speech, free labor, and free men." Except for this third party, the slavery issue became blurred during the campaign as both the Whigs and the Democrats tired to ignore it. Van Buren attracted enough support from New York Democrats to throw that state's electoral vote to Taylor—giving the general a majority in the electoral college. Taylor received 163 ballots to Cass's 129; but in the popular column, Taylor was a minority president—obtaining 1,360,099 votes to 1,511,807 for Cass and Van Buren. Although Van Buren captured no states his more than 290,000 votes indicated the growing antislavery sentiment in the North. In describing his victory, Taylor wrote that he felt "neither exultation or gratification" as the presidency had become "more a bed of thorns than one of roses."

For the second time since the adoption of the Constitution, the end of a presidential term fell on Sunday. Taylor's inauguration, therefore, took place in front of the Capitol on Monday, March 5, 1849. Retiring president Polk talked with Taylor about national problems during their ride to the ceremonies. In the evening, Polk wrote in his diary that the general impressed him as a well-meaning old man, but "exceedingly ignorant of public affairs, and, I should judge, of very ordinary capacity."

Elected by the American people to the highest office known to our laws, I appear here to take the oath prescribed by the Constitution; and, in compliance with a time honored custom, to address those who are now assembled.

The confidence and respect shown by my countrymen in calling me to be the Chief Magistrate of a Republic holding a high rank among the nations of the earth have inspired me with feelings of the most profound gratitude; but when I reflect that the acceptance of the office which their partiality has bestowed imposes the discharge of the most arduous duties and involves the weightiest obligations, I am conscious that the position which I have been called to fill, though sufficient to satisfy the loftiest ambition, is surrounded by fearful responsibilities. Happily, however, in the performance of my new duties I shall not be without able cooperation. The legislative and judicial branches of the Government present prominent examples of distinguished civil attainments and matured experience, and it shall be my endeavor to call to my assistance in the Executive Departments individuals whose talents, integrity, and purity of character will furnish ample guaranties for the faithful and honorable performance of the trusts to be committed to their charge. With such aids and an honest purpose to do whatever is right, I hope to execute diligently, impartially, and for the best interests of the country the manifold duties devolved upon me.

In the discharge of these duties my guide will be the Constitution, which I this day swear to preserve, protect, and defend. For the interpretation of that instrument I shall look to the decisions of the judicial tribunals established by its authority and to the practice of the Government under the earlier Presidents, who had so large a share in its formation. To the example of those illustrious patriots I shall always defer with reverence, and especially to his example who was by so many titles, the Father of his Country.

To command the Army and Navy of the United States; with the advice and consent of the Senate, to make treaties and to appoint ambassadors and other officers; to give to Congress information of the state of the Union and recommend such measures as he shall judge to be necessary; and to take care that the laws shall be faithfully executed; these are the most important functions intrusted to the President by the Constitution, and it may be expected that I shall briefly indicate the principles which will control me in their execution.

Chosen by the body of the people under the assurance that my Administration would be devoted to the welfare of the whole country, and not to the support of any particular section or merely local interest, I this day renew the declarations I have heretofore made and proclaim my fixed determination to maintain to the extent of my ability the Government in its original purity and to adopt as the basis of my public policy those great republican doctrines which constitute the strength of our national existence.

In reference to the Army and Navy, lately employed with so much distinction on active service, care shall be taken to insure the highest condition of efficiency, and in furtherance of that object the military and naval schools, sustained by the liberality of Congress, shall receive the special attention of the Executive.

As American freemen we can not but sympathize in all efforts to extend the blessings of civil and political liberty, but at the same time we are warned by the admonitions of history and the voice of our own beloved Washington to abstain from entangling alliances with foreign nations. In all disputes between conflicting governments it is our interest not less than our duty to remain strictly neutral, while our geographical position, the genius of our institutions and our people, the advancing spirit of civilization, and, above all, the dictates of religion direct us to the cultivation of peaceful and friendly relations with all other powers. It is to be hoped that no international question can now arise which a government confident in its own strength and resolved to protect its own just rights may not settle by wise negotiation; and it eminently becomes a government like our own, founded on the morality and intelligence of its citizens and upheld by their affections, to exhaust every resort of honorable diplomacy before appealing to arms. In the conduct of our foreign relations I shall conform to these views, as I believe them essential to the best interests and the true honor of the country.

The appointing power vested in the President imposes delicate and onerous duties. So far as it is possible to be informed, I shall make honesty, capacity, and fidelity indispensable prerequisites to the bestowal of office, and the absence of either of these qualities shall be deemed sufficient cause for removal.

It shall be my study to recommend such constitutional measures to Congress as may be necessary and proper to secure encouragement and protection to the great interests of agriculture, commerce, and manufactures, to improve our rivers and harbors, to provide for the speedy extinguishment of the public debt, to enforce a strict accountability on the part of all officers of the Government and the utmost economy in all public expenditures; but it is for the wisdom of Congress itself, in which all legislative powers are vested by the Constitution, to regulate these and other matters of domestic policy. I shall look with confidence to the enlightened patriotism of that body to adopt such measures of conciliation as may harmonize conflicting interests and tend to perpetuate that Union which should be the paramount object of our hopes and affections. In any action calculated to promote an object so near the heart of everyone who truly loves his country I will zealously unite with the coordinate branches of the Government.

In conclusion, I congratulate you, my fellow citizens, upon the high state of prosperity to which the goodness of Divine Providence has conducted our common country. Let us invoke a continuance of the same protecting care which has led us from small beginnings to the eminence we this day occupy, and let us seek to deserve that continuance by prudence and moderation in our councils, by well directed attempts to assuage the bitterness which too often marks unavoidable differences of opinion, by the promulgation and practice of just and liberal principles, and by an enlarged patriotism, which shall acknowledge no limits but those of our own widespread Republic.

Franklin Pierce

Inaugural Address

MARCH 4, 1853

Commentary

In 1850, the nation stood equally divided into 15 slave and 15 free states. When California petitioned for admission as a free state, the mounting sectional antagonisms threatened to disrupt the Union. Once more an adjustment resulted—the Compromise of 1850—in which both moderate Northern and Southern leaders rallied to avoid secession. The persuasive Henry Clay, now 73, welded together a series of resolutions to save the Union. His plan proposed the admission of California as a free state; the organization of New Mexico and Utah as territories without mention of slavery; the establishment of more efficient machinery for returning fugitive slaves to their masters; the abolition of the slave trade in the District of Columbia but the continuation of slavery there unless Maryland consented otherwise; and federal compensation to Texas for some territory ceded to New Mexico. Both sides would give up something but the Union would be preserved.

Scenes of incredible drama dominated the Senate chamber as the great Whig and Democratic leaders spoke in one of the most important debates in American history. On March 4, 1850, a grim, dying John Calhoun, too feeble to speak himself, had his speech read, a speech that prophetically proclaimed that the South could not long remain in the Union with honor. In this notable rebuttal of Clay's compromise, Calhoun pessimistically discussed the growing sectional divisions, maintaining that the South, bound by economic interests, had to defend slavery. The Union, so near its end, could be saved, not by eulogies, nor by cries of "Union, Union, glorious Union," but by a full, final settlement that would preserve slavery while giving the South her equal rights in the territories. Would the North agree to do this? It was for her to answer.

On March 7, Daniel Webster rose to speak "not as a Massachusetts man, nor as a Northern man, but as an American . . . I speak to-day for the preservation of the Union." The greatest Senate orator strongly embraced compromise, denouncing those who thought peaceable secession possible as well as abolitionists who scoffed at fugitive slave laws. Mustering his forensic skills, Webster delivered a most eloquent and forceful defense of the Union. Two days later, President Taylor, an opponent of the compromise measures, died. His successor, Millard Fillmore, sympathized with Clay and Webster, thus easing final passage. In the end, moderation triumphed and the nation endured—at least for another decade. But the clairvoyant could note that national political parties, the major link that still united the diverse sections, were beginning to crack.

The Compromise dominated the 1852 presidential campaign. The Democrats deadlocked again as the leading contenders—Lewis Cass, Stephen Douglas, and James Buchanan—could not obtain the two-thirds necessary for nomination. On the forty-ninth ballot, a "dark horse," Franklin Pierce, former senator from New Hampshire, received the convention's endorsement. He and his party pledged complete support for the Compromise, stressing strict enforcement of the Fugitive Slave Law. The Whigs bypassed Fillmore and Webster to choose another military hero. On the fifty-third ballot, with mixed feelings of joy, doubt, and disgust, the party turned to General Winfield Scott, whose greatest asset was that he had avoided making any public statement on the Compromise of 1850. A dull and listless campaign became enlivened briefly when Scott made a tour through several western states, the first time a presidential candidate undertook such a trip. In fact, an excuse had to justify this unusual tactic. And so, Whig congressmen appointed him one of a board to visit Blue Lick Spring, Kentucky, to decide on its fitness as a site for the Western Military Asylum! On Election Day, Pierce carried all but four states, receiving an overwhelming electoral endorsement, 254 to Scott's 54. This solid Democratic victory ominously signaled the breakup of the faction-ridden Whig Party. With the death of Clay and Webster during the campaign, no Whig leader of national stature remained to hold the party together. The initiative taken by Whig leaders in solving the nation's pressing problems of 1850 so divided the rank and file that now, after the shattering election defeat, the party's disintegration appeared inevitable.

When Chief Justice Roger Taney administered the oath to Franklin Pierce on March 4, 1853, Pierce raised his right hand and broke with tradition by affirming rather than swearing. The new president then delivered his carefully prepared inaugural address without a manuscript or notes. Festivities were curtailed in respect for Pierce's son, who had died tragically in January. It is to this grief that the president refers in the first sentence of his speech.

My countrymen:

It a relief to feel that no heart but my own can know the personal regret and bitter sorrow over which I have been borne to a position so suitable for others rather than desirable for myself.

The circumstances under which I have been called for a limited period to preside over the destinies of the Republic fill me with a profound sense of responsibility, but with nothing like shrinking apprehension. I repair to the post assigned me not as to one sought, but in obedience to the unsolicited expression of your will, answerable only for a fearless, faithful, and diligent exercise of my best powers. I ought to be, and am, truly grateful for the rare manifestation of the nation's confidence; but this, so far from lightening my obligations, only adds to their weight. You have summoned me in my weakness; you must sustain me by your strength. When looking for the fulfillment of reasonable requirements, you will not be unmindful of the great changes which have occurred, even within the last quarter of a century, and the consequent augmentation and complexity of duties imposed in the administration both of your home and foreign affairs.

Whether the elements of inherent force in the Republic have kept pace with its unparalleled progression in territory, population, and wealth has been the subject of earnest thought and discussion on both sides of the ocean. Less than sixty-four years ago the Father of his Country made the then recent accession of the important State of North Carolina to the Constitution of the United States, one of the subjects of his special congratulation. At that moment, however, when the agitation consequent upon the Revolutionary struggle had hardly subsided, when we were just emerging from the weakness and embarrassments of the Confederation, there was an evident consciousness of vigor equal to the great mission so wisely and bravely fulfilled by our fathers. It was not a presumptuous assurance, but a calm faith, springing from a clear view of the sources of power in a government constituted like ours. It is no paradox to say that although comparatively weak the new-born nation was intrinsically strong. Inconsiderable in population and apparent resources, it was upheld by a broad and intelligent comprehension of rights and an all pervading purpose to maintain them, stronger than armaments.

It came from the furnace of the Revolution, tempered to the necessities of the times. The thoughts of the men of that day were as practical as their sentiments were patriotic. They wasted no portion of their energies upon idle and delusive speculations, but with a firm and fearless step advanced beyond the governmental landmarks which had hitherto circumscribed the limits of human freedom and planted their standard, where it has stood against dangers which have threatened from abroad, and internal agitation, which has at times fearfully menaced at home. They proved themselves equal to the solution of the great problem, to understand which their minds had been illuminated by the dawning lights of the Revolution. The object sought was not a thing dreamed of; it was a thing realized. They had exhibited only the power to achieve, but, what all history affirms to be so much more unusual, the capacity to maintain. The oppressed throughout the world from that day to the present have turned their eyes hitherward, not to find those lights extinguished or to fear lest they should wane, but to be constantly cheered by their steady and increasing radiance.

In this our country has, in my judgment, thus far fulfilled its highest duty to suffering humanity. It has spoken and will continue to speak, not only by its words, but by its acts, the language of sympathy, encouragement, and hope to those who earnestly listen to tones which pronounce for the largest rational liberty. But after all, the most animating encouragement and potent appeal for freedom will be its own history; its trials and its triumphs. Preeminently, the power of our advocacy reposes in our example; but no example, be it remembered, can be powerful for lasting good, whatever apparent advantages may be gained, which is not based upon eternal principles of right and justice. Our fathers decided for themselves, both upon the hour to declare and the hour to strike. They were their own judges of the circumstances under which it became them to pledge to each other, their lives, their fortunes, and their sacred honor; for the acquisition of the priceless inheritance transmitted to us. The energy with which that great conflict was opened and, under the guidance of a manifest and beneficent Providence the uncomplaining endurance with which it was prosecuted to its consummation were only surpassed by the wisdom and patriotic spirit of concession which characterized all the counsels of the early fathers.

One of the most impressive evidences of that wisdom is to be found in the fact that the actual working of our system has dispelled a degree of solicitude which at the outset disturbed bold hearts and far reaching intellects. The apprehension of dangers from extended territory, multiplied

States, accumulated wealth, and augmented population has proved to be unfounded. The stars upon your banner have become nearly threefold their original number; your densely populated possessions skirt the shores of the two great oceans; and yet this vast increase of people and territory has not only shown itself compatible with the harmonious action of the States and Federal Government in their respective constitutional spheres, but has afforded an additional guaranty of the strength and integrity of both.

With an experience thus suggestive and cheering, the policy of my Administration will not be controlled by any timid forebodings of evil from expansion. Indeed, it is not to be disguised that our attitude as a nation and our position on the globe render the acquisition of certain possessions not within our jurisdiction eminently important for our protection, if not in the future essential for the preservation of the rights of commerce and the peace of the world. Should they be obtained, it will be through no grasping spirit, but with a view to obvious national interest and security, and in a manner entirely consistent with the strictest observance of national faith. We have nothing in our history or position to invite aggression; we have everything to beckon us to the cultivation of relations of peace and amity with all nations. Purposes, therefore, at once just and pacific will be significantly marked in the conduct of our foreign affairs. I intend that my Administration shall leave no blot upon our fair record, and trust I may safely give the assurance that no act within the legitimate scope of my constitutional control will be tolerated on the part of any portion of our citizens which can not challenge a ready justification before the tribunal of the civilized world. An Administration would be unworthy of confidence at home or respect abroad should it cease to be influenced by the conviction that no apparent advantage can be purchased at a price so dear as that of national wrong or dishonor. It is not your privilege as a nation to speak of a distant past. The striking incidents of your history, replete with instruction and furnishing abundant grounds for hopeful confidence, are comprised in a period comparatively brief. But if your past is limited, your future is boundless. Its obligations throng the unexplored pathway of advancement, and will be limitless as duration. Hence a sound and comprehensive policy should embrace not less the distant future than the urgent present.

The great objects of our pursuit as a people are best to be attained by peace, and are entirely consistent with the tranquillity and interests of the rest of mankind. With the neighboring nations upon our continent we should cultivate kindly and fraternal relations. We can desire nothing in regard to them so much as to see them consolidate their strength and pursue the paths of prosperity and happiness. If in the course of their growth we should open new channels of trade and create additional facilities for friendly intercourse, the benefits realized will be equal and mutual. Of the complicated European systems of national polity we have heretofore been independent. From their wars, their tumults, and anxieties we have been, happily, almost entirely exempt. Whilst these are confined to the nations which gave them existence, and within their legitimate jurisdiction, they can not affect us except as they appeal to our sympathies in the cause of human freedom and universal advancement. But the vast interests of commerce are common to all mankind, and the advantages of trade and international intercourse must always present a noble field for the moral influence of a great people.

With these views firmly and honestly carried out, we have a right to expect, and shall under all circumstances require, prompt reciprocity. The rights which belong to us as a nation are not alone to be regarded, but those which pertain to every citizen in his individual capacity, at home and abroad, must be sacredly maintained. So long as he can discern every star in its place upon that ensign, without wealth to purchase for him preferment or title to secure for him place, it will be his privilege, and must be his acknowledged right, to stand unabashed even in the presence of princes, with a proud consciousness that he is himself one of a nation of sovereigns and that he can not in legitimate pursuit wander so far from home that the agent whom he shall leave behind in the place which I now occupy will not see that no rude hand of power or tyrannical passion is laid upon him with impunity. He must realize that upon every sea and on every soil where our enterprise may rightfully seek the protection of our flag American citizenship is an inviolable panoply for the security of American rights. And in this connection it can hardly be necessary to reaffirm a principle which should now be regarded as fundamental. The rights, security, and repose of this Confederacy reject the idea of interference or colonization on this side of the ocean by any foreign power beyond present jurisdiction as utterly inadmissible.

The opportunities of observation furnished by my brief experience as a soldier confirmed in my own mind the opinion, entertained and acted upon by others from the formation of the Government, that the maintenance of large standing armies in our country would be not only dangerous, but unnecessary. They also illustrated the importance, I might well say the absolute necessity, of the military science and practical skill furnished in such an eminent degree by the institution which has made your Army what it is, under the discipline and instruction of officers not more distinguished for their solid attainments, gallantry, and devotion to the public service than for unobtrusive bearing and high moral tone. The Army as organized must be the nucleus around which in every time of need the strength of your military power, the sure bulwark of your defense, a national militia, may be readily formed into a well disciplined and efficient organization. And the skill and self-devotion of the Navy assure you that you may take the performance of the past as a pledge for the future, and may confidently expect that the flag which has waved its untarnished folds over every sea will still float in undiminished honor. But these, like many other subjects, will be appropriately brought at a future time to the attention of the coordinate branches of the Government, to which I shall always look with profound respect and with trustful confidence that they will accord to me the aid and support which I shall so much need and which their experience and wisdom will readily suggest.

In the administration of domestic affairs you expect a devoted integrity in the public service and an observance of rigid economy in all departments, so marked as never justly to be questioned. If this reasonable expectation be not realized, I frankly confess that one of your leading hopes is doomed to disappointment, and that my efforts in a very important particular must result in a humiliating failure. Offices can be properly regarded only in the light of aids for the accomplishment of these objects, and as occupancy can confer no prerogative nor importunate desire for preferment any claim, the public interest imperatively demands that they be considered with sole reference to the duties to be performed. Good citizens may well claim the protection of good laws and the benign influence of good government, but a claim for office is what the people of a republic should never recognize. No reasonable man of any party will expect the Administration to be so regardless of its responsibility and of the obvious elements of success as to retain persons known to be under the influence of political hostility and partisan prejudice in positions which will require not only severe labor, but cordial cooperation. Having no implied engagements to ratify, no rewards to bestow, no resentments to remember, and no personal wishes to consult in selections for official station, I shall fulfill this difficult and delicate trust, admitting no motive as worthy either of my character or position which does not contemplate an efficient discharge of duty and the best interests of my country. I acknowledge my obligations to the masses of my countrymen, and to them alone. Higher objects than personal aggrandizement gave direction and energy to their exertions in the late canvass, and they shall not be disappointed. They require at my hands diligence, integrity, and capacity wherever there are duties to be performed. Without these qualities in their public servants, more stringent laws for the prevention or punishment of fraud, negligence, and peculation will be vain. With them they will be unnecessary.

But these are not the only points to which you look for vigilant watchfulness. The dangers of a concentration of all power in the general government of a confederacy so vast as ours are too obvious to be disregarded. You have a right, therefore, to expect your agents in every department to regard strictly the limits imposed upon them by the Constitution of the United States. The great scheme of our constitutional liberty rests upon a proper distribution of power between the State and Federal authorities, and experience has shown that the harmony and happiness of our people must depend upon a just discrimination between the separate rights and responsibilities of the States and your common rights and obligations under the General Government; and here, in my opinion, are the considerations which should form the true basis of future concord in regard to the questions which have most seriously disturbed public tranquillity. If the Federal Government will confine itself to the exercise of powers clearly granted by the Constitution, it can hardly happen that its action upon any question should endanger the institutions of the States or interfere with their right to manage matters strictly domestic according to the will of their own people.

In expressing briefly my views upon an important subject which has recently agitated the nation to almost a fearful degree, I am moved by no other impulse than a most earnest desire for the perpetuation of that Union which has made us what we are, showering upon us blessings and conferring a power and influence which our fathers could hardly have anticipated, even with their most sanguine hopes directed to a far off future. The sentiments I now announce were not unknown before the expression of the voice which called me here. My own position upon this subject was clear and unequivocal, upon the record of my words and my acts, and it is only recurred to at this time because silence might perhaps be misconstrued. With the Union my best and dearest earthly hopes are entwined. Without it what are we individually or collectively? What becomes of the noblest field ever opened for the advancement of our race in religion, in government, in the arts, and in all that dignifies and adorns mankind? From that radiant constellation which both illumines our own way and points out to struggling nations their course, let but a single star be lost, and, if these be not utter darkness, the luster of the whole is dimmed. Do my countrymen need any assurance that such a catastrophe is not to overtake them while I possess the power to stay it? It is with me an earnest and vital belief that as the Union has been the source, under Providence, of our prosperity to this time, so it is the surest pledge of a continuance of the blessings we have enjoyed, and which we are sacredly bound to transmit undiminished to our children. The field of calm and free discussion in our country is open, and will always be so, but never has been and never can be traversed for good in a spirit of sectionalism and uncharitableness. The founders of the Republic dealt with things as they were presented to them, in a spirit of self-sacrificing patriotism, and, as time has proved, with a comprehensive wisdom which it will always be safe for us to consult. Every measure tending to strengthen the fraternal feelings of all the members of our Union has had my heartfelt approbation. To every theory of society or government, whether the off-spring of feverish ambition or of morbid enthusiasm, calculated to dissolve the bonds of law and affection which unite us, I shall interpose a ready and stern resistance. I believe that involuntary servitude, as it exists in different States of this Confederacy, is recognized by the Constitution. I believe that it stands like any other admitted right, and that the States where it exists are entitled to efficient remedies to enforce the constitutional provisions. I hold that the laws of 1850, commonly called the "compromise measures," are strictly constitutional and to be unhesitatingly carried into effect. I believe that the constituted authorities of this Republic are bound to regard the rights of the South in this respect as they would view any other legal and constitutional right, and that the laws to enforce them should be respected and obeyed, not with a reluctance encouraged by abstract opinions as to their propriety in a different state of society, but cheerfully and according to the decisions of the tribunal to which their exposition belongs. Such have been, and are, my convictions, and upon them I shall act. I fervently hope that the question is at rest, and that no sectional or ambitious or fanatical excitement may again threaten the durability of our institutions or obscure the light of our prosperity.

But let not the foundation of our hope rest upon man's wisdom. It will not be sufficient that sectional prejudices find no place in the public deliberations. It will not be sufficient that the rash counsels of human passion are rejected. It must be felt that there is no national security but in the nation's humble, acknowledged dependence upon God and His overruling providence.

We have been carried in safety through a perilous crisis. Wise counsels, like those which gave us the Constitution, prevailed to uphold it. Let the period be remembered as an admonition, and not as an encouragement, in any section of the Union, to make experiments where experiments are fraught with such fearful hazard. Let it be impressed upon all hearts that, beautiful as our fabric is, no earthly power or wisdom could ever reunite its broken fragments. Standing, as I do, almost within view of the green slopes of Monticello, and, as it were, within reach of the tomb of Washington, with all the cherished memories of the past gathering around me like so many eloquent voices of exhortation from heaven, I can express no better hope for my country than that the kind Providence which smiled upon our fathers may enable their children to preserve the blessings they have inherited.

James Buchanan

Inaugural Address

MARCH 4, 1857

Commentary

In 1854, slavery in the territories again brought the Union close to disruption. A large section of the original Louisiana Purchase—stretching west from Missouri, Iowa, and the Minnesota Territory to the Rocky Mountains—remained without any government. With Pierce's victory, the Democrats controlled Congress, and Stephen Douglas, chairman of the Senate Committee on Territories, decided to grapple with the controversial but pressing problem. Douglas's bill, which was passed on May 30, after three months of bitter debates, divided the area at the fortieth parallel into two territories, Kansas and Nebraska. All questions pertaining to slavery were left to the people living there. The bill repealed the Missouri Compromise of 1820, which had prohibited slavery within the Louisiana Purchase above the 36° 30' line, Missouri's southern border. Congress now sanctioned complete popular sovereignty and abandoned the idea that it could exclude slavery from a territory.

Douglas miscalculated the depth and intensity of Northern opposition to slavery expansion. To many, the Missouri Compromise had become a sacred guarantee. The fury unleashed against the bill and Douglas is unmatched—countless effigies compared him to Benedict Arnold. As the telegraph spread the news of passage, an event occurred in Boston that further deepened the sectional abyss. A runaway slave named Anthony Burns was arrested and ordered reverted to his former master under the provisions of the 1850 Fugitive Slave Law. To Burns's defense came the most distinguished New Englanders, including Theodore Parker and Richard Henry Dana. Riots broke out as attempts to purchase Burns failed. When the federal commissioner ordered his return,

President Pierce sent a revenue cutter to Boston because land travel would have been impossible. Business stopped on that day. Flags, with the union down, hung from houses draped in mourning. Twenty-two militia companies patrolled the streets as some 50,000 Bostonians watched the shackled slave, surrounded by armed U.S. soldiers and Marines, marched to the wharf. As the steamer cast loose, the deathly silence broke when a minister cried out: "Let us pray that God be merciful to the poor slave and the recreant republic." Bitterness in the North against the ill-timed Kansas–Nebraska measure and the Fugitive Slave Law sounded the knell of the Whig Party, which had straddled the slavery question for so long.

Many Northerners favored another party firmly opposed to the further expansion of slavery in the territories. By the end of 1854, the new Republican Party began to spread throughout the North. Composed of antislavery men, free soilers, and former Whigs, the party demanded repeal of the Kansas–Nebraska Act and the Fugitive Slave Law as well as the abolition of slavery in the District of Columbia. At their first national convention, held in Philadelphia in June 1856, the Republicans unanimously chose the dashing, popular explorer John C. Fremont as their presidential nominee. With a campaign slogan of "Free Soil, Free Speech, Free Men, and Fremont," the vibrant Republicans enthusiastically embarked on a moral crusade. No such spirit existed at the Democratic convention. A brief platform reaffirmed the Compromise of 1850, the provisions of the Kansas–Nebraska Act, and pledged the party to noninterference with "domestic institutions" in slave states. James Buchanan received the nomination on the seventeenth ballot, primarily because he had been serving as minister to Great Britain during the Kansas–Nebraska debates. Another group, calling itself the American Party, endorsed Millard Fillmore on a platform favoring popular sovereignty in the territories. In September, what was left of the Whigs met and backed Fillmore as the best means of preventing a civil war. A bitter campaign marked by hysterical charges and countercharges followed. Buchanan won but the Republicans received more than 33 percent of the popular ballots. Eleven free states cast 114 votes for Freemont while five free and every Southern state but one went for Buchanan, giving him 174 votes. Fillmore captured only Maryland. Both houses of Congress remained Democratic. As the South quaked with fear, the Republicans looked forward hopefully to the 1860 campaign.

On Inauguration Day, 1857, Buchanan rode to the Capitol with Pierce. From the East Portico, he read his long address. Those who heard the speech found that the new president had something to say on most great issues of the hour. Above all, he affirmed his decision to uphold the Kansas–Nebraska Act, believing that people should be perfectly free to regulate domestic institutions as they saw fit. In an oblique reference, Buchanan predicted the Supreme Court would shortly settle the issue of slavery in the territories once and for all—although he did not reveal that he had received advance information of the fateful Dred Scott decision. Most startling, though, was his announcement declaring he would serve only one term. Thus, from the very beginning of Buchanan's tenure, politicians sought his successor.

Fellow citizens:

I appear before you this day to take the solemn oath; that I will faithfully execute the office of President of the United States and will to the best of my ability preserve, protect, and defend the Constitution of the United States.

In entering upon this great office I must humbly invoke the God of our fathers for wisdom and firmness to execute its high and responsible duties in such a manner as to restore harmony and ancient friendship among the people of the several States and to preserve our free institutions throughout many generations. Convinced that I owe my election to the inherent love for the Constitution and the Union which still animates the hearts of the American people, let me earnestly ask their powerful support in sustaining all just measures calculated to perpetuate these, the richest political blessings which Heaven has ever bestowed upon any nation. Having determined not to become a candidate for reelection, I shall have no motive to influence my conduct in administering the Government except the desire ably and faithfully to serve my country and to live in grateful memory of my countrymen.

We have recently passed through a Presidential contest in which the passions of our fellow citizens were excited to the highest degree by questions of deep and vital importance; but when the people proclaimed their will the tempest at once subsided and all was calm.

The voice of the majority, speaking in the manner prescribed by the Constitution, was heard, and instant submission followed. Our own country could alone have exhibited so grand and striking a spectacle of the capacity of man for self-government.

What a happy conception, then, was it for Congress to apply this simple rule, that the will of the majority shall govern, to the settlement of the question of domestic slavery in the Territories. Congress is neither to legislate slavery into any Territory or State nor to exclude it therefrom, but to leave the people thereof perfectly free to form and regulate their domestic institutions in their own way, subject only to the Constitution of the United States.

As a natural consequence, Congress has also prescribed that when the Territory of Kansas shall be admitted as a State it shall be received into the Union with or without slavery, as their constitution may prescribe at the time of their admission. A difference of opinion has arisen in regard to the point of time when the people of a Territory shall decide this question for themselves.

This is, happily, a matter of but little practical importance. Besides, it is a judicial question, which legitimately belongs to the Supreme Court of the United States, before whom it is now pending, and will, it is understood, be speedily and finally settled. To their decision, in common with all good citizens, I shall cheerfully submit, whatever this may be, though it has ever been my individual opinion that under the Nebraska–Kansas act the appropriate period will be when the number of actual residents in the Territory shall justify the formation of a constitution with a view to its admission as a State into the Union. But be this as it may, it is the imperative and indispensable duty of the Government of the United States to secure to every resident inhabitant the free and independent expression of his opinion by his vote. This sacred right of each individual must be preserved. That being accomplished, nothing can be fairer than to leave the people of a Territory free from all foreign interference to decide their own destiny for themselves, subject only to the Constitution of the United States.

The whole Territorial question being thus settled upon the principle of popular sovereignty; a principle as ancient as free government itself, everything of a practical nature has been decided. No other question remains for adjustment, because all agree that under the Constitution slavery in the States is beyond the reach of any human power except that of the respective States themselves wherein it exists. May we not, then, hope that the long agitation on this subject is approaching its end, and that the geographical parties to which it has given birth, so much dreaded by the Father of his Country, will speedily become extinct? Most happy will it be for the country when the public mind shall be diverted from this question to others of more pressing and practical importance. Throughout the whole progress of this agitation, which has scarcely known any intermission for more than twenty years, whilst it has been productive of no positive good to any human being it has been the prolific source of great evils to the master, to the slave, and to the whole country. It has alienated and estranged the people of the sister States from each other, and has even seriously endangered the very existence of the Union. Nor has the danger yet entirely ceased. Under our system there is a remedy for all mere political evils in the sound sense and sober judgment of the people. Time is a great corrective. Political subjects which but a few years ago excited and exasperated the public mind have passed away and are now nearly forgotten. But this question of domestic slavery is of far graver importance than any mere political question, because should the agitation continue it may eventually endanger the personal safety of a large portion of our countrymen where the institution exists. In that event no form of government, however admirable in itself and however productive of material benefits, can compensate for the loss of peace and domestic security around the family altar. Let every Union-loving man, therefore, exert his best influence to suppress this agitation, which since the recent legislation of Congress is without any legitimate object.

It is an evil omen of the times that men have undertaken to calculate the mere material value of the Union. Reasoned estimates have been presented of the pecuniary profits and local advantages which would result to different States and sections from its dissolution and of the comparative injuries which such an event would inflict on other States and sections. Even descending to this low and narrow view of the mighty question, all such calculations are at fault. The bare reference to a single consideration will be conclusive on this point. We at present enjoy a free trade throughout our extensive and expanding country such as the world has never witnessed. This trade is conducted on railroads and canals, on noble rivers and arms of the sea, which bind together the North and the South, the East and the West, of our Confederacy. Annihilate this trade, arrest its free progress by the geographical lines of jealous and hostile States, and you destroy the prosperity and onward march of the whole and every part and involve all in one common ruin. But such considerations, important as they are in themselves, sink into insignificance when we reflect on the terrific evils which would result from disunion to every portion of the Confederacy to the North, not more than to the South, to the East not more than to the West. These I shall not attempt to portray, because I feel an humble confidence that the kind Providence which inspired our fathers with wisdom to frame the most perfect form of government and union ever devised by man will not suffer it to perish until it shall have been peacefully instrumental by its example in the extension of civil and religious liberty throughout the world.

Next in importance to the maintenance of the Constitution and the
Union is the duty of preserving the Government free from the taint or even
the suspicion of corruption. Public virtue is the vital spirit of republics,
and history proves that when this has decayed and the love of money has
usurped its place, although the forms of free government may remain for a
season, the substance has departed forever.

Our present financial condition is without a parallel in history. No
nation has ever before been embarrassed from too large a surplus in its
treasury. This almost necessarily gives birth to extravagant legislation. It
produces wild schemes of expenditure and begets a race of speculators and
jobbers, whose ingenuity is exerted in contriving and promoting expedients
to obtain public money. The purity of official agents, whether rightfully or
wrongfully, is suspected, and the character of the government suffers in the
estimation of the people. This is in itself a very great evil.

The natural mode of relief from this embarrassment is to appropriate the surplus in the Treasury to great national objects for which a clear
warrant can be found in the Constitution. Among these I might mention
the extinguishment of the public debt, a reasonable increase of the Navy,
which is at present inadequate to the protection of our vast tonnage afloat,
now greater than that of any other nation, as well as to the defense of our
extended seacoast.

It is beyond all question the true principle that no more revenue ought
to be collected from the people than the amount necessary to defray the
expenses of a wise, economical, and efficient administration of the Government. To reach this point it was necessary to resort to a modification of the
tariff, and this has, I trust, been accomplished in such a manner as to do as
little injury as may have been practicable to our domestic manufactures,
especially those necessary for the defense of the country. Any discrimination against a particular branch for the purpose of benefiting favored corporations, individuals, or interests would have been unjust to the rest of the
community and inconsistent with that spirit of fairness and equality which
ought to govern in the adjustment of a revenue tariff.

But the squandering of the public money sinks into comparative insignificance as a temptation to corruption when compared with the squandering of the public lands.

No nation in the tide of time has ever been blessed with so rich and
noble an inheritance as we enjoy in the public lands. In administering this
important trust, whilst it may be wise to grant portions of them for the im-

provement of the remainder, yet we should never forget that it is our cardinal policy to reserve these lands, as much as may be, for actual settlers, and this at moderate prices. We shall thus not only best promote the prosperity of the new States and Territories, by furnishing them a hardy and independent race of honest and industrious citizens, but shall secure homes for our children and our children's children, as well as for those exiles from foreign shores who may seek in this country to improve their condition and to enjoy the blessings of civil and religious liberty. Such emigrants have done much to promote the growth and prosperity of the country. They have proved faithful both in peace and in war. After becoming citizens they are entitled, under the Constitution and laws, to be placed on a perfect equality with native born citizens, and in this character they should ever be kindly recognized.

The Federal Constitution is a grant from the States to Congress of certain specific powers, and the question whether this grant should be liberally or strictly construed has more or less divided political parties from the beginning. Without entering into the argument, I desire to state at the commencement of my Administration that long experience and observation have convinced me that a strict construction of the powers of the Government is the only true, as well as the only safe, theory of the Constitution. Whenever in our past history doubtful powers have been exercised by Congress, these have never failed to produce injurious and unhappy consequences. Many such instances might be adduced if this were the proper occasion. Neither is it necessary for the public service to strain the language of the Constitution, because all the great and useful powers required for a successful administration of the Government, both in peace and in war, have been granted, either in express terms or by the plainest implication.

Whilst deeply convinced of these truths, I yet consider it clear that under the war making power Congress may appropriate money toward the construction of a military road when this is absolutely necessary for the defense of any State or Territory of the Union against foreign invasion. Under the Constitution Congress has power to declare war; to raise and support armies; to provide and maintain a navy; and to call forth the militia to repel invasions. Thus endowed, in an ample manner, with the war making power, the corresponding duty is required that the United States shall protect each of them the States, against invasion. Now, how is it possible to afford this protection to California and our Pacific possessions except by means of a military road through the Territories of the United States, over which men and munitions of war may be speedily transported from the Atlantic States to meet and to repel the invader? In the event of a war with a naval power much stronger than our own we should then have no other available access to the Pacific Coast, because such a power would instantly close the route across the isthmus of Central America. It is impossible to conceive that whilst the Constitution has expressly required Congress to defend all the States it should yet deny to them, by any fair construction, the only possible means by which one of these States can be defended. Besides, the Government, ever since its origin, has been in the constant practice of constructing military roads. It might also be wise to consider whether the love for the Union which now animates our fellow citizens on the Pacific Coast may not be impaired by our neglect or refusal to provide for them, in their remote and isolated condition, the only means by which the power of the States on this side of the Rocky Mountains can reach them in sufficient time to protect them against invasion. I forbear for the present from expressing an opinion as to the wisest and most economical mode in which the Government can lend its aid in accomplishing this great and necessary work. I believe that many of the difficulties in the way, which now appear formidable, will in a great degree vanish as soon as the nearest and best route shall have been satisfactorily ascertained.

It may be proper that on this occasion I should make some brief remarks in regard to our rights and duties as a member of the great family of nations. In our intercourse with them there are some plain principles, approved by our own experience, from which we should never depart. We ought to cultivate peace, commerce, and friendship with all nations, and this not merely as the best means of promoting our own material interests, but in a spirit of Christian benevolence toward our fellow men, wherever their lot may be cast. Our diplomacy should be direct and frank, neither seeking to obtain more nor accepting less than is our due. We ought to cherish a sacred regard for the independence of all nations, and never attempt to interfere in the domestic concerns of any unless this shall be imperatively required by the great law of self-preservation. To avoid entangling alliances has been a maxim of our policy ever since the days of Washington, and its wisdom's no one will attempt to dispute. In short, we ought to do justice in a kindly spirit to all nations and require justice from them in return.

It is our glory that whilst other nations have extended their dominions by the sword we have never acquired any territory except by fair purchase or, as in the case of Texas, by the voluntary determination of a brave, kindred, and independent people to blend their destinies with our own. Even our acquisitions from Mexico form no exception. Unwilling to take advantage of the fortune of war against a sister republic, we purchased these possessions under the treaty of peace for a sum which was considered at the time a fair equivalent. Our past history forbids that we shall in the future acquire territory unless this be sanctioned by the laws of justice and honor. Acting on this principle, no nation will have a right to interfere or to complain if in the progress of events we shall still further extend our possessions. Hitherto in all our acquisitions the people, under the protection of the American flag, have enjoyed civil and religious liberty, as well as equal and just laws, and have been contented, prosperous, and happy. Their trade with the rest of the world has rapidly increased, and thus every commercial nation has shared largely in their successful progress.

I shall now proceed to take the oath prescribed by the Constitution, whilst humbly invoking the blessing of Divine Providence on this great people.

ABRAHAM LINCOLN

FIRST INAUGURAL ADDRESS

MARCH 4, 1861

COMMENTARY

The 1860 election is the most important in American history; when the re-sults were known, the Union began to shatter. During Buchanan's administra-tion, sectional disputes had become more acrimonious, passions more excited, propagandists in both North and South more active. The Dred Scott decision (1857) and John Brown's raid at Harpers Ferry (1859) further intensified the burning slavery issue. With the fatalism of a Greek tragedy, the nation ap-peared to be rushing toward destruction.

When the Democratic Party assembled at Charleston in April 1860, South-ern delegates refused to accept any platform that did not guarantee federal pro-tection of slavery in the territories. Stephen Douglas controlled a majority of the delegates and would not agree—but his support stopped short of the two-thirds necessary to gain the nomination. After 10 days of futile balloting, the convention adjourned to meet again in Baltimore on June 18. Upon reassem-bling, the party remained divided into Northern and Southern wings. Most Southern delegates now withdrew and the Northern Democrats nominated Douglas and endorsed the party's 1856 platform. The bolters put forth John C. Breckinridge of Kentucky for president on a platform supporting slavery in the territories. With this crucial Democratic split, another bond holding the nation together dissolved. Republican chances for victory now brightened.

The Republican Party nominated Abraham Lincoln, and his rivals for the honor, William Seward and Salmon Chase, rallied behind him. Lincoln, now 51 years old, had served as a Whig representative for one term (1847–1849) and then resumed his law practice in Springfield, Illinois. "Honest Abe" embodied the American success story. Born in a log cabin, self-educated, he rose to become a noted lawyer and shrewd politician. In 1858, Lincoln accepted the Republican nomination for the Senate, opposing Stephen Douglas. In the course of the seven campaign debates with Douglas, held between August 21 and October 15, Lincoln, although he lost the election, established himself as a national figure. When Douglas sought to identify Lincoln with the radical abolitionists, Lincoln declared that he had no intention of interfering with slavery where it then existed. It was expansion into the territories that he opposed—and he stuck to his position during the 1860 campaign.

Many myths now surround this tall, frugal, industrious rail-splitter, and he himself carefully assisted in cultivating stories about his humble origins. But above all, Lincoln was an excellent politician. It is interesting to compare two Lincoln statements about the African American—one made in Chicago, the other in Charleston, Illinois:

> *Chicago, July 10, 1858. Let us discard all this quibbling about this man and the other man, this race and that race and the other race being inferior, and therefore they must be placed in an inferior position. Let us discard all these things and unite as one people throughout this land, until we shall once more stand up declaring that all men are created equal.*

> *Charleston, September 18, 1858. I am not, nor ever have been, in favor of bringing about in any way the social and political equality of the white and black races; that I am not, nor ever have been, in favor of making voters or jurors of Negroes, nor of qualifying them to hold office, nor to intermarry with white people . . . .*
> *And inasmuch as they cannot so live, while they do remain together there must be the position of superior and inferior, and I as much as any other man am in favor of having the superior position assigned to the white race.*

Few who voted for Lincoln at the Republican convention realized that their greatest man had been nominated, a man who would become a towering humanitarian. To the majority of the delegates, he simply appeared to have the best chance of winning.

In addition to Lincoln, Douglas, and Breckinridge, the former Whig-American Party, renamed the Constitutional Union Party, nominated John Bell of

Tennessee on a platform advocating "the Constitution of the country, the union of the states, and the enforcement of the laws." When the returns were tabulated, Lincoln received 180 of the 303 electoral votes—all from free states. Breckinridge carried 11 slave states and 72 votes; Bell ran third with 39, winning three border slave states; Douglas captured only Missouri and three New Jersey votes for a total of 12. In the popular vote column, Lincoln received 1,866,452 ballots against 2,813,741 for his three opponents—39.9 percent of the total. The election clearly shows the sectional voting pattern, almost as if two elections were being held; Lincoln vs. Douglas in the North and West, Breckinridge vs. Bell in the South. Although Lincoln pledged himself and his party to uphold the Union, its future remained in Southern hands.

On December 20, 1860, South Carolina seceded. Lincoln's election, declared the state's governor, would "inevitably destroy our equality in the Union, and ultimately reduce the Southern states to mere provinces of a consolidated despotism, to be governed by a fixed majority in congress hostile to our institutions and fatally bent upon our ruin." The Deep South followed, and, during January 1861, Mississippi, Florida, Alabama, Georgia, Louisiana, and Texas passed secession ordinances. With the exception of South Carolina, this movement certainly was not unanimous. In Alabama, for example, 34 of the 95 delegates to the special convention voted against immediate secession; in Georgia, 133 out of 297. Nevertheless, the zealots triumphed. And the South, which had talked about states rights for so long, now, ironically, established a national government, the Confederate States of America. Throughout this crisis, the Buchanan administration developed no clear policy.

Lincoln left Springfield on February 11, 1861. As he moved toward Washington, he calmly explained to anxious crowds the necessity of preserving the Union. His journey became one continuous ovation. "We mean to treat you as near as we possibly can, as a Washington, Jefferson, and Madison treated you," he told a group of Kentuckians present in the Cincinnati crowd. "We mean to leave you alone, and in no way to interfere with your institutions, to abide by all and every compromise of the Constitution." At Pittsburgh, he remarked that despite the trouble "across the river" no crisis existed. "If the American people will only keep their temper on both sides of the line the troubles will come to an end and they will prosper as heretofore." He reached Washington on February 23. Nine days later, before the stark, unfinished Capitol, Lincoln took his oath of office. In a masterly inaugural address, which had been carefully prepared, he invoked "the mystic chords of memory" in making a direct appeal to Southerners. "In your hands, my dissatisfied fellow countrymen, and

not in mine, is the momentous issue of civil war. The Government will not as-
sail you. You can have no conflict without being yourselves the aggressors."

Fellow citizens of the United States:

In compliance with a custom as old as the Government itself, I appear before you to address you briefly and to take in your presence the oath prescribed by the Constitution of the United States to be taken by the President before he enters on the execution of this office.

I do not consider it necessary at present for me to discuss those matters of administration about which there is no special anxiety or excitement.

Apprehension seems to exist among the people of the Southern States that by the accession of a Republican Administration their property and their peace and personal security are to be endangered. There has never been any reasonable cause for such apprehension. Indeed, the most ample evidence to the contrary has all the while existed and been open to their inspection. It is found in nearly all the published speeches of him who now addresses you. I do but quote from one of those speeches when I declare that I have no purpose, directly or indirectly, to interfere with the institution of slavery in the States where it exists. I believe I have no lawful right to do so, and I have no inclination to do so.

Those who nominated and elected me did so with full knowledge that I had made this and many similar declarations and had never recanted them; and more than this, they placed in the platform for my acceptance, and as a law to themselves and to me, the clear and emphatic resolution which I now read:

"Resolved, That the maintenance inviolate of the rights of the States, and especially the right of each State to order and control its own domestic institutions according to its own judgment exclusively, is essential to that balance of power on which the perfection and endurance of our political fabric depend; and we denounce the lawless invasion by armed force of the soil of any State or Territory, no matter what pretext, as among the gravest of crimes."

I now reiterate these sentiments, and in doing so I only press upon the public attention the most conclusive evidence of which the case is susceptible that the property, peace, and security of no section are to be in any wise endangered by the now incoming Administration. I add, too, that all the protection which, consistently with the Constitution and the laws, can be given will be cheerfully given to all the States when lawfully demanded, for whatever cause, as cheerfully to one section as to another.

There is much controversy about the delivering up of fugitives from service or labor. The clause I now read is as plainly written in the Constitution as any other of its provisions:

"No person held to service or labor in one State, under the laws thereof, escaping into another, shall in consequence of any law or regulation therein be discharged from such service or labor, but shall be delivered up on claim of the party to whom such service or labor may be due."

It is scarcely questioned that this provision was intended by those who made it for the reclaiming of what we call fugitive slaves; and the intention of the lawgiver is the law. All members of Congress swear their support to the whole Constitution, to this provision as much as to any other. To the proposition, then, that slaves whose cases come within the terms of this clause shall be delivered up their oaths are unanimous. Now, if they would make the effort in good temper, could they not with nearly equal unanimity frame and pass a law by means of which to keep good that unanimous oath?

There is some difference of opinion whether this clause should be enforced by national or by State authority, but surely that difference is not a very material one. If the slave is to be surrendered, it can be of but little consequence to him or to others by which authority it is done. And should anyone in any case be content that his oath shall go unkept on a merely unsubstantial controversy as to how it shall be kept?

Again, in any law upon this subject ought not all the safeguards of liberty known in civilized and humane jurisprudence to be introduced, so that a free man be not in any case surrendered as a slave? And might it not be well at the same time to provide by law for the enforcement of that clause in the Constitution which guarantees that the citizens of each State shall be entitled to all privileges and immunities of citizens in the several States?

I take the official oath today with no mental reservations and with no purpose to construe the Constitution or laws by any hypercritical rules; and while I do not choose now to specify particular acts of Congress as proper to be enforced, I do suggest that it will be much safer for all, both in official and private stations, to conform to and abide by all those acts which stand unrepealed than to violate any of them trusting to find impunity in having them held to be unconstitutional.

It is seventy-two years since the first inauguration of a President under our National Constitution. During that period fifteen different and greatly distinguished citizens have in succession administered the executive branch of the Government. They have conducted it through many perils, and generally with great success. Yet, with all this scope of precedent, I now enter upon the same task for the brief constitutional term of four years under great and peculiar difficulty. A disruption of the Federal Union, heretofore only menaced, is now formidably attempted.

I hold that in contemplation of universal law and of the Constitution the Union of these States is perpetual. Perpetuity is implied, if not expressed, in the fundamental law of all national governments. It is safe to assert that no government proper ever had a provision in its organic law for its own termination. Continue to execute all the express provisions of our National Constitution, and the Union will endure forever, it being impossible to destroy it except by some action not provided for in the instrument itself.

Again, if the United States be not a government proper, but an association of States in the nature of contract merely, can it, as a contract, be peaceably unmade by less than all the parties who made it? One party to a contract may violate it, break it so to speak, but does it not require all to lawfully rescind it?

Descending from these general principles, we find the proposition that in legal contemplation the Union is perpetual confirmed by the history of the Union itself. The Union is much older than the Constitution. It was formed, in fact, by the Articles of Association in 1774. It was matured and continued by the Declaration of Independence in 1776. It was further matured, and the faith of all the then thirteen States expressly plighted and engaged that it should be perpetual, by the Articles of Confederation in 1778. And finally, in 1787, one of the declared objects for ordaining and establishing the Constitution was to form a more perfect Union.

But if destruction of the Union by one or by a part only of the States be lawfully possible, the Union is less perfect than before the Constitution, having lost the vital element of perpetuity.

It follows from these views that no State upon its own mere motion can lawfully get out of the Union; that resolves and ordinances to that effect are legally void, and that acts of violence within any State or States against the authority of the United States are insurrectionary or revolutionary, according to circumstances.

I therefore consider that in view of the Constitution and the laws the Union is unbroken, and to the extent of my ability, I shall take care, as the Constitution itself expressly enjoins upon me, that the laws of the Union be faithfully executed in all the States. Doing this I deem to be only a simple duty on my part, and I shall perform it so far as practicable unless my rightful masters, the American people, shall withhold the requisite means or in some authoritative manner direct the contrary. I trust this will not be regarded as a menace, but only as the declared purpose of the Union that it will constitutionally defend and maintain itself.

In doing this there needs to be no bloodshed or violence, and there shall be none unless it be forced upon the national authority. The power confided to me will be used to hold, occupy, and possess the property and places belonging to the Government and to collect the duties and imposts; but beyond what may be necessary for these objects, there will be no invasion, no using of force against or among the people anywhere. Where hostility to the United States in any interior locality shall be so great and universal as to prevent competent resident citizens from holding the Federal offices, there will be no attempt to force obnoxious strangers among the people for that object. While the strict legal right may exist in the Government to enforce the exercise of these offices, the attempt to do so would be so irritating and so nearly impracticable withal that I deem it better to forego for the time the uses of such offices.

The mails, unless repelled, will continue to be furnished in all parts of the Union. So far as possible the people everywhere shall have that sense of perfect security which is most favorable to calm thought and reflection. The course here indicated will be followed unless current events and experience shall show a modification or change to be proper, and in every case and exigency my best discretion will be exercised, according to circumstances actually existing and with a view and a hope of a peaceful solution of the national troubles and the restoration of fraternal sympathies and affections.

That there are persons in one section or another who seek to destroy the Union at all events and are glad of any pretext to do it I will neither affirm nor deny; but if there be such, I need address no word to them. To those, however, who really love the Union may I not speak?

Before entering upon so grave a matter as the destruction of our national fabric, with all its benefits, its memories, and its hopes, would it not be wise to ascertain precisely why we do it? Will you hazard so desperate a step while there is any possibility that any portion of the ills you fly from have no real existence? Will you, while the certain ills you fly to are greater than all the real ones you fly from, will you risk the commission of so fearful a mistake?

All profess to be content in the Union if all constitutional rights can be maintained. Is it true, then, that any right plainly written in the Constitution has been denied? I think not. Happily, the human mind is so constituted that no party can reach to the audacity of doing this. Think, if you can, of a single instance in which a plainly written provision of the Constitution has ever been denied. If by the mere force of numbers a majority should deprive a minority of any clearly written constitutional right, it might in a moral point of view justify revolution; certainly would if such right were a vital one. But such is not our case. All the vital rights of minorities and of individuals are so plainly assured to them by affirmations and negations, guaranties and prohibitions, in the Constitution that controversies never arise concerning them. But no organic law can ever be framed with a provision specifically applicable to every question which may occur in practical administration. No foresight can anticipate nor any document of reasonable length contain express provisions for all possible questions. Shall fugitives from labor be surrendered by national or by State authority? The Constitution does not expressly say. May Congress prohibit slavery in the Territories? The Constitution does not expressly say. Must Congress protect slavery in the Territories? The Constitution does not expressly say.

From questions of this class spring all our constitutional controversies, and we divide upon them into majorities and minorities. If the minority will not acquiesce, the majority must, or the Government must cease. There is no other alternative, for continuing the Government is acquiescence on one side or the other. If a minority in such case will secede rather than acquiesce, they make a precedent which in turn will divide and ruin them, for a minority of their own will secede from them whenever a majority refuses to be controlled by such minority. For instance, why may not any portion of a new confederacy a year or two hence arbitrarily secede again, precisely as portions of the present Union now claim to secede from it? All who cherish disunion sentiments are now being educated to the exact temper of doing this.

Is there such perfect identity of interests among the States to compose a new union as to produce harmony only and prevent renewed secession?

Plainly the central idea of secession is the essence of anarchy. A majority held in restraint by constitutional checks and limitations, and always changing easily with deliberate changes of popular opinions and sentiments, is the only true sovereign of a free people. Whoever rejects it does of necessity fly to anarchy or to despotism. Unanimity is impossible. The rule of a minority, as a permanent arrangement, is wholly inadmissible; so that, rejecting the majority principle, anarchy or despotism in some form is all that is left.

I do not forget the position assumed by some that constitutional questions are to be decided by the Supreme Court, nor do I deny that such decisions must be binding in any case upon the parties to a suit as to the object of that suit, while they are also entitled to very high respect and consideration in all parallel cases by all other departments of the Government. And while it is obviously possible that such decision may be erroneous in any given case, still the evil effect following it, being limited to that particular case, with the chance that it may be overruled and never become a precedent for other cases, can better be borne than could the evils of a different practice. At the same time, the candid citizen must confess that if the policy of the Government upon vital questions affecting the whole people is to be irrevocably fixed by decisions of the Supreme Court, the instant they are made in ordinary litigation between parties in personal actions the people will have ceased to be their own rulers, having to that extent practically resigned their Government into the hands of that eminent tribunal. Nor is there in this view any assault upon the court or the judges. It is a duty from which they may not shrink to decide cases properly brought before them, and it is no fault of theirs if others seek to turn their decisions to political purposes.

One section of our country believes slavery is right and ought to be extended, while the other believes it is wrong and ought not to be extended. This is the only substantial dispute. The fugitive slave clause of the Constitution and the law for the suppression of the foreign slave trade are each as well enforced, perhaps, as any law can ever be in a community where the moral sense of the people imperfectly supports the law itself. The great body of the people abide by the dry legal obligation in both cases, and a few break over in each. This, I think, can not be perfectly cured, and it would be worse in both cases after the separation of the sections than before. The foreign slave trade, now imperfectly suppressed, would be ultimately revived without restriction in one section, while fugitive slaves, now only partially surrendered, would not be surrendered at all by the other.

Physically speaking, we can not separate. We can not remove our respective sections from each other nor build an impassable wall between them. A husband and wife may be divorced and go out of the presence and beyond the reach of each other, but the different parts of our country can not do this. They can not but remain face to face, and intercourse, either amicable or hostile, must continue between them. Is it possible, then, to make that intercourse more advantageous or more satisfactory after separation than before? Can aliens make treaties easier than friends can make laws? Can treaties be more faithfully enforced between aliens than laws can among friends? Suppose you go to war, you can not fight always; and when, after much loss on both sides and no gain on either, you cease fighting, the identical old questions, as to terms of intercourse, are again upon you.

This country, with its institutions, belongs to the people who inhabit it. Whenever they shall grow weary of the existing Government, they can exercise their constitutional right of amending it or their revolutionary right to dismember or overthrow it. I can not be ignorant of the fact that many worthy and patriotic citizens are desirous of having the National Constitution amended. While I make no recommendation of amendments, I fully recognize the rightful authority of the people over the whole subject, to be exercised in either of the modes prescribed in the instrument itself; and I should, under existing circumstances, favor rather than oppose a fair opportunity being afforded the people to act upon it. I will venture to add that to me the convention mode seems preferable, in that it allows amendments to originate with the people themselves, instead of only permitting them to take or reject propositions originated by others, not especially chosen for the purpose, and which might not be precisely such as they would wish to either accept or refuse. I understand a proposed amendment to the Constitution, which amendment, however, I have not seen, has passed Congress, to the effect that the Federal Government shall never interfere with the domestic institutions of the States, including that of persons held to service. To avoid misconstruction of what I have said, I depart from my purpose not to speak of particular amendments so far as to say that, holding such a provision to now be implied constitutional law, I have no objection to its being made express and irrevocable.

The Chief Magistrate derives all his authority from the people, and they have referred none upon him to fix terms for the separation of the States. The people themselves can do this if also they choose, but the Executive as such has nothing to do with it. His duty is to administer the present Government as it came to his hands and to transmit it unimpaired by him to his successor.

Why should there not be a patient confidence in the ultimate justice of the people? Is there any better or equal hope in the world? In our present differences, is either party without faith of being in the right? If the Almighty Ruler of Nations, with His eternal truth and justice, be on your side of the North, or on yours of the South, that truth and that justice will surely prevail by the judgment of this great tribunal of the American people.

By the frame of the Government under which we live this same people have wisely given their public servants but little power for mischief, and have with equal wisdom provided for the return of that little to their own hands at very short intervals. While the people retain their virtue and vigilance no Administration by any extreme of wickedness or folly can very seriously injure the Government in the short space of four years.

My countrymen, one and all, think calmly and well upon this whole subject. Nothing valuable can be lost by taking time. If there be an object to hurry any of you in hot haste to a step which you would never take deliberately, that object will be frustrated by taking time; but no good object can be frustrated by it. Such of you as are now dissatisfied still have the old Constitution unimpaired, and, on the sensitive point, the laws of your own framing under it; while the new Administration will have no immediate power, if it would, to change either. If it were admitted that you who are dissatisfied hold the right side in the dispute, there still is no single good reason for precipitate action. Intelligence, patriotism, Christianity, and a firm reliance on Him who has never yet forsaken this favored land are still competent to adjust in the best way all our present difficulty.

In your hands, my dissatisfied fellow countrymen, and not in mine, is the momentous issue of civil war. The Government will not assail you. You can have no conflict without being yourselves the aggressors. You have no oath registered in heaven to destroy the Government, while I shall have the most solemn one to preserve, protect, and defend it.

I am loath to close. We are not enemies, but friends. We must not be enemies. Though passion may have strained it must not break our bonds of affection. The mystic chords of memory, stretching from every battlefield and patriot grave to every living heart and hearthstone all over this broad land, will yet swell the chorus of the Union, when again touched, as surely they will be, by the better angels of our nature.

——— SECOND INAUGURAL ADDRESS ———

MARCH 4, 1865

COMMENTARY

Lincoln delivered his short but brilliant second inaugural address—just a little under 700 words—on March 4, 1865. For four years, the crusade to save the Union had raged and now it neared a successful conclusion. Four years of death and destruction had created an atmosphere of vindictiveness. But

Lincoln's memorable address stands above the hate that preceded, accompanied, and followed this horrible war: "With malice toward none, with charity for all." In four paragraphs, 26 sentences, he soared above momentary passions to capture something of the larger tragedy involved, embracing that feeling of renewed confidence so necessary in facing the future problems of reconstruction. There was one new and striking feature in the simple inaugural ceremony—the presence of a battalion of African-American troops in the escort party.

Fellow countrymen:

At this second appearing to take the oath of the Presidential office there is less occasion for an extended address than there was at the first. Then a statement somewhat in detail of a course to be pursued seemed fitting and proper. Now, at the expiration of four years, during which public declarations have been constantly called forth on every point and phase of the great contest which still absorbs the attention and engrosses the energies of the nation, little that is new could be presented. The progress of our arms, upon which all else chiefly depends, is as well known to the public as to myself, and it is, I trust, reasonably satisfactory and encouraging to all. With high hope for the future, no prediction in regard to it is ventured.

On the occasion corresponding to this four years ago all thoughts were anxiously directed to an impending civil war. All dreaded it, all sought to avert it. While the inaugural address was being delivered from this place, devoted altogether to saving the Union without war, urgent agents were in the city seeking to destroy it without war; seeking to dissolve the Union and divide effects by negotiation. Both parties deprecated war, but one of them would make war rather than let the nation survive, and the other would accept war rather than let it perish, and the war came.

One-eighth of the whole population were colored slaves, not distributed generally over the Union, but localized in the southern part of it. These slaves constituted a peculiar and powerful interest. All knew that this interest was somehow the cause of the war. To strengthen, perpetuate, and extend this interest was the object for which the insurgents would rend the Union even by war, while the Government claimed no right to do more than to restrict the territorial enlargement of it. Neither party expected for the war the magnitude or the duration which it has already attained. Neither anticipated that the cause of the conflict might cease with or even before the conflict itself should cease. Each looked for an easier triumph, and a result less fundamental and astounding. Both read the same Bible and pray to the same God, and each invokes His aid against the other. It may seem strange that any men should dare to ask a just God's assistance in wringing their bread from the sweat of other men's faces, but let us judge not, that we be not judged. The prayers of both could not be answered. That of neither has been answered fully. The Almighty has His own purposes. Woe unto the world because of offenses; for it must needs be that offenses come, but woe to that man by whom the offense cometh. If we shall suppose that American slavery is one of those offenses which, in the providence of God, must needs come, but which, having continued through His appointed time, He now wills to remove, and that He gives to both North and South this terrible war as the woe due to those by whom the offense came, shall we discern therein any departure from those divine attributes which the believers in a living God always ascribe to Him? Fondly do we hope, fervently do we pray, that this mighty scourge of war may speedily pass away. Yet, if God wills that it continue until all the wealth piled by the bondsman's two hundred and fifty years of unrequited toil shall be sunk, and until every drop of blood drawn with the lash shall be paid by another drawn with the sword, as was said three thousand years ago, so still it must be said, the judgments of the Lord are true and righteous altogether.

With malice toward none, with charity for all, with firmness in the right as God gives us to see the right, let us strive on to finish the work we are in, to bind up the nation's wounds, to care for him who shall have borne the battle and for his widow and his orphan, to do all which may achieve and cherish a just and lasting peace among ourselves and with all nations.

Ulysses S. Grant

First Inaugural Address

MARCH 4, 1869

Commentary

The North's victory in the Civil War meant more than the preservation of the Union; it was the complete triumph of one section over another. The vanquished South had to be reconstructed politically, economically, and socially. Although conditions varied from place to place, the general picture was one of ruin and despair. The scars of war—of a desperate civil war—did not disappear with peace. In fact, a bitterness developed between the sections that still exists. In accepting Lee's surrender at Appomattox on April 9, 1865, General Grant commented that this would be "the last battle of the war." It was for the military phase. The battle over reconstruction now began.

During the war both Lincoln and the Congress had shown concern for Southern reconstruction. In December 1863, the president, using his power to pardon, announced a lenient plan that allowed executive recognition of re-established state governments where 10 percent of the 1860 electorate swore allegiance to the Union. From this proposal and from several statements, it appeared abundantly clear that Lincoln intended to use his presidential authority to make reconstruction a short and merciful process. Radical Republicans, however, excoriated the President for his magnanimity. "He must confine himself to his executive duties," declared Senator Benjamin Wade of Ohio and Representative Henry Davis of Maryland in a biting statement, ". . . to obey and to execute, not make the laws, and leave political reconstruction to Congress." Accordingly, in 1864, Congress, the judge of its own membership, refused to seat representatives from Arkansas and Louisiana, two states that had complied with the president's 10 percent proclamation. A virtual stalemate existed between the chief executive and the legislature when an assassin's bullet ended Lincoln's life on April 14, 1865.

Through an unusual turn of events a former lifelong Southern Democrat now became president of the United States. Andrew Johnson had been a senator from Tennessee but when the Southern states seceded in 1860–1861, he refused to resign his seat—the only Southern senator to oppose secession. In 1862, after Union troops had occupied the state, Lincoln appointed him military governor of Tennessee. When, in 1864, the Republican Party, to emphasize its bipartisan, anti-Confederate character, reformed under the National Union banner, Johnson became the logical choice for second position. Now, Johnson, a man technically without a party, assumed the presidency. At first, the new chief executive cooperated with the Radicals. "Johnson, we have faith in you," Senator Wade told him. But Johnson gradually relied on more moderate advice and soon issued a reconstruction plan reminiscent of Lincoln's liberality. By December 1865, every former Confederate state except Texas had complied with this plan and awaited admission to Congress. Included among the newly elected Southern representatives was Alexander Stephens, former vice president of the Confederate States of America. A head-on collision between the president and the Radicals now seemed inevitable.

When Congress convened in December 1865, it refused to endorse Johnson's actions. "The future condition of the conquered people depends on the will of the conqueror," proclaimed grim Representative Thaddeus Stevens of Pennsylvania, the leader of the Radical faction. "They must come in as new states or remain as conquered provinces. Congress is the only power that can act in the matter." During 1866, differences between the president and the Radicals sharpened, especially as Southern states passed "Black Codes" restricting the rights of the new freedmen. The congressional elections of 1866 settled the crisis. Johnson attempted but failed to rally Northern moderates, particularly as former ex-Confederates and Southern sympathizers endorsed his program. Radical politicians dwelt on this, stressing that the same men who voted for secession would return to Washington if Johnson had his way. Would slavery then be reenacted? Would the Confederate debt be validated? The vindictive Radicals triumphed, receiving an even greater congressional majority. Reconstruction now passed to Congress—two years after the war had ended.

Congress moved boldly ahead in 1867 and 1868, enacting their stringent program over the president's vetoes. The South, with the exception of Tennessee where local Radicals had gained power, was divided into five military districts. Military authority would remain until republican governments, in *which African Americans could vote and hold office, functioned. When Congress approved each new state constitution and when each state accepted the Fourteenth Amendment, then federal troops would be withdrawn. The Radicals also passed several laws curbing the president's powers, fearing he would somehow overturn their work. Actually, Johnson's enemies sought his removal. And when the president ineptly committed a "high misdemeanor" by violating the new Tenure of Office Act, the House of Representatives, on February 24, 1868, brought resolutions of impeachment against him. The trial before the Senate began on March 30, with the chief justice of the United States presiding. On May 16, the Senate cast 35 votes for conviction and 19 for acquittal, one short of the two-thirds needed to remove the president.*

Four days after the dramatic Senate vote, the Republicans nominated General Ulysses S. Grant for the presidency. Their platform endorsed Radical reconstruction and condemned Johnson. "Let us have peace," stated the general in his acceptance message. But passions ran too high and the presidential election of 1868 was perhaps the most bitter in American history. Much to Johnson's disappointment, the Democrats passed him over to choose Governor Horatio Seymour of New York. The party denounced Radical military reconstruction as "unconstitutional, revolutionary and void," and promised a restoration of the South that would be "fair." The great Northern war hero trounced Seymour in the electoral vote, receiving 214 to the governor's 80. Surprisingly, though, Grant's popular majority was only a little more than 300,000 out of 5,715,000. Approximately 700,000 African Americans voted in six Southern states under Radical domination and Grant received most of their votes. His majority depended on that support. As a result of this political situation, the Radicals attempted to make African-American suffrage irrevocable by submitting the Fifteenth Amendment to the states.

It is against this disagreeable and tragic aftermath of the Civil War that on March 4, 1869, the "Lion of Vicksburg" delivered his first inaugural address. After Chief Justice Chase had administered the oath of office the president drew seven pages of foolscap from his coat breast pocket and began to read his message slowly and with great deliberation.

⌒ ᧬ ⌒

Citizens of the United States:

Your suffrages having elected me to the office of President of the United States, I have, in conformity to the Constitution of our country, taken the oath of office prescribed therein. I have taken this oath without mental reservation and with the determination to do to the best of my ability all that is required of me. The responsibilities of the position I feel, but accept them without fear. The office has come to me unsought; I commence its duties untrammeled. I bring to it a conscious desire and determination to fill it to the best of my ability to the satisfaction of the people.

On all leading questions agitating the public mind I will always express my views to Congress and urge them according to my judgment, and when I think it advisable will exercise the constitutional privilege of interposing a veto to defeat measures which I oppose; but all laws will be faithfully executed, whether they meet my approval or not.

I shall on all subjects have a policy to recommend, but none to enforce against the will of the people. Laws are to govern all alike; those opposed as well as those who favor them. I know no method to secure the repeal of bad or obnoxious laws so effective as their stringent execution.

The country having just emerged from a great rebellion, many questions will come before it for settlement in the next four years which preceding Administrations have never had to deal with. In meeting these it is desirable that they should be approached calmly, without prejudice, hate, or sectional pride, remembering that the greatest good to the greatest number is the object to be attained.

This requires security of person, property, and free religious and political opinion in every part of our common country, without regard to local prejudice. All laws to secure these ends will receive my best efforts for their enforcement.

A great debt has been contracted in securing to us and our posterity the Union. The payment of this, principal and interest, as well as the return to a specie basis as soon as it can be accomplished without material detriment to the debtor class or to the country at large, must be provided for. To protect the national honor, every dollar of Government indebtedness should be paid in gold, unless otherwise expressly stipulated in the contract. Let it be understood that no repudiator of one farthing of our public debt will be trusted in public place, and it will go far toward strengthening a credit which ought to be the best in the world, and will ultimately enable us to replace the debt with bonds bearing less interest than we now pay. To this should be added a faithful collection of the revenue, a strict accountability to the Treasury for every dollar collected, and the greatest practicable retrenchment in expenditure in every department of Government.

When we compare the paying capacity of the country now, with the ten States in poverty from the effects of war, but soon to emerge, I trust, into greater prosperity than ever before, with its paying capacity twenty-five years ago, and calculate what it probably will be twenty-five years hence, who can doubt the feasibility of paying every dollar then with more ease than we now pay for useless luxuries? Why, it looks as though Providence had bestowed upon us a strong box in the precious metals locked up in the sterile mountains of the far West, and which we are now forging the key to unlock, to meet the very contingency that is now upon us.

Ultimately it may be necessary to insure the facilities to reach these riches and it may be necessary also that the General Government should give its aid to secure this access; but that should only be when a dollar of obligation to pay secures precisely the same sort of dollar to use now, and not before. Whilst the question of specie payments is in abeyance the prudent business man is careful about contracting debts payable in the distant future. The nation should follow the same rule. A prostrate commerce is to be rebuilt and all industries encouraged.

The young men of the country, those who from their age must be its rulers twenty-five years hence, have a peculiar interest in maintaining the national honor. A moment's reflection as to what will be our commanding influence among the nations of the earth in their day, if they are only true to themselves, should inspire them with national pride. All divisions, geographical, political, and religious; can join in this common sentiment. How the public debt is to be paid or specie payments resumed is not so important as that a plan should be adopted and acquiesced in. A united determination to do is worth more than divided counsels upon the method of doing. Legislation upon this subject may not be necessary now, or even advisable, but it will be when the civil law is more fully restored in all parts of the country and trade resumes its wonted channels.

It will be my endeavor to execute all laws in good faith, to collect all revenues assessed, and to have them properly accounted for and economically disbursed. I will to the best of my ability appoint to office those only who will carry out this design.

In regard to foreign policy, I would deal with nations as equitable law requires individuals to deal with each other, and I would protect the law abiding citizen, whether of native or foreign birth, wherever his rights are jeopardized or the flag of our country floats. I would respect the rights of all nations, demanding equal respect for our own. If others depart from this rule in their dealings with us, we may be compelled to follow their precedent.

The proper treatment of the original occupants of this land, the Indians one deserving of careful study. I will favor any course toward them which tends to their civilization and ultimate citizenship.

The question of suffrage is one which is likely to agitate the public so long as a portion of the citizens of the nation are excluded from its privileges in any State. It seems to me very desirable that this question should be settled now, and I entertain the hope and express the desire that it may be by the ratification of the fifteenth article of amendment to the Constitution.

In conclusion I ask patient forbearance one toward another throughout the land, and a determined effort on the part of every citizen to do his share toward cementing a happy union; and I ask the prayers of the nation to Almighty God in behalf of this consummation.

———— SECOND INAUGURAL ADDRESS ————

MARCH 4, 1873

COMMENTARY

The Grant administration enforced Radical reconstruction. But national and local events began to undo the original aims. Corruption and enforced African-American voting produced a marked reaction among Southern whites to African-American participation in government. Several secret organizations were formed to restrain the Radicals and to start the whites on the road to political supremacy in the South by intimidating the freedmen. The Ku Klux Klan, organized in 1866, was one manifestation of this unrest. Horrified at this turn of events, Congress and the president took notice of this situation through the passage of the Enforcement Acts of 1870–1871. These increased penalties of willful denial to any citizen of rights secured under the fourteenth and fifteenth amendments. The president now had authority to suspend the writ of habeas corpus wherever he thought such action necessary to suppress rebellions against the authority of the United States. Nevertheless terrorism against Radical state officials and African Americans continued.

While the issues of the war slowly retreated into the past, corrupt national and local officials gradually secured the ascendancy and completely overshadowed the chief executive. Grant the politician, unlike Grant the general, proved indecisive and weak. Abuses in the management of the civil service, continued enforcement of a vindictive reconstruction program, scandal, and the excesses of the spoils system caused many liberal Republicans to raise their voices against what they labeled "Grantism." Their demands for reform, especially when it became apparent that Radical reconstruction could be maintained only by federal troops, were instantly rebuked by Republican stalwarts who branded them enemies of the party and sympathizers with treason. But the drift toward general demoralization caused the chief founders and the most preeminent representatives of the Republican Party—Chase, Seward, Sumner, and Greeley—to desert more than a year before the end of Grant's first demonstration. Early in 1872, the Liberal Republican leader called a national convention to meet on May 1. The heterogeneous assemblage, united only in their opposition to "Grantism," nominated Horace Greeley, editor of the New York Tribune, on a Liberal Republican ticket. When the Democrats convened in July, the party reluctantly accepted Greeley with the hope that union with the Liberal Republicans would cause the defeat of Grant.

Greeley made a spirited campaign, promising honesty in government, complete amnesty for former Confederates, and equal rights for all men. The regular Republican machine subjected him to a torrent of abuse, causing Greeley to remark dejectedly that he scarcely knew whether he was running for the presidency or the penitentiary. Greeley was no match for Grant, who won re-election with ease, carrying 31 of the 37 states.

In spite of Grant's victory, the campaign of 1872 demonstrated a sizable movement for reconciliation with the South. In May 1872, the Radical-controlled Congress took note of this by passing a general amnesty act that removed public office-holding disqualifications from all but the most prominent ex-Confederates. Grant now used federal troops less frequently in Southern elections and gradually white Democratic state government replaced those maintained by the Radical Republicans. By the end of Grant's second administration, the Southern African American had lost his political rights and his opportunity for economic equality. "The whole public are tired of the annual autumnal outbreaks in the south," declared Grant in 1875.

Grant's second inauguration occurred on a bitterly cold day. A gale had swept in from the southwest, playing havoc with the elaborate decorations. Nevertheless, some 20,000 people jammed Capitol Plaza to witness the ceremonies. At Chief Justice Chase's signal, Grant rose from his plain red-leather chair, which had been used by Washington, to take the oath. He then read his address. The wind blew violently, at times nearly wrenching the manuscript from his hands.

Fellow citizens:

Under Providence I have been called a second time to act as Executive over this great nation. It has been my endeavor in the past to maintain all the laws, and, so far as lay in my power, to act for the best interests of the whole people. My best efforts will be given in the same direction in the future aided, I trust, by my four years' experience in the office.

When my first term of the office of Chief Executive began, the country had not recovered from the effects of a great internal revolution, and three of the former States of the Union had not been restored to their Federal relations.

It seemed to me wise that no new questions should be raised so long as that condition of affairs existed. Therefore the past four years, so far as I could control events, have been consumed in the effort to restore harmony, public credit, commerce, and all the arts of peace and progress. It is my firm conviction that the civilized world is tending toward republicanism, or government by the people through their chosen representatives, and that our own great Republic is destined to be the guiding star to all others.

Under our Republic we support an army less than that of any European power of any standing and a navy less than that of either of at least five of them. There could be no extension of territory on the continent which would call for an increase of this force, but rather might such extension enable us to diminish it.

The theory of government changes with general progress. Now that the telegraph is made available for communicating thought, together with rapid transit by steam, all parts of a continent are made contiguous for all purposes of government, and communication between the extreme limits of the country made easier than it was throughout the old thirteen States at the beginning of our national existence.

The effects of the late civil strife have been to free the slave and make him a citizen. Yet he is not possessed of the civil rights which citizenship should carry with it. This is wrong, and should be corrected. To this correction I stand committed, so far as Executive influence can avail.

Social equality is not a subject to be legislated upon, nor shall I ask that anything be done to advance the social status of the colored man, except to give him a fair chance to develop what there is good in him, give him access to the schools, and when he travels let him feel assured that his conduct will regulate the treatment and fare he will receive.

The States lately at war with the General Government are now happily rehabilitated, and no Executive control is exercised in any one of them that would not be exercised in any other State under like circumstances.

In the first year of the past Administration the proposition came up for the admission of Santo Domingo as a Territory of the Union. It was not a question of my seeking, but was a proposition from the people of Santo Domingo, and which I entertained. I believe now, as I did then, that it was for the best interest of this country, for the people of Santo Domingo, and all concerned that the proposition should be received favorably. It was, however, rejected constitutionally, and therefore the subject was never brought up again by me.

In future, while I hold my present office, the subject of acquisition of territory must have the support of the people before I will recommend any proposition looking to such acquisition. I say here, however, that I do not share in the apprehension held by many as to the danger of governments becoming weakened and destroyed by reason of their extension of territory. Commerce, education, and rapid transit of thought and matter by telegraph and steam have changed all this. Rather do I believe that our Great Maker is preparing the world, in His own good time, to become one nation, speaking one language, and when armies and navies will be no longer required.

My efforts in the future will be directed to the restoration of good feeling between the different sections of our common country; to the restoration of our currency to a fixed value as compared with the world's standard of values, gold, and if possible, to a par with it; to the construction of cheap routes of transit throughout the land, to the end that the products of all may find a market and leave a living remuneration to the producer; to the maintenance of friendly relations with all our neighbors and with distant nations; to the reestablishment of our commerce and share in the carrying trade upon the ocean; to the encouragement of such manufacturing industries as can be economically pursued in this country, to the end that the exports of home products and industries may pay for our imports, the only sure method of returning to and permanently maintaining a specie basis; to the elevation of labor; and, by a humane course, to bring the aborigines of the country under the benign influences of education and civilization. It is either this or war of extermination: Wars of extermination, engaged in by people pursuing commerce and all industrial pursuits, are expensive even against the weakest people, and are demoralizing and wicked. Our superiority of strength and advantages of civilization should make us lenient toward the Indian. The wrong inflicted upon him should be taken into account and the balance placed to his credit. The moral view of the question should be considered and the question asked, Can not the Indian be made a useful and productive member of society by proper teaching and treatment? If the effort is made in good faith, we will stand better before the civilized nations of the earth and in our own consciences for having made it.

All these things are not to be accomplished by one individual, but they will receive my support and such recommendations to Congress as will in my judgment best serve to carry them into effect. I beg your support and encouragement.

It has been, and is, my earnest desire to correct abuses that have grown up in the civil service of the country. To secure this reformation rules regulating methods of appointment and promotions were established and have been tried. My efforts for such reformation shall be continued to the best of my judgment. The spirit of the rules adopted will be maintained.

I acknowledge before this assemblage, representing, as it does, every section of our country, the obligation I am under to my countrymen for the great honor they have conferred on me by returning me to the highest office within their gift, and the further obligation resting on me to render to them the best services within my power. This I promise, looking forward with the greatest anxiety to the day when I shall be released from responsibilities that at times are almost overwhelming, and from which I have scarcely had a respite since the eventful firing upon Fort Sumter, in April 1861, to the present day. My services were then tendered and accepted under the first call for troops growing out of that event.

I did not ask for place or position, and was entirely without influence or the acquaintance of persons of influence, but was resolved to perform my part in a struggle threatening the very existence of the nation. I performed a conscientious duty, without asking promotion or command, and without a revengeful feeling toward any section or individual.

Notwithstanding this, throughout the war, and from my candidacy for my present office in 1868 to the close of the last Presidential campaign, I have been the subject of abuse and slander scarcely ever equaled in political history, which today I feel that I can afford to disregard in view of your verdict, which I gratefully accept as my vindication.

Rutherford B. Hayes

Inaugural Address

MARCH 5, 1877

Commentary

Grant concluded his second inaugural address by saying: "I have been the sub-
ject of abuse and slander scarcely ever equaled in political history, which today
I feel that I can afford to disregard in view of your verdict, which I gratefully
accept as my vindication." Hardly had Grant begun his new term when outra-
geous misconduct in office by high presidential appointees broke every rule of
decency. Day after day, month after month, public officials fell from their sta-
tions as scandal upon scandal shattered the Republican Party from top to bot-
tom. By the beginning of 1876, Grant's administration approached complete
breakdown as new exposés rocked the very foundations of the government.
"The President was overwhelmed," observed cartoonist Thomas Nast after a
personal visit; "wherever he turned some new dishonor lay concealed."

The Republican nominating convention of 1876 was determined to hold
the executive branch with all its patronage. Governor Rutherford B. Hayes of
Ohio, who had achieved an admirable record as an efficient state administra-
tor, proved the perfect answer for the divided party. Hayes, described perhaps
too harshly by Henry Adams as "a third rate nonentity, whose only recommen-
dation is that he is obnoxious to no one," prudently portrayed himself as the
new image of honest moderate Republicanism. The revived Democratic Party
chose Governor Samuel J. Tilden of New York, a wealthy economic liberal who
had fearlessly opposed corruption in government. Their platform denounced
"Grantism" and pledged the elimination of sectional strife, as well as tariff and
tax reductions. During the campaign, Republicans raised the cry of the "bloody
shirt" against the Democrats—"Soldiers, every scar you have on your heroic

bodies was given you by a Democrat." Tilden's supporters countered with further accusations of fraud and corruption.

Tilden won a popular majority and appeared to be victorious, claiming 184 electoral votes. But disputed returns were submitted from Oregon, Louisiana, South Carolina, and Florida, the latter three states controlled by the Radical Republicans. If all the disputed votes went to Hayes, he would be elected 185 to 184. The well-organized Republican machine, supported by federal troops, sought to hold these Southern states for their candidate while the Democrats claimed that Radical-dominated election boards had fraudulently voided Tilden ballots. As a result, two sets of returns went to Congress from these states.

Congressmen met in December amidst great excitement and confusion. The vague clause in the Constitution provides that "The President of the Senate shall, in the presence of the Senate and the House of Representatives, open all certificates, and the vote shall then be counted." But, counted by whom? If the Republican Senate had the power, Hayes would be chosen. Conversely, the Democrats had a majority in the House and they would sustain Tilden electors. Finally, to meet this unprecedented situation, Congress created a special Electoral Commission consisting of five senators (three Republicans and two Democrats), five representatives (three Democrats and two Republicans), and five justices of the Supreme Court. Four of the justices were designated by name in the bill (two Democrats and two Republicans) with power to choose the fifth justice, the fifteenth Commission member. Justice David Davis, an independent, would have been selected but his election to the U.S. Senate by the Illinois legislature removed him from the Court. Justice Joseph P. Bradley, a Republican, became the fifteenth man. Between February 9 and February 28, 1877, the Commission, voting strictly along party lines, awarded all of the disputed electoral votes to Hayes, who was declared elected. It appears that the Republicans now promised to withdraw all federal troops from the South, thus completely abandoning Radical Reconstruction, if the Democrats ceased obstruction to the final electoral count. In addition, spokesmen for Hayes agreed that he would appoint at least one Southerner to his cabinet. All historians who have studied the electoral crisis of 1876–1877 applaud the extraordinary calm with which the mass of the people accepted the Commission's decision. In many countries, a similar situation might have caused civil war.

March 4, 1877, fell on a Sunday. For religious reason, Hayes requested that his inauguration be postponed until the following day. President Grant and Secretary of State Hamilton Fish, concerned about the interregnum, persuaded

Hayes to go through with a secret oath-taking ceremony on the evening of March 3. It occurred in the Red Room of the White House. Hayes repeated the oath in public on March 5, and then delivered his inaugural address.

Fellow citizens:

We have assembled to repeat the public ceremonial, begun by Washington, observed by all my predecessors, and now a time honored custom, which marks the commencement of a new term of the Presidential office. Called to the duties of this great trust, I proceed, in compliance with usage, to announce some of the leading principles, on the subjects that now chiefly engage the public attention, by which it is my desire to be guided in the discharge of those duties. I shall not undertake to lay down irrevocably principles or measures of administration, but rather to speak of the motives which should animate us, and to suggest certain important ends to be attained in accordance with our institutions and essential to the welfare of our country.

At the outset of the discussions which preceded the recent Presidential election it seemed to me fitting that I should fully make known my sentiments in regard to several of the important questions which then appeared to demand the consideration of the country. Following the example, and in part adopting the language, of one of my predecessors, I wish now, when every motive for misrepresentation has passed away, to repeat what was said before the election, trusting that my countrymen will candidly weigh and understand it, and that they will feel assured that the sentiments declared in accepting the nomination for the Presidency will be the standard of my conduct in the path before me, charged, as I now am, with the grave and difficult task of carrying them out in the practical administration of the Government so far as depends, under the Constitution and laws on the Chief Executive of the nation.

The permanent pacification of the country upon such principles and by such measures as will secure the complete protection of all its citizens in the free enjoyment of all their constitutional rights is now the one subject in our public affairs which all thoughtful and patriotic citizens regard as of supreme importance.

Many of the calamitous efforts of the tremendous revolution which has passed over the Southern States still remain. The immeasurable benefits which will surely follow, sooner or later, the hearty and generous acceptance of the legitimate results of that revolution have not yet been realized.

Difficult and embarrassing questions meet us at the threshold of this subject. The people of those States are still impoverished, and the inestimable blessing of wise, honest, and peaceful local self-government is not fully enjoyed. Whatever difference of opinion may exist as to the cause of this condition of things, the fact is clear that in the progress of events the time has come when such government is the imperative necessity required by all the varied interests, public and private, of those States. But it must not be forgotten that only a local government which recognizes and maintains inviolate the rights of all is a true self-government.

With respect to the two distinct races whose peculiar relations to each other have brought upon us the deplorable complications and perplexities which exist in those States, it must be a government which guards the interests of both races carefully and equally. It must be a government which submits loyally and heartily to the Constitution and the laws, the laws of the nation and the laws of the States themselves, accepting and obeying faithfully the whole Constitution as it is.

Resting upon this sure and substantial foundation, the superstructure of beneficent local governments can be built up, and not otherwise. In furtherance of such obedience to the letter and the spirit of the Constitution, and in behalf of all that its attainment implies, all so-called party interests lose their apparent importance, and party lines may well be permitted to fade into insignificance. The question we have to consider for the immediate welfare of those States of the Union is the question of government or no government; of social order and all the peaceful industries and the happiness that belongs to it, or a return to barbarism. It is a question in which every citizen of the nation is deeply interested, and with respect to which we ought not to be, in a partisan sense, either Republicans or Democrats, but fellow citizens and fellowmen, to whom the interests of a common country and a common humanity are dear.

The sweeping revolution of the entire labor system of a large portion of our country and the advance of 4,000,000 people from a condition of servitude to that of citizenship, upon an equal footing with their former masters, could not occur without presenting problems of the gravest moment, to be dealt with by the emancipated race, by their former masters, and by the General Government, the author of the act of emancipation. That it was a wise, just, and providential act, fraught with good for all concerned, is not generally conceded throughout the country. That a moral obligation rests upon the National Government to employ its constitutional power and influence to establish the rights of the people it has emancipated, and to protect them in the enjoyment of those rights when they are infringed or assailed, is also generally admitted.

The evils which afflict the Southern States can only be removed or remedied by the united and harmonious efforts of both races, actuated by motives of mutual sympathy and regard; and while in duty bound and fully determined to protect the rights of all by every constitutional means at the disposal of my Administration, I am sincerely anxious to use every legitimate influence in favor of honest and efficient local self-government as the true resource of those States for the promotion of the contentment and prosperity of their citizens. In the effort I shall make to accomplish this purpose I ask the cordial cooperation of all who cherish an interest in the welfare of the country, trusting that party ties and the prejudice of race will be freely surrendered in behalf of the great purpose to be accomplished. In the important work of restoring the South it is not the political situation alone that merits attention. The material development of that section of the country has been arrested by the social and political revolution through which it has passed, and now needs and deserves the considerate care of the National Government within the just limits prescribed by the Constitution and wise public economy.

But at the basis of all prosperity, for that as well as for every other part of the country, lies the improvement of the intellectual and moral condition of the people. Universal suffrage should rest upon universal education. To this end, liberal and permanent provision should be made for the support of free schools by the State governments and, if need be, supplemented by legitimate aid from national authority.

Let me assure my countrymen of the Southern States that it is my earnest desire to regard and promote their truest interest, the interests of the white and of the colored people both and equally; and to put forth my best efforts in behalf of a civil policy which will forever wipe out in our political affairs the color line and the distinction between North and South, to the end that we may have not merely a united North or a united South, but a united country.

I ask the attention of the public to the paramount necessity of reform in our civil service; a reform not merely as to certain abuses and practices of so-called official patronage which have come to have the sanction of usage in the several Departments of our Government, but a change in the system of appointment itself; a reform that shall be thorough, radical, and complete; a return to the principles and practices of the founders of the

Government. They neither expected nor desired from public officers any partisan service. They meant that public officers should owe their whole service to the Government and to the people. They meant that the officer should be secure in his tenure as long as his personal character remained untarnished and the performance of his duties satisfactory. They held that appointments to office were not to be made nor expected merely as rewards for partisan services, nor merely on the nomination of members of Congress, as being entitled in any respect to the control of such appointments.

The fact that both the great political parties of the country, in declaring their principles prior to the election, gave a prominent place to the subject of reform of our civil service, recognizing and strongly urging its necessity, in terms almost identical in their specific import with those I have here employed, must be accepted as a conclusive argument in behalf of these measures. It must be regarded as the expression of the united voice and will of the whole country upon this subject, and both political parties are virtually pledged to give it their unreserved support.

The President of the United States of necessity owes his election to office to the suffrage and zealous labors of a political party, the members of which cherish with ardor and regard as of essential importance the principles of their party organization; but he should strive to be always mindful of the fact that he serves his party best who serves the country best.

In furtherance of the reform we seek, and in other important respects a change of great importance, I recommend an amendment to the Constitution prescribing a term of six years for the Presidential office and forbidding a reelection.

With respect to the financial condition of the country, I shall not attempt an extended history of the embarrassment and prostration which we have suffered during the past three years. The depression in all our varied commercial and manufacturing interests throughout the country, which began in September 1873, still continues. It is very gratifying, however, to be able to say that there are indications all around us of a coming change to prosperous times.

Upon the currency question, intimately connected, as it is, with this topic, I may be permitted to repeat here the statement made in my letter of acceptance, that in my judgment the feeling of uncertainty inseparable from an irredeemable paper currency, with its fluctuation of values, is one of the greatest obstacles to a return to prosperous times. The only safe paper currency is one which rests upon a coin basis and is at all times and promptly convertible into coin.

I adhere to the views heretofore expressed by me in favor of Congressional legislation in behalf of an early resumption of specie payments, and I am satisfied not only that this is wise, but that the interests, as well as the public sentiment, of the country imperatively demand it.

Passing from these remarks upon the condition of our own country to consider our relations with other lands, we are reminded by the international complications abroad, threatening the peace of Europe, that our traditional rule of noninterference in the affairs of foreign nations has proved of great value in past times and ought to be strictly observed.

The policy inaugurated by my honored predecessor, President Grant, of submitting to arbitration grave questions in dispute between ourselves and foreign powers points to a new, and incomparably the best, instrumentality for the preservation of peace, and will, as I believe, become a beneficent example of the course to be pursued in similar emergencies by other nations.

If, unhappily, questions of difference should at any time during the period of my Administration arise between the United States and any foreign government, it will certainly be my disposition and my hope to aid in their settlement in the same peaceful and honorable way, thus securing to our country the great blessings of peace and mutual good offices with all the nations of the world.

Fellow citizens, we have reached the close of a political contest marked by the excitement which usually attends the contests between great political parties whose members espouse and advocate with earnest faith their respective creeds. The circumstances were, perhaps, in no respect extraordinary save in the closeness and the consequent uncertainty of the result.

For the first time in the history of the country it has been deemed best, in view of the peculiar circumstances of the case, that the objections and questions in dispute with reference to the counting of the electoral votes should be referred to the decision of a tribunal appointed for this purpose.

That tribunal, established by law for this sole purpose; its members, all of them, men of long-established reputation for integrity and intelligence, and, with the exception of those who are also members of the supreme judiciary, chosen equally from both political parties; its deliberations enlightened by the research and the arguments of able counsel, was entitled to the fullest confidence of the American people. Its decisions have been patiently waited for, and accepted as legally conclusive by the general judgment of the public. For the present, opinion will widely vary as to the wisdom of the several conclusions announced by that tribunal. This is to be anticipated in every instance where matters of dispute are made the subject of arbitration under the forms of law. Human judgment is never unerring, and is rarely regarded as otherwise than wrong by the unsuccessful party in the contest.

The fact that two great political parties have in this way settled a dispute in regard to which good men differ as to the facts and the law no less than as to the proper course to be pursued in solving the question in controversy is an occasion for general rejoicing.

Upon one point there is entire unanimity in public sentiment, that conflicting claims to the Presidency must be amicably and peaceably adjusted, and that when so adjusted the general acquiescence of the nation ought surely to follow.

It has been reserved for a government of the people, where the right of suffrage is universal, to give to the world the first example in history of a great nation, in the midst of the struggle of opposing parties for power, hushing its party tumults to yield the issue of the contest to adjustment according to the forms of law.

Looking for the guidance of that Divine Hand by which the destinies of nations and individuals are shaped, I call upon you, Senators, Representatives, judges, fellow citizens, here and everywhere, to unite with me in an earnest effort to secure to our country the blessings, not only of material prosperity, but of justice, peace, and union; a union depending not upon the constraint of force, but upon the loving devotion of a free people; and that all things may be so ordered and settled upon the best and surest foundations that peace and happiness, truth and justice, religion and piety, may be established among us for all generations.

JAMES A. GARFIELD

INAUGURAL ADDRESS

MARCH 4, 1881

COMMENTARY

National politics from the end of Reconstruction to the Populist revolt of the 1890s is perhaps the dreariest chapter in American history. The major social problems inherent in an industrial society that had subjugated a vast continent were virtually ignored. Both Democratic and Republican office holders offered little choice to the voter as politicians of both parties absorbed themselves in assisting the captains of industry to achieve their objectives. Statesmanship was never so uninspiring or statesmen so inadequate. The drab procession of political nonentities can be compared to a Punch and Judy show: voices change but control of the strings remains the same. Presidential campaigns, with their bombastic oratory, occurred quadrennially, but public debates on pressing issues were usually superficial. "The period was poor in purpose and barren in results," noted Henry Adams in 1905.

In June 1880, the deadlocked Republican convention nominated the moderate Ohio representative James A. Garfield on the thirty-sixth ballot. For vice president, the party leaders selected Chester A. Arthur of New York. The Democrats also settled upon a compromise candidate, General Winfield Hancock, a distinguished Civil War hero. After a dull campaign, where the principal issue seemed the desire to win power and control patronage, Garfield won a majority in the electoral college, 215 to 155 for Hancock. In the popular vote, Garfield barely achieved a majority—4,449,053 to Hancock's 4,442,035.

In The Politicos, *Matthew Josephson writes that the interlude between the election and the inauguration was one of "fabulous intrigue, fabulous even in the quarrelsome annals of the American republic. Behind the scenes, while the public heard only confusing or distorted reports, Guelphs and Ghibelines fought without quarter for control of the new government." Garfield's own diary reveals his bewilderment by the maddening demands for political appointments. His noncommittal inaugural address does not reveal any of the infighting among Republicans spoilsmen. "I have been dealing all these years with ideas," the distraught Garfield told James Blaine. "I have been heretofore treating of the fundamental principles of government and here I am considering all day whether A or B shall be appointed to this or that office. . . . My God! What is there in this place that a man should ever want to get into it?"*

⁓ ⟡ ⁓

Fellow citizens:

We stand today upon an eminence which overlooks a hundred years of national life; a century crowded with perils, but crowned with the triumphs of liberty and law. Before continuing the onward march let us pause on this height for a moment to strengthen our faith and renew our hope by a glance at the pathway along which our people have traveled.

It is now three days more than a hundred years since the adoption of the first written constitution of the United States, the Articles of Confederation and Perpetual Union. The new Republic was then beset with danger on every hand. It had not conquered a place in the family of nations. The decisive battle of the war for independence, whose centennial anniversary will soon be gratefully celebrated at Yorktown, had not yet been fought. The colonists were struggling not only against the armies of a great nation, but against the settled opinions of mankind; for the world did not then believe that the supreme authority of government could be safely intrusted to the guardianship of the people themselves.

We can not overestimate the fervent love of liberty, the intelligent courage, and the sum of common sense with which our fathers made the great experiment of self-government. When they found, after a short trial, that the confederacy of States, was too weak to meet the necessities of a vigorous and expanding republic, they boldly set it aside, and in its stead established a National Union, founded directly upon the will of the people, endowed with full power of self-preservation and ample authority for the accomplishment of its great object.

Under this Constitution the boundaries of freedom have been enlarged, the foundations of order and peace have been strengthened, and the growth of our people in all the better elements of national life has indicated the wisdom of the founders and given new hope to their descendants. Under this Constitution our people long ago made themselves safe against danger from without and secured for their mariners and flag equality of rights on all the seas. Under this Constitution twenty-five States have been added to the Union, with constitutions and laws, framed and enforced by their own citizens, to secure the manifold blessings of local self-government.

The jurisdiction of this Constitution now covers an area fifty times greater than that of the original thirteen States and a population twenty times greater than that of 1780.

The supreme trial of the Constitution came at last under the tremendous pressure of civil war. We ourselves are witnesses that the Union emerged from the blood and fire of that conflict purified and made stronger for all the beneficent purposes of good government.

And now, at the close of this first century of growth, with the inspirations of its history in their hearts, our people have lately reviewed the condition of the nation, passed judgment upon the conduct and opinions of political parties, and have registered their will concerning the future administration of the Government. To interpret and to execute that will in accordance with the Constitution is the paramount duty of the Executive.

Even from this brief review it is manifest that the nation is resolutely facing to the front, resolved to employ its best energies in developing the great possibilities of the future. Sacredly preserving whatever has been gained to liberty and good government during the century, our people are determined to leave behind them all those bitter controversies concerning things which have been irrevocably settled, and the further discussion of which can only stir up strife and delay the onward march.

The supremacy of the nation and its laws should be no longer a subject of debate. That discussion, which for half a century threatened the existence of the Union, was closed at last in the high court of war by a decree from which there is no appeal; that the Constitution and the laws made in pursuance thereof are and shall continue to be the supreme law of the land, binding alike upon the States and the people. This decree does not disturb the autonomy of the States nor interfere with any of their necessary rights of local self-government, but it does fix and establish the permanent supremacy of the Union.

The will of the nation, speaking with the voice of battle and through the amended Constitution, has fulfilled the great promise of 1776 by proclaiming liberty throughout the land to all the inhabitants thereof.

The elevation of the negro race from slavery to the full rights of citizen-ship is the most important political change we have known since the adop-tion of the Constitution of 1787. No thoughtful man can fail to appreciate its beneficent effect upon our institutions and people. It has freed us from the perpetual danger of war and dissolution. It has added immensely to the mor-al and industrial forces of our people. It has liberated the master as well as the slave from a relation which wronged and enfeebled both. It has surrendered to their own guardianship the manhood of more than five million people, and has opened to each one of them a career of freedom and usefulness. It has given new inspiration to the power of self-help in both races by making labor more honorable to the one and more necessary to the other. The influence of this force will grow greater and bear richer fruit with the coming years.

No doubt this great change has caused serious disturbance to our Southern communities. This is to be deplored, though it was perhaps un-avoidable. But those who resisted the change should remember that under our institutions there was no middle ground for the negro race between slavery and equal citizenship. There can be no permanent disfranchised peasantry in the United States. Freedom can never yield its fullness of bless-ings so long as the law or its administration places the smallest obstacle in the pathway of any virtuous citizen.

The emancipated race has already made remarkable progress. With un-questioning devotion to the Union, with a patience and gentleness not born of fear, they have followed the light as God gave them to see the light. They are rapidly laying the material foundations of self-support, widening their circle of intelligence, and beginning to enjoy the blessings that gather around the homes of the industrious poor. They deserve the generous encourage-ment of all good men. So far as my authority can lawfully extend they shall enjoy the full and equal protection of the Constitution and the laws.

The free enjoyment of equal suffrage is still in question, and a frank statement of the issue may aid its solution. It is alleged that in many com-munities negro citizens are practically denied the freedom of the ballot. In so far as the truth of this allegation is admitted, it is answered that in many places honest local government is impossible if the mass of uneducated ne-groes are allowed to vote. These are grave allegations. So far as the latter is true, it is the only palliation that can be offered for opposing the freedom of the ballot. Bad local government is certainly a great evil, which ought to be prevented; but to violate the freedom and sanctities of the suffrage is more than an evil. It is a crime which, if persisted in, will destroy the Government itself. Suicide is not a remedy. If in other lands it be high treason to compass the death of the king, it shall be counted no less a crime here to strangle our sovereign power and stifle its voice.

It has been said that unsettled questions have no pity for the repose of nations. It should be said with the utmost emphasis that this question of the suffrage will never give repose or safety to the States or to the nation until each, within its own jurisdiction, makes and keeps the ballot free and pure by the strong sanctions of the law.

But the danger which arises from ignorance in the voter can not be denied. It covers a field far wider than that of negro suffrage and the present condition of the race. It is a danger that lurks and hides in the sources and fountains of power in every state. We have no standard by which to measure the disaster that may be brought upon us by ignorance and vice in the citizens when joined to corruption and fraud in the suffrage.

The voters of the Union, who make and unmake constitutions, and upon whose will hang the destinies of our governments, can transmit their supreme authority to no successors save the coming generation of voters, who are the sole heirs of sovereign power. If that generation comes to its inheritance blinded by ignorance and corrupted by vice, the fall of the Republic will be certain and remediless.

The census has already sounded the alarm in the appalling figures which mark how dangerously high the tide of illiteracy has risen among our voters and their children.

To the South this question is of supreme importance. But the responsibility for the existence of slavery did not rest upon the South alone. The nation itself is responsible for the extension of the suffrage, and is under special obligations to aid in removing the illiteracy which it has added to the voting population. For the North and South alike there is but one remedy. All the constitutional power of the nation and of the States and all the volunteer forces of the people should be surrendered to meet this danger by the savory influence of universal education.

It is the high privilege and sacred duty of those now living to educate their successors and fit them, by intelligence and virtue, for the inheritance which awaits them.

In this beneficent work sections and races should be forgotten and partisanship should be unknown. Let our people find a new meaning in the divine oracle which declares that a little child shall lead them, for our own little children will soon control the destinies of the Republic.

My countrymen, we do not now differ in our judgment concerning the controversies of past generations, and fifty years hence our children will not be divided in their opinions concerning our controversies. They will surely bless their fathers and their fathers' God that the Union was preserved, that slavery was overthrown, and that both races were made equal before the law. We may hasten or we may retard, but we can not prevent, the final reconciliation. Is it not possible for us now to make a truce with time by anticipating and accepting its inevitable verdict?

Enterprises of the highest importance to our moral and material well being unite us and offer ample employment of our best powers. Let all our people, leaving behind them the battlefields of dead issues, move forward and in their strength of liberty and the restored Union win the grander victories of peace.

The prosperity which now prevails is without parallel in our history. Fruitful seasons have done much to secure it, but they have not done all. The preservation of the public credit and the resumption of specie payments, so successfully attained by the Administration of my predecessors, have enabled our people to secure the blessings which the seasons brought.

By the experience of commercial nations in all ages it has been found that gold and silver afford the only safe foundation for a monetary system. Confusion has recently been created by variations in the relative value of the two metals, but I confidently believe that arrangements can be made between the leading commercial nations which will secure the general use of both metals. Congress should provide that the compulsory coinage of silver now required by law may not disturb our monetary system by driving either metal out of circulation. If possible, such an adjustment should be made that the purchasing power of every coined dollar will be exactly equal to its debt paying power in all the markets of the world.

The chief duty of the National Government in connection with the currency of the country is to coin money and declare its value. Grave doubts have been entertained whether Congress is authorized by the Constitution to make any form of paper money legal tender. The present issue of United States notes has been sustained by the necessities of war; but such paper should depend for its value and currency upon its convenience in use and its prompt redemption in coin at the will of the holder, and not upon its compulsory circulation. These notes are not money, but promises to pay money. If the holders demand it, the promise should be kept.

The refunding of the national debt at a lower rate of interest should be accomplished without compelling the withdrawal of the national bank notes, and thus disturbing the business of the country.

I venture to refer to the position I have occupied on financial questions during a long service in Congress, and to say that time and experience have strengthened the opinions I have so often expressed on these subjects.

The finances of the Government shall suffer no detriment which it may be possible for my Administration to prevent.

The interests of agriculture deserve more attention from the Government than they have yet received. The farms of the United States afford homes and employment for more than one-half our people, and furnish much the largest part of all our exports. As the Government lights our coasts for the protection of mariners and the benefit of commerce, so it should give to the tillers of the soil the best lights of practical science and experience.

Our manufacturers are rapidly making us industrially independent, and are opening to capital and labor new and profitable fields of employment. Their steady and healthy growth should still be matured. Our facilities for transportation should be promoted by the continued improvement of our harbors and great interior waterways and by the increase of our tonnage on the ocean.

The development of the world's commerce has led to an urgent demand for shortening the great sea voyage around Cape Horn by constructing ship canals or railways across the isthmus which unites the continents. Various plans to this end have been suggested and will need consideration, but none of them has been sufficiently matured to warrant the United States in extending pecuniary aid. The subject, however, is one which will immediately engage the attention of the Government with a view to a thorough protection to American interests. We will urge no narrow policy nor seek peculiar or exclusive privileges in any commercial route; but, in the language of my predecessor, I believe it to be the right and duty of the United States to assert and maintain such supervision and authority over any interoceanic canal across the isthmus that connects North and South America as will protect our national interest.

The Constitution guarantees absolute religious freedom. Congress is prohibited from making any law respecting an establishment of religion or prohibiting the free exercise thereof. The Territories of the United States are subject to the direct legislative authority of Congress, and hence the General Government is responsible for any violation of the Constitution in any of them. It is therefore a reproach to the Government that in the most populous of the Territories the constitutional guaranty is not enjoyed by the people and the authority of Congress is set at naught. The Mormon Church not only offends the moral sense of manhood by sanctioning polygamy, but prevents the administration of justice through ordinary instrumentalities of law.

In my judgment, it is the duty of Congress, while respecting to the uttermost the conscientious convictions and religious scruples of every citizen, to prohibit within its jurisdiction all criminal practices, especially of that class which destroy the family relations and endanger social order. Nor can any ecclesiastical organization be safely permitted to usurp in the smallest degree the functions and powers of the National Government.

The civil service can never be placed on a satisfactory basis until it is regulated by law. For the good of the service itself, for the protection of those who are intrusted with the appointing power against the waste of time and obstruction to the public business caused by the inordinate pressure for place, and for the protection of incumbents against intrigue and wrong, I shall at the proper time ask Congress to fix the tenure of the minor offices of the several Executive Departments and prescribe the grounds upon which removals shall be made during the terms for which incumbents have been appointed.

Finally, acting always within the authority and limitations of the Constitution, invading neither the rights of the States nor the reserved rights of the people, it will be the purpose of my Administration to maintain the authority of the nation in all places within its jurisdiction; to enforce obedience to all the laws of the Union in the interests of the people; to demand rigid economy in all the expenditures of the Government, and to require the honest and faithful service of all executive officers, remembering that the offices were created, not for the benefit of incumbents or their supporters, but for the service of the Government.

And now, fellow citizens, I am about to assume the great trust which you have committed to my hands. I appeal to you for that earnest and thoughtful support which makes this Government in fact, as it is in law, a government of the people.

I shall greatly rely upon the wisdom and patriotism of Congress and of those who may share with me the responsibilities and duties of administration, and, above all, upon our efforts to promote the welfare of this great people and their Government I reverently invoke the support and blessings of almighty God.

Grover Cleveland

First Inaugural Address

MARCH 4, 1885

Commentary

On July 2, 1881, Garfield was shot by a disgruntled office seeker. Throughout the summer, the president precariously clung to life. He died on September 19, 1881. During this 80-day period, leading journals sought outstanding legal opinion on the constitutional problems involved in presidential disability. The answers were conflicting and confusing. Although the bulletins of Garfield's physicians indicated that the president could not attend to his office, Vice President Arthur steadfastly refused to assume any presidential responsibility. The important fact, though, is that the U.S. government was virtually paralyzed for 80 days. Fortunately, no urgent business demanded immediate attention.

Public reaction to Garfield's assassination led to the passage of the Pendleton Act of 1883, which established the nonpartisan Civil Service Commission. Although the number of jobs placed under the merit system was relatively small—approximately 10 percent—an auspicious start had been made. Arthur's otherwise placid administration ended with a lively presidential campaign where, again, control of the national government remained the chief issue.

The Republican convention of 1884 bypassed Arthur to choose James Blaine of Maine, a popular politician who had served in Congress and as Garfield's secretary of state. His enthusiastic followers, with their brass bands and "spontaneous" demonstrations, stampeded the convention for him. But Blaine also had made many enemies during his long and often controversial political career. Liberal Republicans, led by such men as Carl Shurz and Edwin Godkin, unalterably opposed Blaine for his stand against further civil service

reform. These "mugwumps" supported the Democratic nominee Grover Cleve-
land. With Cleveland, the Democrats had found a candidate whose life was
"a study in courage." Reform mayor of Buffalo, able governor of New York,
implacable enemy of Tammany Hall, Cleveland was dubbed the "ugly-honest
man of good purpose and undaunted courage." Since no real issues separated
the two candidates, the campaign degenerated into one of personal vilification
and mudslinging. "Everyone takes part," wrote Henry Adams; "we are all do-
ing our best, and swearing at each other like demons. But the amusing thing
is that no one talks about real interests. By common consent they agree to let
these alone." Cleveland narrowly carried New York State and thereby won the
election, receiving 219 electoral votes to Blaine's 182.

March 4, 1885, dawned sunny and mild. Promptly at noon on the steps
of the Capitol, Chief Justice Morrison Waite administered the oath of office
to Grover Cleveland, the first Democratic president since James Buchanan.
Cleveland then delivered his inaugural address without referring to notes or to
a written manuscript.

—— ⌐○⌐ ——

Fellow citizens:

In the presence of this vast assemblage of my countrymen I am about
to supplement and seal by the oath which I shall take the manifestation of
the will of a great and free people. In the exercise of their power and right
of self-government they have committed to one of their fellow citizens a
supreme and sacred trust, and he here consecrates himself to their service.

This impressive ceremony adds little to the solemn sense of responsibility with which I contemplate the duty I owe to all the people of the land.
Nothing can relieve me from anxiety lest by any act of mine their interests
may suffer, and nothing is needed to strengthen my resolution to engage
every faculty and effort in the promotion of their welfare.

Amid the din of party strife the people's choice was made, but its attendant circumstances have demonstrated anew the strength and safety of a
government by the people. In each succeeding year it more clearly appears
that our democratic principle needs no apology, and that in its fearless and
faithful application is to be found the surest guaranty of good government.

But the best results in the operation of a government wherein every
citizen has a share largely depend upon a proper limitation of purely partisan zeal and effort and a correct appreciation of the time when the heat of
the partisan should be merged in the patriotism of the citizen.

Today the executive branch of the Government is transferred to new keeping. But this is still the Government of all the people, and it should be none the less an object of their affectionate solicitude. At this hour the animosities of political strife, the bitterness of partisan defeat, and the exultation of partisan triumph should be supplanted by an ungrudging acquiescence in the popular will and a sober, conscientious concern for the general weal. Moreover, if from this hour we cheerfully and honestly abandon all sectional prejudice and distrust, and determine, with manly confidence in one another, to work out harmoniously the achievements of our national destiny, we shall deserve to realize all the benefits which our happy form of government can bestow.

On this auspicious occasion we may well renew the pledge of our devotion to the Constitution, which, launched by the founders of the Republic and consecrated by their prayers and patriotic devotion, has for almost a century borne the hopes and the aspirations of a great people through prosperity and peace and through the shock of foreign conflicts and the perils of domestic strife and vicissitudes.

By the Father of his Country our Constitution was commended for adoption as the result of a spirit of amity and mutual concession. In that same spirit it should be administered, in order to promote the lasting welfare of the country and to secure the full measure of its priceless benefits to us and to those who will succeed to the blessings of our national life. The large variety of diverse and competing interests subject to Federal control, persistently seeking the recognition of their claims, need give us no fear that the greatest good to the greatest number will fail to be accomplished if in the halls of national legislation that spirit of amity and mutual concession shall prevail in which the Constitution had its birth. If this involves the surrender or postponement of private interests and the abandonment of local advantages, compensation will be found in the assurance that the common interest is subserved and the general welfare advanced.

In the discharge of my official duty I shall endeavor to be guided by a just and unstrained construction of the Constitution, a careful observance of the distinction between the powers granted to the Federal Government and those reserved to the States or to the people, and by a cautious appreciation of those functions which by the Constitution and laws have been especially assigned to the executive branch of the Government.

But he who takes the oath today to preserve, protect, and defend the Constitution of the United States only assumes the solemn obligation which every patriotic citizen; on the farm, in the workshop, in the busy marts of trade, and everywhere, should share with him. The Constitution which prescribes his oath, my countrymen, is yours; the Government you have chosen him to administer for a time is yours; the suffrage which executes the will of freemen is yours; the laws and the entire scheme of our civil rule, from the town meeting to the State capitals and the national capital, is yours. Your every voter, as surely as your Chief Magistrate, under the same high sanction, though in a different sphere, exercises a public trust. Nor is this all. Every citizen owes to the country a vigilant watch and close scrutiny of its public servants and a fair and reasonable estimate of their fidelity and usefulness. Thus is the people's will impressed upon the whole framework of our civil polity—municipal, State, and Federal; and this is the price of our liberty and the inspiration of our faith in the Republic.

It is the duty of those serving the people in public place to closely limit public expenditures to the actual needs of the Government economically administered, because this bounds the right of the Government to exact tribute from the earnings of labor or the property of the citizen, and because public extravagance begets extravagance among the people. We should never be ashamed of the simplicity and prudential economies which are best suited to the operation of a republican form of government and most compatible with the mission of the American people. Those who are selected for a limited time to manage public affairs are still of the people, and may do much by their example to encourage, consistently with the dignity of their official functions, that plain way of life which among their fellow-citizens aids integrity and promotes thrift and prosperity.

The genius of our institutions, the needs of our people in their home life, and the attention which is demanded for the settlement and development of the resources of our vast territory dictate the scrupulous avoidance of any departure from that foreign policy commended by the history, the traditions, and the prosperity of our Republic. It is the policy of independence, favored by our position and defended by our known love of justice and by our power. It is the policy of peace suitable to our interests. It is the policy of neutrality, rejecting any share in foreign broils and ambitions upon other continents and repelling their intrusion here. It is the policy of Monroe and of Washington and Jefferson—peace, commerce and honest friendship with all nations; entangling alliance with none.

A due regard for the interests and prosperity of all the people demands that our finances shall be established upon such a sound and sensible basis as shall secure the safety and confidence of business interests and make the wage of labor sure and steady, and that our system of revenue shall be so adjusted as to relieve the people of unnecessary taxation, having a due regard to the interests of capital invested and workingmen employed in American industries, and preventing the accumulation of a surplus in the Treasury to tempt extravagance and waste.

Care for the property of the nation and for the needs of future settlers requires that the public domain should be protected from purloining schemes and unlawful occupation.

The conscience of the people demands that the Indians within our boundaries shall be fairly and honestly treated as wards of the Government and their education and civilization promoted with a view to their ultimate citizenship, and that polygamy in the Territories, destructive of the family relation and offensive to the moral sense of the civilized world, shall be repressed.

The laws should be rigidly enforced which prohibit the immigration of a servile class to compete with American labor, with no intention of acquiring citizenship, and bringing with them and retaining habits and customs repugnant to our civilization.

The people demand reform in the administration of the Government and the application of business principles to public affairs. As a means to this end, civil service reform should be in good faith enforced. Our citizens have the right to protection from the incompetency of public employees who hold their places solely as the reward of partisan service, and from the corrupting influence of those who promise and the vicious methods of those who expect such rewards; and those who worthily seek public employment have the right to insist that merit and competency shall be recognized instead of party subserviency or the surrender of honest political belief.

In the administration of a government pledged to do equal and exact justice to all men there should be no pretext for anxiety touching the protection of the freedmen in their rights or their security in the enjoyment of their privileges under the Constitution and its amendments. All discussion as to their fitness for the place accorded to them as American citizens is idle and unprofitable except as it suggests the necessity for their improvement. The fact that they are citizens entitles them to all the rights due to that relation and charges them with all its duties, obligations, and responsibilities.

These topics and the constant and ever varying wants of an active and enterprising population may well receive the attention and the patriotic endeavor of all who make and execute the Federal law. Our duties are practical and call for industrious application, an intelligent perception of the claims of public office, and, above all, a firm determination, by united action, to secure to all the people of the land the full benefits of the best form of government ever vouchsafed to man. And let us not trust to human effort alone, but humbly acknowledging the power and goodness of almighty God, who presides over the destiny of nations, and who has at all times been revealed in our country's history, let us invoke His aid and His blessings upon our labors.

Benjamin Harrison

Inaugural Address

MARCH 4, 1889

Commentary

The principal achievements of Cleveland's first administration centered on extension of civil service, vetoing undeserved pensions for Civil War veterans, and tariff revision. In the 1880s the United States faced the unusual problem of having a surplus in the Treasury, indicating that taxes were too high. Extravagant pension bills and "pork barrel" legislation for rivers and harbors would have readily disposed of the surplus, but Cleveland boldly decided to attack the cause of the problem. On December 6, 1887, the president focused the attention of the nation upon the need for tariff reform by devoting the third annual State of the Union message exclusively to this subject. "Our present tariff laws," he declared, "the vicious, inequitable, and illogical source of unnecessary taxation, ought to be at once revised and amended." He pointed out that the existing law protected American industrialists, but, and above all, that the tariff also had correspondingly increased consumer prices and provided an additional "burden upon those with moderate means and the poor, the employed and unemployed, the sick and well, and the young and old." He vividly described the tariff as "a tax which with relentless grasp is fastened upon the clothing of every man, woman, and child in the land." Appealing for immediate reduction—not free trade—Cleveland repeated that his purpose was not humanitarian, but to relieve the people from an unnecessary tax, one which had helped to produce a treasury surplus with a corresponding deflationary economic trend. From the conclusion of his message to Election Day, 1888, the tariff debate raged in and out of Congress.

The Democratic-controlled House Ways and Means Committee, chaired by Roger Mills of Texas, prepared a lowered tariff bill with an estimated total

revenue reduction of $80 million per year. For several months, the House de-
bated, amended, criticized, and praised the administration's Mills Bill. Con-
gressmen representing special interest groups as well as their sectional interests
delivered both partisan and moral appeals for and against enactment. During
the course of these debates and the prolonged testimony before the Ways and
Means Committee, the Republican Party became committed to protection suf-
ficiently high to maintain a domestic monopoly for American industrialist—in
other words, protection for the sake of protection. On July 21, 1888, the Mills
Bill passed the House and was sent to the Senate. But the Republican-controlled
Senate passed the Allison Bill, which maintained a generally high level of duties.
By this time, though, Cleveland's speech and the Mills Bill had become the chief
1888 campaign issue.

As expected, the Democrats renominated Cleveland by acclamation. The
Republicans chose Senator Benjamin Harrison of Indiana and endorsed a tar-
iff plank that frankly advocated high protection. The fairly quiet campaign
was mainly waged on this issue until the introduction of the "Murchison" let-
ter. Falling into a carefully planned Republican trap, the British minister to
Washington, Sir Lionel Sackville-West, advised a purported naturalized citi-
zen of English birth to vote for Cleveland. This inopportune intervention into
American politics by the minister undoubtedly cost Cleveland the support of
many Irish-Americans and, perhaps, the election. Cleveland received 100,000
votes more than Harrison, but Harrison carried the key states of New York
and Indiana, receiving an electoral count of 233 to Cleveland's 168. Harri-
son piously attributed his victory to God, but Republican National Chairman
Matthew Quay, who had purchased untold votes in New York and Indiana,
exclaimed that "providence hadn't a damn thing to do with it," and added that
he supposed Harrison would "never know how close a number of men were
compelled to approach the gates of the penitentiary to make him President."

On March 4, 1889, the grandson of President William Henry Harrison, "Old
Tippecanoe," became the twenty-third president of the United States. Benjamin
Harrison's inaugural address contained a platitudinous restatement of his party's
principles. He spoke of no urgent problems and of no immediate objectives.

⁓ ⌢ ⁓

Fellow citizens:

There is no constitutional or legal requirement that the President shall
take the oath of office in the presence of the people, but there is so manifest
an appropriateness in the public induction to office of the chief executive

officer of the nation that from the beginning of the Government the people, to whose service the official oath consecrates the officer, have been called to witness the solemn ceremonial. The oath taken in the presence of the people becomes a mutual covenant. The officer covenants to serve the whole body of the people by a faithful execution of the laws, so that they may be the unfailing defense and security of those who respect and observe them, and that neither wealth, station, nor the power of combinations shall be able to evade their just penalties or to wrest them from a beneficent public purpose to serve the ends of cruelty or selfishness.

My promise is spoken; yours unspoken, but not the less real and solemn. The people of every State have here their representatives. Surely I do not misinterpret the spirit of the occasion when I assume that the whole body of the people covenant with me and with each other today to support and defend the Constitution and the Union of the States, to yield willing obedience to all the laws and each to every other citizen his equal civil and political rights. Entering thus solemnly into covenant with each other, we may reverently invoke and confidently expect the favor and help of almighty God; that He will give to me wisdom, strength, and fidelity, and to our people a spirit of fraternity and a love of righteousness and peace.

This occasion derives peculiar interest from the fact that the Presidential term which begins this day is the twenty-sixth under our Constitution. The first inauguration of President Washington took place in New York, where Congress was then sitting, on the 30th day of April, 1789, having been deferred by reason of delays attending the organization of the Congress and the canvass of the electoral vote. Our people have already worthily observed the centennials of the Declaration of Independence, of the battle of Yorktown, and of the adoption of the Constitution, and will shortly celebrate in New York the institution of the second great department of our constitutional scheme of government. When the centennial of the institution of the judicial department, by the organization of the Supreme Court, shall have been suitably observed, as I trust it will be, our nation will have fully entered its second century.

I will not attempt to note the marvelous and in great part happy contrasts between our country as it steps over the threshold into its second century of organized existence under the Constitution and that weak but wisely ordered young nation that looked undauntedly down the first century, when all its years stretched out before it.

Our people will not fail at this time to recall the incidents which accompanied the institution of government under the Constitution, or to find inspiration and guidance in the teachings and example of Washington and his great associates, and hope and courage in the contrast which thirty-eight populous and prosperous States offer to the thirteen States, weak in everything except courage and the love of liberty, that then fringed our Atlantic seaboard.

The Territory of Dakota has now a population greater than any of the original States (except Virginia) and greater than the aggregate of five of the smaller States in 1790. The center of population when our national capital was located was east of Baltimore, and it was argued by many well informed persons that it would move eastward rather than westward; yet in 1880 it was found to be near Cincinnati, and the new census about to be taken will show another stride to the westward. That which was the body has come to be only the rich fringe of the nation's robe. But our growth has not been limited to territory, population and aggregate wealth, marvelous as it has been in each of those directions. The masses of our people are better fed, clothed, and housed than their fathers were. The facilities for popular education have been vastly enlarged and more generally diffused.

The virtues of courage and patriotism have given recent proof of their continued presence and increasing power in the hearts and over the lives of our people. The influences of religion have been multiplied and strengthened. The sweet offices of charity have greatly increased. The virtue of temperance is held in higher estimation. We have not attained an ideal condition. Not all of our people are happy and prosperous; not all of them are virtuous and law-abiding. But on the whole the opportunities offered to the individual to secure the comforts of life are better than are found elsewhere and largely better than they were here one hundred years ago.

The surrender of a large measure of sovereignty to the General Government, effected by the adoption of the Constitution, was not accomplished until the suggestions of reason were strongly reenforced by the more imperative voice of experience. The divergent interests of peace speedily demanded a "more perfect union." The merchant, the shipmaster, and the manufacturer discovered and disclosed to our statesmen and to the people that commercial emancipation must be added to the political freedom which had been so bravely won. The commercial policy of the mother country had not relaxed any of its hard and oppressive features. To hold in check the development of our commercial marine, to prevent or retard the establishment and growth of manufactures in the States, and so to secure the American market for their shops and the carrying trade for their ships, was the policy of European statesmen, and was pursued with the most selfish vigor.

Petitions poured in upon Congress urging the imposition of discriminating duties that should encourage the production of needed things at home. The patriotism of the people, which no longer found afield of exercise in war, was energetically directed to the duty of equipping the young Republic for the defense of its independence by making its people self dependent. Societies for the promotion of home manufactures and for encouraging the use of domestics in the dress of the people were organized in many of the States. The revival at the end of the century of the same patriotic interest in the preservation and development of domestic industries and the defense of our working people against injurious foreign competition is an incident worthy of attention. It is not a departure but a return that we have witnessed. The protective policy had then its opponents. The argument was made, as now, that its benefits inured to particular classes or sections.

If the question became in any sense or at any time sectional, it was only because slavery existed in some of the States. But for this there was no reason why the cotton-producing States should not have led or walked abreast with the New England States in the production of cotton fabrics. There was this reason only why the States that divide with Pennsylvania the mineral treasures of the great southeastern and central mountain ranges should have been so tardy in bringing to the smelting furnace and to the mill the coal and iron from their near opposing hillsides. Mill fires were lighted at the funeral pile of slavery. The emancipation proclamation was heard in the depths of the earth as well as in the sky; men were made free, and material things became our better servants.

The sectional element has happily been eliminated from the tariff discussion. We have no longer States that are necessarily only planting States. None are excluded from achieving that diversification of pursuits among the people which brings wealth and contentment. The cotton plantation will not be less valuable when the product is spun in the country town by operatives whose necessities call for diversified crops and create a home demand for garden and agricultural products. Every new mine, furnace, and factory is an extension of the productive capacity of the State more real and valuable than added territory.

Shall the prejudices and paralysis of slavery continue to hang upon the skirts of progress? How long will those who rejoice that slavery no longer exists cherish or tolerate the incapacities it put upon their communities? I look hopefully to the continuance of our protective system and to the consequent development of manufacturing and mining enterprises in the States hitherto wholly given to agriculture as a potent influence in the perfect unification of our people. The men who have invested their capital in these enterprises, the farmers who have felt the benefit of their neighborhood, and the men who work in shop or field will not fail to find and to defend a community of interest.

Is it not quite possible that the farmers and the promoters of the great mining and manufacturing enterprises which have recently been established in the South may yet find that the free ballot of the workingman, without distinction of race, is needed for their defense as well as for his own? I do not doubt that if those men in the South who now accept the tariff views of Clay and the constitutional expositions of Webster would courageously avow and defend their real convictions they would not find it difficult, by friendly instruction and cooperation, to make the black man their efficient and safe ally, not only in establishing correct principles in our national administration, but in preserving for their local communities the benefits of social order and economical and honest government. At least until the good offices of kindness and education have been fairly tried the contrary conclusion can not be plausibly urged.

I have altogether rejected the suggestion of a special Executive policy for any section of our country. It is the duty of the Executive to administer and enforce in the methods and by the instrumentalities pointed out and provided by the Constitution all the laws enacted by Congress. These laws are general and their administration should be uniform and equal. As a citizen may not elect what laws he will obey, neither may the Executive eject which he will enforce. The duty to obey and to execute embraces the Constitution in its entirety and the whole code of laws enacted under it. The evil example of permitting individuals, corporations, or communities to nullify the laws because they cross some selfish or local interest or prejudices is full of danger, not only to the nation at large, but much more to those who use this pernicious expedient to escape their just obligations or to obtain an unjust advantage over others. They will presently themselves be compelled to appeal to the law for protection, and those who would use the law as a defense must not deny that use of it to others.

If our great corporations would more scrupulously observe their legal limitations and duties, they would have less cause to complain of the unlawful limitations of their rights or of violent interference with their operations. The community that by concert, open or secret, among its citizens denies to a portion of its members their plain rights under the law has severed the only safe bond of social order and prosperity. The evil works from a bad center both ways. It demoralizes those who practice it and destroys the faith of those who suffer by it in the efficiency of the law as a safe protector. The man in whose breast that faith has been darkened is naturally the subject of dangerous and uncanny suggestions. Those who use unlawful methods, if moved by no higher motive than the selfishness that prompted them, may well stop and inquire what is to be the end of this.

An unlawful expedient can not become a permanent condition of government. If the educated and influential classes in a community either practice or connive at the systematic violation of laws that seem to them to cross their convenience, what can they expect when the lesson that convenience or a supposed class interest is a sufficient cause for lawlessness has been well learned by the ignorant classes? A community where law is the rule of conduct and where courts, not mobs, execute its penalties is the only attractive field for business investments and honest labor.

Our naturalization laws should be so amended as to make the inquiry into the character and good disposition of persons applying for citizenship more careful and searching. Our existing laws have been in their administration an unimpressive and often an unintelligible form. We accept the man as a citizen without any knowledge of his fitness, and he assumes the duties of citizenship without any knowledge as to what they are. The privileges of American citizenship are so great and its duties so grave that we may well insist upon a good knowledge of every person applying for citizenship and a good knowledge by him of our institutions. We should not cease to be hospitable to immigration, but we should cease to be careless as to the character of it. There are men of all races, even the best, whose coming is necessarily a burden upon our public revenues or a threat to social order. These should be identified and excluded.

We have happily maintained a policy of avoiding all interference with European affairs. We have been only interested spectators of their contentions in diplomacy and in war, ready to use our friendly offices to promote peace, but never obtruding our advice and never attempting unfairly to coin the distresses of other powers into commercial advantage to ourselves. We have a just right to expect that our European policy will be the American policy of European courts.

It is so manifestly incompatible with those precautions for our peace and safety which all the great powers habitually observe and enforce in matters affecting them that a shorter waterway between our eastern and western seaboards should be dominated by any European Government that we may confidently expect that such a purpose will not be entertained by any friendly power.

We shall in the future, as in the past, use every endeavor to maintain and enlarge our friendly relations with all the great powers, but they will not expect us to look kindly upon any project that would leave us subject to the dangers of a hostile observation or environment. We have not sought to dominate or to absorb any of our weaker neighbors, but rather to aid and encourage them to establish free and stable governments resting upon the consent of their own people. We have a clear right to expect, therefore, that no European Government will seek to establish colonial dependencies upon the territory of these independent American States. That which a sense of justice restrains us from seeking they may be reasonably expected willingly to forego.

It must not be assumed, however, that our interests are so exclusively American that our entire inattention to any events that may transpire elsewhere can be taken for granted. Our citizens domiciled for purposes of trade in all countries and in many of the islands of the sea demand and will have our adequate care in their personal and commercial rights. The necessities of our Navy require convenient coaling stations and dock and harbor privileges. These and other trading privileges we will feel free to obtain only by means that do not in any degree partake of coercion, however feeble the government from which we ask such concessions. But having fairly obtained them by methods and for purposes entirely consistent with the most friendly disposition toward all other powers, our consent will be necessary to any modification or impairment of the concession.

We shall neither fail to respect the flag of any friendly nation or the just rights of its citizens, nor to exact the like treatment for our own. Calmness, justice, and consideration should characterize our diplomacy. The offices of an intelligent diplomacy or of friendly arbitration in proper cases should be adequate to the peaceful adjustment of all international difficulties. By such methods we will make our contribution to the world's peace, which no nation values more highly, and avoid the opprobrium which must fall upon the nation that ruthlessly breaks it.

The duty devolved by law upon the President to nominate and, by and with the advice and consent of the Senate, to appoint all public officers whose appointment is not otherwise provided for in the Constitution or by act of Congress has become very burdensome and its wise and efficient discharge full of difficulty. The civil list is so large that a personal knowledge of any large number of the applicants is impossible. The President must rely upon the representations of others, and these are often made inconsiderately and without any just sense of responsibility. I have a right, I think, to insist that those who volunteer or are invited to give advice as to appointments shall exercise consideration and fidelity. A high sense of duty and an ambition to improve the service should characterize all public officers.

There are many ways in which the convenience and comfort of those who have business with our public offices may be promoted by a thoughtful and obliging officer, and I shall expect those whom I may appoint to justify their selection by a conspicuous efficiency in the discharge of their duties. Honorable party service will certainly not be esteemed by me a disqualification for public office, but it will in no case be allowed to serve as a shield of official negligence, incompetency, or delinquency. It is entirely creditable to seek public office by proper methods and with proper motives, and all applicants will be treated with consideration; but I shall need, and the heads of Departments will need, time for inquiry and deliberation. Persistent importunity will not, therefore, be the best support of an application for office. Heads of Departments, bureaus, and all other public officers having any duty connected therewith will be expected to enforce the civil-service law fully and without evasion. Beyond this obvious duty I hope to do something more to advance the reform of the civil service. The ideal, or even my own ideal, I shall probably not attain. Retrospect will be a safer basis of judgment than promises. We shall not, however, I am sure, be able to put our civil service upon a nonpartisan basis until we have secured an incumbency that fair-minded men of the opposition will approve for impartiality and integrity. As the number of such in the civil list is increased removals from office will diminish.

While a Treasury surplus is not the greatest evil, it is a serious evil. Our revenue should be ample to meet the ordinary annual demands upon our Treasury, with a sufficient margin for those extraordinary but scarcely less imperative demands which arise now and then. Expenditure should always be made with economy and only upon public necessity. Wastefulness, profligacy, or favoritism in public expenditures is criminal. But there is nothing in the condition of our country or of our people to suggest that anything presently necessary to the public prosperity, security, or honor should be unduly postponed.

It will be the duty of Congress wisely to forecast and estimate these extraordinary demands, and, having added them to our ordinary expenditures, to so adjust our revenue laws that no considerable annual surplus will remain. We will fortunately be able to apply to the redemption of the public debt any small and unforeseen excess of revenue. This is better than to reduce our income below our necessary expenditures, with the resulting choice between another change of our revenue laws and an increase of the public debt. It is quite possible, I am sure, to effect the necessary reduction in our revenues without breaking down our protective tariff or seriously injuring any domestic industry.

The construction of a sufficient number of modern war ships and of their necessary armament should progress as rapidly as is consistent with care and perfection in plans and workmanship. The spirit, courage, and skill of our naval officers and seamen have many times in our history given to weak ships and inefficient guns a rating greatly beyond that of the naval list. That they will again do so upon occasion I do not doubt; but they ought not, by premeditation or neglect, to be left to the risks and exigencies of an unequal combat. We should encourage the establishment of American steamship lines. The exchanges of commerce demand stated, reliable, and rapid means of communication, and until these are provided the development of our trade with the States lying south of us is impossible.

Our pension laws should give more adequate and discriminating relief to the Union soldiers and sailors and to their widows and orphans. Such occasions as this should remind us that we owe everything to their valor and sacrifice.

It is a subject of congratulation that there is a near prospect of the admission into the Union of the Dakotas and Montana and Washington Territories. This act of justice has been unreasonably delayed in the case of some of them. The people who have settled these Territories are intelligent, enterprising, and patriotic, and the accession these new States will add strength to the nation. It is due to the settlers in the Territories who have availed themselves of the invitations of our land laws to make homes upon the public domain that their titles should be speedily adjusted and their honest entries confirmed by patent.

It is very gratifying to observe the general interest now being manifested in the reform of our election laws. Those who have been for years calling attention to the pressing necessity of throwing about the ballot box and about the elector further safeguards, in order that our elections might not only be free and pure, but might clearly appear to be so, will welcome the accession of any who did not so soon discover the need of reform. The National Congress has not as yet taken control of elections in that case over which the Constitution gives it jurisdiction, but has accepted and adopted the election laws of the several States, provided penalties for their violation and a method of supervision. Only the inefficiency of the State laws or an unfair partisan administration of them could suggest a departure from this policy.

It was clearly, however, in the contemplation of the framers of the Constitution that such an exigency might arise, and provision was wisely made for it. The freedom of the ballot is a condition of our national life, and no power vested in Congress or in the Executive to secure or perpetuate it should remain unused upon occasion. The people of all the Congressional districts have an equal interest that the election in each shall truly express the views and wishes of a majority of the qualified electors residing within it. The results of such elections are not local, and the insistence of electors residing in other districts that they shall be pure and free does not savor at all of impertinence.

If in any of the States the public security is thought to be threatened by ignorance among the electors, the obvious remedy is education. The sympathy and help of our people will not be withheld from any community struggling with special embarrassments or difficulties connected with the suffrage if the remedies proposed proceed upon lawful lines and are promoted by just and honorable methods. How shall those who practice election frauds recover that respect for the sanctity of the ballot which is the first condition and obligation of good citizenship? The man who has come to regard the ballot box as a juggler's hat has renounced his allegiance.

Let us exalt patriotism and moderate our party contentions. Let those who would die for the flag on the field of battle give a better proof of their patriotism and a higher glory to their country by promoting fraternity and justice. A party success that is achieved by unfair methods or by practices that partake of revolution is hurtful and evanescent even from a party standpoint. We should hold our differing opinions in mutual respect, and, having submitted them to the arbitrament of the ballot, should accept an adverse judgment with the same respect that we would have demanded of our opponents if the decision had been in our favor.

No other people have a government more worthy of their respect and love or a land so magnificent in extent, so pleasant to look upon, and so full of generous suggestion to enterprise and labor. God has placed upon our head a diadem and has laid at our feet power and wealth beyond definition or calculation. But we must not forget that we take these gifts upon the condition that justice and mercy shall hold the reins of power and that the upward avenues of hope shall be free to all the people.

I do not mistrust the future. Dangers have been in frequent ambush along our path, but we have uncovered and vanquished them all. Passion has swept some of our communities, but only to give us a new demonstration that the great body of our people are stable, patriotic, and law-abiding. No political party can long pursue advantage at the expense of public honor or by rude and indecent methods without protest and fatal disaffection in its own body. The peaceful agencies of commerce are more fully revealing the necessary unity of all our communities, and the increasing intercourse of our people is promoting mutual respect. We shall find unalloyed pleasure in the revelation which our next census will make of the swift development of the great resources of some of the States. Each State will bring its generous contribution to the great aggregate of the nation's increase. And when the harvests from the fields, the cattle from the hills, and the ores of the earth shall have been weighed, counted, and valued, we will turn from them all to crown with the highest honor the State that has most promoted education, virtue, justice and patriotism among its people.

GROVER CLEVELAND

SECOND INAUGURAL ADDRESS

MARCH 4, 1893

COMMENTARY

*During the first two years of Harrison's administration, the Republicans en-
joyed a majority in both houses of Congress—it is here, under the relentless
leadership of the party bosses, that the power resided. The aloof, conservative, fiercely partisan Harrison, referred to by his contemporaries as a human icicle, seemed almost unaware of the growing farmer unrest and the
plight of the urban laborer. Determined Republican legislators proceeded
to redeem their campaign pledge by passing the McKinley Tariff Act, which
raised duties to a new high. But the growing western bloc wrested an important concession in return for their needed congressional support of the
tariff—a more liberal silver purchase act. To quiet the growing public clamor
against business monopolies, the Republican leaders agreed to the passage
of the Sherman Antitrust Act, carefully making its key clauses so vague that
those who supported it understood that it would be ineffective. Veterans'
organizations, notably the Grand Army of the Republic, were placated by
liberal pensions that literally opened the Treasury doors. "God help the surplus," boastfully exclaimed Harrison's pension commissioner. The electorate
expressed their reaction to the work of "the billion dollar Congress" in the
1890 congressional elections. With the tariff again the main issue, and now
probably better understood by the debt-ridden farmers, the Republicans received an emphatic rebuke, losing control of the House. Nine representatives
of a new party, the Populists, were sent to Washington, certainly an omen
of the growing agrarian discontent. The government, nevertheless, still remained in conservative hands.*

In June 1892, the Republican National Convention meeting at Minne-apolis had no other choice but to renominate Harrison and to extol their record. The Democrats again turned to Cleveland, who like Harrison was selected on the first ballot. An otherwise dull campaign was enlivened with the appearance of a third candidate, James Weaver of Iowa, who ran on the Populist ticket. The radical Populist platform, which demanded federal as-sistance for the farmer and worker, excoriated "the struggles of the two great political parties for power and plunder. . . . The fruits of the toil of millions are boldly stolen to build up colossal fortunes for the few. . . . From the same pro-lific womb of governmental injustice we breed the two great classes—tramps and millionaires." When the votes were in, Cleveland received 5,554,414 to Harrison's 5,190,802, and Weaver polled 1,027,000. Cleveland won 227 elec-toral votes to Harrison's 145 and Weaver's 22. For the first time since before the Civil War, the president and both houses of Congress were Democratic. The Populists carried five states—Kansas, North Dakota, Colorado, Idaho, and Nevada. In large sections of the Midwest and especially in the South, reluctance to vote for a third party caused the election of many Democrats sympathetic to the Populist cause.

On March 4, 1893, as snow whitened the streets of the capital, a slightly heavier Cleveland, his hair a little thinner, delivered his second inaugural ad-dress. Speaking again without notes, he lauded "our stupendous achievements as a people and our country's robust strength." But within the year, fierce in-dustrial strikes, financial panic, increasing agricultural distress, and a bad de-pression would place the conservative president clearly out of touch with the major problems facing the nation.

My fellow citizens:

In obedience of the mandate of my countrymen I am about to dedi-cate myself to their service under the sanction of a solemn oath. Deeply moved by the expression of confidence and personal attachment which has called me to this service, I am sure my gratitude can make no better return than the pledge I now give before God and these witnesses of un-reserved and complete devotion to the interests and welfare of those who have honored me.

I deem it fitting on this occasion, while indicating the opinion I hold concerning public questions of present importance, to also briefly refer to the existence of certain conditions and tendencies among our people which seem to menace the integrity and usefulness of their Government.

While every American citizen must contemplate with the utmost pride and enthusiasm the growth and expansion of our country, the sufficiency of our institutions to stand against the rudest shocks of violence, the wonderful thrift and enterprise of our people, and the demonstrated superiority of our free government, it behooves us to constantly watch for every symptom of insidious infirmity that threatens our national vigor.

The strong man who in the confidence of sturdy health courts the sternest activities of life and rejoices in the hardihood of constant labor may still have lurking near his vitals the unheeded disease that dooms him to sudden collapse.

It can not be doubted that our stupendous achievements as a people and our country's robust strength have given rise to heedlessness of those laws governing our national health which we can no more evade than human life can escape the laws of God and nature.

Manifestly nothing is more vital to our supremacy as a nation and to the beneficent purposes of our Government than a sound and stable currency. Its exposure to degradation should at once arouse to activity the most enlightened statesmanship, and the danger of depreciation in the purchasing power of the wages paid to toil should furnish the strongest incentive to prompt and conservative precaution.

In dealing with our present embarrassing situation as related to this subject we will be wise if we temper our confidence and faith in our national strength and resources with the frank concession that even these will not permit us to defy with impunity the inexorable laws of finance and trade. At the same time, in our efforts to adjust differences of opinion we should be free from intolerance or passion, and our judgments should be unmoved by alluring phrases and unvexed by selfish interests.

I am confident that such an approach to the subject will result in prudent and effective remedial legislation. In the meantime, so far as the executive branch of the Government can intervene, none of the powers with which it is invested will be withheld when their exercise is deemed necessary to maintain our national credit or avert financial disaster.

Closely related to the exaggerated confidence in our country's greatness which tends to a disregard of the rules of national safety, another danger confronts us not less serious. I refer to the prevalence of a popular disposition to expect from the operation of the Government especial and direct individual advantages.

The verdict of our voters which condemned the injustice of maintaining protection for protection's sake enjoins upon the people's servants the duty of exposing and destroying the brood of kindred evils which are the unwholesome progeny of paternalism. This is the bane of republican institutions and the constant peril of our government by the people. It degrades to the purposes of wily craft the plan of rule our fathers established and bequeathed to us as an object of our love and veneration. It perverts the patriotic sentiments of our countrymen and tempts them to pitiful calculation of the sordid gain to be derived from their Government's maintenance. It undermines the self-reliance of our people and substitutes in its place dependence upon governmental favoritism. It stifles the spirit of true Americanism and stupefies every ennobling trait of American citizenship.

The lessons of paternalism ought to be unlearned and the better lesson taught that while the people should patriotically and cheerfully support their Government its functions do not include the support of the people.

The acceptance of this principle leads to a refusal of bounties and subsidies, which burden the labor and thrift of a portion of our citizens to aid ill-advised or languishing enterprises in which they have no concern. It leads also to a challenge of wild and reckless pension expenditure, which overleaps the bounds of grateful recognition of patriotic service and prostitutes to vicious uses the people's prompt and generous impulse to aid those disabled in their country's defense.

Every thoughtful American must realize the importance of checking at its beginning any tendency in public or private station to regard frugality and economy as virtues which we may safely outgrow. The toleration of this idea results in the waste of the people's money by their chosen servants and encourages prodigality and extravagance in the home life of our countrymen.

Under our scheme of government the waste of public money is a crime against the citizen, and the contempt of our people for economy and frugality in their personal affairs deplorably saps the strength and sturdiness of our national character.

It is a plain dictate of honesty and good government that public expenditures should be limited by public necessity, and that this should be measured by the rules of strict economy; and it is equally clear that frugality among the people is the best guaranty of a contented and strong support of free institutions.

One mode of the misappropriation of public funds is avoided when appointments to office, instead of being the rewards of partisan activity, are awarded to those whose efficiency promises a fair return of work for the compensation paid to them. To secure the fitness and competency of appointees to office and remove from political action the demoralizing madness for spoils, civil service reform has found a place in our public policy and laws. The benefits already gained through this instrumentality and the further usefulness it promises entitle it to the hearty support and encouragement of all who desire to see our public service well performed or who hope for the elevation of political sentiment and the purification of political methods.

The existence of immense aggregations of kindred enterprises and combinations of business interests formed for the purpose of limiting production and fixing prices is inconsistent with the fair field which ought to be open to every independent activity. Legitimate strife in business should not be superseded by an enforced concession to the demands of combinations that have the power to destroy, nor should the people to be served lose the benefit of cheapness which usually results from wholesome competition. These aggregations and combinations frequently constitute conspiracies against the interests of the people, and in all their phases they are unnatural and opposed to our American sense of fairness. To the extent that they can be reached and restrained by Federal power the General Government should relieve our citizens from their interference and exactions.

Loyalty to the principles upon which our Government rests positively demands that the equality before the law which it guarantees to every citizen should be justly and in good faith conceded in all parts of the land. The enjoyment of this right follows the badge of citizenship wherever found, and, unimpaired by race or color, it appeals for recognition to American manliness and fairness.

Our relations with the Indians located within our border impose upon us responsibilities we can not escape. Humanity and consistency require us to treat them with forbearance and in our dealings with them to honestly and considerately regard their rights and interests. Every effort should be made to lead them, through the paths of civilization and education, to self-supporting and independent citizenship. In the meantime, as the nation's wards, they should be promptly defended against the cupidity of designing men and shielded from every influence or temptation that retards their advancement.

The people of the United States have decreed that on this day the control of their Government in its legislative and executive branches shall be given to a political party pledged in the most positive terms to the accomplishment of tariff reform. They have thus determined in favor of a more just and equitable system of Federal taxation. The agents they have chosen to carry out their purposes are bound by their promises not less than by the command of their masters to devote themselves unremittingly to this service.

While there should be no surrender of principle, our task must be undertaken wisely and without heedless vindictiveness. Our mission is not punishment, but the rectification of wrong. If in lifting burdens from the daily life of our people we reduce inordinate and unequal advantages too long enjoyed, this is but a necessary incident of our return to right and justice. If we exact from unwilling minds acquiescence in the theory of an honest distribution of the fund of the governmental beneficence treasured up for all, we but insist upon a principle which underlies our free institutions. When we tear aside the delusions and misconceptions which have blinded our countrymen to their condition under vicious tariff laws, we but show them how far they have been led away from the paths of contentment and prosperity. When we proclaim that the necessity for revenue to support the Government furnishes the only justification for taxing the people, we announce a truth so plain that its denial would seem to indicate the extent to which judgment may be influenced by familiarity with perversions of the taxing power. And when we seek to reinstate the self-confidence and business enterprise of our citizens by discrediting an abject dependence upon governmental favor, we strive to stimulate those elements of American character which support the hope of American achievement.

Anxiety for the redemption of the pledges which my party has made and solicitude for the complete justification of the trust the people have reposed in us constrain me to remind those with whom I am to cooperate that we can succeed in doing the work which has been especially set before us only by the most sincere, harmonious, and disinterested effort. Even if insuperable obstacles and opposition prevent the consummation of our task, we shall hardly be excused; and if failure can be traced to our fault or neglect we may be sure the people will hold us to a swift and exacting accountability.

The oath I now take to preserve, protect, and defend the Constitution of the United States not only impressively defines the great responsibility I assume, but suggests obedience to constitutional commands as the rule by which my official conduct must be guided. I shall to the best of my ability and within my sphere of duty preserve the Constitution by loyally protecting every grant of Federal power it contains, by defending all its restraints when attacked by impatience and restlessness, and by enforcing its limitations and reservations in favor of the States and the people.

Fully impressed with the gravity of the duties that confront me and mindful of my weakness, I should be appalled if it were my lot to bear unaided the responsibilities which await me. I am, however, saved from discouragement when I remember that I shall have the support and the counsel and cooperation of wise and patriotic men who will stand at my side in Cabinet places or will represent the people in their legislative halls.

I find also much comfort in remembering that my countrymen are just and generous and in the assurance that they will not condemn those who by sincere devotion to their service deserve their forbearance and approval.

Above all, I know there is a Supreme Being who rules the affairs of men and whose goodness and mercy have always followed the American people, and I know He will not turn from us now if we humbly and reverently seek His powerful aid.

WILLIAM MCKINLEY

FIRST INAUGURAL ADDRESS

MARCH 4, 1897

COMMENTARY

The American farmer in the post-Civil War decades harbored an increasing sense of frustration as government, both state and national, remained indifferent to his or her worsening plight. Operating under conditions of the freest of free competition, the farmer competed for markets but bought manufactured articles from well-protected industries. Farm prices fell dramatically between 1870 and 1896—wheat, which had averaged $1.06 a bushel in 1870, brought only 60 cents in 1896; cotton dropped from 15 cents per pound to six cents. Compounded by droughts, high interest rates, insect plague, fixed overhead, discriminatory railroad rates, plus a dozen other problems, the embittered farmer seethed as Washington continued immune to agricultural conditions. Declining prices and increasing debts had become a constant.

Western agricultural protest movements date back to the 1860s but with the 1890s, the Populists, a new, more aggressive movement, demanded immediate relief through direct political action. "What you farmers need to do," Mary Lease told a Kansas audience, "is to raise less corn and more Hell." One must go back to medieval Europe on the eve of the First Crusade for an emotional response comparable to that generated by the Populists. Almost miraculously, leaders sprang up carrying their message to farm picnics, rural crossroads, and county fairs. William Allen White recalled the Populist fervor during the 1894 congressional elections: "Far into the night the voices rose—women's voices, children's voices, the voices of old men, of youth and maidens', rose on the ebbing prairie breezes, as the crusaders of the revolution rode home, praising the people's will as though it were God's will and cursing wealth for its iniquity."

In the 1894 elections, Populist candidates polled 1,471,590 votes, an increase of about 400,000, or 42 percent, over 1892. Still, results for individual candidates proved disappointing. Many elected Republicans and Democrats sympathized with the Populist views, making it evident that fusion with a major party remained the only way to political power.

The presidential election of 1896 revived political life in America. Free silver became the great rallying cry—the free and unlimited coinage of silver at the ratio to gold of 16 to 1. Resumption by the government of silver coinage would have increased the circulation of paper currency. The resulting inflation, so believed the farmers, would end every agricultural inequity. Free silver became the all-encompassing panacea:

> *The dollar of our daddies,*
> > *Of silver coinage free*
> *Will make us rich and happy*
> > *Will bring prosperity.*

When the Democratic convention assembled in Chicago on July 7, the party seemed not only leaderless but also divided by bitter strife. Cleveland firmly opposed free silver as "dangerous and reckless." But state convention after convention chose delegates pledged to the silver crusade. The uncompromising silver platform plank, adopted 628 to 301, indicated that the bimetallists had won a majority of the delegates. On the evening of July 9, William Jennings Bryan, an Omaha editor and former congressman from Nebraska, rose to defend the platform. Before he finished speaking, the assembled convention knew that they had found their leader. In a stirring address, the 36-year-old Bryan thrilled his listeners as he defended silver. His words rang out in an electrifying challenge:

> *You come to us and tell us that the great cities are in favor of the gold standard. We reply that the great cities rest upon our broad and fertile prairies. Burn down your cities and leave our farms, and your cities will spring up again as if by magic; but destroy our farms, and the grass will grow in the streets of every city in the country.*

And, to the now half-hysterical audience, he concluded with the rousing peroration:

> *Having behind us the producing masses of this nation and the world, the laboring interests, and the toilers everywhere, we will*

answer their demand for a gold standard by saying to them: You
shall not press down upon the brow of labor this crown of thorns—
you shall not crucify mankind upon a cross of gold!

The tumult that followed, as one observer recorded, "was like that of a great sea thundering against the dykes. Twenty thousand men and women went mad with an irresistible enthusiasm." On the fifth ballot, they acclaimed Bryan the choice of the Democratic Party. The Populists assembled the following month and had little alternative but to endorse Bryan and accept free silver as the paramount issue. The forces of agrarian discontent, at long last, had found a spokesman.

The Republicans embraced the banner of the gold standard. "We are unalterably opposed to every measure calculated to debase our currency," declared their platform. "We are therefore opposed to the free coinage of silver." For its nominee, the convention chose William McKinley, governor of Ohio and a former congressman who had been chairman of the Ways and Means Committee that drafted the high, protective Tariff Act of 1890. Although as a congressman McKinley had backed prosilver bills, he now assured eastern Republicans of his complete acceptance of the gold plank. Thirty-four western delegates pledged to free silver, led by Senator Henry Teller of Colorado, bolted the convention and urged their followers to support Bryan. The issue between the parties was clearly drawn.

The ensuing campaign became the most memorable and exciting since that of 1860. Bryan traveled more than 18,000 miles, making over 600 speeches in 29 states. The Democratic strategy attempted to unite the eastern worker with the agrarian masses, but Bryan remained an alien symbol and a sectional candidate east of the Ohio River. Once, Bryan himself referred to the East, and to New York in particular, as "the enemy's country" that he intended to invade. Cleveland, the Democratic standard-bearer in the three proceeding presidential contests, referred to the silverites as "madmen" and "criminals." Nevertheless, Bryan's unorthodox views and his campaign methods drew thousands of listeners—on some days he spoke to as many as 100,000 people. The "Great Commoner," as his followers affectionately called him, assaulted the "money power" and promised the hopes of democracy for all. With his campaign tactics managed by the Ohio industrialist Mark Hanna, McKinley remained at his home in Canton delivering talks to visiting delegations. But armies of well-paid Republican speakers equated a Bryan victory with national disaster—a reign of terror would follow. Vicious cartoons and slanderous articles about Bryan circulated throughout the country. The seemingly indefatigable Bryan continued his travels down to Election Day—to no avail.

McKinley received 271 electoral votes to Bryan's 176. In the popular column, the election appears considerably closer. McKinley polled 7,035,638 to Bryan's 6,467,946. The Democrats carried no state north of the former Confederacy or east of the Mississippi River. The battle had been fought and lost, probably because of the sectional and economically narrow appeal of Bryan and silver.

On March 4, 1897, Republican clubs from all parts of America descended on Washington to witness the McKinley inauguration. As the president unfolded his manuscript and put on his reading glasses, he could see a placecard in the distance boldly proclaiming: "God saved US from Bryan."

Fellow citizens:

In obedience to the will of the people, and in their presence, by the authority vested in me by this oath, I assume the arduous and responsible duties of President of the United States, relying upon the support of my countrymen and invoking the guidance of Almighty God. Our faith teaches that there is no safer reliance than upon the God of our fathers, who has so singularly favored the American people in every national trial, and who will not forsake us so long as we obey His commandments and walk humbly in His footsteps.

The responsibilities of the high trust to which I have been called, always of grave importance, are augmented by the prevailing business conditions entailing idleness upon willing labor and loss to useful enterprises. The country is suffering from industrial disturbances from which speedy relief must be had. Our financial system needs some revision; our money is all good now, but its value must not further be threatened. It should all be put upon an enduring basis, not subject to easy attack, nor its stability to doubt or dispute. Our currency should continue under the supervision of the Government. The several forms of our paper money offer, in my judgment, a constant embarrassment to the Government and a safe balance in the Treasury. Therefore I believe it necessary to devise a system which, without diminishing the circulating medium or offering a premium for its contraction, will present a remedy for those arrangements which, temporary in their nature, might well in the years of our prosperity have been displaced by wiser provisions. With adequate revenue secured, but not until then, we can enter upon such changes in our fiscal laws as will, while insuring safety and volume to our money, no longer impose upon the Government the necessity of maintaining so large a gold reserve, with its attendant and inevitable temptations to speculation. Most of our financial laws are the outgrowth of experience and trial, and should not be amended without investigation and demonstration of the wisdom of the proposed changes. We must be both sure we are right and make haste slowly. If, therefore, Congress, in its wisdom, shall deem it expedient to create a commission to take under early consideration the revision of our coinage, banking and currency laws, and give them that exhaustive, careful and dispassionate examination that their importance demands, I shall cordially concur in such action. If such power is vested in the President, it is my purpose to appoint a commission of prominent, well informed citizens of different parties, who will command public confidence, both on account of their ability and special fitness for the work. Business experience and public training may thus be combined, and the patriotic zeal of the friends of the country be so directed that such a report will be made as to receive the support of all parties, and our finances cease to be the subject of mere partisan contention. The experiment is, at all events, worth a trial, and, in my opinion, it can but prove beneficial to the entire country.

The question of international bimetallism will have early and earnest attention. It will be my constant endeavor to secure it by cooperation with the other great commercial powers of the world. Until that condition is realized when the parity between our gold and silver money springs from and is supported by the relative value of the two metals, the value of the silver already coined and of that which may hereafter be coined, must be kept constantly at par with gold by every resource at our command. The credit of the Government, the integrity of its currency, and the inviolability of its obligations must be preserved. This was the commanding verdict of the people, and it will not be unheeded.

Economy is demanded in every branch of the Government at all times, but especially in periods, like the present, of depression in business and distress among the people. The severest economy must be observed in all public expenditures, and extravagance stopped wherever it is found, and prevented wherever in the future it may be developed. If the revenues are to remain as now, the only relief that can come must be from decreased expenditures. But the present must not become the permanent condition of the Government. It has been our uniform practice to retire, not increase our outstanding obligations, and this policy must again be resumed and vigorously enforced. Our revenues should always be large enough to meet with ease and promptness not only our current needs and the principal and interest of the public debt, but to make proper and liberal provision for that most deserving body of public creditors, the soldiers and sailors and the widows and orphans who are the pensioners of the United States.

The Government should not be permitted to run behind or increase its debt in times like the present. Suitably to provide against this is the mandate of duty; the certain and easy remedy for most of our financial difficulties. A deficiency is inevitable so long as the expenditures of the Government exceed its receipts. It can only be met by loans or an increased revenue. While a large annual surplus of revenue may invite waste and extravagance, inadequate revenue creates distrust and undermines public and private credit. Neither should be encouraged. Between more loans and more revenue there ought to be but one opinion. We should have more revenue, and that without delay, hindrance, or postponement. A surplus in the Treasury created by loans is not a permanent or safe reliance. It will suffice while it lasts, but it can not last long while the outlays of the Government are greater than its receipts, as has been the case during the past two years. Nor must it be forgotten that however much such loans may temporarily relieve the situation, the Government is still indebted for the amount of the surplus thus accrued, which it must ultimately pay, while its ability to pay is not strengthened, but weakened by a continued deficit. Loans are imperative in great emergencies to preserve the Government or its credit, but a failure to supply needed revenue in time of peace for the maintenance of either has no justification.

The best way for the Government to maintain its credit is to pay as it goes, not by resorting to loans but by keeping out of debt; through an adequate income secured by a system of taxation, external or internal, or both. It is the settled policy of the Government, pursued from the beginning and practiced by all parties and Administrations, to raise the bulk of our revenue from taxes upon foreign productions entering the United States for sale and consumption, and avoiding, for the most part, every form of direct taxation, except in time of war. The country is clearly opposed to any needless additions to the subject of internal taxation, and is committed by its latest popular utterance to the system of tariff taxation. There can be no misunderstanding, either, about the principle upon which this tariff taxation shall be levied. Nothing has ever been made plainer at a general election than that the controlling principle in the raising of revenue from duties on imports is zealous care for American interests and American labor. The people have declared that such legislation should be had as will give ample protection and encouragement to the industries and the development of our country. It is, therefore, earnestly hoped and expected that Congress will, at the earliest practicable moment, enact revenue legislation that shall be fair, reasonable, conservative, and just, and which, while supplying sufficient revenue for public purposes, will still be signally beneficial and helpful to every section and every enterprise of the people. To this policy we are all, of whatever party, firmly bound by the voice of the people; a power vastly more potential than the expression of any political platform. The paramount duty of Congress is to stop deficiencies by the restoration of that protective legislation which has always been the firmest prop of the Treasury. The passage of such a law or laws would strengthen the credit of the Government both at home and abroad, and go far toward stopping the drain upon the gold reserve held for the redemption of our currency, which has been heavy and well-nigh constant for several years.

In the revision of the tariff especial attention should be given to the re-enactment and extension of the reciprocity principle of the law of 1890, under which so great a stimulus was given to our foreign trade in new and advantageous markets for our surplus agricultural and manufactured products. The brief trial given this legislation amply justifies a further experiment and additional discretionary power in the making of commercial treaties, the end in view always to be the opening up of new markets for the products of our country, by granting concessions to the products of other lands that we need and cannot produce ourselves, and which do not involve any loss of labor to our own people, but tend to increase their employment.

The depression of the past four years has fallen with especial severity upon the great body of toilers of the country, and upon none more than the holders of small farms. Agriculture has languished and labor suffered. The revival of manufacturing will be a relief to both. No portion of our population is more devoted to the institution of free government nor more loyal in their support, while none bears more cheerfully or fully its proper share in the maintenance of the Government or is better entitled to its wise and liberal care and protection. Legislation helpful to producers is beneficial to all. The depressed condition of industry on the farm and in the mine and factory has lessened the ability of the people to meet the demands upon them, and they rightfully expect that not only a system of revenue shall be established that will secure the largest income with the least burden, but that every means will be taken to decrease, rather than increase, our public expenditures. Business conditions are not the most promising. It will take time to restore the prosperity of former years. If we cannot promptly attain it, we can resolutely turn our faces in that direction and aid its return by friendly legislation. However troublesome the situation may appear, Congress will not, I am sure, be found lacking in disposition or ability to relieve it as far as legislation can do so. The restoration of confidence and the revival of business, which men of all parties so much desire, depend more largely upon the prompt, energetic, and intelligent action of Congress than upon any other single agency affecting the situation.

It is inspiring, too, to remember that no great emergency in the one hundred and eight years of our eventful national life has ever arisen that has not been met with wisdom and courage by the American people, with fidelity to their best interests and highest destiny, and to the honor of the American name. These years of glorious history have exalted mankind and advanced the cause of freedom throughout the world, and immeasurably strengthened the precious free institutions which we enjoy. The people love and will sustain these institutions. The great essential to our happiness and prosperity is that we adhere to the principles upon which the Government was established and insist upon their faithful observance. Equality of rights must prevail, and our laws be always and everywhere respected and obeyed. We may have failed in the discharge of our full duty as citizens of the great Republic, but it is consoling and encouraging to realize that free speech, a free press, free thought, free schools, the free and unmolested right of religious liberty and worship, and free and fair elections are dearer and more universally enjoyed to-day than ever before. These guaranties must be sacredly preserved and wisely strengthened. The constituted authorities must be cheerfully and vigorously upheld. Lynchings must not be tolerated in a great and civilized country like the United States; courts, not mobs, must execute the penalties of the law. The preservation of public order, the right of discussion, the integrity of courts, and the orderly administration of justice must continue forever the rock of safety upon which our Government securely rests.

One of the lessons taught by the late election, which all can rejoice in, is that the citizens of the United States are both law respecting and law abiding people, not easily swerved from the path of patriotism and honor. This is in entire accord with the genius of our institutions, and but emphasizes the advantages of inculcating even a greater love for law and order in the future. Immunity should be granted to none who violate the laws, whether individuals, corporations, or communities; and as the Constitution imposes upon the President the duty of both its own execution, and of the statutes enacted in pursuance of its provisions, I shall endeavor carefully to carry them into effect. The declaration of the party now restored to power has been in the past that of opposition to all combinations of capital organized in trusts, or otherwise, to control arbitrarily the condition of trade among our citizens, and it has supported such legislation as will prevent the execution of all schemes to oppress the people by undue charges on their supplies, or by unjust rates for the transportation of their products to the market. This purpose will be steadily pursued, both by the enforcement of the laws now in existence and the recommendation and support of such new statutes as may be necessary to carry it into effect.

Our naturalization and immigration laws should be further improved to the constant promotion of a safer, a better, and a higher citizenship. A grave peril to the Republic would be a citizenship too ignorant to understand or too vicious to appreciate the great value and beneficence of our institutions and laws, and against all who come here to make war upon them our gates must be promptly and tightly closed. Nor must we be unmindful of the need of improvement among our own citizens, but with the zeal of our forefathers encourage the spread of knowledge and free education. Illiteracy must be banished from the land if we shall attain that high destiny as the foremost of the enlightened nations of the world which, under Providence, we ought to achieve.

Reforms in the civil service must go on; but the changes should be real and genuine, not perfunctory, or prompted by a zeal in behalf of any party simply because it happens to be in power. As a member of Congress I voted and spoke in favor of the present law, and I shall attempt its enforcement in the spirit in which it was enacted. The purpose in view was to secure the most efficient service of the best men who would accept appointment under the Government, retaining faithful and devoted public servants in office, but shielding none, under the authority of any rule or custom, who are inefficient, incompetent, or unworthy. The best interests of the country demand this, and the people heartily approve the law wherever and whenever it has been thus administrated.

Congress should give prompt attention to the restoration of our American merchant marine, once the pride of the seas in all the great ocean highways of commerce. To my mind, few more important subjects so imperatively demand its intelligent consideration. The United States has progressed with marvelous rapidity in every field of enterprise and endeavor until we have become foremost in nearly all the great lines of inland trade, commerce, and industry. Yet, while this is true, our American merchant marine has been steadily declining until it is now lower, both in the percentage of tonnage and the number of vessels employed, than it was prior to the Civil War. Commendable progress has been made of late years in the upbuilding of the American Navy, but we must supplement these efforts by providing as a proper consort for it a merchant marine amply sufficient for our own carrying trade to foreign countries. The question is one that appeals both to our business necessities and the patriotic aspirations of a great people.

It has been the policy of the United States since the foundation of the Government to cultivate relations of peace and amity with all the nations of the world, and this accords with my conception of our duty now. We have cherished the policy of non-interference with affairs of foreign governments wisely inaugurated by Washington, keeping ourselves free from entanglement, either as allies or foes, content to leave undisturbed with them the settlement of their own domestic concerns. It will be our aim to pursue a firm and dignified foreign policy, which shall be just, impartial, ever watchful of our national honor, and always insisting upon the enforcement of the lawful rights of American citizens everywhere. Our diplomacy should seek nothing more and accept nothing less than is due us. We want no wars of conquest; we must avoid the temptation of territorial aggression. War should never be entered upon until every agency of peace has failed; peace is preferable to war in almost every contingency. Arbitration is the true method of settlement of international as well as local or individual differences. It was recognized as the best means of adjustment of differences between employers and employees by the forty-ninth Congress, in 1886, and its application was extended to our diplomatic relations by the unanimous concurrence of the Senate and House of the fifty-first Congress in 1890. The latter resolution was accepted as the basis of negotiations with us by the British House of Commons in 1893, and upon our invitation a treaty of arbitration between the United States and Great Britain was signed at Washington and transmitted to the Senate for its ratification in January last. Since this treaty is clearly the result of our own initiative; since it has been recognized as the leading feature of our foreign policy throughout our entire national history, the adjustment of difficulties by judicial methods rather than force of arms, and since it presents to the world the glorious example of reason and peace, not passion and war, controlling the relations between two of the greatest nations in the world, an example certain to be followed by others, I respectfully urge the early action of the Senate thereon, not merely as a matter of policy, but as a duty to mankind. The importance and moral influence of the ratification of such a treaty can hardly be overestimated in the cause of advancing civilization. It may well engage the best thought of the statesmen and people of every country, and I cannot but consider it fortunate that it was reserved to the United States to have the leadership in so grand a work.

It has been the uniform practice of each President to avoid, as far as possible, the convening of Congress in extraordinary session. It is an example which, under ordinary circumstances and in the absence of a public necessity, is to be commended. But a failure to convene the representatives of the people in Congress in extra session when it involves neglect of a public duty places the responsibility of such neglect upon the Executive himself. The condition of the public Treasury, as has been indicated, demands the immediate consideration of Congress. It alone has the power to provide revenues for the Government. Not to convene it under such circumstances I can view in no other sense than the neglect of a plain duty. I do not sympathize with the sentiment that Congress in session is dangerous to our general business interests. Its members are the agents of the people, and their presence at the seat of Government in the execution of the sovereign will should not operate as an injury, but a benefit. There could be no better time to put the Government upon a sound financial and economic basis than now. The people have only recently voted that this should be done, and nothing is more binding upon the agents of their will than the obligation of immediate action. It has always seemed to me that the postponement of the meeting of Congress until more than a year after it has been chosen deprived Congress too often of the inspiration of the popular will and the country of the corresponding benefits. It is evident, therefore, that to postpone action in the presence of so great a necessity would be unwise on the part of the Executive because unjust to the interests of the people. Our action now will be freer from mere partisan consideration than if the question of tariff revision was postponed until the regular session of Congress. We are nearly two years from a Congressional election, and politics cannot so greatly distract us as if such contest was immediately pending. We can approach the problem calmly and patriotically, without fearing its effect upon an early election.

Our fellow citizens who may disagree with us upon the character of this legislation prefer to have the question settled now, even against their preconceived views, and perhaps settled so reasonably, as I trust and believe it will be, as to insure great permanence, than to have further uncertainty menacing the vast and varied business interests of the United States. Again, whatever action Congress may take will be given a fair opportunity for trial before the people are called to pass judgment upon it, and this I consider a great essential to the rightful and lasting settlement of the question. In view of these considerations, I shall deem it my duty as President to convene Congress in extraordinary session on Monday, the 15th day of March, 1897.

In conclusion, I congratulate the country upon the fraternal spirit of the people and the manifestations of good will everywhere so apparent. The recent election not only most fortunately demonstrated the obliteration of sectional or geographical lines, but to some extent also the prejudices which for years have distracted our councils and marred our true greatness as a nation. The triumph of the people, whose verdict is carried into effect today, is not the triumph of one section, nor wholly of one party, but of all sections and all the people. The North and the South no longer divide on the old lines, but upon principles and policies; and in this fact surely every lover of the country can find cause for true felicitation.

Let us rejoice in and cultivate this spirit; it is ennobling and will be both a gain and a blessing to our beloved country. It will be my constant aim to do nothing, and permit nothing to be done, that will arrest or disturb this growing sentiment of unity and cooperation, this revival of esteem and affiliation which now animates so many thousands in both the old antagonistic sections, but I shall cheerfully do everything possible to promote and increase it. Let me again repeat the words of the oath administered by the Chief Justice which, in their respective spheres, so far as applicable, I would have all my countrymen observe—I will faithfully execute the office of President of the United States, and will, to the best of my ability, preserve, protect, and defend the Constitution of the United States. This is the obligation I have reverently taken before the Lord Most High. To keep it will be my single purpose, my constant prayer; and I shall confidently rely upon the forbearance and assistance of all the people in the discharge of my solemn responsibilities.

——— SECOND INAUGURAL ADDRESS ———

MARCH 4, 1901

COMMENTARY

In 1900, the Republicans renominated William McKinley, "the advance agent of prosperity," on a platform that boasted of four momentous years. New responsibilities had been thrust upon America as a result of the successful conclusion of the Spanish-American War—Spain ceded Puerto Rico, Guam, and the Philippines to the United States and surrendered all claim to Cuba. America gained a colonial empire! Above all, prosperity prevailed, attributed by the party to their sound money program and high tariff policy. Nominating Theodore Roosevelt, the hero of the Battle of San Juan, for vice president, the convention delegates rejoiced in the "new and noble responsibility" that had fallen to the American people.

An anti-imperialist bloc had vigorously fought the whole idea of overseas expansion, especially the annexation of the Philippines. Stalwart dissenters from all walks of life eloquently argued that annexation would mean a reversal of the fundamental American belief that a government rests on the consent of the governed. Imperialistic arguments, though, had caught the nation's imagination. "It is His will," maintained McKinley in defending the acquisition of an overseas empire. There was nothing left for the nation to do but "to take them all, and to educate the Filipinos, and to uplift and civilize and Christianize them, and by God's grace do the very best we can by them as our fellowmen for whom Christ also died." And so, with Divine guidance pointing the way, the United States assumed "the white man's burden."

The Democrats again chose William Jennings Bryan. This time imperialism replaced the fervent silver crusade of his last campaign. "We condemn and denounce the Philippine policy of the present Administration," declared the Democratic platform. "We assert that no nation can long endure half republic and half empire and we warn the American people that imperialism abroad will lead quickly and inevitably to despotism at home." The warning went unheeded. Prosperity, allied with pride in empire and fear of Bryan's free silver views, caused another McKinley victory. McKinley polled 7,219,525 votes to Bryan's 6,358,747. In the electoral college, McKinley carried every state except the "Solid South" and the four silver states of Colorado, Montana, Idaho, and Nevada. The Republican slogans of "Four years more of the Full Dinner Pail" and "Let Well Enough Alone" had prevailed.

The drizzle quickened to a downpour when, on March 4, 1901, William McKinley took his second oath of office. In a strong voice, he delivered his inaugural address.

My fellow citizens:

When we assembled here on the 4th of March 1897, there was great anxiety with regard to our currency and credit. None exists now. Then our Treasury receipts were inadequate to meet the current obligations of the Government.

Now they are sufficient for all public needs, and we have a surplus instead of a deficit. Then I felt constrained to convene the Congress in extraordinary session to devise revenues to pay the ordinary expenses of the Government. Now I have the satisfaction to announce that the Congress just closed has reduced taxation in the sum of $41,000,000. Then there was deep solicitude because of the long depression in our manufacturing, mining, agricultural, and mercantile industries and the consequent distress of our laboring population. Now every avenue of production is crowded with activity, labor is well employed, and American products find good markets at home and abroad.

Our diversified productions, however, are increasing in such unprecedented volume as to admonish us of the necessity of still further enlarging our foreign markets by broader commercial relations. For this purpose reciprocal trade arrangements with other nations should in liberal spirit be carefully cultivated and promoted.

The national verdict of 1896 has for the most part been executed. Whatever remains unfulfilled is a continuing obligation resting with undiminished force upon the Executive and the Congress. But fortunate as our condition is, its permanence can only be assured by sound business methods and strict economy in national administration and legislation. We should not permit our great prosperity to lead us to reckless ventures in business or profligacy in public expenditures. While the Congress determines the objects and the sum of appropriations, the officials of the executive departments are responsible for honest and faithful disbursement, and it should be their constant care to avoid waste and extravagance.

Honesty, capacity and industry are nowhere more indispensable than in public employment. These should be fundamental requisites to original appointment and the surest guaranties against removal.

Four years ago we stood on the brink of war without the people knowing it and without any preparation or effort at preparation for the impending peril. I did all that in honor could be done to avert the war, but without avail. It became inevitable; and the Congress at its first regular session, without party division, provided money in anticipation of the crisis and in preparation to meet it. It came. The result was signally favorable to American arms and in the highest degree honorable to the Government. It imposed upon us obligations from which we cannot escape and from which it would be dishonorable to seek escape. We are now at peace with the world, and it is my fervent prayer that if differences arise between us and other powers they may be settled by peaceful arbitration and that hereafter we may be spared the horrors of war.

Intrusted by the people for a second time with the office of President, I enter upon its administration appreciating the great responsibilities which attach to this renewed honor and commission, promising unreserved devotion on my part to their faithful discharge and reverently invoking for my guidance the direction and favor of almighty God. I should shrink from the duties this day assumed if I did not feel that in their performance I should have the cooperation of the wise and patriotic men of all parties. It encourages me for the great task which I now undertake to believe that those who voluntarily committed to me the trust imposed upon the Chief Executive of the Republic will give to me generous support in my duties to preserve, protect, and defend, the Constitution of the United States and to care that the laws be faithfully executed. The national purpose is indicated through a national election. It is the constitutional method of ascertaining the public will. When once it is registered it is a law to us all, and faithful observance should follow its decrees.

Strong hearts and helpful hands are needed, and, fortunately, we have them in every part of our beloved country. We are reunited. Sectionalism has disappeared. Division on public questions can no longer be traced by the war maps of 1861. These old differences less and less disturb the judgment. Existing problems demand the thought and quicken the conscience of the country, and the responsibility for their presence, as well as for their righteous settlement, rests upon us all; no more upon me than upon you. There are some national questions in the solution of which patriotism should exclude partisanship. Magnifying their difficulties will not take them off our hands nor facilitate their adjustment. Distrust of the capacity, integrity, and high purposes of the American people will not be an inspiring theme for future political contests. Dark pictures and gloomy forebodings are worse than useless. These only becloud, they do not help to point the way of safety and honor. Hope maketh not ashamed. The prophets of evil were not the builders of the Republic, nor in its crises since have they saved or served it. The faith of the fathers was a mighty force in its creation, and the faith of their descendants has wrought its progress and furnished its defenders. They are obstructionists who despair, and who would destroy confidence in the ability of our people to solve wisely and for civilization the mighty problems resting upon them. The American people, intrenched in freedom at home, take their love for it with them wherever they go, and they reject as mistaken and unworthy the doctrine that we lose our own liberties by securing the enduring foundations of liberty to others. Our institutions will not deteriorate by extension, and our sense of justice will not abate under tropic suns in distant seas. As heretofore, so hereafter will the nation demonstrate its fitness to administer any new estate which events devolve upon it, and in the fear of God will take occasion by the hand and make the bounds of freedom wider yet. If there are those among us who would make our way more difficult, we must not be disheartened, but the more earnestly dedicate ourselves to the task upon which we have rightly entered. The path of progress is seldom smooth. New things are often found hard to do. Our fathers found them so. We find them so. They are inconvenient. They cost us something. But are we not made better for the effort and sacrifice, and are not those we serve lifted up and blessed?

We will be consoled with the fact that opposition has confronted every onward movement of the Republic from its opening hour until now, but without success. The Republic has marched on and on, and its step has exalted freedom and humanity. We are undergoing the same ordeal as did our predecessors nearly a century ago. We are following the course they blazed. They triumphed. Will their successors falter and plead organic impotency in the nation? Surely after 125 years of achievement for mankind we will not now surrender our equality with other powers on matters fundamental and essential to nationality. With no such purpose was the nation created. In no such spirit has it developed its full and independent sovereignty. We adhere to the principle of equality among ourselves, and by no act of ours will we assign to ourselves a subordinate rank in the family of nations.

My fellow citizens, the public events of the past four years have gone into history. They are too near to justify recital. Some of them were unforeseen; many of them momentous and far-reaching in their consequences to ourselves and our relations with the rest of the world. The part which the United States bore so honorably in the thrilling scenes in China, while new to American life, has been in harmony with its true spirit and best traditions, and in dealing with the results its policy will be that of moderation and fairness.

We face at this moment a most important question that of the future relations of the United States and Cuba. With our near neighbors we must remain close friends. The declaration of the purposes of this Government in the resolution of April 20, 1898, must be made good. Ever since the evacuation of the island by the army of Spain, the Executive, with all practicable speed, has been assisting its people in the successive steps necessary to the establishment of a free and independent government prepared to assume and perform the obligations of international law which now rest upon the United States under the treaty of Paris. The convention elected by the people to frame a constitution is approaching the completion of its labors. The transfer of American control to the new government is of such great importance, involving an obligation resulting from our intervention and the treaty of peace, that I am glad to be advised by the recent act of Congress of the policy which the legislative branch of the Government deems essential to the best interests of Cuba and the United States. The principles which led to our intervention require that the fundamental law upon which the new government rests should be adapted to secure a government capable of performing the duties and discharging the functions of a separate nation, of observing its international obligations of protecting life and property, insuring order, safety, and liberty, and conforming to the established and historical policy of the United States in its relation to Cuba.

The peace which we are pledged to leave to the Cuban people must carry with it the guaranties of permanence. We became sponsors for the pacification of the island, and we remain accountable to the Cubans, no less than to our own country and people, for the reconstruction of Cuba as a free commonwealth on abiding foundations of right, justice, liberty, and assured order. Our enfranchisement of the people will not be completed until free Cuba shall be a reality, not a name; a perfect entity, not a hasty experiment bearing within itself the elements of failure.

While the treaty of peace with Spain was ratified on the 6th of February 1899, and ratifications were exchanged nearly two years ago, the Congress has indicated no form of government for the Philippine Islands. It has, however, provided an army to enable the Executive to suppress insurrection, restore peace, give security to the inhabitants, and establish the authority of the United States throughout the archipelago. It has authorized the organization of native troops as auxiliary to the regular force. It has been advised from time to time of the acts of the military and naval officers in the islands, of my action in appointing civil commissions, of the instructions with which they were charged, of their duties and powers, of their recommendations, and of their several acts under executive commission, together with the very complete general information they have submitted. These reports fully set forth the conditions, past and present, in the islands, and the instructions clearly show the principles which will guide the Executive until the Congress shall, as it is required to do by the treaty, determine the civil rights and political status of the native inhabitants. The Congress having added the sanction of its authority to the powers already possessed and exercised by the Executive under the Constitution, thereby leaving with the Executive the responsibility for the government of the Philippines, I shall continue the efforts already begun until order shall be restored throughout the islands, and as fast as conditions permit will establish local governments, in the formation of which the full co-operation of the people has been already invited, and when established will encourage the people to administer them. The settled purpose, long ago proclaimed, to afford the inhabitants of the islands self-government as fast as they were ready for it will be pursued with earnestness and fidelity. Already something has been accomplished in this direction. The Government's representatives, civil and military, are doing faithful and noble work in their mission of emancipation and merit the approval and support of their countrymen. The most liberal terms of amnesty have already been communicated to the insurgents, and the way is still open for those who have raised their arms against the Government for honorable submission to its authority. Our countrymen should not be deceived. We are not waging war against the inhabitants of the Philippine Islands. A portion of them are making war against the United States. By far the greater part of the inhabitants recognize American sovereignty and welcome it as a guaranty of order and of security for life, property, liberty, freedom of conscience, and the pursuit of happiness. To them full protection will be given. They shall not be abandoned. We will not leave the destiny of the loyal millions the islands to the disloyal thousands who are in rebellion against the United States. Order under civil institutions will come as soon as those who now break the peace shall keep it. Force will not be needed or used when those who make war against us shall make it no more. May it end without further bloodshed, and there be ushered in the reign of peace to be made permanent by a government of liberty under law.

THEODORE ROOSEVELT

INAUGURAL ADDRESS

MARCH 4, 1905

COMMENTARY

With the assassination of William McKinley in September 1901, Theodore Roosevelt, not quite 43, became the youngest and one of the most colorful presidents of the United States. Rancher, soldier, naturalist, scholar, plus a dozen other things, Roosevelt had achieved national fame during the Spanish-American War. His reputation was sufficient to elect him governor of New York in 1898. In 1900, the New York Republican bosses wished to have this dynamic man out of state politics so they pushed him for the vice presidential nomination. "I would greatly rather be anything else," said Roosevelt, perhaps thinking that no vice president subsequently had been elected to the presidency since 1837. He accepted, though, and waged a good campaign. Within six months of his election to this secondary post, he was suddenly elevated to the highest office in the land. Roosevelt's first statement as president gave comfort, at least temporarily, to many Republican conservatives and politicians. "I wish to say that it shall be my aim to continue absolutely unbroken, the policy of President McKinley." But the days of the post-Civil War sedentary and docile presidents had ended. Roosevelt, with his inexhaustible energy and tremendous personal magnetism, was bound to arouse greater interest and greater antagonism than his predecessors.

The public soon became intrigued with their president. Cartoonists were never at a loss for ideas and journalists predicted collapse unless he slowed his pace. From beneath the glamour emerged a strong national leader who dramatized the immense powers connected with his office. Roosevelt's administration proceeded to attack the growing trend toward industrial mergers by recommending legislation abolishing the abuses of these combinations. De-manding a "square deal" for all Americans, the president pledged enforcement of existing antitrust laws and stricter supervision of big business. "We do not wish to destroy corporations but we do wish to make them subserve the public good." More than any other president, Roosevelt forwarded conservation by withdrawing millions of acres of forest lands from public sale. He captured the popular fancy by calling for, among other things, the construction of an Isth-mian canal, a bigger navy and a better army, pensions for Civil War veterans, extension of civil service, and a strong foreign policy. In 1904, the Republican convention nominated him by acclamation.

The Democratic Party, ignoring Bryan, attempted to appeal to conserva-tives by nominating Alton B. Parker, the distinguished presiding judge of the New York State Court of Appeals. Parker repudiated free silver and guaranteed that he would support business interests if elected. The 1904 campaign proved exceedingly dull. Roosevelt did not go on the stump and Parker, relatively un-known outside of his state, remained at his home making speeches to visiting groups. Roosevelt won an overwhelming victory, carrying every state outside of the Solid South. More than 57 percent of the voters endorsed this strong and vigorous personality, giving him a popular majority of 2,540,067.

On March 4, 1905, Roosevelt delivered his simple inaugural address, which he had written with great care. It was his day and, as he had wished, he was now president in his own right.

My fellow citizens:

No people on earth have more cause to be thankful than ours, and this is said reverently, in no spirit of boastfulness in our own strength, but with gratitude to the Giver of Good who has blessed us with the conditions which have enabled us to achieve so large a measure of well-being and of happiness. To us as a people it has been granted to lay the foundations of our national life in a new continent. We are the heirs of the ages, and yet we have had to pay few of the penalties which in old countries are exacted by the dead hand of a bygone civilization. We have not been obliged to fight for our existence against any alien race; and yet our life has called for the vigor and effort without which the manlier and hardier virtues wither away. Under such conditions it would be our own fault if we failed; and the success which we have had in the past, the success which we confidently believe the future will bring, should cause in us no feeling of vainglory, but rather a deep and abiding realization of all which life has offered us; a full acknowledgment of the responsibility which is ours; and a fixed determination to show that under a free government a mighty people can thrive best, alike as regards the things of the body and the things of the soul.

Much has been given us, and much will rightfully be expected from us. We have duties to others and duties to ourselves; and we can shirk neither. We have become a great nation, forced by the fact of its greatness into relations with the other nations of the earth, and we must behave as beseems a people with such responsibilities. Toward all other nations, large and small, our attitude must be one of cordial and sincere friendship. We must show not only in our words, but in our deeds, that we are earnestly desirous of securing their good will by acting toward them in a spirit of just and generous recognition of all their rights. But justice and generosity in a nation, as in an individual, count most when shown not by the weak but by the strong. While ever careful to refrain from wrongdoing others, we must be no less insistent that we are not wronged ourselves. We wish peace, but we wish the peace of justice, the peace of righteousness. We wish it because we think it is right and not because we are afraid. No weak nation that acts manfully and justly should ever have cause to fear us, and no strong power should ever be able to single us out as a subject for insolent aggression.

Our relations with the other powers of the world are important; but still more important are our relations among ourselves. Such growth in wealth, in population, and in power as this nation has seen during the century and a quarter of its national life is inevitably accompanied by a like growth in the problems which are ever before every nation that rises to greatness. Power invariably means both responsibility and danger. Our forefathers faced certain perils which we have outgrown. We now face other perils, the very existence of which it was impossible that they should foresee. Modern life is both complex and intense, and the tremendous changes wrought by the extraordinary industrial development of the last half century are felt in every fiber of our social and political being. Never before have men tried so vast and formidable an experiment as that of administering the affairs of a continent under the forms of a Democratic republic. The conditions which have told for our marvelous material well-being, which have developed to a very high degree our energy, self-reliance, and individual initiative, have also brought the care and anxiety inseparable from the accumulation of great wealth in industrial centers. Upon the success of our experiment much depends, not only as regards our own welfare, but as regards the welfare of mankind. If we fail, the cause of free self-government throughout the world will rock to its foundations, and therefore our responsibility is heavy, to ourselves, to the world as it is today, and to the generations yet unborn. There is no good reason why we should fear the future, but there is every reason why we should face it seriously, neither hiding from ourselves the gravity of the problems before us nor fearing to approach these problems with the unbending, unflinching purpose to solve them aright.

Yet, after all, though the problems are new, though the tasks set before us differ from the tasks set before our fathers who founded and preserved this Republic, the spirit in which these tasks must be undertaken and these problems faced, if our duty is to be well done, remains essentially unchanged. We know that self-government is difficult. We know that no people needs such high traits of character as that people which seeks to govern its affairs aright through the freely expressed will of the freemen who compose it. But we have faith that we shall not prove false to the memories of the men of the mighty past. They did their work, they left us the splendid heritage we now enjoy. We in our turn have an assured confidence that we shall be able to leave this heritage unwasted and enlarged to our children and our children's children. To do so we must show, not merely in great crises, but in the everyday affairs of life, the qualities of practical intelligence, of courage, of hardihood, and endurance, and above all the power of devotion to a lofty ideal, which made great the men who founded this Republic in the days of Washington, which made great the men who preserved this Republic in the days of Abraham Lincoln.

WILLIAM HOWARD TAFT

INAUGURAL ADDRESS

MARCH 4, 1909

COMMENTARY

When Roosevelt received the news of his election victory on November 8, 1904, he announced, perhaps a bit hastily, that "under no circumstances will I be a candidate for or accept another nomination." During 1906 and 1907 repeated reports circulated that the president planned to retract his declaration. But Roosevelt kept his word. By January 1908, he had decided that his secretary of war, William Howard Taft, would faithfully pursue his policies, and so designated him the heir apparent. The Republican convention, meeting in Chicago in June, obediently nominated Taft on the first ballot on a platform calling for a continuation of Roosevelt's programs. The Democrats again nominated William Jennings Bryan, declaring that popular government had been jeopardized by Roosevelt's personal selection of his successor. Both Bryan and Taft made extensive speaking tours but there was never much doubt of the final outcome. The nation remained prosperous and Bryan could not find an issue to rouse the voters. Taft received a popular vote of 7,677,788 to Bryan's 6,407,982. The electoral count gave 321 to Taft and 162 to Bryan. "I can never forget that the power I now exercise," Taft later wrote Roosevelt, "was voluntarily transferred from you to me and that I am under obligation to you to see that your judgment in selecting me as your successor and bringing about the succession shall be vindicated according to the standards which you and I . . . have always formulated."

When Taft took the oath of office on March 4, 1909, he faced a country that had forged ahead to the front rank of the manufacturing nations. The new industrial age had brought many material benefits to society—between 1900 and 1909 automobile output had increased some 3,500 percent, with a corresponding increase in the demand for glass, steel, rubber, and petroleum products. At the same time, these material benefits raised fundamental questions for a democratic nation. Could America ignore the social problems inherent in an industrial society? Essentially, the spirit of the era was optimistic and the nation's progressive leaders believed that the ideas of Jeffersonian democracy could be adjusted to the hard facts of the twentieth-century world. Roosevelt's administrations are significant because he helped shape the idea of a positive state where the national government assumes an expanded position in economic questions affecting the masses. "Under this interpretation of executive power," wrote Roosevelt, "I did and caused to be done many things not previously done by the President and the heads of departments. I did not usurp power, but I did greatly broaden the use of executive power. In other words, I acted for the public welfare, I acted for the common well-being of all our people." It remained to be seen whether his successor could continue in this direction.

My fellow citizens:

Anyone who has taken the oath I have just taken must feel a heavy weight of responsibility. If not, he has no conception of the powers and duties of the office upon which he is about to enter, or he is lacking in a proper sense of the obligation which the oath imposes.

The office of an inaugural address is to give a summary outline of the main policies of the new administration, so far as they can be anticipated. I have had the honor to be one of the advisers of my distinguished predecessor, and, as such, to hold up his hands in the reforms he has initiated. I should be untrue to myself, to my promises, and to the declarations of the party platform upon which I was elected to office, if I did not make the maintenance and enforcement of those reforms a most important feature of my administration. They were directed to the suppression of the lawlessness and abuses of power of the great combinations of capital invested in railroads and in industrial enterprises carrying on interstate commerce. The steps which my predecessor took and the legislation passed on his recommendation have accomplished much, have caused a general halt in the vicious policies which created popular alarm, and have brought about in the business affected a much higher regard for existing law.

To render the reforms lasting, however, and to secure at the same time freedom from alarm on the part of those pursuing proper and progressive business methods, further legislative and executive action are needed. Relief of the railroads from certain restrictions of the antitrust law have been urged by my predecessor and will be urged by me. On the other hand, the administration is pledged to legislation looking to a proper federal supervision and restriction to prevent excessive issues of bonds and stock by companies owning and operating interstate commerce railroads.

Then, too, a reorganization of the Department of Justice, of the Bureau of Corporations in the Department of Commerce and Labor, and of the Interstate Commerce Commission, looking to effective cooperation of these agencies, is needed to secure a more rapid and certain enforcement of the laws affecting interstate railroads and industrial combinations.

I hope to be able to submit at the first regular session of the incoming Congress, in December next, definite suggestions in respect to the needed amendments to the antitrust and the interstate commerce law and the changes required in the executive departments concerned in their enforcement.

It is believed that with the changes to be recommended American business can be assured of that measure of stability and certainty in respect to those things that may be done and those that are prohibited which is essential to the life and growth of all business. Such a plan must include the right of the people to avail themselves of those methods of combining capital and effort deemed necessary to reach the highest degree of economic efficiency, at the same time differentiating between combinations based upon legitimate economic reasons and those formed with the intent of creating monopolies and artificially controlling prices.

The work of formulating into practical shape such changes is creative work of the highest order, and requires all the deliberation possible in the interval. I believe that the amendments to be proposed are just as necessary in the protection of legitimate business as in the clinching of the reforms which properly bear the name of my predecessor.

A matter of most pressing importance is the revision of the tariff. In accordance with the promises of the platform upon which I was elected, I shall call Congress into extra session to meet on the 15th day of March, in order that consideration may be at once given to a bill revising the Dingley Act. This should secure an adequate revenue and adjust the duties in such a manner as to afford to labor and to all industries in this country, whether of the farm, mine or factory, protection by tariff equal to the difference between the cost of production abroad and the cost of production here, and have a provision which shall put into force, upon executive determination of certain facts, a higher or maximum tariff against those countries whose trade policy toward us equitably requires such discrimination. It is thought that there has been such a change in conditions since the enactment of the Dingley Act, drafted on a similarly protective principle, that the measure of the tariff above stated will permit the reduction of rates in certain schedules and will require the advancement of few, if any.

The proposal to revise the tariff made in such an authoritative way as to lead the business community to count upon it necessarily halts all those branches of business directly affected; and as these are most important, it disturbs the whole business of the country. It is imperatively necessary, therefore, that a tariff bill be drawn in good faith in accordance with promises made before the election by the party in power, and as promptly passed as due consideration will permit. It is not that the tariff is more important in the long run than the perfecting of the reforms in respect to antitrust legislation and interstate commerce regulation, but the need for action when the revision of the tariff has been determined upon is more immediate to avoid embarrassment of business. To secure the needed speed in the passage of the tariff bill, it would seem wise to attempt no other legislation at the extra session. I venture this as a suggestion only, for the course to be taken by Congress, upon the call of the Executive, is wholly within its discretion.

In the mailing of a tariff bill the prime motive is taxation and the securing thereby of a revenue. Due largely to the business depression which followed the financial panic of 1907, the revenue from customs and other sources has decreased to such an extent that the expenditures for the current fiscal year will exceed the receipts by $100,000,000. It is imperative that such a deficit shall not continue, and the framers of the tariff bill must, of course, have in mind the total revenues likely to be produced by it and so arrange the duties as to secure an adequate income. Should it be impossible to do so by import duties, new kinds of taxation must be adopted, and among these I recommend a graduated inheritance tax as correct in principle and as certain and easy of collection.

The obligation on the part of those responsible for the expenditures made to carry on the Government, to be as economical as possible, and to make the burden of taxation as light as possible, is plain, and should be affirmed in every declaration of government policy. This is especially true when we are face to face with a heavy deficit. But when the desire to win the popular approval leads to the cutting off of expenditures really needed to make the Government effective and to enable it to accomplish its proper objects, the result is as much to be condemned as the waste of government funds in unnecessary expenditure. The scope of a modern government in what it can and ought to accomplish for its people has been widened far beyond the principles laid down by the old laissez faire school of political writers, and this widening has met popular approval.

In the Department of Agriculture the use of scientific experiments on a large scale and the spread of information derived from them for the improvement of general agriculture must go on.

The importance of supervising business of great railways and industrial combinations and the necessary investigation and prosecution of unlawful business methods are another necessary tax upon Government which did not exist half a century ago.

The putting into force of laws which shall secure the conservation of our resources, so far as they may be within the jurisdiction of the Federal Government, including the most important work of saving and restoring our forests and the great improvement of waterways, are all proper government functions which must involve large expenditure if properly performed. While some of them, like the reclamation of arid lands, are made to pay for themselves, others are of such an indirect benefit that this cannot be expected of them. A permanent improvement, like the Panama Canal, should be treated as a distinct enterprise, and should be paid for by the proceeds of bonds, the issue of which will distribute its cost between the present and future generations in accordance with the benefits derived. It may well be submitted to the serious consideration of Congress whether the deepening and control of the channel of a great river system, like that of the Ohio or of the Mississippi, when definite and practical plans for the enterprise have been approved and determined upon, should not be provided for in the same way.

Then, too, there are expenditures of Government absolutely necessary if our country is to maintain its proper place among the nations of the world, and is to exercise its proper influence in defense of its own trade interests in the maintenance of traditional American policy against the colonization of European monarchies in this hemisphere, and in the promotion of peace and international morality. I refer to the cost of maintaining a proper army, a proper navy, and suitable fortifications upon the mainland of the United States and in its dependencies.

We should have an army so organized and so officered as to be capable in time of emergency, in cooperation with the national militia and under the provisions of a proper national volunteer law, rapidly to expand into a force sufficient to resist all probable invasion from abroad and to furnish a respectable expeditionary force if necessary in the maintenance of our traditional American policy which bears the name of President Monroe.

Our fortifications are yet in a state of only partial completeness, and the number of men to man them is insufficient. In a few years however, the usual annual appropriations for our coast defenses, both on the mainland and in the dependencies, will make them sufficient to resist all direct attack, and by that time we may hope that the men to man them will be provided as a necessary adjunct. The distance of our shores from Europe and Asia of course reduces the necessity for maintaining under arms a great army, but it does not take away the requirement of mere prudence; that we should have an army sufficiently large and so constituted as to form a nucleus out of which a suitable force can quickly grow.

What has been said of the army may be affirmed in even a more emphatic way of the navy. A modern navy can not be improvised. It must be built and in existence when the emergency arises which calls for its use and operation. My distinguished predecessor has in many speeches and messages set out with great force and striking language the necessity for maintaining a strong navy commensurate with the coast line, the governmental resources, and the foreign trade of our Nation; and I wish to reiterate all the reasons which he has presented in favor of the policy of maintaining a strong navy as the best conservator of our peace with other nations, and the best means of securing respect for the assertion of our rights, the defense of our interests, and the exercise of our influence in international matters.

Our international policy is always to promote peace. We shall enter into any war with a full consciousness of the awful consequences that it always entails, whether successful or not, and we, of course, shall make every effort consistent with national honor and the highest national interest to avoid a resort to arms. We favor every instrumentality, like that of the Hague Tribunal and arbitration treaties made with a view to its use in all international controversies, in order to maintain peace and to avoid war. But we should be blind to existing conditions and should allow ourselves to become foolish idealists if we did not realize that, with all the nations of the world armed and prepared for war, we must be ourselves in a similar condition, in order to prevent other nations from taking advantage of us and of our inability to defend our interests and assert our rights with a strong hand.

In the international controversies that are likely to arise in the Orient growing out of the question of the open door and other issues the United

States can maintain her interests intact and can secure respect for her just demands. She will not be able to do so, however, if it is understood that she never intends to back up her assertion of right and her defense of her interest by anything but mere verbal protest and diplomatic note. For these reasons the expenses of the army and navy and of coast defenses should always be considered as something which the Government must pay for, and they should not be cut off through mere consideration of economy. Our Government is able to afford a suitable army and a suitable navy. It may maintain them without the slightest danger to the Republic or the cause of free institutions, and fear of additional taxation ought not to change a proper policy in this regard.

The policy of the United States in the Spanish war and since has given it a position of influence among the nations that it never had before, and should be constantly exerted to securing to its bona fide citizens, whether native or naturalized, respect for them as such in foreign countries. We should make every effort to prevent humiliating and degrading prohibition against any of our citizens wishing temporarily to sojourn in foreign countries because of race or religion.

The admission of Asiatic immigrants who cannot be amalgamated with our population has been made the subject either of prohibitory clauses in our treaties and statutes or of strict administrative regulation secured by diplomatic negotiation. I sincerely hope that we may continue to minimize the evils likely to arise from such immigration without unnecessary friction and by mutual concessions between self-respecting governments. Meantime we must take every precaution to prevent, or failing that, to punish outbursts of race feeling among our people against foreigners of whatever nationality who have by our grant a treaty right to pursue lawful business here and to be protected against lawless assault or injury.

This leads me to point out a serious defect in the present federal jurisdiction, which ought to be remedied at once. Having assured to other countries by treaty the protection of our laws for such of their subjects or citizens as we permit to come within our jurisdiction, we now leave to a state or a city, not under the control of the Federal Government, the duty of performing our international obligations in this respect. By proper legislation we may, and ought to, place in the hands of the Federal Executive the means of enforcing the treaty rights of such aliens in the courts of the Federal Government. It puts our Government in a pusillanimous position to make definite engagements to protect aliens and then to excuse the fail-

ure to perform those engagements by an explanation that the duty to keep
them is in States or cities, not within our control. If we would promise we
must put ourselves in a position to perform our promise. We cannot permit
the possible failure of justice, due to local prejudice in any State or municipal government, to expose us to the risk of a war which might be avoided
if federal jurisdiction was asserted by suitable legislation by Congress and
carried out by proper proceedings instituted by the Executive in the courts
of the National Government.

One of the reforms to be carried out during the incoming administration is a change of our monetary and banking laws, so as to secure greater
elasticity in the forms of currency available for trade and to prevent the
limitations of law from operating to increase the embarrassment of a financial panic. The monetary commission, lately appointed, is giving full
consideration to existing conditions and to all proposed remedies, and will
doubtless suggest one that will meet the requirements of business and of
public interest.

We may hope that the report will embody neither the narrow dew of
those who believe that the sole purpose of the new system should be to secure
a large return on banking capital or of those who would have greater expansion of currency with little regard to provisions for its immediate redemption
or ultimate security. There is no subject of economic discussion so intricate
and so likely to evoke differing views and dogmatic statements as this one.
The commission, in studying the general influence of currency on business
and of business on currency, have wisely extended their investigations in
European banking and monetary methods. The information that they have
derived from such experts as they have found abroad will undoubtedly be
found helpful in the solution of the difficult problem they have in hand.

The incoming Congress should promptly fulfill the promise of the Republican platform and pass a proper postal savings bank bill. It will not be
unwise or excessive paternalism. The promise to repay by the Government
will furnish an inducement to savings deposits which private enterprise can
not supply and at such a low rate of interest as not to withdraw custom
from existing banks. It will substantially increase the funds available for
investment as capital in useful enterprises. It will furnish absolute security
which makes the proposed scheme of government guaranty of deposits so
alluring, without its pernicious results.

I sincerely hope that the incoming Congress will be alive, as it should
be, to the importance of our foreign trade and of encouraging it in every

way feasible. The possibility of increasing this trade in the Orient, in the Philippines, and in South America are known to everyone who has given the matter attention. The direct effect of free trade between this country and the Philippines will be marked upon our sales of cottons, agricultural machinery, and other manufactures. The necessity of the establishment of direct lines of steamers between North and South America has been brought to the attention of Congress by my predecessor and by Mr. Root before and after his noteworthy visit to that continent, and I sincerely hope that Congress may be induced to see the wisdom of a tentative effort to establish such lines by the use of mail subsidies.

The importance of the part which the Departments of Agriculture and of Commerce and Labor may play in ridding the markets of Europe of pro- hibitions and discriminations against the importation of our products is fully understood, and it is hoped that the use of the maximum and mini- mum feature of our tariff law to be soon passed will be effective to remove many of those restrictions.

The Panama Canal will have a most important bearing upon the trade between the eastern and far western sections of our country, and will greatly increase the facilities for transportation between the eastern and the western seaboard, and may possibly revolutionize the transcontinental rates with respect to bulky merchandise. It will also have a most beneficial effect to increase the trade between the eastern seaboard of the United States and the western coast of South America, and, indeed, with some of the important ports on the east coast of South America reached by rail from the west coast.

The work on the canal is making most satisfactory progress. The type of the canal as a lock canal was fixed by Congress after a full consideration of the conflicting reports of the majority and minority of the consulting board, and after the recommendation of the War Department and the Ex- ecutive upon those reports. Recent suggestion that something had occurred on the Isthmus to make the lock type of the canal less feasible than it was supposed to be when the reports were made and the policy determined on led to a visit to the Isthmus of a board of competent engineers to examine the Gatun dam and locks, which are the key of the lock type. The report of that board shows nothing has occurred in the nature of newly revealed evidence which should change the views once formed in the original dis- cussion. The construction will go on under a most effective organization controlled by Colonel Goethals and his fellow army engineers associated with him, and will certainly be completed early in the next administration, if not before.

Some type of canal must be constructed. The lock type has been selected. We are all in favor of having it built as promptly as possible. We must not now, therefore, keep up a fire in the rear of the agents whom we have authorized to do our work on the Isthmus. We must hold up their hands, and speaking for the incoming administration I wish to say that I propose to devote all the energy possible and under my control to pushing of this work on the plans which have been adopted, and to stand behind the men who are doing faithful, hard work to bring about the early completion of this, the greatest constructive enterprise of modern times.

The governments of our dependencies in Porto Rico and the Philippines are progressing as favorably as could be desired. The prosperity of Porto Rico continues unabated. The business conditions in the Philippines are not all that we could wish them to be, but with the passage of the new tariff bill permitting free trade between the United States and the archipelago, with such limitations on sugar and tobacco as shall prevent injury to domestic interests in those products, we can count on an improvement in business conditions in the Philippines and the development of a mutually profitable trade between this country and the islands. Meantime our Government in each dependency is upholding the traditions of civil liberty and increasing popular control which might be expected under American auspices. The work which we are doing there redounds to our credit as a nation.

I look forward with hope to increasing the already good feeling between the South and the other sections of the country. My chief purpose is not to effect a change in the electoral vote of the Southern States. That is a secondary consideration. What I look forward to is an increase in the tolerance of political views of all kinds and their advocacy throughout the South, and the existence of a respectable political opposition in every State; even more than this, to an increased feeling on the part of all the people in the South that this Government is their Government, and that its officers in their states are their officers.

The consideration of this question can not, however, be complete and full without reference to the negro race, its progress and its present condition. The thirteenth amendment secured them freedom; the fourteenth amendment due process of law, protection of property, and the pursuit of happiness; and the fifteenth amendment attempted to secure the negro against any deprivation of the privilege to vote because he was a negro.

The thirteenth and fourteenth amendments have been generally enforced and have secured the objects for which they are intended. While the fifteenth amendment has not been generally observed in the past, it ought to be observed, and the tendency of Southern legislation today is toward the enactment of electoral qualifications which shall square with that amendment. Of course, the mere adoption of a constitutional law is only one step in the right direction. It must be fairly and justly enforced as well. In time both will come. Hence it is clear to all that the domination of an ignorant, irresponsible element can be prevented by constitutional laws which shall exclude from voting both negroes and whites not having education or other qualifications thought to be necessary for a proper electorate. The danger of the control of an ignorant electorate has therefore passed. With this change, the interest which many of the Southern white citizens take in the welfare of the negroes has increased. The colored men must base their hope on the results of their own industry, self-restraint, thrift, and business success, as well as upon the aid and comfort and sympathy which they may receive from their white neighbors of the South.

There was a time when Northerners who sympathized with the negro in his necessary struggle for better conditions sought to give him the suffrage as a protection to enforce its exercise against the prevailing sentiment of the South. The movement proved to be a failure. What remains is the fifteenth amendment to the Constitution and the right to have statutes of States specifying qualifications for electors subjected to the test of compliance with that amendment. This is a great protection to the negro. It never will be repealed, and it never ought to be repealed. If it had not passed, it might be difficult now to adopt it; but with it in our fundamental law, the policy of Southern legislation must and will tend to obey it, and so long as the statutes of the States meet the test of this amendment and are not otherwise in conflict with the Constitution and laws of the United States, it is not the disposition or within the province of the Federal Government to interfere with the regulation by Southern States of their domestic affairs. There is in the South a stronger feeling than ever among the intelligent well-to-do, and influential element in favor of the industrial education of the negro and the encouragement of the race to make themselves useful members of the community. The progress which the negro has made in the last fifty years, from slavery, when its statistics are reviewed, is marvelous, and it furnishes every reason to hope that in the next twenty-five years a still greater improvement in his condition as a productive member of society, on the farm, and in the shop, and in other occupations may come.

The negroes are now Americans. Their ancestors came here years ago against their will, and this is their only country and their only flag. They have shown themselves anxious to live for it and to die for it. Encountering the race feeling against them, subjected at times to cruel injustice growing out of it, they may well have our profound sympathy and aid in the struggle they are making. We are charged with the sacred duty of making their path as smooth and easy as we can. Any recognition of their distinguished men, any appointment to office from among their number, is properly taken as an encouragement and an appreciation of their progress, and this just policy should be pursued when suitable occasion offers.

But it may well admit of doubt whether, in the case of any race, an appointment of one of their number to a local office in a community in which the race feeling is so widespread and acute as to interfere with the ease and facility with which the local government business can be done by the appointee is of sufficient benefit by way of encouragement to the race to outweigh the recurrence and increase of race feeling which such an appointment is likely to engender. Therefore the Executive, in recognizing the negro race by appointments, must exercise a careful discretion not thereby to do it more harm than good. On the other hand, we must be careful not to encourage the mere pretense of race feeling manufactured in the interest of individual political ambition.

Personally, I have not the slightest race prejudice or feeling, and recognition of its existence only awakens in my heart a deeper sympathy for those who have to bear it or suffer from it, and I question the wisdom of a policy which is likely to increase it. Meantime, if nothing is done to prevent it, a better feeling between the negroes and the whites in the South will continue to grow, and more and more of the white people will come to realize that the future of the South is to be much benefited by the industrial and intellectual progress of the negro. The exercise of political franchises by those of this race who are intelligent and well to do will be acquiesced in, and the right to vote will be withheld only from the ignorant and irresponsible of both races.

There is one other matter to which I shall refer. It was made the subject of great controversy during the election and calls for at least a passing reference now. My distinguished predecessor has given much attention to the cause of labor, with whose struggle for better things he has shown the sincerest sympathy. At his instance Congress has passed the bill fixing the liability of interstate carriers to their employees for injury sustained in the course of employment, abolishing the rule of fellow servant and the common-law rule as to contributory negligence, and substituting therefor the so-called rule of comparative negligence. It has also passed a law fixing the compensation of government employees for injuries sustained in the employ of the Government through the negligence of the superior. It has also passed a model child-labor law for the District of Columbia. In previous administrations an arbitration law for interstate commerce railroads and their employees, and laws for the application of safety devices to save the lives and limbs of employees of interstate railroads had been passed. Additional legislation of this kind was passed by the outgoing Congress.

I wish to say that insofar as I can I hope to promote the enactment of further legislation of this character. I am strongly convinced that the Government should make itself as responsible to employees injured in its employ as an interstate railway corporation is made responsible by federal law to its employees; and I shall be glad, whenever any additional reasonable safety device can be invented to reduce the loss of life and limb among railway employees, to urge Congress to require its adoption by interstate railways.

Another labor question has arisen which has awakened the most excited discussion. That is in respect to the power of the federal courts to issue injunctions in industrial disputes. As to that, my convictions are fixed. Take away from the courts, if it could be taken away, the power to issue injunctions in labor disputes, and it would create a privileged class among the laborers and save the lawless among their number from a most needful remedy available to all men for the protection of their business against lawless invasion. The proposition that business is not a property or pecuniary right which can be protected by equitable injunction is utterly without foundation in precedent or reason. The proposition is usually linked with one to make the secondary boycott lawful. Such a proposition is at variance with the American instinct, and will find no support, in my judgment, when submitted to the American people. The secondary boycott is an instrument of tyranny, and ought not to be made legitimate.

The issue of a temporary restraining order without notice has in several instances been abused by its inconsiderate exercise, and to remedy this the platform upon which I was elected recommends the formulation in a statute of the conditions under which such a temporary restraining order ought to issue. A statute can and ought to be framed to embody the best modern practice, and can bring the subject so closely to the attention of the court as to make abuses of the process unlikely in the future. The American people, if I understand them, insist that the authority of the courts shall be sustained, and are opposed to any change in the procedure by which the powers of a court may be weakened and the fearless and effective administration of justice be interfered with.

Having thus reviewed the questions likely to recur during my administration, and having expressed in a summary way the position which I expect to take in recommendations to Congress and in my conduct as an Executive, I invoke the considerate sympathy and support of my fellow-citizens and the aid of the Almighty God in the discharge of my responsible duties.

WOODROW WILSON

FIRST INAUGURAL ADDRESS

MARCH 4, 1913

COMMENTARY

Taft entered the presidency in 1909 after a solid election victory, but within two years only eastern conservative Republicans remained loyal to him. Progressives within the party were aroused by the president's support of the high, protective Payne-Aldrich Tariff Act (1909) despite his campaign pledge of downward revision. Taft's dismissal of the zealous conservationist Chief Forester Gifford Pinchot further widened the breach. These progressives, led by Senator Robert La Follette of Wisconsin, were convinced that Roosevelt's policies had been violated. Taft championed many liberal reforms—the Mann-Elkins Act of 1910, which strengthened the jurisdiction of the Interstate Commerce Commission, the Postal Savings Bank of 1910, as well as an antitrust program under which 90 proceedings were initiated against monopolies. Nevertheless, insurgent hostility grew. The president seemed to ignore major social reforms, especially the plight of the farmer and laborer, and increasingly accepted recommendations from the business community. The surprising triumph of these Republican insurgents in the 1910 congressional elections, as well as heavy Democratic gains, clearly indicated that the president's prestige had been weakened. Emboldened by their success and looking forward to the capture of the Republican Party in 1912, Taft's critics formed the National Progressive Republican League in 1911.

Theodore Roosevelt was now under increasing pressure from his friends to seek the 1912 Republican nomination. Roosevelt, who returned from an African hunting trip and a triumphal tour through Europe in June 1910, had avoided open criticism of his hand-picked successor. In several speeches, however, he enunciated his new creed, called the New Nationalism. "I stand for a square deal," he said. "But I mean not merely that I stand for fair play under the present rules of the game, but that I stand for having those rules changed so as to work for a more substantial equality of opportunity and reward." This new Roosevelt approach to social problems meant the abandonment of laissez faire and the assumption by the national government of new responsibilities. The Republican Progressives were overjoyed, especially as the rift between Taft and Roosevelt now widened. The restless energy of the former president, combined with additional evidence of Taft's conservatism, convinced Roosevelt of the necessity of entering the 1912 Republican primaries. "My hat is in the ring," he announced in February 1912.

The ensuing four months witnessed a lively fight for Republican delegates, a fight described by Roosevelt as "the most momentous struggle since the close of the Civil War." "This wrenches my soul," responded Taft. "I am here to reply to an old and true friend who has made many charges. I deny those charges. . . . I do not want to fight Theodore Roosevelt, but I am going to fight." A majority of states holding direct primaries chose pro-Roosevelt delegates, but the Old Guard controlled the convention machinery. Taft was renominated on the first ballot. Convinced that he had been cheated out of the nomination by corrupt politicians, Roosevelt now vowed to "find out whether the Republican Party is the party of the plain people or the party of the bosses." Amidst the hysterical shouts of his frenzied supporters, he announced his willingness to run on a third ticket "even if only one State should support me." On August 6, 1912, the new party, called the Progressive Party, obediently nominated their hero. "We have put forth," Roosevelt declared to the hastily summoned convention, "a platform which shall be a contract with the people." This dramatic split within Republican ranks virtually assured the victory of the Democratic candidate.

The Democrats, realizing that the White House was within their grasp, battled fiercely before selecting their nominee. On the forty-sixth ballot, the convention chose Governor Woodrow Wilson of New Jersey. The party's standard-bearer, a former president of Princeton University, had made an impressive record as a progressive governor championing a workmen's compensation act, a direct primary law, ballot reform, and a state corrupt practices act. The ensuing campaign was the first serious three-cornered presidential contest since 1860. Roosevelt's New Nationalism called for the extension of federal powers while Wilson's New Freedom stressed his faith in the states. Neither denied the need for political and social change. Taft had privately conceded defeat by July, as it grew *apparent that the real contest was between Wilson and Roosevelt. Wilson carried 40 states, receiving 435 electoral votes. Roosevelt won 88 electoral votes, and Taft carried only Vermont and Utah with their 8 votes. Despite this sweeping electoral triumph, Wilson received but 42 percent of the popular vote. His victory was the direct result of the Republican split. Wilson polled 6,286,124 votes, Roosevelt 4,126,020, Taft 3,483,922, and Eugene V. Debs, the Socialist candidate, 897,000. The Democrats also carried the House of Representatives by 290 to 145 and the Senate by 51 to 45. The election demonstrated a clear-cut victory for the progressives and an overwhelming defeat for defenders of the status quo.*

Wilson insisted that his inauguration be made as simple as possible. He decided against an inaugural ball; no president since Pierce had objected to this established institution. On March 4, 1913, Chief Justice White administered the oath and then Wilson delivered his simple but sincere address. Just before the ceremonies began, the president-elect noticed that the police had kept the people far back, leaving a wide open space before the speaker's platform. "Let the people come forward," Wilson instructed a guard. And they did. Many admirers seized upon this sentence as the symbol of the new administration.

My fellow citizens:

There has been a change of government. It began two years ago, when the House of Representatives became Democratic by a decisive majority. It has now been completed. The Senate about to assemble will also be Democratic. The offices of President and Vice President have been put into the hands of Democrats. What does the change mean? That is the question that is uppermost in our minds to-day. That is the question I am going to try to answer, in order, if I may, to interpret the occasion.

It means much more than the mere success of a party. The success of a party means little except when the Nation is using that party for a large and definite purpose. No one can mistake the purpose for which the Nation now seeks to use the Democratic Party. It seeks to use it to interpret a change in its own plans and point of view. Some old things with which we had grown familiar, and which had begun to creep into the very habit of our thought and of our lives, have altered their aspect as we have latterly looked critically upon them, with fresh, awakened eyes; have dropped their disguises and shown themselves alien and sinister. Some new things, as we look frankly upon them, willing to comprehend their real character, have come to assume the aspect of things long believed in and familiar, stuff of our own convictions. We have been refreshed by a new insight into our own life.

We see that in many things that life is very great. It is incomparably great in its material aspects, in its body of wealth, in the diversity and sweep of its energy, in the industries which have been conceived and built up by the genius of individual men and the limitless enterprise of groups of men. It is great, also, very great, in its moral force. Nowhere else in the world have noble men and women exhibited in more striking forms the beauty and the energy of sympathy and helpfulness and counsel in their efforts to rectify wrong, alleviate suffering, and set the weak in the way of strength and hope. We have built up, moreover, a great system of government, which has stood through a long age as in many respects a model for those who seek to set liberty upon foundations that will endure against fortuitous change, against storm and accident. Our life contains every great thing, and contains it in rich abundance.

But the evil has come with the good, and much fine gold has been corroded. With riches has come inexcusable waste. We have squandered a great part of what we might have used, and have not stopped to conserve the exceeding bounty of nature, without which our genius for enterprise would have been worthless and impotent, scorning to be careful, shamefully prodigal as well as admirably efficient. We have been proud of our industrial achievements, but we have not hitherto stopped thoughtfully enough to count the human cost, the cost of lives snuffed out, of energies overtaxed and broken, the fearful physical and spiritual cost to the men and women and children upon whom the dead weight and burden of it all has fallen pitilessly the years through. The groans and agony of it all had not yet reached our ears, the solemn, moving undertone of our life, coming up out of the mines and factories, and out of every home where the struggle had its intimate and familiar seat. With the great Government went many deep secret things which we too long delayed to look into and scrutinize with candid, fearless eyes. The great Government we loved has too often been made use of for private and selfish purposes, and those who used it had forgotten the people.

At last a vision has been vouchsafed us of our life as a whole. We see the bad with the good, the debased and decadent with the sound and vital. With this vision we approach new affairs. Our duty is to cleanse, to reconsider, to restore, to correct the evil without impairing the good, to purify and humanize every process of our common life without weakening or sentimentalizing it. There has been something crude and heartless and unfeeling in our haste to succeed and be great. Our thought has been Let every man look out for himself, let every generation look out for itself, while we reared giant machinery which made it impossible that any but those who stood at the levers of control should have a chance to look out for themselves. We had not forgotten our morals. We remembered well enough that we had set up a policy which was meant to serve the humblest as well as the most powerful, with an eye single to the standards of justice and fair play, and remembered it with pride. But we were very heedless and in a hurry to be great.

We have come now to the sober second thought. The scales of heedlessness have fallen from our eyes. We have made up our minds to square every process of our national life again with the standards we so proudly set up at the beginning and have always carried at our hearts. Our work is a work of restoration.

We have itemized with some degree of particularity the things that ought to be altered and here are some of the chief items: A tariff which cuts us off from our proper part in the commerce of the world, violates the just principles of taxation, and makes the Government a facile instrument in the hand of private interests; a banking and currency system based upon the necessity of the Government to sell its bonds fifty years ago and perfectly adapted to concentrating cash and restricting credits; an industrial system which, take it on all its sides, financial as well as administrative, holds capital in leading strings, restricts the liberties and limits the opportunities of labor, and exploits without renewing or conserving the natural resources of the country; a body of agricultural activities never yet given the efficiency of great business undertakings or served as it should be through the instrumentality of science taken directly to the farm, or afforded the facilities of credit best suited to its practical needs; watercourses undeveloped, waste places unreclaimed, forests untended, fast disappearing without plan or prospect of renewal, unregarded waste heaps at every mine. We have studied as perhaps no other nation has the most effective means of production, but we have not studied cost or economy as we should either as organizers of industry, as statesmen, or as individuals.

Nor have we studied and perfected the means by which government may be put at the service of humanity, in safeguarding the health of the Nation, the health of its men and its women and its children, as well as their rights in the struggle for existence. This is no sentimental duty. The firm basis of government is justice, not pity. These are matters of justice. There can be no equality or opportunity, the first essential of justice in the body politic, if men and women and children be not shielded in their lives, their very vitality, from the consequences of great industrial and social processes which they can not alter, control, or singly cope with. Society must see to it that it does not itself crush or weaken or damage its own constituent parts. The first duty of law is to keep sound the society it serves. Sanitary laws, pure food laws, and laws determining conditions of labor which individuals are powerless to determine for themselves are intimate parts of the very business of justice and legal efficiency.

These are some of the things we ought to do, and not leave the others undone, the old fashioned, never to be neglected, fundamental safeguarding of property and of individual right. This is the high enterprise of the new day: To lift everything that concerns our life as a Nation to the light that shines from the hearthfire of every man's conscience and vision of the right. It is inconceivable that we should do this as partisans; it is inconceivable we should do it in ignorance of the facts as they are or in blind haste. We shall restore, not destroy. We shall deal with our economic system as it is and as it may be modified, not as it might be if we had a clean sheet of paper to write upon; and step by step we shall make it what it should be, in the spirit of those who question their own wisdom and seek counsel and knowledge, not shallow self-satisfaction or the excitement of excursions whither they can not tell. Justice, and only justice, shall always be our motto.

And yet it will be no cool process of mere science. The Nation has been deeply stirred, stirred by a solemn passion, stirred by the knowledge of wrong, of ideals lost, of government too often debauched and made an instrument of evil. The feelings with which we face this new age of right and opportunity sweep across our heartstrings like some air out of God's own presence, where justice and mercy are reconciled and the judge and the brother are one. We know our task to be no mere task of politics but a task which shall search us through and through, whether we be able to understand our time and the need of our people, whether we be indeed their spokesmen and interpreters, whether we have the pure heart to comprehend and the rectified will to choose our high course of action.

This is not a day of triumph. It is a day of dedication. Here muster, not the forces of party, but the forces of humanity. Men's hearts wait upon us; men's lives hang in the balance; men's hopes call upon us to say what we will do. Who shall live up to the great trust? Who dares fail to try? I summon all honest men, all patriotic, all forward-looking men, to my side. God helping me, I will not fail them, if they will but counsel and sustain me.

───── SECOND INAUGURAL ADDRESS ─────

MARCH 5, 1917

COMMENTARY

Wilson's talent for leadership, combined with the progressive temper of the times, resulted in an amazing spurt of legislation. After four years in the White House, the president confidently stated that "no equal period in our history has been so fruitful of important reforms in our economic and industrial life or so full of significant changes in the spirit and purpose of our political action." This adroit chief executive had established his firm control over both Congress and the Democratic Party. Tariff reductions, banking reforms, stronger antimonopoly legislation, assistance to agriculture, and conservation legislation—the major progressive demands—had been enacted into law. Wilson thought the New Freedom legislation had righted fundamental wrongs. Although more advanced progressives questioned whether Wilson understood the far-reaching social and economic tensions of the day, there can be no doubt that his first administration represents the climax of an era of reform and the end of an era of peace.

Outbreak of war in Europe in August 1914 stunned Americans. Europe had been on the brink of a conflict for more than a decade, but when the clash came most Americans were shocked at the thought of organized slaughter. On August 19, Wilson appealed to the nation to remain impartial in thought, as well as in action. Nevertheless, sentiment against Germany grew. The president himself, an ardent admirer of the British parliamentary system, privately confided as early as August 30, 1914, that "if Germany wins, it will change the course of our civilization, and make the United States a military nation." Both the American people and the administration, however, desired neutrality. Throughout 1915 and 1916, the president, his patience often frayed by provoking British and German incidents, attempted to follow this course.

Wilson received the Democratic nomination by acclamation on June 15, 1916. The platform proudly recounted the achievements of the first Democratic administration since 1897. Above all, the delegates acclaimed Wilson's handling of the problems caused by the European conflict. "He kept us out of war" became the party's rallying cry. To oppose the president, the Republicans selected Charles Evans Hughes, an associate justice of the U.S. Supreme Court and former reform governor of New York. Although Theodore Roosevelt returned to the Republican fold, many of his 1912 supporters backed Wilson. The election proved extremely close. But Wilson managed to transform his plurality of 1912 into a resounding majority, receiving 9,129,600 votes as opposed to 8,538,221 for Hughes, a gain for Wilson of nearly 3 million. The electoral vote stood 277 to 254, the closest division since 1876. Democrats again captured both houses of Congress. The president accepted his reelection as an endorsement of his domestic policies and as a mandate to keep the nation out of war, at least as long as that remained possible.

On Sunday, March 4, 1917, Woodrow Wilson took his second oath with only the cabinet and a few personal friends present. The following day, more than 50,000 people heard the president repeat the oath and deliver his short inaugural address.

My fellow citizens:

The four years which have elapsed since last I stood in this place have been crowded with counsel and action of the most vital interest and consequence. Perhaps no equal period in our history has been so fruitful of important reforms in our economic and industrial life or so full of significant changes in the spirit and purpose of our political action. We have sought very thoughtfully to set our house in order, correct the grosser errors and abuses of our industrial life, liberate and quicken the processes of our national genius and energy, and lift our politics to a broader view of the people's essential interests.

It is a record of singular variety and singular distinction. But I shall not attempt to review it. It speaks for itself and will be of increasing influence as the years go by. This is not the time for retrospect. It is time rather to speak our thoughts and purposes concerning the present and the immediate future.

Although we have centered counsel and action with such unusual concentration and success upon the great problems of domestic legislation to which we addressed ourselves four years ago, other matters have more and more forced themselves upon our attention; matters lying outside our own life as a nation and over which we had no control, but which, despite our wish to keep free of them, have drawn us more and more irresistibly into their own current and influence.

It has been impossible to avoid them. They have affected the life of the whole world. They have shaken men everywhere with a passion and an apprehension they never knew before. It has been hard to preserve calm counsel while the thought of our own people swayed this way and that under their influence. We are a composite and cosmopolitan people. We are of the blood of all the nations that are at war. The currents of our thoughts as well as the currents of our trade run quick at all seasons back and forth between us and them. The war inevitably set its mark from the first alike upon our minds, our industries, our commerce, our politics and our social action. To be indifferent to it, or independent of it, was out of the question.

And yet all the while we have been conscious that we were not part of it. In that consciousness, despite many divisions, we have drawn closer together. We have been deeply wronged upon the seas, but we have not wished to wrong or injure in return; have retained throughout the consciousness of standing in some sort apart, intent upon an interest that transcended the immediate issues of the war itself.

As some of the injuries done us have become intolerable we have still been clear that we wished nothing for ourselves that we were not ready to demand for all mankind; fair dealing, justice, the freedom to live and to be at ease against organized wrong.

It is in this spirit and with this thought that we have grown more and more aware, more and more certain that the part we wished to play was the part of those who mean to vindicate and fortify peace. We have been obliged to arm ourselves to make good our claim to a certain minimum of right and of freedom of action. We stand firm in armed neutrality since it seems that in no other way we can demonstrate what it is we insist upon and cannot forget. We may even be drawn on, by circumstances, not by our own purpose or desire, to a more active assertion of our rights as we see them and a more immediate association with the great struggle itself. But nothing will alter our thought or our purpose. They are too clear to be obscured. They are too deeply rooted in the principles of our national life to be altered. We desire neither conquest nor advantage. We wish nothing that can be had only at the cost of another people. We always professed unselfish purpose and we covet the opportunity to prove our professions are sincere.

There are many things still to be done at home, to clarify our own politics and add new vitality to the industrial processes of our own life, and we shall do them as time and opportunity serve, but we realize that the greatest things that remain to be done must be done with the whole world for stage and in cooperation with the wide and universal forces of mankind, and we are making our spirits ready for those things.

We are provincials no longer. The tragic events of the thirty months of vital turmoil through which we have just passed have made us citizens of the world. There can be no turning back. Our own fortunes as a nation are involved whether we would have it so or not.

And yet we are not the less Americans on that account. We shall be the more American if we but remain true to the principles in which we have been bred. They are not the principles of a province or of a single continent. We have known and boasted all along that they were the principles of a liberated mankind. These, therefore, are the things we shall stand for, whether in war or in peace:

That all nations are equally interested in the peace of the world and in the political stability of free peoples, and equally responsible for their maintenance; that the essential principle of peace is the actual equality of nations in all matters of right or privilege; that peace cannot securely or justly rest upon an armed balance of power; that governments derive all their just powers from the consent of the governed and that no other powers should be supported by the common thought, purpose or power of the family of nations; that the seas should be equally free and safe for the use of all peoples, under rules set up by common agreement and consent, and that, so far as practicable, they should be accessible to all upon equal terms; that national armaments shall be limited to the necessities of national order and domestic safety; that the community of interest and of power upon which peace must henceforth depend imposes upon each nation the duty of seeing to it that all influences proceeding from its own citizens meant to encourage or assist revolution in other states should be sternly and effectually suppressed and prevented.

I need not argue these principles to you, my fellow countrymen; they are your own part and parcel of your own thinking and your own motives in affairs. They spring up native amongst us. Upon this as a platform of purpose and of action we can stand together. And it is imperative that we should stand together. We are being forged into a new unity amidst the fires that now blaze throughout the world. In their ardent heat we shall, in God's Providence, let us hope, be purged of faction and division, purified of the errant humors of party and of private interest, and shall stand forth in the days to come with a new dignity of national pride and spirit. Let each man see to it that the dedication is in his own heart, the high purpose of the nation in his own mind, ruler of his own will and desire.

I stand here and have taken the high and solemn oath to which you have been audience because the people of the United States have chosen me for this august delegation of power and have by their gracious judgment named me their leader in affairs.

I know now what the task means. I realize to the full the responsibility which it involves. I pray God I may be given the wisdom and the prudence to do my duty in the true spirit of this great people. I am their servant and can succeed only as they sustain and guide me by their confidence and their counsel. The thing I shall count upon, the thing without which neither counsel nor action will avail, is the unity of America, an America united in feeling, in purpose and in its vision of duty, of opportunity and of service.

We are to beware of all men who would turn the tasks and the necessities of the nation to their own private profit or use them for the building up of private power.

United alike in the conception of our duty and in the high resolve to perform it in the face of all men, let us dedicate ourselves to the great task to which we must now set our hand. For myself I beg your tolerance, your countenance and your united aid.

The shadows that now lie dark upon our path will soon be dispelled, and we shall walk with the light all about us if we be but true to ourselves—to ourselves as we have wished to be known in the counsels of the world and in the thought of all those who love liberty and justice and the right exalted.

WARREN G. HARDING

INAUGURAL ADDRESS

MARCH 4, 1921

COMMENTARY

The election of 1920 represents a repudiation of Wilsonian idealism. After being involved in a horrible war, the nation had grown tired of crusades to "make the world safe for democracy." Combined Allied war losses were staggering. Of the 65 million men mobilized for combat, 10 million had been killed and some 20 million wounded. The war left in its wake a bitter disillusionment. Wilson had spoken of a new dawning for democracy, but the harsh realities of the peace treaties embittered many. At home, the president's hope for a better world through the League of Nations had been defeated by the Senate. Strikes flared up throughout the country, involving more than 4 million workers in 1919. Programs lagged for easing men back into peacetime activities. Wilson had become, in Mark Sullivan's words, "the symbol of the exaltation that has turned sour, personification of the rapture that has now become gall, sacrificial whipping boy for the present bitterness."

By the beginning of 1920, most political observers predicted that any Republican candidate would be elected. Meeting in Chicago on June 8, the Republican convention chose Senator Warren Harding of Ohio on the tenth ballot. Harding, a handsome, gregarious, and amiable party regular, with a notably undistinguished senatorial record, represented this return to "normalcy." He made no pretense to intellectualism and even friends described him as a second-rater. Above all, Harding "looked like a president" and appeared willing to cooperate with the party bosses. Governor Calvin Coolidge of Massachusetts was nominated for vice president. Coolidge had gained nationwide prominence for his statement in connection with the 1919 Boston police strike:

"There is no right to strike against the public safety, by any body, any where, any time." The Republican platform remained intentionally vague on the important League of Nations issue. It pledged the party "to such agreement with other nations of the world as shall meet the full duty of America to civilization and humanity."

The deeply divided Democratic convention selected Governor James Cox of Ohio on the forty-ninth ballot and the vice presidential nomination went to the wartime assistant secretary of the Navy, Franklin D. Roosevelt, then 38 years old. Cox and Roosevelt waged a vigorous campaign that took them to every section of the country. They supported Wilson's domestic policies and the League of Nations. Harding, on the other hand, remained at his Marion home making few speeches marked by extremely vague and often meaningless phrases. William McAdoo did not exaggerate when he said that Harding's speeches left "the impression of an army of pompous phrases moving over the landscape in search of an idea; sometimes these meandering words would actually capture a straggling thought and bear it triumphantly, a prisoner in their midst, until it died of servitude and overwork." But the election results were a foregone conclusion. Harding swept the country, carrying 37 states and receiving 16,152,220 votes to 9,147,353 for Cox. Harding captured New York City's five boroughs as well as every county on the Pacific Coast. For the first time in history, Tennessee went Republican. The Republicans also won majorities in both the House and Senate. Joseph Tumulty, Wilson's former secretary, commented, "It wasn't a landslide, it was an earthquake."

<hr />

My countrymen:

When one surveys the world about him after the great storm, noting the marks of destruction and yet rejoicing in the ruggedness of the things which withstood it, if he is an American he breathes the clarified atmosphere with a strange mingling of regret and new hope. We have seen a world passion spend its fury, but we contemplate our Republic unshaken, and hold our civilization secure. Liberty, liberty within the law, and civilization are inseparable, and though both were threatened we find them now secure; and there comes to Americans the profound assurance that our representative government is the highest expression and surest guaranty of both.

Standing in this presence, mindful of the solemnity of this occasion, feeling the emotions which no one may know until he senses the great weight of responsibility for himself, I must utter my belief in the divine inspiration of the founding fathers. Surely there must have been God's intent in the making of this new world Republic. Ours is an organic law which had but one ambiguity, and we saw that effaced in a baptism of sacrifice and blood, with union maintained, the Nation supreme, and its concord inspiring. We have seen the world rivet its hopeful gaze on the great truths on which the founders wrought. We have seen civil, human, and religious liberty verified and glorified. In the beginning the Old World scoffed at our experiment; today our foundations of political and social belief stand unshaken, a precious inheritance to ourselves, an inspiring example of freedom and civilization to all mankind. Let us express renewed and strengthened devotion, in grateful reverence for the immortal beginning, and utter our confidence in the supreme fulfillment.

The recorded progress of our Republic, materially and spiritually, in itself proves the wisdom of the inherited policy of non-involvement in Old World affairs. Confident of our ability to work out our own destiny, and jealously guarding our right to do so, we seek no part in directing the destinies of the Old World. We do not mean to be entangled. We will accept no responsibility except as our own conscience and judgment, in each instance, may determine.

Our eyes never will be blind to a developing menace, our ears never deaf to the call of civilization. We recognize the new order in the world, with the closer contacts which progress has wrought. We sense the call of the human heart for fellowship, fraternity, and cooperation. We crave friendship and harbor no hate. But America, our America, the America builded on the foundation laid by the inspired fathers, can be a party to no permanent military alliance. It can enter into no political commitments, nor assume any economic obligations which will subject our decisions to any other than our own authority.

I am sure our own people will not misunderstand, nor will the world misconstrue. We have no thought to impede the paths to closer relationship. We wish to promote understanding. We want to do our part in making offensive warfare so hateful that Governments and peoples who resort to it must prove the righteousness of their cause or stand as outlaws before the bar of civilization.

We are ready to associate ourselves with the nations of the world, great and small, for conference, for counsel; to seek the expressed views of world opinion; to recommend a way to approximate disarmament and relieve the crushing burdens of military and naval establishments. We elect to participate in suggesting plans for mediation, conciliation, and arbitration, and would gladly join in that expressed conscience of progress, which seeks to clarify and write the laws of international relationship, and establish a world court for the disposition of such justiciable questions as nations are agreed to submit thereto. In expressing aspirations, in seeking practical plans, in translating humanity's new concept of righteousness and justice and its hatred of war into recommended action we are ready most heartily to unite, but every commitment must be made in the exercise of our national sovereignty. Since freedom impelled, and independence inspired, and nationality exalted, a world supergovernment is contrary to everything we cherish and can have no sanction by our Republic. This is not selfishness, it is sanctity. It is not aloofness, it is security. It is not suspicion of others, it is patriotic adherence to the things which made us what we are.

Today, better than ever before, we know the aspirations of humankind, and share them. We have come to a new realization of our place in the world and a new appraisal of our Nation by the world. The unselfishness of these United States is a thing proven; our devotion to peace for ourselves and for the world is well established; our concern for preserved civilization has had its impassioned and heroic expression. There was no American failure to resist the attempted reversion of civilization; there will be no failure today or tomorrow.

The success of our popular government rests wholly upon the correct interpretation of the deliberate, intelligent, dependable popular will of America. In a deliberate questioning of a suggested change of national policy, where internationality was to supersede nationality, we turned to a referendum, to the American people. There was ample discussion, and there is a public mandate in manifest understanding.

America is ready to encourage, eager to initiate, anxious to participate in any seemly program likely to lessen the probability of war, and promote that brotherhood of mankind which must be God's highest conception of human relationship. Because we cherish ideals of justice and peace, because we appraise international comity and helpful relationship no less highly than any people of the world, we aspire to a high place in the moral leadership of civilization, and we hold a maintained America, the proven Republic, the unshaken temple of representative democracy, to be not only an inspiration and example, but the highest agency of strengthening good will and promoting accord on both continents.

Mankind needs a worldwide benediction of understanding. It is needed among individuals, among peoples, among governments, and it will inaugurate an era of good feeling to make the birth of a new order. In such understanding men will strive confidently for the promotion of their better relationships and nations will promote the comities so essential to peace.

We must understand that ties of trade bind nations in closest intimacy, and none may receive except as he gives. We have not strengthened ours in accordance with our resources or our genius, notably on our own continent, where a galaxy of Republics reflects the glory of new world democracy, but in the new order of finance and trade we mean to promote enlarged activities and seek expanded confidence.

Perhaps we can make no more helpful contribution by example than prove a Republic's capacity to emerge from the wreckage of war. While the world's embittered travail did not leave us devastated lands nor desolated cities, left no gaping wounds, no breast with hate, it did involve us in the delirium of expenditure, in expanded currency and credits, in unbalanced industry, in unspeakable waste, and disturbed relationships. While it uncovered our portion of hateful selfishness at home, it also revealed the heart of America as sound and fearless, and beating in confidence unfailing.

Amid it all we have riveted the gaze of all civilization to the unselfishness and the righteousness of representative democracy, where our freedom never has made offensive warfare, never has sought territorial aggrandizement through force, never has turned to the arbitrament of arms until reason has been exhausted. When the Governments of the earth shall have established a freedom like our own and shall have sanctioned the pursuit of peace as we have practiced it, I believe the last sorrow and the final sacrifice of international warfare will have been written.

Let me speak to the maimed and wounded soldiers who are present today, and through them convey to their comrades the gratitude of the Republic for their sacrifices in its defense. A generous country will never forget the services you rendered, and you may hope for a policy under Government that will relieve any maimed successors from taking your places on another such occasion as this.

Our supreme task is the resumption of our onward, normal way. Reconstruction, readjustment, restoration all these must follow. I would like to hasten them. If it will lighten the spirit and add to the resolution with which we take up the task, let me repeat for our Nation, we shall give no people just cause to make war upon us; we hold no national prejudices; we entertain no spirit of revenge; we do not hate; we do not covet; we dream of no conquest, nor boast of armed prowess.

If, despite this attitude, war is again forced upon us, I earnestly hope a way may be found which will unify our individual and collective strength and consecrate all America, materially and spiritually, body and soul, to national defense. I can vision the ideal republic, where every man and woman is called under the flag for assignment to duty for whatever service, military or civic, the individual is best fitted; where we may call to universal service every plant, agency, or facility, all in the sublime sacrifice for country, and not one penny of war profit shall inure to the benefit of private individual, corporation, or combination, but all above the normal shall flow into the defense chest of the Nation. There is something inherently wrong, something out of accord with the ideals of representative democracy, when one portion of our citizenship turns its activities to private gain amid defensive war while another is fighting, sacrificing, or dying for national preservation.

Out of such universal service will come a new unity of spirit and purpose, a new confidence and consecration, which would make our defense impregnable, our triumph assured. Then we should have little or no disorganization of our economic, industrial, and commercial systems at home, no staggering war debts, no swollen fortunes to flout the sacrifices of our soldiers, no excuse for sedition, no pitiable slackerism, no outrage of treason. Envy and jealousy would have no soil for their menacing development, and revolution would be without the passion which engenders it.

A regret for the mistakes of yesterday must not, however, blind us to the tasks of today. War never left such an aftermath. There has been staggering loss of life and measureless wastage of materials. Nations are still groping for return to stable ways. Discouraging indebtedness confronts us like all the war torn nations, and these obligations must be provided for. No civilization can survive repudiation.

We can reduce the abnormal expenditures, and we will. We can strike at war taxation, and we must. We must face the grim necessity, with full knowledge that the task is to be solved, and we must proceed with a full realization that no statute enacted by man can repeal the inexorable laws of nature. Our most dangerous tendency is to expect too much of government, and at the same time do for it too little. We contemplate the immediate task of putting our public household in order. We need a rigid and yet sane economy, combined with fiscal justice, and it must be attended by individual prudence and thrift, which are so essential to this trying hour and reassuring for the future.

The business world reflects the disturbance of war's reaction. Herein flows the lifeblood of material existence. The economic mechanism is intricate and its parts interdependent, and has suffered the shocks and jars incident to abnormal demands, credit inflations, and price upheavals. The normal balances have been impaired, the channels of distribution have been clogged, the relations of labor and management have been strained. We must seek the readjustment with care and courage. Our people must give and take. Prices must reflect the receding fever of war activities. Perhaps we never shall know the old levels of wages again, because war invariably readjusts compensations, and the necessaries of life will show their inseparable relationship, but we must strive for normalcy to reach stability. All the penalties will not be light, nor evenly distributed. There is no way of making them so. There is no instant step from disorder to order. We must face a condition of grim reality, charge off our losses and start afresh. It is the oldest lesson of civilization. I would like government to do all it can to mitigate; then, in understanding, in mutuality of interest, in concern for the common good, our tasks will be solved. No altered system will work a miracle. Any wild experiment will only add to the confusion. Our best assurance lies in efficient administration of our proven system.

The forward course of the business cycle is unmistakable. Peoples are turning from destruction to production. Industry has sensed the changed order and our own people are turning to resume their normal, onward way. The call is for productive America to go on. I know that Congress and the Administration will favor every wise Government policy to aid the resumption and encourage continued progress.

I speak for administrative efficiency, for lightened tax burdens, for sound commercial practices, for adequate credit facilities, for sympathetic concern for all agricultural problems, for the omission of unnecessary interference of Government with business, for an end to Government's experiment in business, and for more efficient business in Government administration. With all of this must attend a mindfulness of the human side of all activities, so that social, industrial, and economic justice will be squared with the purposes of a righteous people.

With the nation-wide induction of womanhood into our political life, we may count upon her intuitions, her refinements, her intelligence, and her influence to exalt the social order. We count upon her exercise of the full privileges and the performance of the duties of citizenship to speed the attainment of the highest state.

I wish for an America no less alert in guarding against dangers from within than it is watchful against enemies from without. Our fundamental law recognizes no class, no group, no section; there must be none in legislation or administration. The supreme inspiration is the common weal. Humanity hungers for international peace, and we crave it with all mankind. My most reverent prayer for America is for industrial peace, with its rewards, widely and generally distributed, amid the inspirations of equal opportunity. No one justly may deny the equality of opportunity which made us what we are. We have mistaken unpreparedness to embrace it to be a challenge of the reality, and due concern for making all citizens fit for participation will give added strength of citizenship and magnify our achievement.

If revolution insists upon overturning established order, let other peoples make the tragic experiment. There is no place for it in America. When World War threatened civilization we pledged our resources and our lives to its preservation, and when revolution threatens we unfurl the flag of law and order and renew our consecration. Ours is a constitutional freedom where the popular will is the law supreme and minorities are sacredly protected. Our revisions, reformations, and evolutions reflect a deliberate judgment and an orderly progress, and we mean to cure our ills, but never destroy or permit destruction by force.

I had rather submit our industrial controversies to the conference table in advance than to a settlement table after conflict and suffering. The earth is thirsting for the cup of good will, understanding is its fountain source. I would like to acclaim an era of good feeling amid dependable prosperity and all the blessings which attend.

It has been proved again and again that we cannot, while throwing our markets open to the world, maintain American standards of living and opportunity, and hold our industrial eminence in such unequal competition. There is a luring fallacy in the theory of banished barriers of trade, but preserved American standards require our higher production costs to be reflected in our tariffs on imports. Today, as never before, when peoples are seeking trade restoration and expansion, we must adjust our tariffs to the new order. We seek participation in the world's exchanges, because therein lies our way to widened influence and the triumphs of peace. We know full well we cannot sell where we do not buy, and we cannot sell successfully where we do not carry. Opportunity is calling not alone for the restoration, but for a new era in production, transportation and trade. We shall answer it best by meeting the demand of a surpassing home market, by promoting self-reliance in production, and by bidding enterprise, genius, and efficiency to carry our cargoes in American bottoms to the marts of the world.

We would not have an America living within and for herself alone, but we would have her self-reliant, independent, and ever nobler, stronger, and richer. Believing in our higher standards, reared through constitutional liberty and maintained opportunity, we invite the world to the same heights. But pride in things wrought is no reflex of a completed task. Common welfare is the goal of our national endeavor. Wealth is not inimical to welfare; it ought to be its friendliest agency. There never can be equality of rewards or possessions so long as the human plan contains varied talents and differing degrees of industry and thrift, but ours ought to be a country free from the great blotches of distressed poverty. We ought to find a way to guard against the perils and penalties of unemployment. We want an America of homes, illumined with hope and happiness, where mothers, freed from the necessity for long hours of toil beyond their own doors, may preside as befits the hearthstone of American citizenship. We want the cradle of American childhood rocked under conditions so wholesome and so hopeful that no blight may touch it in its development, and we want to provide that no selfish interest, no material necessity, no lack of opportunity shall prevent the gaining of that education so essential to best citizenship.

There is no short cut to the making of these ideals into glad realities. The world has witnessed again and again the futility and the mischief of ill-considered remedies for social and economic disorders. But we are mindful today as never before of the friction of modern industrialism, and we must learn its causes and reduce its evil consequences by sober and tested methods. Where genius has made for great possibilities, justice and happiness must be reflected in a greater common welfare.

Service is the supreme commitment of life. I would rejoice to acclaim the era of the Golden Rule and crown it with the autocracy of service. I pledge an administration wherein all the agencies of Government are called to serve, and ever promote an understanding of Government purely as an expression of the popular will.

One cannot stand in this presence and be unmindful of the tremendous responsibility. The world upheaval has added heavily to our tasks. But with the realization comes the surge of high resolve, and there is reassurance in belief in the God-given destiny of our Republic. If I felt that there is to be sole responsibility in the Executive for the America of tomorrow I should shrink from the burden. But here are a hundred millions, with common concern and shared responsibility, answerable to God and country. The Republic summons them to their duty, and I invite cooperation.

I accept my part with single mindedness of purpose and humility of spirit, and implore the favor and guidance of God in His Heaven. With these I am unafraid, and confidently face the future.

I have taken the solemn oath of office on that passage of Holy Writ wherein it is asked: What doth the Lord require of thee but to do justly, and to love mercy, and to walk humbly with thy God? This I plight to God and country.

CALVIN COOLIDGE

INAUGURAL ADDRESS

MARCH 4, 1925

COMMENTARY

By the spring of 1923, Washington buzzed with rumors about alleged scandals within the highest echelons of government. After Harding's death in August, investigations confirmed the suspicions. But Calvin Coolidge, with his homey virtue, rural simplicity, and Yankee twang, suggested a return to honesty briefly interrupted by the Harding years. "I want things as they used to be—before," said the new president. This dour, unimaginative man represented the essence of conservatism. Serene faith in the wisdom of the business class, plus governmental economies, a balanced budget, lower taxes, and a protective tariff, won him wide support. When the Republican convention met on June 10, 1924, Coolidge, though having held office less than 10 months, was overwhelmingly nominated for a full term.

No such unanimity marked the Democratic convention that assembled in New York on June 24. A serious disagreement over a resolution asking for the denunciation of the Ku Klux Klan by name divided the delegates. The revived Klan had carried its programs of racial and religious discrimination into politics, scoring dramatic victories in the rural South and West. After a bitter debate, the resolution was defeated but the strife shattered the party. John W. Davis, a conservative New York lawyer whose firm served as counsel for J. P. Morgan, was chosen as the nominee after a record 103 ballots and 17 days. Remnants of the progressive movement who found that they could not vote for either Davis or Coolidge formed a new Progressive Party and nominated Senator Robert M. La Follette of Wisconsin for president. La Follette opposed "the control of government and industry by private monopoly." His platform called for sweeping social and political changes, including banking reforms and public ownership of water power. However, the electorate did not wish to jeopardize the status quo. After a relatively dull campaign, characterized by public indifference to politics, only 51.1 percent of the eligible voters went to the polls and Coolidge was decisively elected. His popular vote exceeded the total of his two opponents' by more than 2 million. The president was justified in his complacent statement that the election revealed "a state of contentment seldom before seen."

Coolidge's dislike of progressive doctrines and his desire to reduce the role of government in the economy of the nation are clearly revealed in his inaugural address, delivered on March 4, 1925.

My countrymen:

No one can contemplate current conditions without finding much that is satisfying and still more that is encouraging. Our own country is leading the world in the general readjustment to the results of the great conflict. Many of its burdens will bear heavily upon us for years, and the secondary and indirect effects we must expect to experience for some time. But we are beginning to comprehend more definitely what course should be pursued, what remedies ought to be applied, what actions should be taken for our deliverance, and are clearly manifesting a determined will faithfully and conscientiously to adopt these methods of relief. Already we have sufficiently rearranged our domestic affairs so that confidence has returned, business has revived, and we appear to be entering an era of prosperity which is gradually reaching into every part of the Nation. Realizing that we can not live unto ourselves alone, we have contributed of our resources and our counsel to the relief of the suffering and the settlement of the disputes among the European nations. Because of what America is and what America has done, a firmer courage, a higher hope, inspires the heart of all humanity.

These results have not occurred by mere chance. They have been secured by a constant and enlightened effort marked by many sacrifices and extending over many generations. We can not continue these brilliant successes in the future, unless we continue to learn from the past. It is necessary to keep the former experiences of our country both at home and abroad continually before us, if we are to have any science of government. If we wish to erect new structures, we must have a definite knowledge of the old foundations. We must realize that human nature is about the most constant thing in the universe and that the essentials of human relationship do not change. We must frequently take our bearings from these fixed stars of our political firmament if we expect to hold a true course. If we examine carefully what we have done, we can determine the more accurately what we can do.

We stand at the opening of the one hundred and fiftieth year since our national consciousness first asserted itself by unmistakable action with an array of force. The old sentiment of detached and dependent colonies disappeared in the new sentiment of a united and independent Nation. Men began to discard the narrow confines of a local charter for the broader opportunities of a national constitution. Under the eternal urge of freedom we became an independent Nation. A little less than fifty years later that freedom and independence were reasserted in the face of all the world, and guarded, supported, and secured by the Monroe Doctrine. The narrow fringe of States along the Atlantic seaboard advanced its frontiers across the hills and plains of an intervening continent until it passed down the golden slope to the Pacific. We made freedom a birthright. We extended our domain over distant islands in order to safeguard our own interests and accepted the consequent obligation to bestow justice and liberty upon less favored peoples. In the defense of our own ideals and in the general cause of liberty we entered the Great War. When victory had been fully secured, we withdrew to our own shores unrecompensed save in the consciousness of duty done.

Throughout all these experiences we have enlarged our freedom, we have strengthened our independence. We have been, and propose to be, more and more American. We believe that we can best serve our own country and most successfully discharge our obligations to humanity by continuing to be openly and candidly, intensely and scrupulously, American. If we have any heritage, it has been that. If we have any destiny, we have found it in that direction.

But if we wish to continue to be distinctively American, we must continue to make that term comprehensive enough to embrace the legitimate desires of a civilized and enlightened people determined in all their relations to pursue a conscientious and religious life. We can not permit ourselves to be narrowed and dwarfed by slogans and phrases. It is not the adjective, but the substantive, which is of real importance. It is not the name of the action, but the result of the action, which is the chief concern. It will be well not to be too much disturbed by the thought of either isolation or entanglement of pacifists and militarists. The physical configuration of the earth has separated us from all of the Old World, but the common brotherhood of man, the highest law of all our being, has united us by inseparable bonds with all humanity. Our country represents nothing but peaceful intentions toward all the earth, but it ought not to fail to maintain such a military force as comports with the dignity and security of a great people. It ought to be a balanced force, intensely modern, capable of defense by sea and land, beneath the surface and in the air. But it should be so conducted that all the world may see in it, not a menace, but an instrument of security and peace.

This Nation believes thoroughly in an honorable peace under which the rights of its citizens are to be everywhere protected. It has never found that the necessary enjoyment of such a peace could be maintained only by a great and threatening array of arms. In common with other nations, it is now more determined than ever to promote peace through friendliness and good will, through mutual understandings and mutual forbearance. We have never practiced the policy of competitive armaments. We have recently committed ourselves by covenants with the other great nations to a limitation of our sea power. As one result of this, our Navy ranks larger, in comparison, than it ever did before. Removing the burden of expense and jealousy, which must always accrue from a keen rivalry, is one of the most effective methods of diminishing that unreasonable hysteria and misunderstanding which are the most potent means of fomenting war. This policy represents a new departure in the world. It is a thought, an ideal, which has led to an entirely new line of action. It will not be easy to maintain. Some never moved from their old positions, some are constantly slipping back to the old ways of thought and the old action of seizing a musket and relying on force. America has taken the lead in this new direction, and that lead America must continue to hold. If we expect others to rely on our fairness and justice we must show that we rely on their fairness and justice.

If we are to judge by past experience, there is much to be hoped for in international relations from frequent conferences and consultations. We have before us the beneficial results of the Washington conference and the various consultations recently held upon European affairs, some of which were in response to our suggestions and in some of which we were active participants. Even the failures can not but be accounted useful and an immeasurable advance over threatened or actual warfare. I am strongly in favor of continuation of this policy, whenever conditions are such that there is even a promise that practical and favorable results might be secured.

In conformity with the principle that a display of reason rather than a threat of force should be the determining factor in the intercourse among nations, we have long advocated the peaceful settlement of disputes by methods of arbitration and have negotiated many treaties to secure that result. The same considerations should lead to our adherence to the Permanent Court of International Justice. Where great principles are involved, where great movements are under way which promise much for the welfare of humanity by reason of the very fact that many other nations have given such movements their actual support, we ought not to withhold our own sanction because of any small and inessential difference, but only upon the ground of the most important and compelling fundamental reasons. We can not barter away our independence or our sovereignty, but we ought to engage in no refinements of logic, no sophistries, and no subterfuges, to argue away the undoubted duty of this country by reason of the might of its numbers, the power of its resources, and its position of leadership in the world, actively and comprehensively to signify its approval and to bear its full share of the responsibility of a candid and disinterested attempt at the establishment of a tribunal for the administration of even handed justice between nation and nation. The weight of our enormous influence must be cast upon the side of a reign not of force but of law and trial, not by battle but by reason.

We have never any wish to interfere in the political conditions of any other countries. Especially are we determined not to become implicated in the political controversies of the Old World. With a great deal of hesitation, we have responded to appeals for help to maintain order, protect life and property, and establish responsible government in some of the small countries of the Western Hemisphere. Our private citizens have advanced large sums of money to assist in the necessary financing and relief of the Old World. We have not failed, nor shall we fail to respond, whenever necessary to mitigate human suffering and assist in the rehabilitation of distressed nations. These, too, are requirements which must be met by reason of our vast powers and the place we hold in the world.

Some of the best thought of mankind has long been seeking for a formula for permanent peace. Undoubtedly the clarification of the principles of international law would be helpful, and the efforts of scholars to prepare such a work for adoption by the various nations should have our sympathy and support. Much may be hoped for from the earnest studies of those who

advocate the outlawing of aggressive war. But all these plans and preparations, these treaties and covenants, will not of themselves be adequate.
One of the greatest dangers to peace lies in the economic pressure to which
people find themselves subjected. One of the most practical things to be
done in the world is to seek arrangements under which such pressure may
be removed, so that opportunity may be renewed and hope may be revived.
There must be some assurance that effort and endeavor will be followed by
success and prosperity. In the making and financing of such adjustments
there is not only an opportunity, but a real duty, for America to respond
with her counsel and her resources. Conditions must be provided under
which people can make a living and work out of their difficulties. But there
is another element, more important than all, without which there can not
be the slightest hope of a permanent peace. That element lies in the heart of
humanity. Unless the desire for peace be cherished there, unless this fundamental and only natural source of brotherly love be cultivated to its highest
degree, all artificial efforts will be in vain. Peace will come when there is
realization that only under a reign of law, based on righteousness and supported by the religious conviction of the brotherhood of man, can there be
any hope of a complete and satisfying life. Parchment will fail, the sword
will fail, it is only the spiritual nature of man that can be triumphant.

It seems altogether probable that we can contribute most to these important objects by maintaining our position of political detachment and
independence. We are not identified with any Old World interests. This position should be made more and more clear in our relations with all foreign
countries. We are at peace with all of them. Our program is never to oppress,
but always to assist. But while we do justice to others, we must require that
justice be done to us. With us a treaty of peace means peace, and a treaty of
amity means amity. We have made great contributions to the settlement of
contentious differences in both Europe and Asia. But there is a very definite point beyond which we can not go. We can only help those who help
themselves. Mindful of these limitations, the one great duty that stands out
requires us to use our enormous powers to trim the balance of the world.

While we can look with a great deal of pleasure upon what we have
done abroad, we must remember that our continued success in that direction depends upon what we do at home. Since its very outset, it has been
found necessary to conduct our Government by means of political parties.
That system would not have survived from generation to generation if it
had not been fundamentally sound and provided the best instrumentalities

for the most complete expression of the popular will. It is not necessary to claim that it has always worked perfectly. It is enough to know that nothing better has been devised. No one would deny that there should be full and free expression and an opportunity for independence of action within the party. There is no salvation in a narrow and bigoted partisanship. But if there is to be responsible party government, the party label must be something more than a mere device for securing office. Unless those who are elected under the same party designation are willing to assume sufficient responsibility and exhibit sufficient loyalty and coherence, so that they can cooperate with each other in the support of the broad general principles, of the party platform, the election is merely a mockery, no decision is made at the polls, and there is no representation of the popular will. Common honesty and good faith with the people who support a party at the polls require that party, when it enters office, to assume the control of that portion of the Government to which it has been elected. Any other course is bad faith and a violation of the party pledges.

When the country has bestowed its confidence upon a party by making it a majority in the Congress, it has a right to expect such unity of action as will make the party majority an effective instrument of government. This Administration has come into power with a very clear and definite mandate from the people. The expression of the popular will in favor of maintaining our constitutional guarantees was overwhelming and decisive. There was a manifestation of such faith in the integrity of the courts that we can consider that issue rejected for some time to come. Likewise, the policy of public ownership of railroads and certain electric utilities met with unmistakable defeat. The people declared that they wanted their rights to have not a political but a judicial determination, and their independence and freedom continued and supported by having the ownership and control of their property, not in the Government, but in their own hands. As they always do when they have a fair chance, the people demonstrated that they are sound and are determined to have a sound government.

When we turn from what was rejected to inquire what was accepted, the policy that stands out with the greatest clearness is that of economy in public expenditure with reduction and reform of taxation. The principle involved in this effort is that of conservation. The resources of this country are almost beyond computation. No mind can comprehend them. But the cost of our combined governments is likewise almost beyond definition. Not only those who are now making their tax returns, but those who meet the enhanced cost of existence in their monthly bills, know by hard experience what this great burden is and what it does. No matter what others may want, these people want a drastic economy. They are opposed to waste. They know that extravagance lengthens the hours and diminishes the rewards of their labor. I favor the policy of economy, not because I wish to save money, but because I wish to save people. The men and women of this country who toil are the ones who bear the cost of the Government. Every dollar that we carelessly waste means that their life will be so much the more meager. Every dollar that we prudently save means that their life will be so much the more abundant. Economy is idealism in its most practical form.

If extravagance were not reflected in taxation, and through taxation both directly and indirectly injuriously affecting the people, it would not be of so much consequence. The wisest and soundest method of solving our tax problem is through economy. Fortunately, of all the great nations this country is best in a position to adopt that simple remedy. We do not any longer need wartime revenues. The collection of any taxes which are not absolutely required, which do not beyond reasonable doubt contribute to the public welfare, is only a species of legalized larceny. Under this republic the rewards of industry belong to those who earn them. The only constitutional tax is the tax which ministers to public necessity. The property of the country belongs to the people of the country. Their title is absolute. They do not support any privileged class; they do not need to maintain great military forces; they ought not to be burdened with a great array of public employees. They are not required to make any contribution to Government expenditures except that which they voluntarily assess upon themselves through the action of their own representatives. Whenever taxes become burdensome a remedy can be applied by the people; but if they do not act for themselves, no one can be very successful in acting for them.

The time is arriving when we can have further tax reduction, when, unless we wish to hamper the people in their right to earn a living, we must have tax reform. The method of raising revenue ought not to impede the transaction of business; it ought to encourage it. I am opposed to extremely high rates, because they produce little or no revenue, because they are bad for the country, and, finally, because they are wrong. We can not finance the country, we can not improve social conditions, through any system of injustice, even if we attempt to inflict it upon the rich. Those who suffer the most harm will be the poor. This country believes in prosperity. It is absurd to suppose that it is envious of those who are already prosperous. The wise and correct course to follow in taxation and all other economic legislation is not to destroy those who have already secured success but to create conditions under which every one will have a better chance to be successful. The verdict of the country has been given on this question. That verdict stands. We shall do well to heed it.

These questions involve moral issues. We need not concern ourselves much about the rights of property if we will faithfully observe the rights of persons. Under our institutions their rights are supreme. It is not property but the right to hold property, both great and small, which our Constitution guarantees. All owners of property are charged with a service. These rights and duties have been revealed, through the conscience of society, to have a divine sanction. The very stability of our society rests upon production and conservation. For individuals or for governments to waste and squander their resources is to deny these rights and disregard these obligations. The result of economic dissipation to a nation is always moral decay.

These policies of better international understandings, greater economy, and lower taxes have contributed largely to peaceful and prosperous industrial relations. Under the helpful influences of restrictive immigration and a protective tariff, employment is plentiful, the rate of pay is high, and wage earners are in a state of contentment seldom before seen. Our transportation systems have been gradually recovering and have been able to meet all the requirements of the service. Agriculture has been very slow in reviving, but the price of cereals at last indicates that the day of its deliverance is at hand.

We are not without our problems, but our most important problem is not to secure new advantages but to maintain those which we already possess. Our system of government made up of three separate and independent departments, our divided sovereignty composed of Nation and State, the matchless wisdom that is enshrined in our Constitution, all these need constant effort and tireless vigilance for their protection and support.

In a republic the first rule for the guidance of the citizen is obedience to law. Under a despotism the law may be imposed upon the subject. He has no voice in its making, no influence in its administration, it does not represent him. Under a free government the citizen makes his own laws, chooses his own administrators, which do represent him. Those who want their rights respected under the Constitution and the law ought to set the example themselves of observing the Constitution and the law. While there may be those of high intelligence who violate the law at times, the barbarian and the defective always violate it. Those who disregard the rules of society are not exhibiting a superior intelligence, are not promoting freedom and independence, are not following the path of civilization, but are displaying the traits of ignorance, of servitude, of savagery, and treading the way that leads back to the jungle.

The essence of a republic is representative government. Our Congress represents the people and the States. In all legislative affairs it is the natural collaborator with the President. In spite of all the criticism which often falls to its lot, I do not hesitate to say that there is no more independent and effective legislative body in the world. It is, and should be, jealous of its prerogative. I welcome its cooperation, and expect to share with it not only the responsibility, but the credit, for our common effort to secure beneficial legislation.

These are some of the principles which America represents. We have not by any means put them fully into practice, but we have strongly signified our belief in them. The encouraging feature of our country is not that it has reached its destination, but that it has overwhelmingly expressed its determination to proceed in the right direction. It is true that we could, with profit, be less sectional and more national in our thought. It would be well if we could replace much that is only a false and ignorant prejudice with a true and enlightened pride of race. But the last election showed that appeals to class and nationality had little effect. We were all found loyal to a common citizenship. The fundamental precept of liberty is toleration. We can not permit any inquisition either within or without the law or apply any religious test to the holding of office. The mind of America must be forever free.

It is in such contemplations, my fellow countrymen, which are not exhaustive but only representative, that I find ample warrant for satisfaction and encouragement. We should not let the much that is to do obscure the much which has been done. The past and present show faith and hope and courage fully justified. Here stands our country, an example of tranquillity at home, a patron of tranquillity abroad. Here stands its Government, aware of its might but obedient to its conscience. Here it will continue to stand, seeking peace and prosperity, solicitous for the welfare of the wage earner, promoting enterprise, developing waterways and natural resources, attentive to the intuitive counsel of womanhood, encouraging education, desiring the advancement of religion, supporting the cause of justice and honor among the nations. America seeks no earthly empire built on blood and force. No ambition, no temptation, lures her to thought of foreign dominions. The legions which she sends forth are armed, not with the sword, but with the cross. The higher state to which she seeks the allegiance of all mankind is not of human, but of divine origin. She cherishes no purpose save to merit the favor of almighty God.

HERBERT HOOVER

INAUGURAL ADDRESS

MARCH 4, 1929

COMMENTARY

Coolidge laconically announced in the summer of 1927 that "I do not choose to run for president in 1928." The Republican Party took the president at his word. Meeting in Kansas City on June 12, 1928, the rank and file of the GOP chose Herbert Hoover as their standard-bearer. Hoover, who had gained fame as an able war administrator and as an effective secretary of commerce in both the Harding and Coolidge cabinets, satisfied the American dream of the self-made man. Born in a simple Iowa cabin, orphaned at an early age, he worked his way through college and quickly accumulated a fortune as a successful mining engineer. The party platform proudly took credit for the prosperity that most Americans enjoyed. With business booming, the Republicans looked forward to another presidential victory.

The Democrats selected the colorful governor of New York, Alfred E. Smith. A Catholic, the first of his religion to be nominated for the presidency by a major party, Smith had risen in New York politics through his loyalty to the Tammany machine. As governor, he became the spokesman for the new urban masses by supporting progressive social reforms. In an age when the prejudices of the Ku Klux Klan were powerful, Smith faced an impossible fight. A vicious whispering campaign claimed that if Smith won, the Catholic Church would rule America, and scurrilous pamphlets slandered him for his religious convictions. Within Smith's own party, the southern wing found a New York Roman Catholic who opposed Prohibition totally unacceptable. On Election Day, five southern states went Republican for the first time since Reconstruction. Even New York disavowed its favorite son. Smith won fewer electoral votes than any

Democratic candidate since Horace Greeley in 1872. Considering the conservatism and prosperity of the twenties, it may be comforting to note that Smith received a larger popular vote than any preceding Democrat.

On March 4, 1929, Herbert Hoover entered the first elective office he had ever held. The New York Herald Tribune *printed a cartoon that day depicting Uncle Sam with one hand on the shoulder of a boy, labeled "An Orphan at 10"; his other hand is on Herbert Hoover, "President of the United States at 54." The caption read: "While such things are possible there is nothing very wrong with our country." In his later years, Hoover described his Inauguration Day as "cold and rainy. American tradition still insisted upon an outdoor ceremonial at the Capitol, and by the time we arrived at the White House both Mrs. Hoover and I were thoroughly soaked . . . . In my inaugural address, I was somewhat hampered by the fact that I was succeeding a President of my own party . . . and I could not in good taste say anything that indicated certain differences in our points of view. I therefore confined myself mostly to American ideals and aspirations." The cartoon theme as well as American ideals and aspirations would be put to the severest test before Hoover's administration ended.*

My countrymen:

This occasion is not alone the administration of the most sacred oath which can be assumed by an American citizen. It is a dedication and consecration under God to the highest office in service of our people. I assume this trust in the humility of knowledge that only through the guidance of Almighty Providence can I hope to discharge its ever increasing burdens.

It is in keeping with tradition throughout our history that I should express simply and directly the opinions which I hold concerning some of the matters of present importance.

OUR PROGRESS

If we survey the situation of our Nation both at home and abroad, we find many satisfactions; we find some causes for concern. We have emerged from the losses of the Great War and the reconstruction following it with increased virility and strength. From this strength we have contributed to the recovery and progress of the world. What America has done has given renewed hope and courage to all who have faith in government by the people. In the large view, we have reached a higher degree of comfort and security than ever existed before in the history of the world. Through liberation from widespread poverty we have reached a higher degree of individual freedom than ever before. The devotion to and concern for our institutions are deep and sincere. We are steadily building a new race; a new civilization great in its own attainments. The influence and high purposes of our Nation are respected among the peoples of the world. We aspire to distinction in the world, but to a distinction based upon confidence in our sense of justice as well as our accomplishments within our own borders and in our own lives. For wise guidance in this great period of recovery the Nation is deeply indebted to Calvin Coolidge.

But all this majestic advance should not obscure the constant dangers from which self-government must be safeguarded. The strong man must at all times be alert to the attack of insidious disease.

THE FAILURE OF OUR SYSTEM OF CRIMINAL JUSTICE

The most malign of all these dangers today is disregard and disobedience of law. Crime is increasing. Confidence in rigid and speedy justice is decreasing. I am not prepared to believe that this indicates any decay in the moral fiber of the American people. I am not prepared to believe that it indicates an impotence of the Federal Government to enforce its laws.

It is only in part due to the additional burdens imposed upon our judicial system by the eighteenth amendment. The problem is much wider than that. Many influences had increasingly complicated and weakened our law enforcement organization long before the adoption of the eighteenth amendment.

To reestablish the vigor and effectiveness of law enforcement we must critically consider the entire Federal machinery of justice, the redistribution of its functions, the simplification of its procedure, the provision of additional special tribunals, the better selection of juries, and the more effective organization of our agencies of investigation and prosecution that justice may be sure and that it may be swift. While the authority of the Federal Government extends to but part of our vast system of national, State, and local justice, yet the standards which the Federal Government establishes have the most profound influence upon the whole structure.

We are fortunate in the ability and integrity of our Federal judges and attorneys. But the system which these officers are called upon to administer is in many respects ill adapted to present day conditions. Its intricate and involved rules of procedure have become the refuge of both big and little criminals.

There is a belief abroad that by invoking technicalities, subterfuge, and delay, the ends of justice may be thwarted by those who can pay the cost.

Reform, reorganization and strengthening of our whole judicial and enforcement system, both in civil and criminal sides, have been advocated for years by statesmen, judges, and bar associations. First steps toward that end should not longer be delayed. Rigid and expeditious justice is the first safeguard of freedom, the basis of all ordered liberty, the vital force of progress. It must not come to be in our Republic that it can be defeated by the indifference of the citizen, by exploitation of the delays and entanglements of the law, or by combinations of criminals. Justice must not fail because the agencies of enforcement are either delinquent or inefficiently organized. To consider these evils, to find their remedy, is the most sore necessity of our times.

ENFORCEMENT OF THE EIGHTEENTH AMENDMENT

Of the undoubted abuses which have grown up under the eighteenth amendment, part are due to the causes I have just mentioned; but part are due to the failure of some States to accept their share of responsibility for concurrent enforcement and to the failure of many State and local officials to accept the obligation under their oath of office zealously to enforce the laws. With the failures from these many causes has come a dangerous expansion in the criminal elements who have found enlarged opportunities in dealing in illegal liquor.

But a large responsibility rests directly upon our citizens. There would be little traffic in illegal liquor if only criminals patronized it. We must awake to the fact that this patronage from large numbers of law-abiding citizens is supplying the rewards and stimulating crime.

I have been selected by you to execute and enforce the laws of the country. I propose to do so to the extent of my own abilities, but the measure of success that the Government shall attain will depend upon the moral support which you, as citizens, extend. The duty of citizens to support the laws of the land is coequal with the duty of their Government to enforce the laws which exist. No greater national service can be given by men and women of good will who, I know, are not unmindful of the responsibilities of citizenship—than that they should, by their example, assist in stamping out crime and outlawry by refusing participation in and condemning all transactions with illegal liquor. Our whole system of self-government will crumble either if officials elect what laws they will enforce or citizens elect what laws they will support. The worst evil of disregard for some law is that it destroys respect for all law. For our citizens to patronize the violation of a particular law on the ground that they are opposed to it is destructive of the very basis of all that protection of life, of homes and property which they rightly claim under other laws. If citizens do not like a law, their duty as honest men and women is to discourage its violation; their right is openly to work for its repeal.

To those of criminal mind there can be no appeal but vigorous enforcement of the law. Fortunately they are but a small percentage of our people. Their activities must be stopped.

A NATIONAL INVESTIGATION

I propose to appoint a national commission for a searching investigation of the whole structure of our Federal system of jurisprudence, to include the method of enforcement of the eighteenth amendment and the causes of abuse under it. Its purpose will be to make such recommendations for reorganization of the administration of Federal laws and court procedure as may be found desirable. In the meantime it is essential that a large part of the enforcement activities be transferred from the Treasury Department to the Department of Justice as a beginning of more effective organization.

THE RELATION OF GOVERNMENT TO BUSINESS

The election has again confirmed the determination of the American people that regulation of private enterprise and not Government ownership or operation is the course rightly to be pursued in our relation to business. In recent years we have established a differentiation in the whole method of business regulation between the industries which produce and distribute commodities on the one hand and public utilities on the other. In the former, our laws insist upon effective competition; in the latter, because we substantially confer a monopoly by limiting competition, we must regulate their services and rates. The rigid enforcement of the laws applicable to both groups is the very base of equal opportunity and freedom from domination for all our people, and it is just as essential for the stability and prosperity of business itself as for the protection of the public at large. Such regulation should be extended by the Federal Government within the limitations of the Constitution and only when the individual States are without power to protect their citizens through their own authority. On the other hand, we should be fearless when the authority rests only in the Federal Government.

COOPERATION BY THE GOVERNMENT

The larger purpose of our economic thought should be to establish more firmly stability and security of business and employment and thereby remove poverty still further from our borders. Our people have in recent years developed a new found capacity for cooperation among themselves to effect high purposes in public welfare. It is an advance toward the highest conception of self-government. Self-government does not and should not imply the use of political agencies alone. Progress is born of cooperation in the community not from governmental restraints. The Government should assist and encourage these movements of collective self-help by itself cooperating with them. Business has by cooperation made great progress in the advancement of service, in stability, in regularity of employment and in the correction of its own abuses. Such progress, however, can continue only so long as business manifests its respect for law.

There is an equally important field of cooperation by the Federal Government with the multitude of agencies, State, municipal and private, in the systematic development of those processes which directly affect public health, recreation, education, and the home. We have need further to perfect the means by which Government can be adapted to human service.

EDUCATION

Although education is primarily a responsibility of the States and local communities, and rightly so, yet the Nation as a whole is vitally concerned in its development everywhere to the highest standards and to complete universality. Self government can succeed only through an instructed electorate. Our objective is not simply to overcome illiteracy. The Nation has marched far beyond that. The more complex the problems of the Nation become, the greater is the need for more and more advanced instruction. Moreover, as our numbers increase and as our life expands with science and invention, we must discover more and more leaders for every walk of life. We can not hope to succeed in directing this increasingly complex civilization unless we can draw all the talent of leadership from the whole people. One civilization after another has been wrecked upon the attempt to secure sufficient leadership from a single group or class. If we would prevent the growth of class distinctions and would constantly refresh our leadership with the ideals of our people, we must draw constantly from the general mass. The full opportunity for every boy and girl to rise through the selective processes of education can alone secure to us this leadership.

PUBLIC HEALTH

In public health the discoveries of science have opened a new era. Many sections of our country and many groups of our citizens suffer from diseases the eradication of which are mere matters of administration and moderate expenditure. Public health service should be as fully organized and as universally incorporated into our governmental system as is public education. The returns are a thousand fold in economic benefits, and infinitely more in reduction of suffering and promotion of human happiness.

WORLD PEACE

The United States fully accepts the profound truth that our own progress, prosperity, and peace are interlocked with the progress, prosperity, and peace of all humanity. The whole world is at peace. The dangers to a continuation of this peace today are largely the fear and suspicion which still haunt the world. No suspicion or fear can be rightly directed toward our country.

Those who have a true understanding of America know that we have no desire for territorial expansion, for economic or other domination of other peoples. Such purposes are repugnant to our ideals of human freedom. Our form of government is ill adapted to the responsibilities which inevitably follow permanent limitation of the independence of other peoples. Superficial observers seem to find no destiny for our abounding increase in population, in wealth and power except that of imperialism. They fail to see that the American people are engrossed in the building for themselves of a new economic system, a new social system, a new political system all of which are characterized by aspirations of freedom of opportunity and thereby are the negation of imperialism. They fail to realize that because of our abounding prosperity our youth are pressing more and more into our institutions of learning; that our people are seeking a larger vision through art, literature, science, and travel; that they are moving toward stronger moral and spiritual life—that from these things our sympathies are broadening beyond the bounds of our Nation and race toward their true expression in a real brotherhood of man. They fail to see that the idealism of America will lead it to no narrow or selfish channel, but inspire it to do its full share as a nation toward the advancement of civilization. It will do that not by mere declaration but by taking a practical part in supporting all useful international undertakings. We not only desire peace with the world, but to see peace maintained throughout the world. We wish to advance the reign of justice and reason toward the extinction of force.

The recent treaty for the renunciation of war as an instrument of national policy sets an advanced standard in our conception of the relations of nations. Its acceptance should pave the way to greater limitation of armament, the offer of which we sincerely extend to the world. But its full realization also implies a greater and greater perfection in the instrumentalities for pacific settlement of controversies between nations. In the creation and use of these instrumentalities we should support every sound method of conciliation, arbitration, and judicial settlement. American statesmen were among the first to propose and they have constantly urged upon the world, the establishment of a tribunal for the settlement of controversies of a justiciable character. The Permanent Court of International Justice in its major purpose is thus peculiarly identified with American ideals and with American statesmanship. No more potent instrumentality for this purpose has ever been conceived and no other is practicable of establishment. The reservations placed upon our adherence should not be misinterpreted. The United States seeks by these reservations no special privilege or advantage but only to clarify our relation to advisory opinions and other matters which are subsidiary to the major purpose of the court. The way should, and I believe will, be found by which we may take our proper place in a movement so fundamental to the progress of peace.

Our people have determined that we should make no political engagements such as membership in the League of Nations, which may commit us in advance as a nation to become involved in the settlements of controversies between other countries. They adhere to the belief that the independence of America from such obligations increases its ability and availability for service in all fields of human progress.

I have lately returned from a journey among our sister Republics of the Western Hemisphere. I have received unbounded hospitality and courtesy as their expression of friendliness to our country. We are held by particular bonds of sympathy and common interest with them. They are each of them building a racial character and a culture which is an impressive contribution to human progress. We wish only for the maintenance of their independence, the growth of their stability, and their prosperity. While we have had wars in the Western Hemisphere, yet on the whole the record is in encouraging contrast with that of other parts of the world. Fortunately the New World is largely free from the inheritances of fear and distrust which have so troubled the Old World. We should keep it so.

It is impossible, my countrymen, to speak of peace without profound emotion. In thousands of homes in America, in millions of homes around the world, there are vacant chairs. It would be a shameful confession of our unworthiness if it should develop that we have abandoned the hope for which all these men died. Surely civilization is old enough, surely mankind is mature enough so that we ought in our own lifetime to find a way to permanent peace. Abroad, to west and east, are nations whose sons mingled their blood with the blood of our sons on the battlefields. Most of these nations have contributed to our race, to our culture, our knowledge, and our progress. From one of them we derive our very language and from many of them much of the genius of our institutions. Their desire for peace is as deep and sincere as our own.

Peace can be contributed to by respect for our ability in defense. Peace can be promoted by the limitation of arms and by the creation of the instrumentalities for peaceful settlement of controversies. But it will become a reality only through self-restraint and active effort in friendliness and helpfulness. I covet for this administration a record of having further contributed to advance the cause of peace.

PARTY RESPONSIBILITIES

In our form of democracy the expression of the popular will can be effected only through the instrumentality of political parties. We maintain party government not to promote intolerant partisanship but because opportunity must be given for expression of the popular will, and organization provided for the execution of its mandates and for accountability of government to the people. It follows that the government both in the executive and the legislative branches must carry out in good faith the platforms upon which the party was entrusted with power. But the government is that of the whole people; the party is the instrument through which policies are determined and men chosen to bring them into being. The animosities of elections should have no place in our Government, for government must concern itself alone with the common weal.

SPECIAL SESSION OF THE CONGRESS

Action upon some of the proposals upon which the Republican Party was returned to power, particularly further agricultural relief and limited changes in the tariff, cannot in justice to our farmers, our labor, and our manufacturers be postponed. I shall therefore request a special session of Congress for the consideration of these two questions. I shall deal with each of them upon the assembly of the Congress.

OTHER MANDATES FROM THE ELECTION

It appears to me that the more important further mandates from the recent election were the maintenance of the integrity of the Constitution; the vigorous enforcement of the laws; the continuance of economy in public expenditure; the continued regulation of business to prevent domination in the community; the denial of ownership or operation of business by the Government in competition with its citizens; the avoidance of policies which would involve us in the controversies of foreign nations; the more effective reorganization of the departments of the Federal Government; the expansion of public works; and the promotion of welfare activities affecting education and the home.

These were the more tangible determinations of the election, but beyond them was the confidence and belief of the people that we would not neglect the support of the embedded ideals and aspirations of America. These ideals and aspirations are the touchstones upon which the day-to-day administration and legislative acts of government must be tested. More than this, the Government must, so far as lies within its proper powers, give leadership to the realization of these ideals and to the fruition of these aspirations. No one can adequately reduce these things of the spirit to phrases or to a catalogue of definitions. We do know what the attainments of these ideals should be: The preservation of self-government and its full foundations in local government; the perfection of justice whether in economic or in social fields; the maintenance of ordered liberty; the denial of domination by any group or class; the building up and preservation of equality of opportunity; the stimulation of initiative and individuality; absolute integrity in public affairs; the choice of officials for fitness to office; the direction of economic progress toward prosperity for the further lessening of poverty; the freedom of public opinion; the sustaining of education and of the advancement of knowledge; the growth of religious spirit and the tolerance of all faiths; the strengthening of the home; the advancement of peace.

There is no short road to the realization of these aspirations. Ours is a progressive people, but with a determination that progress must be based upon the foundation of experience. Ill-considered remedies for our faults bring only penalties after them. But if we hold the faith of the men in our mighty past who created these ideals, we shall leave them heightened and strengthened for our children.

CONCLUSION

This is not the time and place for extended discussion. The questions before our country are problems of progress to higher standards; they are not the problems of degeneration. They demand thought and they serve to quicken the conscience and enlist our sense of responsibility for their settlement. And that responsibility rests upon you, my countrymen, as much as upon those of us who have been selected for office.

Ours is a land rich in resources; stimulating in its glorious beauty; filled with millions of happy homes; blessed with comfort and opportunity. In no nation are the institutions of progress more advanced. In no nation are the fruits of accomplishment more secure. In no nation is the government more worthy of respect. No country is more loved by its people. I have an abiding faith in their capacity, integrity and high purpose. I have no fears for the future of our country. It is bright with hope.

In the presence of my countrymen, mindful of the solemnity of this occasion, knowing what the task means and the responsibility which it involves, I beg your tolerance, your aid, and your cooperation. I ask the help of almighty God in this service to my country to which you have called me.

FRANKLIN DELANO ROOSEVELT

FIRST INAUGURAL ADDRESS

MARCH 4, 1933

COMMENTARY

The 1932 presidential election came in the midst of the greatest depression experienced by the American people. Never before in the history of the United States had pessimism been so universal. The descent from the heights of prosperity of the late 1920s had been rapid and disillusioning, bringing fear and uncertainty.

When the bottom dropped from the stock market in October 1929, stocks and bonds, ironically called securities, steadily declined for the next three and one-half years, carrying with them speculators, big and little, wiping out thousands of accounts, and causing staggering losses that ran into billions of dollars. Despite repeated assurances from business and government leaders of the underlying soundness of the economy, the market did not rally. "I see nothing in the present situation," commented Secretary of the Treasury Andrew Mellon, "that is either menacing or warrants pessimism." And Willis H. Booth, president of the Merchants' Association of New York, envisioned "no fundamental reason why business should not find itself again on the upgrade early in 1930." Unfortunately, the only upgrade occurred in unemployment figures, and, in March 1930, the estimates ranged from nearly 3,250,000 to 4 million. One year later, these had risen to 7.5 million. By March 1932, approximately 12 million men and women faced locked doors. The peak came early in 1933, with the unemployed numbering between 13.5 million and 16 million. Commodity prices had dropped sharply, foreign trade fell off factories curtailed production or closed their doors, and private construction practically ceased. In the hard-hit cities, long lines of hungry people waited before charity soup kitchens, and thousands, unable to pay rent, huddled in empty lots. A million or more Americans wandered aimlessly throughout the country in search of jobs. Confronted with mounting despair, the nation experienced a total depression.

President Herbert Hoover had attempted to use governmental power and prestige to check the deteriorating situation, but conditions worsened. Critics of Hoover claim that his policies moved too slowly and lacked imagination. His defenders maintain that, regardless of the president's efforts, the depression just had to run its course. But millions of Americans would not wait for the economic system to right itself. The depression had caused not only financial disaster but, perhaps more important, a loss in personal pride, status, and self-satisfaction. Prompt and immediate action was demanded. All indications pointed to a sweeping Democratic victory in the 1932 elections.

The Republicans knew their position was difficult but they renominated Hoover and stood on his record, giving unstinted praise to the policies that had guided the nation for the preceding four years. The Democrats convened in Chicago in June, confident of victory. After a masterly preconvention campaign managed by James A. Farley and Louis Howe, Franklin D. Roosevelt won the nomination on the fourth ballot. The 50-year-old governor of New York, a distant relative of Theodore Roosevelt, shattered precedent by flying to the convention to accept the nomination in person. "I pledge you," he told the delegates, "I pledge myself, to a new deal for the American people."

Roosevelt toured the nation talking about relief, tariff reform regulation of utilities, and economic reorganization. Throughout his campaign, he declared his unalterable support of private capitalism, insisting that reforms were necessary to prevent revolutionary movements from developing out of the economic debacle. Hoover, on the other hand, denounced proposals for additional federal controls and reemphasized his belief in the common good to be achieved through the voluntary cooperation of individuals. But the depression was only one real campaign issue. On Election Day, the nation gave Roosevelt a smashing victory, 22,809,038 votes to Hoover's 15,758,901. Hoover carried only six states, losing the electoral vote 472 to 59. The Democrats also elected heavy majorities to both houses of Congress. The people wanted a change and they had placed their faith in Franklin Roosevelt.

Between Election Day and the swearing in of the new president, the depression deepened. Numerous bank failures, the result of sudden panic by depositors, added to the growing alarm. By March 4, 1933, bank holidays had been declared in all but two states. Stock and grain markets were closed and business lay stagnant. On Inauguration Day, hunger marchers paraded in New York and

Chicago as if in a ghastly mockery of the Washington ceremonies. It seemed that all the fears brought by the depression had come to a climax. "World literally rocking beneath our feet," noted journalist Agnes Meyer. "Hard on H[oover] to go out of office to the sound of crashing banks. Like the tragic end of a tragic story. . . . H's administration is Greek in its fatality."

Roosevelt's inaugural address gave hope to a disillusioned America. His assured tone and absolute confidence in the recovery of the country provided a needed tonic for a confused people. The president's encouraging voice urged immediate steps to end unemployment, to aid the farmer, and to bring about national recovery. If the Congress failed to respond, he promised to seek broad executive powers "to wage a war against the emergency, as great as the power that would be given to me if we were in fact invaded by a foreign foe." This vigorous assertion of national leadership, combined with Roosevelt's forceful presentation, inspired confidence and renewed faith in the democratic system of government. Not since Washington had a president started his term of office with such popular support.

I am certain that my fellow Americans expect that on my induction into the Presidency I will address them with a candor and a decision which the present situation of our Nation impels. This is preeminently the time to speak the truth, the whole truth, frankly and boldly. Nor need we shrink from honestly facing conditions in our country today. This great Nation will endure as it has endured, will revive and will prosper. So, first of all, let me assert my firm belief that the only thing we have to fear is fear itself; nameless, unreasoning, unjustified terror which paralyzes needed efforts to convert retreat into advance. In every dark hour of our national life a leadership of frankness and vigor has met with that understanding and support of the people themselves which is essential to victory. I am convinced that you will again give that support to leadership in these critical days.

In such a spirit on my part and on yours we face our common difficulties. They concern, thank God, only material things. Values have shrunken to fantastic levels; taxes have risen; our ability to pay has fallen; government of all kinds is faced by serious curtailment of income; the means of exchange are frozen in the currents of trade; the withered leaves of industrial enterprise lie on every side; farmers find no markets for their produce; the savings of many years in thousands of families are gone.

More important, a host of unemployed citizens face the grim problem of existence, and an equally great number toil with little return. Only a foolish optimist can deny the dark realities of the moment.

Yet our distress comes from no failure of substance. We are stricken by no plague of locusts. Compared with the perils which our forefathers conquered because they believed and were not afraid, we have still much to be thankful for. Nature still offers her bounty and human efforts have multiplied it. Plenty is at our doorstep, but a generous use of it languishes in the very sight of the supply. Primarily this is because the rulers of the exchange of mankind's goods have failed, through their own stubbornness and their own incompetence, have admitted their failure, and abdicated. Practices of the unscrupulous money changers stand indicted in the court of public opinion, rejected by the hearts and minds of men.

True they have tried, but their efforts have been cast in the pattern of an outworn tradition. Faced by failure of credit they have proposed only the lending of more money. Stripped of the lure of profit by which to induce our people to follow their false leadership, they have resorted to exhortations, pleading tearfully for restored confidence. They know only the rules of a generation of self-seekers. They have no vision, and when there is no vision the people perish.

The money changers have fled from their high seats in the temple of our civilization. We may now restore that temple to the ancient truths. The measure of the restoration lies in the extent to which we apply social values more noble than mere monetary profit.

Happiness lies not in the mere possession of money; it lies in the joy of achievement, in the thrill of creative effort. The joy and moral stimulation of work no longer must be forgotten in the mad chase of evanescent profits. These dark days will be worth all they cost us if they teach us that our true destiny is not to be ministered unto but to minister to ourselves and to our fellow men.

Recognition of the falsity of material wealth as the standard of success goes hand in hand with the abandonment of the false belief that public office and high political position are to be valued only by the standards of pride of place and personal profit; and there must be an end to a conduct in banking and in business which too often has given to a sacred trust the likeness of callous and selfish wrongdoing. Small wonder that confidence languishes, for it thrives only on honesty, on honor, on the sacredness of obligations, on faithful protection, on unselfish performance; without them it cannot live.

Restoration calls, however, not for changes in ethics alone. This Nation asks for action, and action now.

Our greatest primary task is to put people to work. This is no unsolvable problem if we face it wisely and courageously. It can be accomplished in part by direct recruiting by the Government itself, treating the task as we would treat the emergency of a war, but at the same time, through this employment, accomplishing greatly needed projects to stimulate and reorganize the use of our natural resources.

Hand in hand with this we must frankly recognize the overbalance of population in our industrial centers and, by engaging on a national scale in a redistribution, endeavor to provide a better use of the land for those best fitted for the land. The task can be helped by definite efforts to raise the values of agricultural products and with this the power to purchase the output of our cities. It can be helped by preventing realistically the tragedy of the growing loss through foreclosure of our small homes and our farms. It can be helped by insistence that the Federal, State, and local governments act forthwith on the demand that their cost be drastically reduced. It can be helped by the unifying of relief activities which today are often scattered, uneconomical, and unequal. It can be helped by national planning for and supervision of all forms of transportation and of communications and other utilities which have a definitely public character. There are many ways in which it can be helped, but it can never be helped merely by talking about it. We must act and act quickly.

Finally, in our progress toward a resumption of work we require two safeguards against a return of the evils of the old order; there must be a strict supervision of all banking and credits and investments; there must be an end to speculation with other people's money, and there must be provision for an adequate but sound currency.

There are the lines of attack. I shall presently urge upon a new Congress in special session detailed measures for their fulfillment, and I shall seek the immediate assistance of the several States.

Through this program of action we address ourselves to putting our own national house in order and making income balance outgo. Our international trade relations, though vastly important, are in point of time and necessity secondary to the establishment of a sound national economy. I favor as a practical policy the putting of first things first. I shall spare no effort to restore world trade by international economic readjustment, but the emergency at home cannot wait on that accomplishment.

The basic thought that guides these specific means of national recovery is not narrowly nationalistic. It is the insistence, as a first consideration, upon the interdependence of the various elements in all parts of the United States; a recognition of the old and permanently important manifestation of the American spirit of the pioneer. It is the way to recovery. It is the immediate way. It is the strongest assurance that the recovery will endure.

In the field of world policy I would dedicate this Nation to the policy of the good neighbor; the neighbor who resolutely respects himself and, because he does so, respects the rights of others; the neighbor who respects his obligations and respects the sanctity of his agreements in and with a world of neighbors.

If I read the temper of our people correctly, we now realize as we have never realized before our interdependence on each other; that we can not merely take but we must give as well; that if we are to go forward, we must move as a trained and loyal army willing to sacrifice for the good of a common discipline, because without such discipline no progress is made, no leadership becomes effective. We are, I know, ready and willing to submit our lives and property to such discipline, because it makes possible a leadership which aims at a larger good. This I propose to offer, pledging that the larger purposes will bind upon us all as a sacred obligation with a unity of duty hitherto evoked only in time of armed strife.

With this pledge taken, I assume unhesitatingly the leadership of this great army of our people dedicated to a disciplined attack upon our common problems.

Action in this image and to this end is feasible under the form of government which we have inherited from our ancestors. Our Constitution is so simple and practical that it is possible always to meet extraordinary needs by changes in emphasis and arrangement without loss of essential form. That is why our constitutional system has proved itself the most superbly enduring political mechanism the modern world has produced. It has met every stress of vast expansion of territory, of foreign wars, of bitter internal strife, of world relations.

It is to be hoped that the normal balance of executive and legislative authority may be wholly adequate to meet the unprecedented task before us. But it may be that an unprecedented demand and need for undelayed action may call for temporary departure from that normal balance of public procedure.

I am prepared under my constitutional duty to recommend the measures that a stricken nation in the midst of a stricken world may require. These measures, or such other measures as the Congress may build out of its experience and wisdom, I shall seek, within my constitutional authority, to bring to speedy adoption.

But in the event that the Congress shall fail to take one of these two courses, and in the event that the national emergency is still critical, I shall not evade the clear course of duty that will then confront me. I shall ask the Congress for the one remaining instrument to meet the crisis; broad Executive power to wage a war against the emergency, as great as the power that would be given to me if we were in fact invaded by a foreign foe.

For the trust reposed in me I will return the courage and the devotion that befit the time. I can do no less.

We face the arduous days that lie before us in the warm courage of the national unity; with the clear consciousness of seeking old and precious moral values; with the clean satisfaction that comes from the stem performance of duty by old and young alike. We aim at the assurance of a rounded and permanent national life.

We do not distrust the future of essential democracy. The people of the United States have not failed. In their need they have registered a mandate that they want direct, vigorous action. They have asked for discipline and direction under leadership. They have made me the present instrument of their wishes. In the spirit of the gift I take it.

In this dedication of a Nation we humbly ask the blessing of God. May He protect each and every one of us. May He guide me in the days to come.

——— SECOND INAUGURAL ADDRESS ———

JANUARY 20, 1937

COMMENTARY

On Inauguration Day, 1937, Franklin D. Roosevelt could look at a multitude of faces no longer taut, drawn, and anxious. For four years the New Deal had passed a bewildering number of laws and created dozens of agencies to meet the problems of relief, recovery, and reform. Although these policies did not completely alleviate depression conditions, hope had returned to America. Unemployment was reduced and the government's vast relief programs cared for the millions still without work. Farm prices rose dramatically—corn sold at $1.26 a bushel compared to 24 cents in 1933. Wheat reached 51 cents per bushel; it had been 47 cents four years earlier. Weekly factory wages had increased an estimated 65 percent. In some quarters, however, the New Deal policies of positive government and increased taxes aroused deep bitterness, but the people as a whole had more income than at any time since the depression first struck the country.

The 1936 Democratic nominee was never in doubt. The national convention met at Philadelphia in June and renominated Roosevelt by acclamation. The Republicans chose Governor Alfred M. Landon of Kansas and their platform endorsed many New Deal projects, including Social Security, the right of labor to collective bargaining, wage-and-hour laws, soil conservation, and the enforcement of antitrust laws. But they caustically denounced the continued growth of federal power and Roosevelt's "socialistic experiments," labeling his administration an "unconstitutional dictatorship." "America is in peril," the GOP warned.

A lively and bitter campaign followed. Republican orators claimed that the New Deal destroyed the American way of life and deprived individuals of their freedom. The Democrats campaigned on the theme that conditions were better than they had been in 1932. Enthusiastic crowds mobbed the president when he toured the country. "You look happier today than you did four years ago," he would say, and the frenzied rallies would become almost uncontrollable.

On November 3, 1936, the nation gave FDR the greatest landslide victory in the history of presidential elections to that date. In the popular vote, Roosevelt polled 27,478,945 to Landon's 16,674,665. Only Maine and Vermont returned majorities for Landon. The president's triumph further increased the Democratic ranks in Congress. Of the 435 House seats, 333 went to Democrats. In the Senate, Democratic membership soared to 75. Roosevelt now stood at the pinnacle of his career. As the unchallenged leader of a vast coalition, he held a mandate to fulfill his promises as the master builder for a still-damaged and troubled America.

Roosevelt's second inaugural occurred on January 20, 1937, in accordance with the Twentieth Amendment, designed to shorten the time between the election and the inauguration of the chief executive. The president declared that his program of social reform was, by no means, complete. In 1933, his prime objective had been recovery. His new objective envisioned a consolidation of what had been accomplished plus an extension of the New Deal's social and economic programs. "In this nation," he said, "I see tens of millions of its citizens . . . who at this very moment are denied the greater part of what the very lowest standards of today call the necessities of life. . . . I see one-third of a nation *ill-housed, ill-clad, ill-nourished." But the president saw these bleak conditions as a challenge. "It is not in despair that I paint you that picture. I paint it for you in hope—because the Nation, seeing and understanding the injustice in it, proposes to paint it out."*

When four years ago we met to inaugurate a President, the Republic, single minded in anxiety, stood in spirit here. We dedicated ourselves to the fulfillment of a vision; to speed the time when there would be for all the people that security and peace essential to the pursuit of happiness. We of the Republic pledged ourselves to drive from the temple of our ancient faith those who had profaned it; to end by action, tireless and unafraid, the stagnation and despair of that day. We did those first things first.

Our covenant with ourselves did not stop there. Instinctively we recognized a deeper need, the need to find through government the instrument of our united purpose to solve for the individual the ever rising problems of a complex civilization. Repeated attempts at their solution without the aid of government had left us baffled and bewildered. For, without that aid, we had been unable to create those moral controls over the services of science which are necessary to make science a useful servant instead of a ruthless master of mankind. To do this we knew that we must find practical controls over blind economic forces and blindly selfish men.

We of the Republic sensed the truth that democratic government has innate capacity to protect its people against disasters once considered inevitable, to solve problems once considered unsolvable. We would not admit that we could not find a way to master economic epidemics just as, after centuries of fatalistic suffering, we had found a way to master epidemics of disease. We refused to leave the problems of our common welfare to be solved by the winds of chance and the hurricanes of disaster. In this we Americans were discovering no wholly new truth; we were writing a new chapter in our book of self-government.

This year marks the one hundred and fiftieth anniversary of the Constitutional Convention which made us a nation. At that Convention our forefathers found the way out of the chaos which followed the Revolutionary War; they created a strong government with powers of united action sufficient then and now to solve problems utterly beyond individual or local solution. A century and a half ago they established the Federal Government in order to promote the general welfare and secure the blessings of liberty to the American people. Today we invoke those same powers of government to achieve the same objectives.

Four years of new experience have not belied our historic instinct. They hold out the clear hope that government within communities, government within the separate States, and government of the United States can do the things the times require, without yielding its democracy. Our tasks in the last four years did not force democracy to take a holiday.

Nearly all of us recognize that as intricacies of human relationships increase, so power to govern them also must increase; power to stop evil; power to do good. The essential democracy of our Nation and the safety of our people depend not upon the absence of power, but upon lodging it with those whom the people can change or continue at stated intervals through an honest and free system of elections. The Constitution of 1787 did not make our democracy impotent.

In fact, in these last four years, we have made the exercise of all power more democratic; for we have begun to bring private autocratic powers into their proper subordination to the public's government. The legend that they were invincible, above and beyond the processes of a democracy, has been shattered. They have been challenged and beaten.

Our progress out of the depression is obvious. But that is not all that you and I mean by the new order of things. Our pledge was not merely to do a patchwork job with secondhand materials. By using the new materials of social justice we have undertaken to erect on the old foundations a more enduring structure for the better use of future generations.

In that purpose we have been helped by achievements of mind and spirit. Old truths have been relearned; untruths have been unlearned. We have always known that heedless self-interest was bad morals; we know now that it is bad economics. Out of the collapse of a prosperity whose builders boasted their practicality has come the conviction that in the long run economic morality pays. We are beginning to wipe out the line that divides the practical from the ideal; and in so doing we are fashioning an instrument of unimagined power for the establishment of a morally better world.

This new understanding undermines the old admiration of worldly success as such. We are beginning to abandon our tolerance of the abuse of power by those who betray for profit the elementary decencies of life.

In this process evil things formerly accepted will not be so easily condoned. Hard-headedness will not so easily excuse hardheartedness. We are moving toward an era of good feeling. But we realize that there can be no era of good feeling save among men of good will. For these reasons I am justified in believing that the greatest change we have witnessed has been the change in the moral climate of America.

Among men of good will, science and democracy together offer an ever richer life and ever larger satisfaction to the individual. With this change in our moral climate and our rediscovered ability to improve our economic order, we have set our feet upon the road of enduring progress. Shall we pause now and turn our back upon the road that lies ahead? Shall we call this the promised land or shall we continue on our way? For each age is a dream that is dying, or one that is coming to birth.

Many voices are heard as we face a great decision. Comfort says, tarry a while. Opportunism says, this is a good spot. Timidity asks, how difficult is the road ahead?

True, we have come far from the days of stagnation and despair. Vitality has been preserved. Courage and confidence have been restored. Mental and moral horizons have been extended. But our present gains were won under the pressure of more than ordinary circumstances. Advance became imperative under the goad of fear and suffering. The times were on the side of progress.

To hold to progress today, however, is more difficult. Dulled conscience, irresponsibility, and ruthless self-interest already reappear. Such symptoms of prosperity may become portents of disaster. Prosperity already tests the persistence of our progressive purpose. Let us ask again, have we reached the goal of our vision of that fourth day of March 1933? Have we found our happy valley?

I see a great nation, upon a great continent, blessed with a great wealth of natural resources. Its hundred and thirty million people are at peace among themselves; they are making their country a good neighbor among the nations. I see a United States which can demonstrate that, under democratic methods of government, national wealth can be translated into a spreading volume of human comforts hitherto unknown, and the lowest standard of living can be raised far above the level of mere subsistence.

But here is the challenge to our democracy. In this nation I see tens of millions of its citizens, a substantial part of its whole population, who at this very moment are denied the greater part of what the very lowest standards of today call the necessities of life. I see millions of families trying to live on incomes so meager that the pall of family disaster hangs over them day by day; I see millions whose daily lives in city and on farm continue under conditions labeled indecent by a so-called polite society half a century ago; I see millions denied education, recreation, and the opportunity to better their lot and the lot of their children; I see millions lacking the means to buy the products of farm and factory and by their poverty denying work and productiveness to many other millions; I see one-third of a nation ill-housed, ill-clad, ill-nourished.

It is not in despair that I paint you that picture. I paint it for you in hope—because the Nation, seeing and understanding the injustice in it, proposes to paint it out. We are determined to make every American citizen the subject of his country's interest and concern; and we will never regard any faithful law abiding group within our borders as superfluous. The test of our progress is not whether we add more to the abundance of those who have much; it is whether we provide enough for those who have too little.

If I know aught of the spirit and purpose of our Nation, we will not listen to comfort, opportunism and timidity. We will carry on.

Overwhelmingly, we of the Republic are men and women of good will; men and women who have more than warm hearts of dedication; men and women who have cool heads and willing hands of practical purpose as well. They will insist that every agency of popular government use effective instruments to carry out their will.

Government is competent when all who compose it work as trustees for the whole people. It can make constant progress when it keeps abreast of all the facts. It can obtain justified support and legitimate criticism when the people receive true information of all that government does.

If I know aught of the will of our people, they will demand that these conditions of effective government shall be created and maintained. They will demand a nation uncorrupted by cancers of injustice and, therefore, strong among the nations in its example of the will to peace.

Today we reconsecrate our country to long cherished ideals in a suddenly changed civilization. In every land there are always at work forces that drive men apart and forces that draw men together. In our personal ambitions we are individualists. But in our seeking for economic and political progress as a nation, we all go up, or else we all go down, as one people.

To maintain a democracy of effort requires a vast amount of patience in dealing with differing methods, a vast amount of humility. But out of the confusion of many voices rises an understanding of dominant public need. Then political leadership can voice common ideals, and aid in their realization.

In taking again the oath of office as President of the United States, I assume the solemn obligation of leading the American people forward along the road over which they have chosen to advance. While this duty rests upon me I shall do my utmost to speak their purpose and to do their will, seeking Divine guidance to help us each and every one to give light to them that sit in darkness and to guide our feet into the way of peace.

——— THIRD INAUGURAL ADDRESS ———

JANUARY 20, 1941

COMMENTARY

Franklin Roosevelt's second inaugural dddress made no mention whatsoever of foreign affairs. Nevertheless, events in Europe and Asia had overshadowed his administration, and the mounting international crisis convinced him to seek an unprecedented third term in 1940.

Throughout the 1930s the United States clung to an isolationist policy, believing that even if war should come abroad, the nation would be able to remain neutral. The bitter memories of the past world war and the dread of a future one, suggested by the rubble of Madrid and Shanghai, helped to create a public opinion that earnestly searched for peace. But the European events of 1939, climaxed by the German invasion of Poland, indicated to many Americans that their own interests were more deeply involved in foreign developments than they had realized. President Roosevelt reflected this change when he declared: "The nation will remain a neutral nation, but I cannot ask that every American remain neutral in thought as well. . . . Even a neutral cannot be asked to close his mind or conscience." Following his statement, a special session of Congress repealed the ban on sales of munitions to foreign countries (November 1939). Neutrality was rapidly discarded as the United States, led by a president determined to aid the European democracies, edged closer toward war.

Against this background, Americans observed their inalienable right to choose a president. The Democratic convention assembled in Chicago during July, and renominated Roosevelt on the first ballot. "My conscience," he declared, "will not allow me to turn my back upon a call to service." The Republicans passed over the claims of their party stalwarts to choose

Wendell L. Willkie, a one-time Democrat and a public-utility executive who had gained national attention for his criticisms of the Tennessee Valley Authority. Willkie accepted most of the New Deal domestic legislation but derided the administration for its inefficiency and bureaucracy. Above all, he pictured the dangers of a third-term candidate. Both parties supported the national defense program, aid to Great Britain, and hemispheric preparedness. Both opposed involvement in a foreign war. Although Roosevelt swept to another victory, receiving some 27 million votes to Willkie's 22 million, the election was closer than any since 1916.

Between the election and the inauguration, many of the hard-fought New Deal domestic issues became obscured by the growing Axis menace. Aware of the desperate British need for arms, Roosevelt established the Office of Production Management in December to coordinate defense production and to speed all material aid "short of war." When Germany protested, the president went on the radio to stress the Fascist threat to America, proclaiming that the United States must be "the great arsenal for democracy." On January 6, 1941, Roosevelt recommended a "lend-lease" program enabling any country whose defense the president deemed vital to that of the United States to receive arms and supplies by sale, transfer, or lease. Two weeks later, he explained in his third inaugural address that "In this day the task of the people is to save the Nation and its institutions from disruption from without." To the United States and the listening world, Roosevelt asserted that there must be no doubts about the future of freedom, warning belligerent nations that "our strong purpose is to protect and to perpetuate the integrity of democracy." The usual festive inaugural parade contained a grim, somber note as armored cars and tanks passed in review.

On each national day of inauguration since 1789, the people have renewed their sense of dedication to the United States. In Washington's day the task of the people was to create and weld together a nation. In Lincoln's day the task of the people was to preserve that Nation from disruption from within. In this day the task of the people is to save that Nation and its institutions from disruption from without.

To us there has come a time, in the midst of swift happenings, to pause for a moment and take stock; to recall what our place in history has been, and to rediscover what we are and what we may be. If we do not, we risk the real peril of inaction.

Lives of nations are determined not by the count of years, but by the lifetime of the human spirit. The life of a man is three-score years and ten: a little more, a little less. The life of a nation is the fullness of the measure of its will to live.

There are men who doubt this. There are men who believe that democracy, as a form of Government and a frame of life, is limited or measured by a kind of mystical and artificial fate that, for some unexplained reason, tyranny and slavery have become the surging wave of the future; and that freedom is an ebbing tide. But we Americans know that this is not true.

Eight years ago, when the life of this Republic seemed frozen by a fatalistic terror, we proved that this is not true. We were in the midst of shock, but we acted. We acted quickly, boldly, decisively.

These later years have been living years, fruitful years for the people of this democracy. For they have brought to us greater security and, I hope, a better understanding that life's ideals are to be measured in other than material things.

Most vital to our present and our future is this experience of a democracy which successfully survived crisis at home; put away many evil things; built new structures on enduring lines; and, through it all, maintained the fact of its democracy.

For action has been taken within the three way framework of the Constitution of the United States. The coordinate branches of the Government continue freely to function. The Bill of Rights remains inviolate. The freedom of elections is wholly maintained. Prophets of the downfall of American democracy have seen their dire predictions come to naught.

Democracy is not dying.

We know it because we have seen it revive and grow.

We know it cannot die because it is built on the unhampered initiative of individual men and women joined together in a common enterprise; an enterprise undertaken and carried through by the free expression of a free majority.

We know it because democracy alone, of all forms of government, enlists the full force of men's enlightened will.

We know it because democracy alone has constructed an unlimited civilization capable of infinite progress in the improvement of human life.

We know it because, if we look below the surface, we sense it still spreading on every continent; for it is the most humane, the most advanced, and in the end the most unconquerable of all forms of human society.

A nation, like a person, has a body; a body that must be fed and clothed and housed, invigorated and rested, in a manner that measures up to the objectives of our time.

A nation, like a person, has a mind; a mind that must be kept informed and alert, that must know itself, that understands the hopes and the needs of its neighbors; all the other nations that live within the narrowing circle of the world.

And a nation, like a person, has something deeper; something more permanent; something larger than the sum of all its parts. It is that something which matters most to its future, which calls forth the most sacred guarding of its present.

It is a thing for which we find it difficult, even impossible, to hit upon a single, simple word. And yet we all understand what it is, the spirit, the faith of America. It is the product of centuries. It was born in the multitudes of those who came from many lands. Some of high degree but mostly plain people, who sought here, early and late, to find freedom more freely.

The democratic aspiration is no mere recent phase in human history. It is human history. It permeated the ancient life of early peoples. It blazed anew in the middle ages. It was written in Magna Charta.

In the Americas its impact has been irresistible. America has been the New World in all tongues, to all peoples, not because this continent was a new found land, but because all those who came here believed they could create upon this continent a new life; a life that should be new in freedom.

Its vitality was written into our own Mayflower Compact, into the Declaration of Independence, into the Constitution of the United States, into the Gettysburg Address.

Those who first came here to carry out the longings of their spirit, and the millions who followed, and the stock that sprang from them; all have moved forward constantly and consistently toward an ideal which in itself has gained stature and clarity with each generation.

The hopes of the Republic cannot forever tolerate either undeserved poverty or self-serving wealth.

We know that we still have far to go; that we must more greatly build the security and the opportunity and the knowledge of every citizen, in the measure justified by the resources and the capacity of the land. But it is not enough to achieve these purposes alone. It is not enough to clothe and feed the body of this Nation, and instruct and inform its mind. For there is also the spirit. And of the three, the greatest is the spirit.

Without the body and the mind, as all men know, the Nation could not live. But if the spirit of America were killed, even though the Nation's body and mind, constricted in an alien world, lived on, the America we know would have perished.

That spirit, that faith, speaks to us in our daily lives in ways often unnoticed, because they seem so obvious. It speaks to us here in the Capital of the Nation. It speaks to us through the processes of governing in the sovereignties of forty-eight States. It speaks to us in our counties, in our cities, in our towns, and in our villages. It speaks to us from the other nations of the hemisphere, and from those across the seas; the enslaved, as well as the free. Sometimes we fail to hear or heed these voices of freedom because to us the privilege of our freedom is such an old, old story.

The destiny of America was proclaimed in words of prophecy spoken by our first President in his first inaugural in 1789; words almost directed, it would seem, to this year of 1941. The preservation of the sacred fire of liberty and the destiny of the republican model of government are justly considered deeply; finally, staked on the experiment intrusted to the hands of the American people.

If we lose that sacred fire, if we let it be smothered with doubt and fear, then we shall reject the destiny which Washington strove so valiantly and so triumphantly to establish. The preservation of the spirit and faith of the Nation does, and will, furnish the highest justification for every sacrifice that we may make in the cause of national defense.

In the face of great perils never before encountered, our strong purpose is to protect and to perpetuate the integrity of democracy. For this we muster the spirit of America, and the faith of America. We do not retreat. We are not content to stand still. As Americans, we go forward, in the service of our country, by the will of God.

——— FOURTH INAUGURAL ADDRESS ———

JANUARY 20, 1945

COMMENTARY

On January 20, 1945, Franklin Roosevelt delivered his shortest inaugural address—573 words. For three years, American soldiers had fought to defeat the Axis powers in Europe, Africa, and Asia, as well as on the seven seas. At home, unemployment disappeared as the civilian labor force swelled to a record 54.5 million. Factories and shipyards produced staggering amounts of war materials. Gradually, the Axis powers retreated. The war had required a mighty effort and the nation successfully met the challenge.

In the fall of 1944, with the war entering its final phase, Americans went to the polls to choose a president. For the first time, a candidate asked for a fourth term. For the first time, too, American soldiers cast ballots in the field. The Democrats chose Senator Harry S. Truman of Missouri as Roosevelt's running mate. Standing on its record in both domestic and foreign affairs, the party pledged to seek a lasting peace. Governor Thomas E. Dewey of New York won the Republican nomination on the first ballot. The two parties fundamentally agreed on most basic issues, causing the campaign to turn on the question of who was most qualified to conclude the war and formulate the peace. On November 7, some 48 million Americans voted and reelected Roosevelt by a plurality of nearly 3.6 million votes.

Roosevelt's fourth inaugural was held on the south portico of the White House instead of at the Capitol. The simple ceremony lasted about five minutes. Robert E. Sherwood writes that the president worked over his short address "with more care and more interest than he had shown in the preparation of any speech in two years. I had the feeling that he was summing up his most profound beliefs when he said, 'We have learned to be citizens of the world, members of the human community. We have learned the simple truth, as Emerson said, that "the only way to have a friend is to be one." ' "

Mr. Chief Justice, Mr. Vice President, my friends:

You will understand and, I believe, agree with my wish that the form of this inauguration be simple and its words brief.

We Americans of today, together with our allies, are passing through a period of supreme test. It is a test of our courage, of our resolve, of our wisdom, of our essential democracy. If we meet that test, successfully and honorably, we shall perform a service of historic importance which men and women and children will honor throughout all time. As I stand here today, having taken the solemn oath of office in the presence of my fellow countrymen, in the presence of our God, I know that it is America's purpose that we shall not fail.

In the days and in the years that are to come we shall work for a just and honorable peace, a durable peace, as today we work and fight for total victory in war. We can and we will achieve such a peace.

We shall strive for perfection. We shall not achieve it immediately, but we still shall strive. We may make mistakes, but they must never be mistakes which result from faintness of heart or abandonment of moral principle.

I remember that my old schoolmaster, Dr. Peabody, said in days that seemed to us then to be secure and untroubled, things in life will not always run smoothly. Sometimes we will be rising toward the heights; then all will seem to reverse itself and start downward. The great fact to remember is that the trend of civilization itself is forever upward; that a line drawn through the middle of the peaks and the valleys of the centuries always has an upward trend.

Our Constitution of 1787 was not a perfect instrument; it is not perfect yet. But it provided a firm base upon which all manner of men, of all races and colors and creeds, could build our solid structure of democracy.

And so today, in this year of war, 1945, we have learned lessons, at a fearful cost, and we shall profit by them.

We have learned that we cannot live alone, at peace; that our own well-being is dependent on the well-being of other nations far away. We have learned that we must live as men, not as ostriches, nor as dogs in the manger.

We have learned to be citizens of the world, members of the human community.

We have learned the simple truth, as Emerson said, that "the only way to have a friend is to be one." We can gain no lasting peace if we approach it with suspicion and mistrust or with fear.

We can gain it only if we proceed with the understanding, the confidence and the courage which flow from conviction.

The almighty God has blessed our land in many ways. He has given our people stout hearts and strong arms with which to strike mighty blows for freedom and truth. He has given to our country a faith which has become the hope of all peoples in an anguished world.

So we pray to Him now for the vision to see our way clearly; to see the way that leads to a better life for ourselves and for all our fellow men; to the achievement of His will to peace on earth.

HARRY S. TRUMAN

INAUGURAL ADDRESS

JANUARY 20, 1949

COMMENTARY

*"I don't know whether you fellows ever had a load of hay or a bull fall on you,"
Harry Truman told reporters the day after Franklin Roosevelt's death, "but last
night the moon, the stars and all the planets fell on me." Truman's selection as
the vice presidential nominee in 1944 occurred mainly because he was the least
objectionable of the several candidates. His birth in the border state of Missouri made him acceptable to both North and South. Veterans' organizations
pointed with pride to his service as an artillery officer in France during World
War I. In 1924, when Truman ran for county judge, the Ku Klux Klan had
opposed him and this now pleased liberals at the Democratic convention. Boss
politicians from large cities noted that Tom Pendergast's Kansas City machine
had supported Truman. But reformers were equally gratified that the machine
scandals had not involved him. While senator, Truman enthusiastically supported the New Deal, establishing a pro-labor and pro-farm voting record that
satisfied these powerful groups. In addition, he had won nationwide attention
as chairman of a special Senate committee investigating national defense. And
so Harry Truman, because no powerful group opposed him, became the 1944
Democratic nominee for vice president. During his eleven-and-one-half-week
service in that office, Roosevelt had not kept him informed about the many
important international decisions that were taking place. Largely unprepared
for the presidency, Truman faced the momentous problems of postwar America
and set out, as he said, to "do my darndest."*

    *The war in the Pacific continued through the summer of 1945. Truman,
Stalin, and Clement Attlee, Churchill's successor, met at Potsdam, near Berlin,*

in July. Agreeing on arrangements for a joint occupation of Germany, they also demanded that Japan surrender unconditionally. When Japan refused, President Truman, in perhaps the most agonizing decision of modern history, ordered an atomic bomb dropped on the industrial city of Hiroshima on August 6, 1945. Three days later, another bomb wiped out Nagasaki. The two blasts killed around 100,000 people. On August 14, Truman announced that Japan had accepted the Potsdam terms and on September 2, in Tokyo Bay, General Douglas MacArthur presided over the formal surrender ceremonies. The most costly and terrifying war in history had ended; the hope for a better world now dawned.

The difficulties of transition from the controlled economy of war to the relatively free economy of peace were many. The chief domestic problems involved demobilization and shortages. In 1945, the supply of meat had reached a new low; razor blades, nylons, electrical appliances, automobiles, and cigarettes were virtually unobtainable. Inflation became alarming as Americans had earned money at unprecedented rates, and now tried to spend it as never before. Government figures showed a rise of 33 percent in living costs between 1941 and 1945. The postwar years witnessed widespread labor-management disputes as workers sought to preserve their wartime gains in earnings. Industry, on the other hand, pressed for relief from scores of federal controls. In 1946, 4.7 million workers went on strike, losing working time that amounted to 110.7 million "man-days." Through all the conflicts of reconverting to a peacetime economy, Truman's political strength steadily declined. On November 5, 1946, the Republicans, making use of the slogan "Had enough?" won control of both houses of Congress for the first time since 1930.

Truman attempted to continue the work of the New Deal in the domestic field. His instincts led him to sympathize with the liberal principles of his predecessor, but the mood of the country appeared to be increasingly conservative. In several messages to Congress, he proposed additional federal aid for housing and education, and a fair-employment practices law to prohibit discrimination based on race, religion, or national origin. But the president was often at odds with Congress, especially with southern Democrats and most Republicans who claimed these programs would create a welfare state. With regard to prices, each party blamed the postwar inflation on the other. Between the middle of 1946 and October 1947, food costs rose 40 percent and clothing 19 percent. Truman proposed a return to wartime wage and price ceilings. Congress, however, passed a much milder bill in December 1947. The sharpest conflict between the president and Congress occurred over labor legislation. Influenced by the mass work stoppages, the Republican-dominated Eightieth Congress passed a strong antilabor bill over the president's veto called the National Labor Relations Act of 1947, or Taft-Hartley Act. Labor organizations bitterly denounced the bill, which, among other things, banned secondary boycotts, established new rules for collective bargaining, and required unions to file complete financial statements with the Department of Labor. The Taft-Hartley Act promised to be one of the major issues in the 1948 elections, as unions labeled it the "slave labor act" and pledged to defeat all who had supported it.

Many Democratic politicians agreed that Harry Truman could not be elected president in 1948, conceding that the Republicans would gain control of the White House after 16 years. Polls taken before the Democratic convention showed that the president's popularity had reached an all-time low. But Truman delegates controlled the convention and gave him the nomination on the first ballot. "I was in a position to control the nomination," wrote Truman. "When I had made up my mind to run, those in the party who turned against me could do nothing to prevent it." The Democratic platform contained a strong civil rights plank, committing the party to support federal laws against lynching, poll taxes, and discrimination in employment. A jubilant Republican convention renominated Governor Thomas Dewey, confident that he would be the next president. To add to the woe of the Democrats, two other groups entered the race, each threatening to cut into Truman's vote. Henry Wallace, vice president during Roosevelt's third term, led the Progressive Party that was pledged to improve relations with the Soviet Union. It appeared that Wallace would receive many votes that usually went to the Democrats. In addition, some southern delegates bolted the Democratic convention over the civil rights plank and formed the States' Rights Party, nominating Governor J. Strom Thurmond of South Carolina for the presidency.

Several presidential candidates have had to cope with splits within their parties, but Truman faced a situation unprecedented in political history. In spite of this handicap, predictions of defeat, and inadequate campaign funds, Truman, in a most surprising political upset, won the election. The final figures showed that he had received 24,105,695 votes, carrying 28 states. Dewey had 21,069,170 votes and 16 states. Wallace and Thurmond polled slightly over one million votes each, with Thurmond capturing Louisiana, Mississippi, Alabama, and South Carolina. Perhaps Truman's greatest achievement was winning without the assistance of the Solid South. Particularly interesting is that not only did the Democrats regain control of Congress, but also won 21 out of

33 gubernatorial contests. The political temper of the nation remained liberal. Shortly after his dramatic election, Truman quipped, "I am just an ordinary human being who has been lucky."

"The oath taking ceremony," wrote Truman in his autobiography, "was scheduled for noon, but in the rotunda of the Capitol the gathering of diplomats, members of Congress, justices of the Supreme Court, and governmental officials was so great, and so many amenities had to be exchanged, that the signal for the Marine Band to play 'Hail to the Chief' was not actually given until twelve-fourteen. . . . The words were the same I had repeated three years and nine months earlier when I had been called so unexpectedly to the White House, but then only a handful of people were with me in the Cabinet Room. I raised my hand; once more I swore faithfully to defend the Constitution of the United States, repeating the short and simple oath, and kissed the Bible. Then I stepped to the rostrum to begin my inaugural address."

Mr. Vice President, Mr. Chief Justice, and fellow citizens:

I accept with humility the honor which the American people have conferred upon me. I accept it with a deep resolve to do all that I can for the welfare of this Nation and for the peace of the world.

In performing the duties of my office, I need the help and prayers of every one of you. I ask for your encouragement and your support. The tasks we face are difficult, and we can accomplish them only if we work together.

Each period of our national history has had its special challenges. Those that confront us now are as momentous as any in the past. Today marks the beginning not only of a new administration, but of a period that will be eventful, perhaps decisive, for us and for the world.

It may be our lot to experience, and in large measure to bring about, a major turning point in the long history of the human race. The first half of this century has been marked by unprecedented and brutal attacks on the rights of man, and by the two most frightful wars in history. The supreme need of our time is for men to learn to live together in peace and harmony.

The peoples of the earth face the future with grave uncertainty, composed almost equally of great hopes and great fears. In this time of doubt, they look to the United States as never before for good will, strength, and wise leadership.

It is fitting, therefore, that we take this occasion to proclaim to the world the essential principles of the faith by which we live, and to declare our aims to all peoples.

The American people stand firm in the faith which has inspired this Nation from the beginning. We believe that all men have a right to equal justice under law and equal opportunity to share in the common good. We believe that all men have the right to freedom of thought and expression. We believe that all men are created equal because they are created in the image of God.

From this faith we will not be moved.

The American people desire, and are determined to work for, a world in which all nations and all peoples are free to govern themselves as they see fit, and to achieve a decent and satisfying life. Above all else, our people desire, and are determined to work for, peace on earth, a just and lasting peace, based on genuine agreement freely arrived at by equals.

In the pursuit of these aims, the United States and other like minded nations find themselves directly opposed by a regime with contrary aims and a totally different concept of life.

That regime adheres to a false philosophy which purports to offer freedom, security, and greater opportunity to mankind. Misled by this philosophy, many peoples have sacrificed their liberties only to learn to their sorrow that deceit and mockery, poverty and tyranny, are their reward.

That false philosophy is communism.

Communism is based on the belief that man is so weak and inadequate that he is unable to govern himself, and therefore requires the rule of strong masters.

Democracy is based on the conviction that man has the moral and intellectual capacity, as well as the inalienable right, to govern himself with reason and justice.

Communism subjects the individual to arrest without lawful cause, punishment without trial, and forced labor as the chattel of the state. It decrees what information he shall receive, what art he shall produce, what leaders he shall follow, and what thoughts he shall think.

Democracy maintains that government is established for the benefit of the individual, and is charged with the responsibility of protecting the rights of the individual and his freedom in the exercise of his abilities.

Communism maintains that social wrongs can be corrected only by violence.

Democracy has proved that social justice can be achieved through peaceful change.

Communism holds that the world is so deeply divided into opposing classes that war is inevitable.

Democracy holds that free nations can settle differences justly and maintain lasting peace.

These differences between communism and democracy do not concern the United States alone. People everywhere are coming to realize that what is involved is material well being, human dignity, and the right to believe in and worship God.

I state these differences, not to draw issues of belief as such, but because the actions resulting from the Communist philosophy are a threat to the efforts of free nations to bring about world recovery and lasting peace.

Since the end of hostilities, the United States has invested its substance and its energy in a great constructive effort to restore peace, stability, and freedom to the world.

We have sought no territory and we have imposed our will on none. We have asked for no privileges we would not extend to others.

We have constantly and vigorously supported the United Nations and related agencies as a means of applying democratic principles to international relations. We have consistently advocated and relied upon peaceful settlement of disputes among nations.

We have made every effort to secure agreement on effective international control of our most powerful weapon, and we have worked steadily for the limitation and control of all armaments.

We have encouraged, by precept and example, the expansion of world trade on a sound and fair basis.

Almost a year ago, in company with 16 free nations of Europe, we launched the greatest cooperative economic program in history. The purpose of that unprecedented effort is to invigorate and strengthen democracy in Europe, so that the free people of that continent can resume their rightful place in the forefront of civilization and can contribute once more to the security and welfare of the world.

Our efforts have brought new hope to all mankind. We have beaten back despair and defeatism. We have saved a number of countries from losing their liberty. Hundreds of millions of people all over the world now agree with us, that we need not have war—that we can have peace.

The initiative is ours.

We are moving on with other nations to build an even stronger structure of international order and justice. We shall have as our partners countries which, no longer solely concerned with the problem of national survival, are now working to improve the standards of living of all their people. We are ready to undertake new projects to strengthen the free world.

In the coming years, our program for peace and freedom will emphasize four major courses of action.

First, we will continue to give unfaltering support to the United Nations and related agencies, and we will continue to search for ways to strengthen their authority and increase their effectiveness. We believe that the United Nations will be strengthened by the new nations which are being formed in lands now advancing toward self-government under democratic principles.

Second, we will continue our programs for world economic recovery.

This means, first of all, that we must keep our full weight behind the European recovery program. We are confident of the success of this major venture in world recovery. We believe that our partners in this effort will achieve the status of self-supporting nations once again.

In addition, we must carry out our plans for reducing the barriers to world trade and increasing its volume. Economic recovery and peace itself depend on increased world trade.

Third, we will strengthen freedom-loving nations against the dangers of aggression.

We are now working out with a number of countries a joint agreement designed to strengthen the security of the North Atlantic area. Such an agreement would take the form of a collective defense arrangement within the terms of the United Nations Charter.

We have already established such a defense pact for the Western Hemisphere by the treaty of Rio de Janeiro.

The primary purpose of these agreements is to provide unmistakable proof of the joint determination of the free countries to resist armed attack from any quarter. Each country participating in these arrangements must contribute all it can to the common defense.

If we can make it sufficiently clear, in advance, that any armed attack affecting our national security would be met with overwhelming force, the armed attack might never occur.

I hope soon to send to the Senate a treaty respecting the North Atlantic security plan.

In addition, we will provide military advice and equipment to free nations which will cooperate with us in the maintenance of peace and security.

Fourth, we must embark on a bold new program for making the benefits of our scientific advances and industrial progress available for the improvement and growth of underdeveloped areas.

More than half the people of the world are living in conditions approaching misery. Their food is inadequate. They are victims of disease.

Their economic life is primitive and stagnant. Their poverty is a handicap and a threat both to them and to more prosperous areas.

For the first time in history, humanity possesses the knowledge and the skill to relieve the suffering of these people.

The United States is preeminent among nations in the development of industrial and scientific techniques. The material resources which we can afford to use for the assistance of other peoples are limited. But our imponderable resources in technical knowledge are constantly growing and are inexhaustible.

I believe that we should make available to peace loving peoples the benefits of our store of technical knowledge in order to help them realize their aspirations for a better life. And, in cooperation with other nations, we should foster capital investment in areas needing development.

Our aim should be to help the free peoples of the world, through their own efforts, to produce more food, more clothing, more materials for housing, and more mechanical power to lighten their burdens.

We invite other countries to pool their technological resources in this undertaking. Their contributions will be warmly welcomed. This should be a cooperative enterprise in which all nations work together through the United Nations and its specialized agencies wherever practicable. It must be a worldwide effort for the achievement of peace, plenty, and freedom.

With the cooperation of business, private capital, agriculture, and labor in this country, this program can greatly increase the industrial activity in other nations and can raise substantially their standards of living. Such new economic developments must be devised and controlled to benefit the peoples of the areas in which they are established. Guarantees to the investor must be balanced by guarantees in the interest of the people whose resources and whose labor go into these developments.

The old imperialism, exploitation for foreign profit, has no place in our plans. What we envisage is a program of development based on the concepts of democratic fair dealing.

All countries, including our own, will greatly benefit from a constructive program for the better use of the world's human and natural resources. Experience shows that our commerce with other countries expands as they progress industrially and economically.

Greater production is the key to prosperity and peace. And the key to greater production is a wider and more vigorous application of modern scientific and technical knowledge.

Only by helping the least fortunate of its members to help themselves can the human family achieve the decent, satisfying life that is the right of all people.

Democracy alone can supply the vitalizing force to stir the peoples of the world into triumphant action, not only against their human oppressors, but also against their ancient enemies hunger, misery, and despair.

On the basis of these four major courses of action we hope to help create the conditions that will lead eventually to personal freedom and happiness for all mankind.

If we are to be successful in carrying out these policies, it is clear that we must have continued prosperity in this country and we must keep ourselves strong.

Slowly but surely we are weaving a world fabric of international security and growing prosperity.

We are aided by all who wish to live in freedom from fear, even by those who live today in fear under their own governments; We are aided by all who want relief from the lies of propaganda, who desire truth and sincerity; We are aided by all who desire self-government and a voice in deciding their own affairs; We are aided by all who long for economic security; for the security and abundance that men in free societies can enjoy; We are aided by all who desire freedom of speech, freedom of religion, and freedom to live their own lives for useful ends. Our allies are the millions who hunger and thirst after righteousness.

In due time, as our stability becomes manifest, as more and more nations come to know the benefits of democracy and to participate in growing abundance, I believe that those countries which now oppose us will abandon their delusions and join with the free nations of the world in a just settlement of international differences.

Events have brought our American democracy to new influence and new responsibilities. They will test our courage, our devotion to duty, and our concept of liberty. But I say to all men, what we have achieved in liberty, we will surpass in greater liberty. Steadfast in our faith in the Almighty, we will advance toward a world where man's freedom is secure.

To that end we will devote our strength, our resources, and our firmness of resolve. With God's help, the future of mankind will be assured in a world of justice, harmony and peace.

Dwight D. Eisenhower

First Inaugural Address

JANUARY 20, 1953

Commentary

The cold war turned hot on June 25, 1950, 7,000 miles from the United States. Soldiers of the Communist-organized "People's Democratic Republic" of North Korea, using Russian-made tanks, drove across the thirty-eighth parallel into South Korea. Twenty-eight hours after the invasion, the United Nations Security Council ordered a cease-fire, which the Korean Communists ignored. Both the United States and the United Nations had assisted in establishing the South Korean Republic in 1947, and Marshall Plan aid and technical advice had been furnished to the young country. If the United States permitted South Korea to be overrun, would the Soviet Union incite a series of incursions in other parts of the world? Was this the ominous test to see if the democracies would resist Communist aggression? On June 27, President Truman firmly announced his decision to send American air and sea forces into combat. The same day, an emergency session of the Security Council requested United Nations members to furnish armed forces to assist South Korea. On June 30, Truman ordered U.S. ground troops into action. The Security Council voted to place the United States in charge of the United Nations fighting force, and the president appointed General Douglas MacArthur military commander. Reminded that only Congress has the power to declare war, Truman very carefully called this a "police action, not a war."

The fighting in Korea can be divided into three broad phases: retreat, counterattack, and Chinese intervention. Throughout the summer of 1950, American marines fell back across South Korea until they occupied only a small beachhead, approximately the size of Connecticut. On September 15, the United Nations launched an amphibious landing at Inchon on the Korean western coast. At the same time, American Marines broke out of the beachhead and regained lost ground. The United Nations forces now began an all-out counterattack, driving into North Korea. By the end of 1950, most of that area had been captured. Then, the Chinese Communists chose to plunge into the fighting by sending waves of "volunteers," forcing the United Nations troops to retreat across the rugged Korean terrain to new defensive positions along the thirty-eighth parallel. For more than two years they occupied this position without appreciable change, while attempts at negotiating a cease-fire dragged on. Finally, on July 27, 1953, both sides agreed to an armistice that kept Korea divided along a line not very different from the original thirty-eighth parallel.

The Korean War became intensely unpopular in the United States. By the end of 1952, America had suffered more than 100,000 casualties, including some 22,000 combat deaths. Critics blamed the Truman administration for having failed to define the "line of containment" against Communist expansion and especially Secretary of State Dean Acheson for his statement in January 1950 that Korea was not essential to American security. Senator Joseph McCarthy of Wisconsin even hurled the unsubstantiated charge that Truman had pro-Russians and even Russian spies as advisors. Most Americans agreed, however, that armed intervention had to take place to demonstrate to the world's Communist leaders that America would use force to stop their expansionist plans.

Although foreign events dominated Truman's second administration, Americans were also concerned about domestic legislation. On January 5, 1949, the president announced that "every segment of our economy and every individual has a right to expect from our Government a fair deal." He then proceeded to outline a program that elaborated and extended the New Deal measures. Congress followed through by passing federal low-rent housing and slum-clearance bills; legislation that increased the minimum wage from 40 cents to 75 cents per hour; extension of rent control to March 31, 1951, for the millions who lived in rented apartments and houses; and a revision of the Social Security Act, which brought approximately 10 million new persons under coverage. But the administration could not secure repeal of the Taft-Hartley Act or enact a strong civil rights bill because of a congressional alliance between southern Democrats and conservative Republicans. Once the Korean conflict began, new outlays for armaments took precedence over domestic federal projects. Nevertheless, there were huge outpourings of consumer goods from private industry, ranging from automobiles and television sets to hula-hoops.

During Truman's second administration, the subjects of communism in government and internal subversion became partisan issues. Communists and *those who sympathized with them faced government checks and congressional investigations. On October 14, 1949, a federal court convicted 11 leaders of the American Communist Party for violating the Smith Act of 1940, which made it a crime to advocate or teach the overthrow of the U.S. government by force or violence. In March 1950, a Senate subcommittee began an investigation of charges made by Senator Joseph McCarthy that "the State Department is infested with Communists" who "handed over" China to Russia. Although the subcommittee majority denounced McCarthy and cleared the State Department, he continued his reckless charges from the Senate floor where immunity protected him from libel suits. The senator, through his smear campaigns against many prominent individuals, stirred up a feeling of distrust and suspicion. He even accused General Eisenhower, on June 15, 1951, of assisting the Russians in obtaining their aim of world domination.*

For 20 years, the Democratic Party had welded the votes of farmers, city machines, and the South into quadrennial victories. In 1952, this same coalition was defeated. The Republicans chose as their candidate General Dwight D. Eisenhower, popular wartime hero, former chief of staff, and NATO commander. His selection took place after a bitter primary fight that almost split the party. Conservative Republicans supported Senator Robert A. Taft of Ohio for the nomination, but the liberal faction managed to defeat him at the convention. The Democrats turned to a new leader, Governor Adlai Stevenson of Illinois, Truman's personal choice as his successor. Beginning with pledges of high purpose, the campaign ended in deep bitterness and recrimination. The two dominating issues were peace and prosperity—in other words, what to do about the bloody and seemingly interminable Korean War and how to maintain a prosperous economy under the burdens imposed by the world threat of communism. Eisenhower promised a new approach, while Stevenson asserted that a Republican administration would mean depression and retreat from the New and Fair Deals. On Election Day, Eisenhower won a tremendous popular vote— 33,824,351 to Stevenson's 27,314,987. For the first time since 1928 a Republican candidate split the solid Democratic South. Stevenson carried only nine states and won 89 electoral votes to Ike's decisive 442. But there was something unique in this election upheaval. The election represented an Eisenhower rather than a Republican triumph. Republicans won the narrowest of margins in the Senate and a slim majority in the House. Voters clearly favored the new leadership that Eisenhower promised, but they appeared less enthusiastic about his party.

In his autobiography, Eisenhower gives this description of events immediately preceding his inaugural:

[On the morning of the inaugural] I decided to write a brief prayer to read before my Inaugural Address. When I told [my wife] Mamie of this idea she agreed enthusiastically, and within five or ten minutes I had written a text on a scratch pad and had it typed. I read it to my son and daughter-in-law and one or two close friends. They thought it was most fitting for the occasion, and it was with this hastily written prayer that I began my first Inaugural Address. It was then time to go to the White House. When Mamie and I dismounted from our car, President and Mrs. Truman came to the front steps; we exchanged greetings and the President and I reentered the first car, while Mamie and Mrs. Truman rode in the second.

To reach the Capitol, custom decreed that the outgoing and incoming presidents ride down Pennsylvania Avenue together. The only comment of any consequence that I can recall during the short ride to the Capitol was asking the President the identity of the person who had ordered my son back from the combat area of Korea to be present at the inauguration. The President replied, "I did," and I thanked him sincerely for his thoughtfulness.

My friends, before I begin the expression of those thoughts that I deem appropriate to this moment, would you permit me the privilege of uttering a little private prayer of my own. And I ask that you bow your heads.

Almighty God, as we stand here at this moment my future associates in the executive branch of government join me in beseeching that Thou will make full and complete our dedication to the service of the people in this throng, and their fellow citizens everywhere.

Give us, we pray, the power to discern clearly right from wrong, and allow all our words and actions to be governed thereby, and by the laws of this land. Especially we pray that our concern shall be for all the people regardless of station, race, or calling.

May cooperation be permitted and be the mutual aim of those who, under the concepts of our Constitution, hold to differing political faiths; so that all may work for the good of our beloved country and Thy glory. Amen.

My fellow citizens:

The world and we have passed the midway point of a century of continuing challenge. We sense with all our faculties that forces of good and evil are massed and armed and opposed as rarely before in history.

This fact defines the meaning of this day. We are summoned by this honored and historic ceremony to witness more than the act of one citizen swearing his oath of service, in the presence of God. We are called as a people to give testimony in the sight of the world to our faith that the future shall belong to the free.

Since this century's beginning, a time of tempest has seemed to come upon the continents of the earth. Masses of Asia have awakened to strike off shackles of the past. Great nations of Europe have fought their bloodiest wars. Thrones have toppled and their vast empires have disappeared. New nations have been born.

For our own country, it has been a time of recurring trial. We have grown in power and in responsibility. We have passed through the anxieties of depression and of war to a summit unmatched in man's history. Seeking to secure peace in the world, we have had to fight through the forests of the Argonne, to the shores of Iwo Jima, and to the cold mountains of Korea.

In the swift rush of great events, we find ourselves groping to know the full sense and meaning of these times in which we live. In our quest of understanding, we beseech God's guidance. We summon all our knowledge of the past and we scan all signs of the future. We bring all our wit and all our will to meet the question. How far have we come in man's long pilgrimage from darkness toward light? Are we nearing the light; a day of freedom and of peace for all mankind? Or are the shadows of another night closing in upon us?

Great as are the preoccupations absorbing us at home, concerned as we are with matters that deeply affect our livelihood today and our vision of the future, each of these domestic problems is dwarfed by, and often even created by, this question that involves all humankind.

This trial comes at a moment when man's power to achieve good or to inflict evil surpasses the brightest hopes and the sharpest fears of all ages. We can turn rivers in their courses, level mountains to the plains. Oceans and land and sky are avenues for our colossal commerce. Disease diminishes and life lengthens.

Yet the promise of this life is imperiled by the very genius that has made it possible. Nations amass wealth. Labor sweats to create, and turns out devices to level not only mountains but also cities. Science seems ready to confer upon us, as its final gift, the power to erase human life from this planet.

At such a time in history, we who are free must proclaim anew our faith. This faith is the abiding creed of our fathers. It is our faith in the deathless dignity of man, governed by eternal moral and natural laws.

This faith defines our full view of life. It establishes, beyond debate, those gifts of the Creator that are man's inalienable rights, and that make all men equal in His sight.

In the light of this equality, we know that the virtues most cherished by free people; love of truth, pride of work, devotion to country; all are treasures equally precious in the lives of the most humble and of the most exalted. The men who mine coal and fire furnaces and balance ledgers and turn lathes and pick cotton and heal the sick and plant corn, all serve as proudly; and as profitably, for America as the statesmen who draft treaties and the legislators who enact laws.

This faith rules our whole way of life. It decrees that we, the people, elect leaders not to rule but to serve. It asserts that we have the right to choice of our own work and to the reward of our own toil. It inspires the initiative that makes our productivity the wonder of the world. And it warns that any man who seeks to deny equality among all his brothers betrays the spirit of the free and invites the mockery of the tyrant.

It is because we, all of us, hold to these principles that the political changes accomplished this day do not imply turbulence, upheaval or disorder. Rather this change expresses a purpose of strengthening our dedication and devotion to the precepts of our founding documents, a conscious renewal of faith in our country and in the watchfulness of a Divine Providence.

The enemies of this faith know no god but force, no devotion but its use. They tutor men in treason. They feed upon the hunger of others. Whatever defies them, they torture, especially the truth.

Here, then, is joined no argument between slightly differing philosophies. This conflict strikes directly at the faith of our fathers and the lives of our sons. No principle or treasure that we hold, from the spiritual knowledge of our free schools and churches to the creative magic of free labor and capital, nothing lies safely beyond the reach of this struggle. Freedom is pitted against slavery; lightness against the dark.

The faith we hold belongs not to us alone but to the free of all the world. This common bond binds the grower of rice in Burma and the planter of wheat in Iowa, the shepherd in southern Italy and the mountaineer in the Andes. It confers a common dignity upon the French soldier who dies in Indo-China, the British soldier killed in Malaya, the American life given in Korea.

We know, beyond this, that we are linked to all free peoples not merely by a noble idea but by a simple need. No free people can for long cling to any privilege or enjoy any safety in economic solitude. For all our own material might, even we need markets in the world for the surpluses of our farms and our factories. Equally, we need for these same farms and factories vital materials and products of distant lands. This basic law of interdependence, so manifest in the commerce of peace, applies with thousand fold intensity in the event of war.

So we are persuaded by necessity and by belief that the strength of all free peoples lies in unity; their danger, in discord. To produce this unity, to meet the challenge of our time, destiny has laid upon our country the responsibility of the free world's leadership.

So it is proper that we assure our friends once again that, in the discharge of this responsibility, we Americans know and we observe the difference between world leadership and imperialism; between firmness and truculence; between a thoughtfully calculated goal and spasmodic reaction to the stimulus of emergencies.

We wish our friends the world over to know this above all—we face the threat, not with dread and confusion, but with confidence and conviction.

We feel this moral strength because we know that we are not helpless prisoners of history. We are free men. We shall remain free, never to be proven guilty of the one capital offense against freedom, a lack of stanch faith.

In pleading our just cause before the bar of history and in pressing our labor for world peace, we shall be guided by certain fixed principles.

These principles are:

1. Abhorring war as a chosen way to balk the purposes of those who threaten us, we hold it to be the first task of statesmanship to develop the strength that will deter the forces of aggression and promote the conditions of peace. For, as it must be the supreme purpose of all free men, so it must be the dedication of their leaders, to save humanity from preying upon itself. In the light of this principle, we stand ready to engage with any and all others in joint effort to remove the causes of mutual fear and distrust among nations, so as to make possible drastic reduction of armaments. The sole requisites for undertaking such effort are that, in their purpose, they be aimed logically and honestly toward secure peace for all; and that, in their result, they provide methods by which every participating nation will prove good faith in carrying out its pledge.

2. Realizing that common sense and common decency alike dictate the futility of appeasement, we shall never try to placate an aggressor by the false and wicked bargain of trading honor for security. Americans, indeed all free men, remember that in the final choice a soldier's pack is not so heavy a burden as a prisoner's chains.

3. Knowing that only a United States that is strong and immensely productive can help defend freedom in our world, we view our Nation's strength and security as a trust upon which rests the hope of free men everywhere. It is the firm duty of each of our free citizens and of every free citizen everywhere to place the cause of his country before the comfort, the convenience of himself.

4. Honoring the identity and the special heritage of each nation in the world, we shall never use our strength to try to impress upon another people our own cherished political and economic institutions.

5. Assessing realistically the needs and capacities of proven friends of freedom, we shall strive to help them to achieve their own security and well-being. Likewise, we shall count upon them to assume, within the limits of their resources, their full and just burdens in the common defense of freedom.

6. Recognizing economic health as an indispensable basis of military strength and the free world's peace, we shall strive to foster everywhere, and to practice ourselves, policies that encourage productivity and profitable trade. For the impoverishment of any single people in the world means danger to the well being of all other peoples.

7. Appreciating that economic need, military security and political wisdom combine to suggest regional groupings of free peoples, we hope, within the framework of the United Nations, to help strengthen such special bonds the world over. The nature of these ties must vary with the different problems of different areas. In the Western Hemisphere, we enthusiastically join with all our neighbors in the work of perfecting a community of fraternal trust and common purpose. In Europe, we ask that enlightened and inspired leaders of the Western nations strive with renewed vigor to make the unity of their peoples a reality. Only as free Europe unitedly marshals its strength can it effectively safeguard, even with our help, its spiritual and cultural heritage.

8. Conceiving the defense of freedom, like freedom itself, to be one and indivisible, we hold all continents and peoples in equal regard and honor. We reject any insinuation that one race or another, one people or another, is in any sense inferior or expendable.

9. Respecting the United Nations as the living sign of all people's hope for peace, we shall strive to make it not merely an eloquent symbol but an effective force. And in our quest for an honorable peace, we shall neither compromise, nor tire, nor ever cease.

By these rules of conduct, we hope to be known to all peoples. By their observance, an earth of peace may become not a vision but a fact. This hope, this supreme aspiration, must rule the way we live.

We must be ready to dare all for our country. For history does not long entrust the care of freedom to the weak or the timid. We must acquire proficiency in defense and display stamina in purpose. We must be willing, individually and as a Nation, to accept whatever sacrifices may be required of us. A people that values its privileges above its principles soon loses both.

These basic precepts are not lofty abstractions, far removed from matters of daily living. They are laws of spiritual strength that generate and define our material strength. Patriotism means equipped forces and a prepared citizenry. Moral stamina means more energy and more productivity, on the farm and in the factory. Love of liberty means the guarding of every resource that makes freedom possible; from the sanctity of our families and the wealth of our soil to the genius of our scientists.

And so each citizen plays an indispensable role. The productivity of our heads, our hands, and our hearts is the source of all the strength we can command, for both the enrichment of our lives and the winning of the peace.

No person, no home, no community can be beyond the reach of this call. We are summoned to act in wisdom and in conscience, to work with industry, to teach with persuasion, to preach with conviction, to weigh our every deed with care and with compassion. For this truth must be clear before us: whatever America hopes to bring to pass in the world must first come to pass in the heart of America.

The peace we seek, then, is nothing less than the practice and fulfillment of our whole faith among ourselves and in our dealings with others. This signifies more than the stilling of guns, easing the sorrow of war. More than escape from death, it is a way of life. More than a haven for the weary, it is a hope for the brave.

This is the hope that beckons us onward in this century of trial. This is the work that awaits us all, to be done with bravery, with charity, and with prayer to almighty God.

——— SECOND INAUGURAL ADDRESS ———

JANUARY 21, 1957

COMMENTARY

Eisenhower brought to the White House a respect for Congress and a traditional concept of the separation of powers. He referred to himself on several occasions as a "constitutional President." "I firmly believe" he said, "that the great mass of the people believe in, you might say, the moderate attack. I believe that they feel they ought to avoid extremes. That is what I stand for." Essentially a pragmatic man, his first administration did not see any major changes in domestic policy. Many of Eisenhower's advisors, especially his initial cabinet appointments, came from the business world and they brought to their office a philosophy, perhaps best summed up by Defense Secretary Charles E. Wilson's comment, "what was good for the country was good for General Motors, and vice versa."

Before Eisenhower had completed his first year in office, a bitter struggle developed between the White House and Senator McCarthy. As chairman of the Senate Committee on Government Operations and of the Permanent Subcommittee on Investigations, the senator continued his unsubstantiated accusations that the federal payroll contained known Communists and fellow travelers. Through his charges, ranging from the assertion that State Department overseas libraries circulated Communist literature to the suggestion that Russian agents directed our intelligence operations, the senator spread fear and dissension throughout the country. In Indiana, a member of the State Textbook Commission went so far as to charge that "there is a Communist directive in education now to stress the story of Robin Hood. They want to stress it because he robbed the rich and gave it to the poor. That's the Communist line. It's just a smearing of law and order." The president tried to hold himself aloof as he did not consider it his function to battle congressional figures in the public arena. He felt time and patience would defeat McCarthy.

In 1954, the Senate conducted two hearings on charges made against Senator McCarthy. The first was to examine the allegation that he had tried to secure favors from the Department of the Army for a former consultant to his subcommittee. The second hearing was called to determine whether his conduct had brought the Senate into disrepute. The sensational first hearing, 2 million words, consumed 160 hours and lasted 36 days. Some 85,000 spectators were admitted to the sessions, while the daily television audience averaged some 20 million. Each side vehemently denied charges made by the other. Although the Senate voted, 67 to 22, on December 2, 1954, to "condemn" McCarthy for conduct unbecoming a senator, each side claimed victory. Eisenhower remained convinced that emotionalism would eventually give way to common sense, and he steadfastly opposed becoming publicly involved. After his censure, McCarthy stayed in the Senate until his death in 1957, but his influence declined sharply.

In foreign policy, the Eisenhower administration carried forward President Truman's main points and the dominating news remained the apparently endless bickering with the Communist world. On March 6, 1953, Premier

Josef Stalin died. Almost immediately, his successor, Georgi Malenkov, began to speak about coexistence. Softer language became the byword in the United Nations. Although short-lived, these peace overtures probably caused the Chinese Communists to agree to a truce in Korea in July 1953, ending the three-year war. The Communists, however, continued to gain in other areas of Asia. In Indo-China, the war between the French Vietnamese and the Communist Vietminh entered its eighth year, with the United States paying approximately 60 percent of the French military costs. Finally, in July 1954, an armistice divided Vietnam into a Communist North and a free South. Six months later, the Chinese Reds began to threaten the islands of Quemoy, Matsu, and Formosa, the last strongholds of Chiang Kaishek's Nationalists. High officials in the Eisenhower administration, including Secretary of State John Foster Dulles, now spoke about sending American troops to help Chiang.

In 1955, the Chinese Communists launched an amphibious assault against the Nationalist-held Tachen Islands, about 200 miles north of Formosa. The president immediately responded and on January 29, 1955, obtained blanket authority from Congress to use American military power to protect Formosa. Eisenhower declared that any attack on the Nationalists would "have to run over" the U.S. Pacific fleet. On December 2, 1954, a new mutual defense pact was concluded with Chiang. In addition, on February 1, 1955, the Senate ratified the Southeast Asia Defense Treaty, which bound the United States to protect Pakistan, Thailand, South Vietnam, Laos, and Cambodia against Communist advances. The Chinese did not invade Formosa; they renewed their threats intermittently but war seemed averted.

When he first came to office, Eisenhower described himself as "President of 160 million Americans," a sort of referee above partisan politics. On several occasions, he expressed his disdain for bickering with Congress. But after the Democratic congressional victories in 1954, the president clearly stated his philosophy of government—liberal in terms of people's needs, but conservative in use of their money. No one doubted that the Republicans would renominate Eisenhower in 1956. The big question remained, though, would he accept? He had suffered two major illnesses, a heart attack in 1955 and an ileitis operation in June 1956. Never before had the health of a president been so candidly debated. Democratic leaders claimed that Eisenhower was much sicker than Republican officials admitted, while Republicans assured the country that he remained capable of performing all executive functions. The Republican convention unanimously renominated him on the first ballot. The Democrats, after a hard-fought preconvention contest, renominated Adlai Stevenson. The outcome was another extraordinary display of the general's personal popularity. Eisenhower won by a landslide, receiving 57.4 percent of the total and 457 electoral votes. But the Democrats captured both houses of Congress and, for the first time since 1848, a president had been elected without his party gaining control of at least one branch of the legislature.

On January 21, 1957, Washington again staged one of the great folk festivals of American life—the inauguration of a president. Ceremonial and spectacular in the grand manner, it began with the solemn oath-taking before the Capitol and concluded with an afternoon-long parade witnessed by hundreds of thousands. But, President Eisenhower commented afterward, "A second inauguration on the same scale as the first one seemed to me to be rather odd, because a man is merely continuing, and it isn't a change."

THE PRICE OF PEACE

Mr. Chairman, Mr. Vice President, Mr. Chief Justice, Mr. Speaker, members of my family and friends, my countrymen, and the friends of my country, wherever they may be:

We meet again, as upon a like moment four years ago, and again you have witnessed my solemn oath of service to you. I too am a witness today, testifying in your name to the principles and purposes to which we, as a people, are pledged.

Before all else, we seek, upon our common labor as a nation, the blessings of Almighty God. And the hopes in our hearts fashion the deepest prayers of our whole people.

May we pursue the right, without self-righteousness; May we know unity, without conformity; May we grow in strength, without pride in self; May we, in our dealings with all peoples of the earth, ever speak truth and serve justice.

And so shall America, in the sight of all men of good will, prove true to the honorable purposes that bind and rule us as a people in all this time of trial through which we pass.

We live in a land of plenty, but rarely has this earth known such peril as today. In our nation, work and wealth abound. Our population grows. Commerce crowds our rivers and rails, our skies, harbors, and highways. Our soil is fertile, our agriculture productive. The air rings with the song of our industry; rolling mills and blast furnaces, dynamos, dams, and assembly lines; the chorus of America the bountiful. This is our home, yet this is not the whole of our world. For our world is where our full destiny lies with men, of all people and all nations, who are or would be free. And for them, and so for us, this is no time of ease or of rest.

In too much of the earth there is want, discord, danger. New forces and new nations stir and strive across the earth, with power to bring, by their fate, great good or great evil to the free world's future. From the deserts of North Africa to the islands of the South Pacific one third of all mankind has entered upon an historic struggle for a new freedom; freedom from grinding poverty. Across all continents, nearly a billion people seek, sometimes almost in desperation, for the skills and knowledge and assistance by which they may satisfy from their own resources, the material wants common to all mankind.

No nation, however old or great, escapes this tempest of change and turmoil. Some, impoverished by the recent World War, seek to restore their means of livelihood. In the heart of Europe, Germany still stands tragically divided. So is the whole continent divided. And so, too, is all the world. The divisive force is International Communism and the power that it controls.

The designs of that power, dark in purpose, are clear in practice. It strives to seal forever the fate of those it has enslaved. It strives to break the ties that unite the free. And it strives to capture, to exploit for its own greater power, all forces of change in the world, especially the needs of the hungry and the hopes of the oppressed.

Yet the world of International Communism has itself been shaken by a fierce and mighty force: the readiness of men who love freedom to pledge their lives to that love. Through the night of their bondage, the unconquerable will of heroes has struck with the swift, sharp thrust of lightning. Budapest is no longer merely the name of a city; henceforth it is a new and shining symbol of man's yearning to be free. Thus, across all the globe there harshly blow the winds of change. And we, though fortunate be our lot, know that we can never turn our backs to them.

We look upon this shaken earth, and we declare our firm and fixed purpose; the building of a peace with justice in a world where moral law prevails. The building of such a peace is a bold and solemn purpose. To proclaim it is easy. To serve it will be hard. And to attain it, we must be aware of its full meaning, and ready to pay its full price. We know clearly what we seek, and why.

We seek peace, knowing that peace is the climate of freedom. And now, as in no other age, we seek it because we have been warned, by the power of modern weapons, that peace may be the only climate possible for human life itself.

Yet this peace we seek cannot be born of fear alone: it must be rooted in the lives of nations. There must be justice, sensed and shared by all peoples, for, without justice the world can know only a tense and unstable truce. There must be law, steadily invoked and respected by all nations, for without law, the world promises only such meager justice as the pity of the strong upon the weak. But the law of which we speak, comprehending the values of freedom, affirms the equality of all nations, great and small.

Splendid as can be the blessings of such a peace, high will be its cost; in toil patiently sustained, in help honorably given, in sacrifice calmly borne. We are called to meet the price of this peace.

To counter the threat of those who seek to rule by force, we must pay the costs of our own needed military strength, and help to build the security of others.

We must use our skills and knowledge and, at times, our substance, to help others rise from misery, however far the scene of suffering may be from our shores. For wherever in the world a people knows desperate want, there must appear at least the spark of hope, the hope of progress, or there will surely rise at last the flames of conflict.

We recognize and accept our own deep involvement in the destiny of men everywhere. We are accordingly pledged to honor, and to strive to fortify, the authority of the United Nations. For in that body rests the best hope of our age for the assertion of that law by which all nations may live in dignity.

And, beyond this general resolve, we are called to act a responsible role in the world's great concerns or conflicts; whether they touch upon the affairs of a vast region, the fate of an island in the Pacific, or the use of a canal in the Middle East. Only in respecting the hopes and cultures of others will we practice the equality of all nations. Only as we show willingness and wisdom in giving counsel, in receiving counsel, and in sharing burdens, will we wisely perform the work of peace.

For one truth must rule all we think and all we do. No people can live to itself alone. The unity of all who dwell in freedom is their only sure defense. The economic need of all nations, in mutual dependence, makes isolation an impossibility; not even America's prosperity could long survive if other nations did not also prosper. No nation can longer be a fortress, lone and strong and safe. And any people, seeking such shelter for themselves, can now build only their own prison. Our pledge to these principles is constant, because we believe in their rightness.

We do not fear this world of change. America is no stranger to much of its spirit. Everywhere we see the seeds of the same growth that America itself has known. The American experiment has, for generations, fired the passion and the courage of millions elsewhere seeking freedom, equality, and opportunity. And the American story of material progress has helped excite the longing of all needy peoples for some satisfaction of their human wants. These hopes that we have helped to inspire, we can help to fulfill. In this confidence, we speak plainly to all peoples.

We cherish our friendship with all nations that are or would be free. We respect, no less, their independence. And when, in time of want or peril, they ask our help, they may honorably receive it; for we no more seek to buy their sovereignty than we would sell our own. Sovereignty is never bartered among freemen.

We honor the aspirations of those nations which, now captive, long for freedom. We seek neither their military alliance nor any artificial imitation of our society. And they can know the warmth of the welcome that awaits them when, as must be, they join again the ranks of freedom.

We honor, no less in this divided world than in a less tormented time, the people of Russia. We do not dread, rather do we welcome, their progress in education and industry. We wish them success in their demands for more intellectual freedom, greater security before their own laws, fuller enjoyment of the rewards of their own toil. For as such things come to pass, the more certain will be the coming of that day when our peoples may freely meet in friendship.

So we voice our hope and our belief that we can help to heal this divided world. Thus may the nations cease to live in trembling before the menace of force. Thus may the weight of fear and the weight of arms be taken from the burdened shoulders of mankind.

This, nothing less, is the labor to which we are called and our strength dedicated. And so the prayer of our people carries far beyond our own frontiers, to the wide world of our duty and our destiny.

May the light of freedom, coming to all darkened lands, flame brightly; until at last the darkness is no more. May the turbulence of our age yield to a true time of peace, when men and nations shall share a life that honors the dignity of each, the brotherhood of all.

JOHN F. KENNEDY

INAUGURAL ADDRESS

JANUARY 20, 1961

COMMENTARY

In his second inaugural address, Eisenhower pointed to the American dilemma of living in a land of plenty and a world of peril. Throughout his new administration, the precarious international situation continued. An almost paradoxical policy of competitive coexistence with the Soviets emerged in which both nations attempted to win the friendship of the world's uncommitted peoples. At the start of his second term, unrest in the Near East and Russian arms shipments to Egypt threatened to disrupt the balance of power. The president warned the Communists not to begin a war in that troubled area as they would unleash a chain of circumstances that would almost surely involve the United States in military action. He requested, and Congress voted, military and economic aid to the Near Eastern countries to prevent and protect them from overt armed aggression from any nation controlled by international Communism. In Latin America, Communist-influenced disorders largely went unnoticed until rioters mobbed and stoned Vice President Richard Nixon in Lima and Caracas during May 1958. A revolt in Cuba the following January brought Fidel Castro to power. Castro sought and received Russian economic and military aid. The possibility of Communist subversion in the Western Hemisphere caused the administration to review and strengthen technical and economic assistance to Latin America.

On October 4, 1957, the Russians launched the first man-made satellite, thrusting it into orbit around the Earth. The satellite, or "Sputnik," 22 inches in diameter, weighed 184.3 pounds and circled the Earth once every 95 minutes, traveling at a speed of 18,000 miles per hour. This achievement marked a major technological triumph over the United States, sending a shudder of dismay through the country. While American overall scientific achievements far over-shadowed those of the Soviets, the Russians, by doing the sensational, seized the propaganda initiative. Before Americans had completely digested the first Sput-nik, the Russians put up a much heavier one. On November 3, they launched a second satellite, weighing 1,120 pounds. This time, a live dog was placed inside a sealed compartment, and instruments strapped to the animal recorded its reac-tions to space conditions. Indeed, American technology had been challenged.

The United States and the Soviets now engaged in a contest to outdistance each other in dramatic leaps into space. American scientists finally achieved success on January 31, 1958, with the launching of the Explorer I satellite. Within three months, two other small satellites had gone into orbit. In May, the Russians outmatched this by sending up the 1.5-ton Sputnik 111. The United States followed with "lunar probes" and the first successful long-distance flight (6,000 miles) of an Atlas intercontinental ballistic missile. In December 1958, the United States orbited an Atlas rocket, and the following month the Rus-sians sent up a "lunik"—a rocket that passed the Moon and orbited around the Sun. The struggle between East and West continued in the diplomatic and economic fields, and now the race for space was added to the contest.

As the decade ended, the principal unresolved question remained: Would the cold war thaw? On November 17, 1958, Russian premier Nikita Khrushchev threatened to sign a separate peace treaty with Communist East Germany and to turn over the Russian sector of Berlin to that country. A new crisis began after the premier issued an ultimatum to the United States, England, and France to with-draw their troops from Berlin within six months. But in spite of these threats, the demands for a summit conference intensified. Many thought that only a meet-ing between Eisenhower and Khrushchev would lessen world tensions. Finally, on August 3, 1959, President Eisenhower and Premier Khrushchev announced reciprocal visits to begin with the premier's trip to the United States. Khrushchev arrived on September 15 and remained for 13 hectic days filled with a cross-country trip, speeches, and a three-day conference with the president.

Before his projected trip to the Soviet Union, Eisenhower, on December 3, 1959, began a 22,000 mile, 11-nation journey that took him as far as India. During these 19 days, the popularity of the general soared to new heights. A staggering crowd of 1.5 million cheered the president in New Delhi. After the trip, a joint communiqué announced that leaders of the United States, England, and France would meet with the Soviet leader for a Big Four talk beginning on May 16, 1960, in Paris.

Eleven days before the meeting, however, the Russians declared that they had shot down an unarmed high-altitude American U-2 plane, which had been flying over the Soviet Union on an intelligence mission. The pilot, Francis Powers, had been captured alive. Khrushchev displayed the wreckage of the plane and threatened retaliation against any nation that provided bases for these American flights. After several contradictory explanations, the United States admitted full responsibility.

The summit conference convened on May 16 as scheduled, but hopes for success appeared dashed. Khrushchev demanded an apology and withdrew his invitation to Eisenhower to visit Russia. Although the president suspended future flights, the Russian insults continued. In spite of the mediating efforts of Britain's prime minister Harold Macmillan and French president Charles De Gaulle, the summit conference ended in failure.

In 1960, Americans again faced the task of choosing a president. The Republicans nominated Vice President Richard M. Nixon, and shortly thereafter the Democrats selected Senator John F. Kennedy of Massachusetts. With characteristic boldness, Kennedy had the Democratic convention choose Senator Lyndon Johnson, his most formidable rival, for the vice presidential spot. This wise move united the party after acrimonious primary fights. The main issue of the strenuous campaign became one of personality, as there appeared to be no major policy differences separating the two men. Both candidates, for example, endorsed Eisenhower's foreign policy commitments. Both promised a higher standard of living, a more workable farm program, equal rights for all citizens, and aid to education. Each claimed, however, that he could do the job better. A series of four widely publicized television debates climaxed the campaign. On Election Day, Kennedy was elected by a margin of only 112,000 votes out of approximately 67 million cast—the closest contest in 76 years. Kennedy won 49.7 percent of the total to Nixon's 49.6 percent. His electoral victory was more decisive, with 303 votes to Nixon's 219. Kennedy and Johnson won despite the enormous popularity of Eisenhower and the executive experience of Vice President Nixon. At the time, the nation enjoyed peace and prosperity.

At 43, John Kennedy, the youngest man ever elected to the presidency and the first Catholic to hold the office, took over the power vested for eight years in Dwight Eisenhower, who, at 70, was the oldest White House occupant. A blanket of seven inches of newly fallen snow, bitter winds, and subfreezing temperature held down the crowds that watched the ceremonies in front of the newly renovated East Front of the Capitol. The new chief executive promised no swift miracles, but he declared his intention to face the challenging problems of the sixties with vigor and determination. As Richard Cardinal Cushing of Boston delivered the invocation asking divine protection for the president, a short circuit caused wisps of fine blue smoke to shoot out from under the lectern, almost as an ominous portent.

⸻

Vice President Johnson, Mr. Speaker, Mr. Chief Justice, President Eisenhower, Vice President Nixon, President Truman, reverend clergy, fellow citizens:

We observe today not a victory of party, but a celebration of freedom symbolizing an end, as well as a beginning, signifying renewal, as well as change. For I have sworn before you and almighty God the same solemn oath our forebears l prescribed nearly a century and three quarters ago.

The world is very different now. For man holds in his mortal hands the power to abolish all forms of human poverty and all forms of human life. And yet the same revolutionary beliefs for which our forebears fought are still at issue around the globe; the belief that the rights of man come not from the generosity of the state, but from the hand of God.

We dare not forget today that we are the heirs of that first revolution. Let the word go forth from this time and place, to friend and foe alike, that the torch has been passed to a new generation of Americans; born in this century, tempered by war, disciplined by a hard and bitter peace, proud of our ancient heritage; and unwilling to witness or permit the slow undoing of those human rights to which this Nation has always been committed, and to which we are committed today at home and around the world.

Let every nation know, whether it wishes us well or ill, that we shall pay any price, bear any burden, meet any hardship, support any friend, oppose any foe, in order to assure the survival and the success of liberty. This much we pledge, and more.

To those old allies whose cultural and spiritual origins we share, we pledge the loyalty of faithful friends. United, there is little we cannot do in a host of cooperative ventures. Divided, there is little we can do, for we dare not meet a powerful challenge at odds and split asunder.

To those new States whom we welcome to the ranks of the free, we pledge our word that one form of colonial control shall not have passed away merely to be replaced by a far more iron tyranny. We shall not always expect to find them supporting our view. But we shall always hope to find them strongly supporting their own freedom; and to remember that, in the past, those who foolishly sought power by riding the back of the tiger ended up inside.

To those peoples in the huts and villages across the globe struggling to break the bonds of mass misery, we pledge our best efforts to help them help themselves, for whatever period is required; not because the Communists may be doing it, not because we seek their votes, but because it is right. If a free society cannot help the many who are poor, it cannot save the few who are rich.

To our sister republics south of our border, we offer a special pledge, to convert our good words into good deeds, in a new alliance for progress; to assist free men and free governments in casting off the chains of poverty. But this peaceful revolution of hope cannot become the prey of hostile powers. Let all our neighbors know that we shall join with them to oppose aggression or subversion anywhere in the Americas. And let every other power know that this Hemisphere intends to remain the master of its own house.

To that world assembly of sovereign states, the United Nations, our last best hope in an age where the instruments of war have far outpaced the instruments of peace, we renew our pledge of support; to prevent it from becoming merely a forum for invective; to strengthen its shield of the new and the weak; and to enlarge the area in which its writ may run.

Finally, to those nations who would make themselves our adversary, we offer not a pledge but a request; that both sides begin anew the quest for peace, before the dark powers of destruction unleashed by science engulf all humanity in planned or accidental self destruction.

We dare not tempt them with weakness. For only when our arms are sufficient beyond doubt can we be certain beyond doubt that they will never be employed.

But neither can two great and powerful groups of nations take comfort from our present course; both sides overburdened by the cost of modern weapons, both rightly alarmed by the steady spread of the deadly atom, yet both racing to alter that uncertain balance of terror that stays the hand of mankind's final war.

So let us begin anew, remembering on both sides that civility is not a sign of weakness, and sincerity is always subject to proof. Let us never negotiate out of fear. But let us never fear to negotiate.

Let both sides explore what problems unite us instead of belaboring those problems which divide us.

Let both sides, for the first time, formulate serious and precise proposals for the inspection and control of arms; and bring the absolute power to destroy other nations under the absolute control of all nations.

Let both sides seek to invoke the wonders of science instead of its terrors. Together let us explore the stars, conquer the deserts, eradicate disease, tap the ocean depths, and encourage the arts and commerce.

Let both sides unite to heed in all corners of the earth the command of Isaiah to undo the heavy burdens and to let the oppressed go free.

And if a beachhead of cooperation may push back the jungle of suspicion, let both sides join in creating a new endeavor, not a new balance of power, but a new world of law, where the strong are just and the weak secure and the peace preserved.

All this will not be finished in the first hundred days. Nor will it be finished in the first thousand days, nor in the life of this Administration, nor even perhaps in our lifetime on this planet. But let us begin.

In your hands, my fellow citizens, more than in mine, will rest the final success or failure of our course. Since this country was founded, each generation of Americans has been summoned to give testimony to its national loyalty. The graves of young Americans who answered the call to service surround the globe.

Now the trumpet summons us again; not as a call to bear arms, though arms we need; not as a call to battle, though embattled we are; but a call to bear the burden of a long twilight struggle, year in and year out, rejoicing in hope, patient in tribulation; a struggle against the common enemies of man; tyranny, poverty, disease, and war itself.

Can we forge against these enemies a grand and global alliance, North and South, East and West, that can assure a more fruitful life for all mankind? Will you join in that historic effort?

In the long history of the world, only a few generations have been granted the role of defending freedom in its hour of maximum danger. I do not shrink from this responsibility, I welcome it. I do not believe that any of us would exchange places with any other people or any other generation. The energy, the faith, the devotion which we bring to this endeavor will light our country and all who serve it, and the glow from that fire can truly light the world.

And so, my fellow Americans, ask not what your country can do for you, ask what you can do for your country.

My fellow citizens of the world, ask not what America will do for you, but what together we can do for the freedom of man.

Finally, whether you are citizens of America or citizens of the world, ask of us the same high standards of strength and sacrifice which we ask of you. With a good conscience our only sure reward, with history the final judge of our deeds, let us go forth to lead the land we love, asking His blessing and His help, but knowing that here on earth God's work must truly be our own.

Lyndon Baines Johnson

Inaugural Address

JANUARY 20, 1965

COMMENTARY

Kennedy won the 1960 election by the narrowest of margins, but after a few months in office he seemed glamorously invincible. Most of the Kennedy family turned out to work for his success and they brought charm, wit, and sophistication to the White House. Young and buoyantly hopeful, the president spoke about American ideals to a prosperous and peaceful nation. He spoke about progressive social legislation, assistance to emerging backward nations as they "hoist freedom's banner," and about civil rights. As the social revolution of the sixties gained momentum, Kennedy became the first president publicly committed to the Supreme Court decisions declaring segregation unconstitutional. The president stood firm on the belief that these decisions were morally right. By authorizing the Justice Department to intervene as an active litigant in civil rights cases, he threw the full force of his executive authority into the fight against segregation. "Our job," said the president, "is to turn the American vision of a society in which no man has to suffer discrimination based on race into a living reality everywhere in our land. And that means we must secure to every American equal access to all parts of our public life—to the voting booth, to the schoolroom, to jobs, to housing, to all public facilities including lunch counters."

Kennedy believed that Americans, especially the young, should help the people of underdeveloped lands with their hands as well as money. Soon after taking office he took steps to establish a Peace Corps. Young men and women who joined it would apply their special skills in working side by side with the less fortunate, teaching then improved ways of doing such things as road building and harvesting crops. Thousands volunteered, and within a few months the first Peace Corps groups arrived in Latin America and Africa.

In foreign affairs, however, the administration faced several critical situations and defeat. By spring 1961, American prestige had suffered two major blows. In Laos, armed forces of the American-supported government gave ground before Soviet-backed rebels. In Cuba, Premier Fidel Castro, with military supplies and aid from the Russians, crushed a feeble American-supported effort of Cuban exiles to liberate their homeland.

Meanwhile, hopes of any real agreement with the Soviet Union on disarmament languished. In the face of growing tension, Kennedy met with Premier Khrushchev in June 1961. The talks produced no agreements to ease the situation. Indeed, Khrushchev shortly demanded that the Western powers recognize East and West Germany as separate nations, threatening to sign a separate peace treaty with East Germany and place Allied routes into Berlin under East German control. The United States promptly took steps to increase its military strength, and with its Allies, stood firm in Berlin. At this point, the Communists sealed off the Western sector to halt the flow of refugees from behind the iron curtain.

The Soviet Union resumed testing of high-altitude nuclear weapons in September 1961, ending a three-year voluntary ban. The United States followed suit but began its tests underground in order to postpone, as long as possible, any addition to the radioactive fallout. Finally, in July 1963, after months of patient talks, the United States signed a nuclear test ban treaty with the Soviet Union—perhaps the greatest achievement of the Kennedy administration.

On November 22, 1963, an assassin's rifle shots took the life of President Kennedy as he rode in an open car in a Dallas motorcade. Vice President Lyndon Johnson took the oath as the thirty-sixth president aboard the plane that took him and the dead president's body back to Washington. On November 24, the casket was taken from the White House to the rotunda of the Capitol, where 250,000 people filed past in tribute. The same day, the accused assassin was shot while being moved through the Dallas City jail corridors—a shooting witnessed by millions of television viewers. On November 25, after three days of unparalleled worldwide mourning, Kennedy was buried in Arlington National Cemetery. Indeed, the tragedy of this fateful weekend, a weekend that inspired an outpouring of poems, essays, and sermons, will never be dulled for those who lived through it.

President Johnson appeared before a joint session of Congress on November 27, pledging to continue the Kennedy policies, and asked for early action on the pending civil rights and tax-cut bills. Before the session ended, Congress passed the Civil Rights Act of 1964, which represents a historic victory for the American conscience. The act was a commitment to make real the equal opportunity guaranteed to the African American a century earlier. Headway was made in federal tax reforms, in support for education, conservation, and urban mass transit. Johnson's first year in the White House saw dramatic changes in foreign affairs, many of them inimical to peace. Premier Khrushchev, who appeared to be leading the Soviet Union toward understanding with the United States, was deposed; Communist China exploded its first atomic device; the United Nations seemed sorely beset by fiscal problems; and developments in South Vietnam moved depressingly downhill.

The main domestic issue during 1964 was the presidential contest. In a surprising series of primary victories, the conservative wing of the Republican Party, led by Senator Barry Goldwater of Arizona, gained control of the convention machinery. In July, much to the surprise of the party's shattered and disunited liberals, the delegates nominated Goldwater for president on the first ballot. During the campaign, Goldwater promised "a choice, not an echo." Assaulting "big government" and the social and welfare programs of the last 30 years, he called for laissez-faire economic policies. In foreign affairs, he asserted his course would be more aggressive, rejecting accommodations with the Communists. Most Republican newspapers and magazines refused to support the senator because, as the Chicago Daily News *phrased it, "He is a leader remote from the mainstream of America."*

On November 2, Johnson received an overwhelming popular endorsement, a popular vote that exceeded 42.1 million, a record-breaking 61.1 percent of the total. Johnson's 486 electoral votes to Goldwater's 52 was surpassed only by the Roosevelt landslide of 1936. Goldwater received 26 million votes, or 7.5 million fewer than Richard Nixon in 1960, indicating massive desertions from the Republican ranks. In the main, Johnson's triumph represented gains for moderates and liberals throughout the nation.

The swearing-in ceremony was held at noon, January 20, 1965, on the Capitol steps. After Hubert Humphrey had been sworn in as vice president, President Johnson rose to take the oath from Chief Justice Earl Warren as Mrs. Johnson held the Bible. Then, the president delivered his 22-minute inaugural address, which sought to interpret "the majesty and the meaning of this moment." Speaking in measured and solemn tones that tended to discourage applause, Johnson described an American covenant founded on justice, liberty, and union. Perhaps, in depicting a potentially rosy future in which strife would cease, want disappear, and the brotherhood of man prevail, the president set forth the program and the dream of the "Great Society."

My fellow countrymen:

On this occasion, the oath I have taken before you and before God is not mine alone, but ours together. We are one nation and one people. Our fate as a nation and our future as a people rest not upon one citizen, but upon all citizens. This is the majesty and the meaning of this moment.

For every generation, there is a destiny. For some, history decides. For this generation, the choice must be our own. Even now, a rocket moves toward Mars. It reminds us that the world will not be the same for our children, or even for ourselves in a short span of years. The next man to stand here will look out on a scene different from our own, because ours is a time of change; rapid and fantastic change bearing the secrets of nature, multiplying the nations, placing in uncertain hands new weapons for mastery and destruction, shaking old values, and uprooting old ways. Our destiny in the midst of change will rest on the unchanged character of our people, and on their faith.

THE AMERICAN COVENANT

They came here, the exile and the stranger, brave but frightened; to find a place where a man could be his own man. They made a covenant with this land. Conceived in justice, written in liberty, bound in union, it was meant one day to inspire the hopes of all mankind; and it binds us still. If we keep its terms, we shall flourish.

JUSTICE AND CHANGE

First, justice was the promise that all who made the journey would share in the fruits of the land. In a land of great wealth, families must not live in hopeless poverty. In a land rich in harvest, children just must not go hungry. In a land of healing miracles, neighbors must not suffer and die unattended. In a great land of learning and scholars, young people must be taught to read and write.

For the more than thirty years that I have served this Nation, I have believed that this injustice to our people, this waste of our resources, was our real enemy. For thirty years or more, with the resources I have had, I have vigilantly fought against it. I have learned, and I know, that it will not surrender easily.

But change has given us new weapons. Before this generation of Americans is finished, this enemy will not only retreat, it will be conquered.

Justice requires us to remember that when any citizen denies his fellow, saying, his color is not mine or his beliefs are strange and different, in that moment he betrays America, though his forebears created this Nation.

LIBERTY AND CHANGE

Liberty was the second article of our covenant. It was self-government. It was our Bill of Rights. But it was more. America would be a place where each man could be proud to be himself; stretching his talents, rejoicing in his work, important in the life of his neighbors and his nation.

This has become more difficult in a world where change and growth seem to tower beyond the control and even the judgment of men. We must work to provide the knowledge and the surroundings which can enlarge the possibilities of every citizen.

The American covenant called on us to help show the way for the liberation of man. And that is today our goal. Thus, if as a nation there is much outside our control, as a people no stranger is outside our hope.

Change has brought new meaning to that old mission. We can never again stand aside, prideful in isolation. Terrific dangers and troubles that we once called foreign, now constantly live among us. If American lives must end, and American treasure be spilled, in countries we barely know, that is the price that change has demanded of conviction and of our enduring covenant.

Think of our world as it looks from the rocket that is heading toward Mars. It is like a child's globe, hanging in space, the continents stuck to its side like colored maps. We are all fellow passengers on a dot of earth. And each of us, in the span of time, has really only a moment among our companions.

How incredible it is that in this fragile existence, we should hate and destroy one another. There are possibilities enough for all who will abandon mastery over others to pursue mastery over nature. There is world enough for all to seek their happiness in their own way.

Our Nation's course is abundantly clear. We aspire to nothing that belongs to others. We seek no dominion over our fellow man. but man's dominion over tyranny and misery.

But more is required. Men want to be a part of a common enterprise; a cause greater than themselves. Each of us must find a way to advance the purpose of the Nation, thus finding new purpose for ourselves. Without this, we shall become a nation of strangers.

UNION AND CHANGE

The third article was union. To those who were small and few against the wilderness, the success of liberty demanded the strength of union. Two centuries of change have made this true again.

No longer need capitalist and worker, farmer and clerk, city and countryside, struggle to divide our bounty. By working shoulder to shoulder, together we can increase the bounty of all. We have discovered that every child who learns, every man who finds work, every sick body that is made whole; like a candle added to an altar, brightens the hope of all the faithful.

So let us reject any among us who seek to reopen old wounds and to rekindle old hatreds. They stand in the way of a seeking nation.

Let us now join reason to faith and action to experience, to transform our unity of interest into a unity of purpose. For the hour and the day and the time are here to achieve progress without strife, to achieve change without hatred; not without difference of opinion, but without the deep and abiding divisions which scar the union for generations.

THE AMERICAN BELIEF

Under this covenant of justice, liberty, and union we have become a nation; prosperous, great, and mighty. And we have kept our freedom. But we have no promise from God that our greatness will endure. We have been allowed by Him to seek greatness with the sweat of our hands and the strength of our spirit.

I do not believe that the Great Society is the ordered, changeless, and sterile battalion of the ants. It is the excitement of becoming; always becoming, trying, probing, falling, resting, and trying again, but always trying and always gaining.

In each generation, with toil and tears, we have had to earn our heritage again.

If we fail now, we shall have forgotten in abundance what we learned in hardship: that democracy rests on faith, that freedom asks more than it gives, and that the judgment of God is harshest on those who are most favored.

If we succeed, it will not be because of what we have, but it will be because of what we are; not because of what we own, but, rather because of what we believe.

For we are a nation of believers. Underneath the clamor of building and the rush of our day's pursuits, we are believers in justice and liberty and union, and in our own Union. We believe that every man must someday be free. And we believe in ourselves.

Our enemies have always made the same mistake. In my lifetime, in depression and in war, they have awaited our defeat. Each time, from the secret places of the American heart, came forth the faith they could not see or that they could not even imagine. It brought us victory. And it will again.

For this is what America is all about. It is the uncrossed desert and the unclimbed ridge. It is the star that is not reached and the harvest sleeping in the unplowed ground. Is our world gone? We say farewell. Is a new world coming? We welcome it, and we will bend it to the hopes of man.

To these trusted public servants and to my family and those close friends of mine who have followed me down a long, winding road, and to all the people of this Union and the world, I will repeat today what I said on that sorrowful day in November 1963, I will lead and I will do the best I can.

But you must look within your own hearts to the old promises and to the old dream. They will lead you best of all. For myself, I ask only, in the words of an ancient leader, give me now wisdom and knowledge, that I may go out and come in before this people, for who can judge this thy people, that is so great?

RICHARD MILHOUS NIXON

FIRST INAUGURAL ADDRESS

JANUARY 20, 1969

COMMENTARY

The 1968 presidential campaign raised concern over the viability of the U.S. political system. By the time the year had run its course, a sitting president announced he would not seek reelection; a presidential candidate and a prominent civil rights leader each had been murdered; and a national party convention was disrupted by riots and bloodshed. Journalist James Reston noted, "The main issue is not Vietnam itself, or in the cities, but in the feeling that the political system for dealing with these things has broken down."

On March 31, 1968, President Lyndon Johnson announced that he would not seek reelection. The escalating war in Vietnam had convinced many Americans that the nation's leaders had badly underestimated the military capacity of the North Vietnamese. Johnson had resisted demands from "hawks" who wanted to use atomic weapons to end the war and from "doves" who wanted a unilateral cease-fire and immediate peace negotiations. By April 1968, U.S. forces in Vietnam soared to 543,000 and U.S. combat deaths had surpassed 23,000. The Gallup Poll reported a major shift in public opinion. In February 1968, self-described "hawks" had outnumbered "doves" 60 percent to 24 percent. A month later, 42 percent described themselves as "doves" compared to 41 percent as "hawks." And, on March 2, Senator Eugene McCarthy of Minnesota, a passionate critic of the Johnson administration's Vietnam policy, electrified the nation by holding the president's victory in the New Hampshire Democratic primary to less than a majority. Four weeks later, Johnson announced that he did not want "the presidency to become involved in the partisan divisions that are developing in this political year. . . . Accordingly, I shall not seek, and I will not accept, the nomination of my party for another term as your President."

For a moment, it seemed as though the anti-Vietnam forces had won. Within days after the New Hampshire primary, Senator Robert F. Kennedy of New York announced he would seek the Democratic presidential nomination. Also, Vice President Hubert Humphrey, with the encouragement of President Johnson, entered the contest. Humphrey received the support of Democratic party leaders, labor unions, and of many delegates that were selected by state-party organizations. Kennedy drew large and enthusiastic audiences during an extensive speaking tour, but his decision to contest the nomination with Senator McCarthy divided the antiwar movement.

In the midst of this bitter political battle in which the Vietnam War was the dominant issue, attention suddenly shifted back to the nation's racial struggle. On April 4, Dr. Martin Luther King Jr. was assassinated in Memphis, Tennessee. His death shocked the United States, producing an outpouring of grief matched in recent memory by the death of John Kennedy. Among blacks, it also produced anger. Rioting, looting, and arson engulfed the nation. Forty-three people died, more than 3,000 were injured, and as many as 27,000 were arrested. In the largest military deployment for a civil emergency in American history, over 21,000 federal troops and 34,000 state guardsmen were called out before the riots subsided.

Despite the racial conflicts, the contest for the Democratic nomination continued. By June 4, Robert Kennedy had won five of six presidential prima-ries, including one in California. Shortly after midnight on June 5, he spoke to his followers in a Los Angeles hotel. As he left, he fell victim to an assassin's bul-let. Kennedy's campaign had inspired enthusiasm rarely seen in political life. It seemed that he had shaped a set of ideas about the American underclass—the "Kennedy legacy"—that would become central to American liberalism. The passions that he aroused made his violent death a shattering experience for many Americans.

Hubert Humphrey's nomination by the Democrats was never in doubt after Kennedy's death. The convention chose him on the first ballot. Humphrey selected Senator Edmund Muskie of Maine as his running mate. However, a bitter platform dispute divided the party over what to do in Vietnam. A bloody confrontation between antiwar demonstrators and more than 5,000 Illinois National Guardsmen took place outside the Chicago International Amphithe-ater where the convention met. These riots were seen by millions who watched as the drama unfolded on television. Humphrey accepted the nomination of a party wracked by internal disorder. Eugene McCarthy refused to appear with him at the traditional reconciliation scene of losers with winners, and all pretense of party unity was shattered.

Richard Nixon made a remarkable comeback at the Republican convention. Nixon, whose political career seemed at an end after his losses in the 1960 presidential election and the California gubernatorial campaign two years later, reemerged as the spokesman for what he called "Middle America." Attempts by both Governor Nelson A. Rockefeller of New York and Governor Ronald Reagan of California to deny him the nomination failed. Nixon won the nomination on the first ballot. He followed his "southern strategy" by choosing the little-known Governor Spiro T. Agnew of Maryland as his running mate. Nixon's acceptance speech focused on the "forgotten Americans"—the workers and taxpayers who were angered by the Vietnam protesters, domestic violence, and the rising cost of living. He promised that his "new leadership" would bring an honorable end to the war in Vietnam.

Nixon's positions on social issues took supporters away from George Wallace, the segregationist governor of Alabama, who was running as a third-party candidate. Wallace based his campaign on a host of conservative grievances, not all of them connected to race. He was by no means a sectional candidate, as his name appeared on all 50 state ballots. Wallace opposed the forced busing of students to achieve school integration, the proliferation of government regulations, and the permissiveness of authorities toward race riots and anti-war demonstrators. He pledged deliverance from African Americans, radicals, bureaucrats, hippies, integrationists, and "pointy headed professors" whose fuzzy thinking had caused the nation's problems.

Humphrey's campaign was a disaster. Antiwar hecklers interrupted his speeches. He contradicted himself on the administration's Vietnam policy. At one point, he endorsed an immediate halt in the bombing raids and said "we can start to remove some of the American forces in early 1969 or late 1968." A July 1968 Gallup Poll found that 66 percent of Democrats and 65 percent of Republicans supported this position. However, a furious President Johnson corrected him. "No one can predict," he angrily said, "when Americans would begin to leave Vietnam." Humphrey could not disengage himself from the Johnson administration and it seemed that the administration had lost the confidence of the nation.

Nixon was heavily favored. He promised to heed the "quiet voice of the great majority of Americans . . . the non-shooters, the non-demonstrators." He made it into an "us versus them" contest, the "us" being middle America—the white, middle-class, patriotic "forgotten Americans." Nixon won 32 states with 301 electoral votes. In the popular vote, Nixon received 43.4 percent, the lowest for a winning candidate since Woodrow Wilson in the three-way election of 1912. A white backlash did take place, validating Nixon's strategy. Of the 13 states in the once solid Democratic South, Humphrey carried only Texas. Five southern states went to Wallace and seven to Nixon. While 95 percent of black voters cast their ballot for Humphrey, less than 35 percent of whites did so. Three out of 10 white Johnson voters in 1964 cast their vote for either Nixon or Wallace in 1968. In his memoirs, Nixon stressed that 57 percent of the voters had voted for either him or Wallace, meaning that a majority favored a change. However, the type of change wanted by the American people remained unclear.

Inauguration Day 1969 was grey and penetratingly cold. Eight years earlier, then vice president Richard Nixon had driven down Pennsylvania Avenue to the Capitol for the inauguration of John Kennedy, but then he was leaving Washington after the Kennedy victory. At noon, Mrs. Nixon held two family Bibles printed in 1828 and 1873, which had been handed down from generation to generation. They were opened to the second chapter of Isaiah, the fourth verse: "They shall beat their swords into plowshares and their spears into pruning hooks: nation shall not lift up sword against nation, neither shall they learn war anymore." Richard Nixon placed his left hand on the Bible as Chief Justice Earl Warren administered the oath of office.

Senator Dirksen, Mr. Chief Justice, Mr. Vice President, President Johnson, Vice President Humphrey, my fellow Americans and my fellow citizens of the world community:

I ask you to share with me today the majesty of this moment. In the orderly transfer of power, we celebrate the unity that keeps us free.

Each moment in history is a fleeting time, precious and unique. But some stand out as moments of beginning, in which courses are set that shape decades or centuries. This can be such a moment.

Forces now are converging that make possible, for the first time, the hope that many of man's deepest aspirations can at last be realized. The spiraling pace of change allows us to contemplate, within our own lifetime, advances that once would have taken centuries.

In throwing wide the horizons of space, we have discovered new horizons on earth.

For the first time, because the people of the world want peace, and the leaders of the world are afraid of war, the times are on the side of peace.

Eight years from now America will celebrate its 200th anniversary as a nation. Within the lifetime of most people now living, mankind will celebrate that great new year which comes only once in a thousand years, the beginning of the third millennium.

What kind of nation we will be, what kind of world we will live in, whether we shape the future in the image of our hopes, is ours to determine by our actions and our choices.

The greatest honor history can bestow is the title of peacemaker. This honor now beckons America; the chance to help lead the world at last out of the valley of turmoil, and onto that high ground of peace that man has dreamed of since the dawn of civilization.

If we succeed, generations to come will say of us now living that we mastered our moment, that we helped make the world safe for mankind. This is our summons to greatness. I believe the American people are ready to answer this call.

The second third of this century has been a time of proud achievement. We have made enormous strides in science and industry and agriculture. We have shared our wealth more broadly than ever. We have learned at last to manage a modern economy to assure its continued growth.

We have given freedom new reach, and we have begun to make its promise real for black as well as for white. We see the hope of tomorrow in the youth of today. I know America's youth. I believe in them. We can be proud that they are better educated, more committed, more passionately driven by conscience than any generation in our history.

No people has ever been so close to the achievement of a just and abundant society, or so possessed of the will to achieve it. Because our strengths are so great, we can afford to appraise our weaknesses with candor and to approach them with hope.

Standing in this same place a third of a century ago, Franklin Delano Roosevelt addressed a Nation ravaged by depression and gripped in fear. He could say in surveying the Nation's troubles, they concern, thank God, only material things.

Our crisis today is the reverse. We have found ourselves rich in goods, but ragged in spirit; reaching with magnificent precision for the moon, but falling into raucous discord on earth.

We are caught in war, wanting peace. We are torn by division, wanting unity. We see around us empty lives, wanting fulfillment. We see tasks that need doing, waiting for hands to do them. To a crisis of the spirit, we need an answer of the spirit. To find that answer, we need only look within ourselves.

When we listen to the better angels of our nature, we find that they celebrate the simple things, the basic things such as goodness, decency, love, kindness. Greatness comes in simple trappings. The simple things are the ones most needed today if we are to surmount what divides us, and cement what unites us. To lower our voices would be a simple thing.

In these difficult years, America has suffered from a fever of words; from inflated rhetoric that promises more than it can deliver; from angry rhetoric that fans discontents into hatreds; from bombastic rhetoric that postures instead of persuading.

We cannot learn from one another until we stop shouting at one another; until we speak quietly enough so that our words can be heard as well as our voices.

For its part, government will listen. We will strive to listen in new ways; to the voices of quiet anguish, the voices that speak without words, the voices of the heart; to the injured voices, the anxious voices, the voices that have despaired of being heard. Those who have been left out, we will try to bring in. Those left behind, we will help to catch up. For all of our people, we will set as our goal the decent order that makes progress possible and our lives secure.

As we reach toward our hopes, our task is to build on what has gone before; not turning away from the old, but turning toward the new.

In this past third of a century, government has passed more laws, spent more money, initiated more programs, than in all our previous history.

In pursuing our goals of full employment, better housing, excellence in education; in rebuilding our cities and improving our rural areas; in protecting our environment and enhancing the quality of life; in all these and more, we will and must press urgently forward.

We shall plan now for the day when our wealth can be transferred from the destruction of war abroad to the urgent needs of our people at home.

The American dream does not come to those who fall asleep. But we are approaching the limits of what government alone can do.

Our greatest need now is to reach beyond government, and to enlist the legions of the concerned and the committed. What has to be done, has to be done by government and people together or it will not be done at all. The lesson of past agony is that without the people we can do nothing; with the people we can do everything.

To match the magnitude of our tasks, we need the energies of our people; enlisted not only in grand enterprises, but more importantly in those small, splendid efforts that make headlines in the neighborhood newspaper instead of the national journal.

With these, we can build a great cathedral of the spirit; each of us raising it one stone at a time, as he reaches out to his neighbor, helping, caring, doing.

I do not offer a life of uninspiring ease. I do not call for a life of grim sacrifice. I ask you to join in a high adventure; one as rich as humanity itself, and as exciting as the times we live in.

The essence of freedom is that each of us shares in the shaping of his own destiny.

Until he has been part of a cause larger than himself, no man is truly whole.

The way to fulfillment is in the use of our talents; we achieve nobility in the spirit that inspires that use.

As we measure what can be done, we shall promise only what we know we can produce, but as we chart our goals we shall be lifted by our dreams.

No man can be fully free while his neighbor is not. To go forward at all is to go forward together.

This means black and white together, as one nation, not two. The laws have caught up with our conscience. What remains is to give life to what is in the law; to ensure at last that as all are born equal in dignity before God, all are born equal in dignity before man.

As we learn to go forward together at home, let us also seek to go forward together with all mankind.

Let us take as our goal. Where peace is unknown, make it welcome; where peace is fragile, make it strong; where peace is temporary, make it permanent.

After a period of confrontation, we are entering an era of negotiation. Let all nations know that during this administration our lines of communication will be open.

We seek an open world. Open to ideas, open to the exchange of goods and people. A world in which no people, great or small, will live in angry isolation.

We cannot expect to make everyone our friend, but we can try to make no one our enemy.

Those who would be our adversaries, we invite to a peaceful competition; not in conquering territory or extending dominion, but in enriching the life of man.

As we explore the reaches of space, let us go to the new worlds together; not as new worlds to be conquered, but as a new adventure to be shared.

With those who are willing to join, let us cooperate to reduce the burden of arms, to strengthen the structure of peace, to lift up the poor and the hungry.

But to all those who would be tempted by weakness, let us leave no doubt that we will be as strong as we need to be for as long as we need to be.

Over the past twenty years, since I first came to this Capital as a fresh-man Congressman, I have visited most of the nations of the world.

I have come to know the leaders of the world, and the great forces, the hatreds, the fears that divide the world.

I know that peace does not come through wishing for it; that there is no substitute for days and even years of patient and prolonged diplomacy.

I also know the people of the world. I have seen the hunger of a home-less child, the pain of a man wounded in battle, the grief of a mother who has lost her son. I know these have no ideology, no race.

I know America. I know the heart of America is good.

I speak from my own heart, and the heart of my country, the deep con-cern we have for those who suffer, and those who sorrow.

I have taken an oath today in the presence of God and my countrymen to uphold and defend the Constitution of the United States. To that oath I now add this sacred commitment: I shall consecrate my office, my energies, and all the wisdom I can summon, to the cause of peace among nations.

Let this message be heard by strong and weak alike. The peace we seek to win is not victory over any other people, but the peace that comes with healing in its wings; with compassion for those who have suffered; with understanding for those who have opposed us; with the opportunity for all the peoples of this earth to choose their own destiny.

Only a few short weeks ago, we shared the glory of man's first sight of the world as God sees it, as a single sphere reflecting light in the darkness. As the Apollo astronauts flew over the moon's gray surface on Christmas Eve, they spoke to us of the beauty of earth; and in that voice so clear across the lunar distance, we heard them invoke God's blessing on its goodness.

In that moment, their view from the moon moved poet Archibald MacLeish to write:

> To see the earth as it truly is, small and blue and beautiful in that
> eternal silence where it floats, is to see ourselves as riders on the
> earth together, brothers on that bright loveliness in the eternal
> cold; brothers who know now they are truly brothers.

In that moment of surpassing technological triumph, men turned their thoughts toward home and humanity; seeing in that far perspective that man's destiny on earth is not divisible; telling us that however far we reach into the cosmos, our destiny lies not in the stars but on Earth itself, in our own hands, in our own hearts.

We have endured a long night of the American spirit. But as our eyes catch the dimness of the first rays of dawn, let us not curse the remaining dark. Let us gather the light.

Our destiny offers, not the cup of despair, but the chalice of opportunity. So let us seize it, not in fear, but in gladness and riders on the earth together, let us go forward, firm in our faith, steadfast in our purpose, cautious of the dangers; but sustained by our confidence in the will of God and the promise of man.

—— SECOND INAUGURAL ADDRESS ——

JANUARY 20, 1973

COMMENTARY

Throughout 1972, the Gallup Poll showed that a majority of Americans supported Richard Nixon and his policies and that he would be reelected. In December, 62 percent of those surveyed approved of the way Nixon handled his job as president, and this figure had remained above 50 percent throughout the year.

As president, Nixon prided himself on mastering grand strategies in foreign policy. However, a settlement of the Vietnam War, although his priority upon taking office, remained elusive. He wanted to negotiate an agreement that would bring American troops home but he wanted only "peace with honor," which meant preserving a pro-American South Vietnamese government. This strategy, called "Vietnamization," involved a gradual withdrawal of American troops, peace talks, and shifting the fighting to the South Vietnamese army. But it just did not work.

The North Vietnamese continually insisted on complete American withdrawal and the abandonment of the South Vietnamese military government. Continued American bombing raids forced the Vietcong (the South Vietnamese Communists) deeper into neighboring Cambodia. This caused an overthrow of the neutral Cambodian government and a civil war that involved the Vietcong. On April 30, 1970, Nixon ordered American troops into Cambodia proclaiming that he would not allow "the world's most powerful nation" to act "like a pitiful helpless giant." The wave of protests that followed included the Kent State University tragedy in which the Ohio National Guard opened fire on antiwar demonstrators, and another march on Washington by more than

100,000 war protestors. After two months, American troops left Cambodia having achieved little.

As the 1972 presidential election neared, the Nixon administration stepped up its efforts to produce a breakthrough in negotiations with the North Vietnamese. On October 26, only days before the election, Secretary of State Henry Kissinger announced from the Paris talks that "peace is at hand." Several weeks later (after the election), negotiations broke down. Finally, after massive American bombing raids against Hanoi and other North Vietnamese targets, the North Vietnamese returned to the conference table. And on January 27, 1973, they signed a vague agreement ending the war. Although the agreement was not implemented, it gave Nixon the excuse for withdrawing American troops from Vietnam.

Throughout 1972, Nixon was obsessed with winning the presidential election. In 1968, he had won in a three-way race, receiving a plurality of the popular vote. Now, in an anticipated two-candidate race, Nixon had to dramatically increase his popular vote. With the aid of his chief political advisor, Attorney General John Mitchell, Nixon devised a reelection plan that was aimed at the "real majority" in the United States—the "unyoung, unblack, and unpoor," the mature, white, middle-class citizen who was disgusted with campus protests, school integration, street crime, and rising health care costs. In particular, they planned to win over those who had voted for George Wallace in 1968. They hoped to establish a permanent Republican majority by also appealing to blue-collar workers in northern cities. To achieve these goals, Nixon decided to run his reelection campaign independent of the Republican Party. His staff set up the Committee to Reelect the President. The Committee directed the campaign, raised the needed money, and had easy access to the president. To his annoyance, it became known as CREEP instead of CRP.

Nixon was far more interested in his Democratic opponent than in any campaign issue. The opponents Nixon most feared were Senator Edmund Muskie of Maine and Governor George Wallace of Alabama. He hoped that the Democrats would nominate George McGovern, the liberal senator from South Dakota. Nixon later wrote: "If by some miracle [McGovern] would be nominated, I had no doubt that he would be the easiest Democrat to beat." And, using CREEP, Nixon set out to manipulate the Democratic Party into nominating its weakest candidate.

As the election of 1972 approached, Nixon's majority seemed to be falling into place. The president warned federal officials to stop pressing for school desegregation through "forced busing." He threatened to seek legislation, even a constitutional amendment, to prevent federal courts from promoting racial *balance through busing. He also declared that efforts to compel school integration in northern suburbs were "counterproductive, and not in the interest of better racial relations." And when George Wallace decided to seek the presidency through the Democratic primaries, Democratic Party chairman Larry O'Brien immediately disavowed his candidacy. Labor leader George Meany called Wallace a "bigot and racist." Wallace swept the southern Democratic primaries and finished a strong second in Pennsylvania and Indiana. An early March Gallup Poll of Democrats showed Wallace with a 15 percent approval rating, running third in a list of 11 potential nominees. Then, on May 15, Wallace was shot five times at point-blank range at a political rally in Maryland. The governor was paralyzed and too ill to continue the race. Former Texas governor John Connally, now a key Nixon political adviser, noted, "We might well say that this was the day the election was won."*

At the beginning of 1972, Senator Edmund Muskie of Maine was the leading contender for the Democratic nomination. He had solid financial backing, a large and experienced staff, and the endorsement of the party's leading figures. Muskie planned to enter every primary. His supporters felt that the senator had won the nomination even before the first primary in New Hampshire. The Manchester Union Leader *was the daily newspaper that was read by 40 percent of New Hampshire's population. In late February, it published a phony letter saying that Muskie's wife had stated that Maine did not have a black problem but it did have "Cannocks," a derogatory term for French-Canadian Americans who made up a substantial number of that state's population. A week before the primary, Muskie cried while defending his wife. The evening news showed that moment, as well as a triumphant Nixon with Prime Minister Chou En-lai on the president's historic visit to China. The contrast between the two images was unfortunate for Muskie. He won the New Hampshire primary with 46.4 percent to McGovern's 37 percent. However, this was less than the clear majority he needed in a state where he was well known. Muskie's campaign all but ended. A year later, the nation learned that CREEP, as part of its "dirty tricks" operation, with Nixon's approval, had been responsible for the incident that triggered Muskie's emotional outburst.*

To Nixon's relief, the Democratic Party now turned to its New Left faction. On July 10, the Democrats nominated Senator George McGovern who was chiefly known for his long record of outspoken opposition to the Vietnam War. McGovern pledged himself to advancing the rights of minorities, expanding social welfare legislation, and closing high income tax loopholes. He proposed giving $1,000 each year to everyone "from the poorest migrant workers to the Rockefellers," to tax it back from the rich and redistribute it to the needy. McGovern favored amnesty for Vietnam draft evaders and a woman's right to choose abortion, and he proposed removing criminal penalties for marijuana use. He promised an immediate end to the bombing in Vietnam and vowed that within 90 days of his inauguration every American prisoner would be out of Vietnam. McGovern chose Senator Thomas Eagleton of Missouri as his running mate. Almost immediately, it was learned that Eagleton had undergone psychiatric treatment for depression, which had included several hospitalizations and electroshock therapy. After saying that he continued to support Eagleton, McGovern replaced him with Sargent Shriver, a brother-in-law of the Kennedys and the first director of the Peace Corps. The McGovern campaign never recovered.

In August, Nixon and Vice President Spiro T. Agnew were renominated at the Republican convention in Miami Beach. They had an insurmountable lead. Nixon became the favorite not only of Republicans but of many Democrats and Independents. He carried every state except Massachusetts and the District of Columbia, receiving 520 electoral votes to McGovern's 17. Nixon received 60.7 percent of the popular vote, which was second only to Lyndon B. Johnson's record-breaking 61.1 percent in the landslide of 1964. Nixon swept the Solid South, completely capturing the Wallace vote. However, Nixon noted in his diary that he was overcome by "a curious feeling, perhaps a foreboding that muted my enjoyment of this triumphal moment."

The 1972 election cannot be fully explained without mentioning the Watergate scandal, the most important political event of the year. It occurred in Washington, D.C., on June 17 at the hotel and office complex known as the Watergate. Seven men, including two former White House aides and a member of CREEP, were apprehended and indicted for breaking into the headquarters of the Democratic National Committee. They were later tried and convicted. They seem to have been trying to place a listening device in the telephone of Larry O'Brien, chairman of the Democratic Party. Apparently, Nixon wanted to know how much O'Brien knew about the president's dealings with billionaire Howard Hughes, a contributor to Nixon's campaign and a friend of O'Brien's. It seemed farfetched that the Republican Party, much less the president of the United States, had anything to do with this illegal act. Administration officials dismissed the Watergate break-in as a "caper" and a "third-rate burglary attempt" of no significance. "I can say categorically," the president stated on August 29, "that no one in the White House staff, no one in this administration, presently employed, was involved in this very bizarre incident." However, the president was lying, and he had authorized a cover-up soon after the burglary. This botched illegal entry led to the unraveling of Nixon's presidency—and to his 1974 resignation in the face of imminent impeachment by Congress.

On January 20, 1973, Richard Nixon was inaugurated for his second term. In his memoirs, there is no mention of the event. He had hoped to be able to announce that peace had been achieved in Vietnam but this was not possible. The hoopla that ordinarily occurs at inaugurals was distinctly absent. Nixon's inaugural address was short and somber.

Mr. Vice President, Mr. Speaker, Mr. Chief Justice, Senator Cook, Mrs. Eisenhower, and my fellow citizens of this great and good country we share together:

When we met here four years ago, America was bleak in spirit, depressed by the prospect of seemingly endless war abroad and of destructive conflict at home. As we meet here today, we stand on the threshold of a new era of peace in the world.

The central question before us is: How shall we use that peace? Let us resolve that this era we are about to enter will not be what other postwar periods have so often been: a time of retreat and isolation that leads to stagnation at home and invites new danger abroad.

Let us resolve that this will be what it can become: a time of great responsibilities greatly borne, in which we renew the spirit and the promise of America as we enter our third century as a nation.

This past year saw far-reaching results from our new policies for peace. By continuing to revitalize our traditional friendships, and by our missions to Peking and to Moscow, we were able to establish the base for a new and more durable pattern of relationships among the nations of the world. Because of America's bold initiatives, 1972 will be long remembered as the year of the greatest progress since the end of World War II toward a lasting peace in the world.

The peace we seek in the world is not the flimsy peace which is merely an interlude between wars, but a peace which can endure for generations to come.

It is important that we understand both the necessity and the limitations of America's role in maintaining that peace. Unless we in America work to preserve the peace, there will be no peace. Unless we in America work to preserve freedom, there will be no freedom.

But let us clearly understand the new nature of America's role, as a result of the new policies we have adopted over these past four years. We shall respect our treaty commitments. We shall support vigorously the principle that no country has the right to impose its will or rule on another by force.

We shall continue, in this era of negotiation, to work for the limitation of nuclear arms, and to reduce the danger of confrontation between the great powers. We shall do our share in defending peace and freedom in the world. But we shall expect others to do their share.

The time has passed when America will make every other nation's conflict our own, or make every other nation's future our responsibility, or presume to tell the people of other nations how to manage their own affairs.

Just as we respect the right of each nation to determine its own future, we also recognize the responsibility of each nation to secure its own future.

Just as America's role is indispensable in preserving the world's peace, so is each nation's role indispensable in preserving its own peace.

Together with the rest of the world, let us resolve to move forward from the beginnings we have made. Let us continue to bring down the walls of hostility which have divided the world for too long, and to build in their place bridges of understanding; so that despite profound differences between systems of government, the people of the world can be friends.

Let us build a structure of peace in the world in which the weak are as safe as the strong; in which each respects the right of the other to live by a different system; in which those who would influence others will do so by the strength of their ideas, and not by the force of their arms.

Let us accept that high responsibility not as a burden, but gladly—gladly because the chance to build such a peace is the noblest endeavor in which a nation can engage; gladly, also, because only if we act greatly in meeting our responsibilities abroad will we remain a great Nation, and only if we remain a great Nation will we act greatly in meeting our challenges at home.

We have the chance today to do more than ever before in our history to make life better in America; to ensure better education, better health, better housing, better transportation, a cleaner environment; to restore respect for law, to make our communities more livable; and to insure the God given right of every American to full and equal opportunity.

Because the range of our needs is so great; because the reach of our opportunities is so great; let us be bold in our determination to meet those needs in new ways.

Just as building a structure of peace abroad has required turning away from old policies that failed, so building a new era of progress at home requires turning away from old policies that have failed.

Abroad, the shift from old policies to new has not been a retreat from our responsibilities, but a better way to peace.

And at home, the shift from old policies to new will not be a retreat from our responsibilities, but a better way to progress.

Abroad and at home, the key to those new responsibilities lies in the placing and the division of responsibility. We have lived too long with the consequences of attempting to gather all power and responsibility in Washington.

Abroad and at home, the time has come to turn away from the condescending policies of paternalism of Washington knows best.

A person can be expected to act responsibly only if he has responsibility. This is human nature. So let us encourage individuals at home and nations abroad to do more for themselves, to decide more for themselves. Let us locate responsibility in more places. Let us measure what we will do for others by what they will do for themselves.

That is why today I offer no promise of a purely governmental solution for every problem. We have lived too long with that false promise. In trusting too much in government, we have asked of it more than it can deliver. This leads only to inflated expectations, to reduced individual effort, and to a disappointment and frustration that erode confidence both in what government can do and in what people can do.

Government must learn to take less from people so that people can do more for themselves.

Let us remember that America was built not by government, but by people not by welfare, but by work not by shirking responsibility, but by seeking responsibility.

In our own lives, let each of us ask not just what will government do for me, but what can I do for myself?

In the challenges we face together, let each of us ask not just how can government help, but how can I help?

Your National Government has a great and vital role to play. And I pledge to you that where this Government should act, we will act boldly and we will lead boldly. But just as important is the role that each and every one of us must play, as an individual and as a member of his own community.

From this day forward, let each of us make a solemn commitment in his own heart: to bear his responsibility, to do his part, to live his ideals so that together, we can see the dawn of a new age of progress for America, and together, as we celebrate our 200th anniversary as a nation, we can do so proud in the fulfillment of our promise to ourselves and to the world.

As America's longest and most difficult war comes to an end, let us again learn to debate our differences with civility and decency. And let each of us reach out for that one precious quality government cannot provide—a new level of respect for the rights and feelings of one another, a new level of respect for the individual human dignity which is the cherished birthright of every American.

Above all else, the time has come for us to renew our faith in ourselves and in America. In recent years, that faith has been challenged.

Our children have been taught to be ashamed of their country, ashamed of their parents, ashamed of America's record at home and of its role in the world.

At every turn, we have been beset by those who find everything wrong with America and little that is right. But I am confident that this will not be the judgment of history on these remarkable times in which we are privileged to live.

America's record in this century has been unparalleled in the world's history for its responsibility, for its generosity, for its creativity and for its progress.

Let us be proud that our system has produced and provided more freedom and more abundance, more widely shared, than any other system in the history of the world.

Let us be proud that in each of the four wars in which we have been engaged in this century, including the one we are now bringing to an end, we have fought not for our selfish advantage, but to help others resist aggression.

Let us be proud that by our bold, new initiatives, and by our steadfastness for peace with honor, we have made a breakthrough toward creating in the world what the world has not known before; a structure of peace that can last, not merely for our time, but for generations to come.

We are embarking here today on an era that presents challenges great as those any nation, or any generation, has ever faced.

We shall answer to God, to history, and to our conscience for the way in which we use these years.

As I stand in this place, so hallowed by history, I think of others who have stood here before me. I think of the dreams they had for America, and I think of how each recognized that he needed help far beyond himself in order to make those dreams come true.

Today, I ask your prayers that in the years ahead I may have God's help in making decisions that are right for America, and I pray for your help so that together we may be worthy of our challenge.

Let us pledge together to make these next four years the best four years in America's history, so that on its 200th birthday America will be as young and as vital as when it began, and as bright a beacon of hope for all the world.

Let us go forward from here confident in hope, strong in our faith in one another, sustained by our faith in God who created us, and striving always to serve His purpose.

JIMMY CARTER

INAUGURAL ADDRESS

JANUARY 20, 1977

COMMENTARY

The 1976 election was the first in which the federal government subsidized a campaign. A new law provided for public funds derived from a checkoff on the federal income tax form. This law was intended to attract office-seekers who otherwise could not afford to get involved in presidential politics. The Democratic Party also implemented a plan of "affirmative action" to ensure that each state's delegation to their national nominating convention be representative of the population-at-large. Seventy percent of the delegates to the 1976 Democratic convention were chosen under this new procedure. However, the most striking feature of the 1976 election was the turnout—the lowest proportion of eligible voters since 1948. Alienated from the political process by the Watergate scandal and distrustful of both candidates, 72 million registered voters made their feelings known on Election Day by staying home.

Jimmy Carter, former governor of Georgia, won the Democratic nomination because he had a superb grasp of the complex rules of the new primary system. He sensed the mood of the nation's disillusionment, which was caused by the Vietnam War and the Watergate scandal. The fact that the public had little perception of what Carter was really like enabled him to shape an image to meet the demands of the new political reality. Carter built his organization in key states with little money and only a few aides. He decided to base his campaign in his hometown of Plains, Georgia, allowing reporters to see for themselves the virtues of a friendly, small, rural, southern town. As he campaigned for the nomination across the country, Carter emphasized his personal character. He pledged that he would never lie to the American people, and that he was committed to "open government." His autobiography, Why Not the Best?, *gave an idyllic portrait of his roots and a confirmation and description of his deep Christian faith. Carter proclaimed himself as a new kind of political leader, one who could heal the nation's wounds. But, he was deliberately vague on issues. As he stated on* Face the Nation *in March 1976, the voters "just feel that I'm the sort of person they can trust, and if they are liberal, I think I'm compatible with their views. If they are moderate, the same; and if the voter is conservative, I think they'll still feel that I'm a good president." It seemed inconceivable that the Democrats would choose someone who held no current office, had no strong power base, and who came from the Deep South.*

In January 1976, a Gallup Poll of Democrats reported that only 4 percent favored Carter as their party's candidate. The following week, Carter won the caucuses in Iowa with 27.6 percent of those who designated a candidate. "None of the above" received just less than 30 percent. Nevertheless, Time *proclaimed him the Democratic front-runner. In New Hampshire the following month, Carter defeated five other candidates in the race, receiving 28.4 percent of the total vote. Both* Time *and* Newsweek *placed him on the cover. In the Massachusetts primary the following week, Carter ran a poor fourth (13.9 percent) but* Time *declared that this defeat had only "slowed the momentum" and Carter had to "recapture the forward thrust." Although only a fraction of Democrats has expressed their opinion, Carter now received three times the television news coverage and four times the newspaper reporting of his competitors combined. The news media had declared Carter the front-runner and the others became the challengers. In the "make or break" Pennsylvania preferential vote, Carter received 37 percent of the vote. A* Washington Post *exit poll showed that 46 percent of the voters would have favored Hubert Humphrey, had he been a candidate. Nevertheless, the "Anyone but Carter" effort by labor leaders and political professionals failed. Carter won the nomination on the first ballot at the Democratic convention. He chose Senator Walter Mondale of Minnesota as his running mate.*

Carter's opponent in the November election was President Gerald Ford. Appointed vice president under the Twenty-fifth Amendment to replace Spiro Agnew, Ford became president after Nixon's resignation on August 9, 1974. After taking the oath of office, he declared that "our national nightmare is over." However, his pardon of Nixon one month later dissipated much of the initial goodwill. Whatever might be said about the merit of his pardon decision, it evoked memories of Watergate and concern that Ford might have made a deal with Nixon. Although

Ford obtained the Republican nomination on the first ballot, he had to ward off a powerful challenge from former California governor Ronald Reagan who had the support of the party's conservative wing. At the August convention, Ford won the nomination by the razor-thin margin of 1,187 votes to Reagan's 1,070. Ford selected Senator Robert (Bob) Dole of Kansas as his running mate.

What followed was a lackluster campaign. Ford's strategy consisted of trying to act presidential by making almost daily announcements against the backdrop of the White House Rose Garden or the Oval Office. Carter presented himself as an outsider and repeatedly promised voters, "I'll never tell a lie." So shallow were Carter's speeches that he left himself open to Ford's charge that "he wavers, he wanders, he wiggles, and he waffles." During the primaries, Carter seemed above reproach, almost too perfect. However, after the nomination, he emerged as an ordinary politician, making deals and promises. This unfocused campaign bored many voters. Differences on substantive policy issues did not emerge and the headlines and evening television news shows featured the mishaps and possible misdeeds of each candidate. Carter's mammoth lead in public opinion polls dwindled by Election Day. Perhaps unhappiness with the economy, and a general disenchantment with Ford, enabled Carter to win a narrow victory—50 percent of the popular vote to Ford's 47.9 percent and 297 electoral votes to Ford's 240. This was the closest electoral vote victory since Woodrow Wilson's 1916 victory over Charles Evans Hughes.

Carter probably won the election because he was able to reclaim the South for the Democrats. Carter not only won the South but he won a larger share of the vote there than any Democrat in the last 25 years. Even more impressive, Carter won nearly twice the percentage of the southern vote (54 percent) that McGovern had received in 1972 (29 percent). Ironically, Carter, the outsider, won with the traditional Democratic vote: 82 percent of registered Democrats voted for him as did 85 percent of nonwhites; 63 percent of union families; 58 percent of manual laborers; and 57 percent of Catholics. While it is difficult to point to one factor in such a close election, Carter did extremely well with men, winning a greater share of their vote than any Democrat during the last 25 years, with the exception of Lyndon Johnson. After voting nearly alike in 1972, men and women diverged in 1976. Ford would have been elected by a 51–48 percent margin in an all-female America. If credit for putting Carter in the White House can be claimed by any single group, nonwhites might justifiably make such a claim. They voted for Carter by more than a 5 to 1 margin, contributing to Carter's electoral win in New York, Louisiana, Mississippi, and Texas. White voters alone would have elected Ford by a comfortable 52–46 percent.

In describing his inauguration, Carter wrote in his diary, "Even though I had been preparing to be President, I was genuinely surprised when in the benediction, the Bishop from Minnesota referred to 'blessings on President Carter.' Just the phrase, 'President Carter,' was startling to me." For the swearing-in ceremony, Carter used his campaign name, "Jimmy Carter," rather than the formal James Earl Carter Jr. He took the oath of office on a Bible that had been in the family for four generations. After an unusually brief inaugural address, the traditional parade down Pennsylvania Avenue to the White House began. Carter, attempting to emulate Jefferson's efforts to identify with the "common man," broke with tradition by walking the mile and a half with his wife and daughter at his side. Not since Jefferson had a president walked in his inaugural parade.

For myself and for our Nation, I want to thank my predecessor for all he has done to heal our land.

In this outward and physical ceremony we attest once again to the inner and spiritual strength of our Nation. As my high school teacher, Miss Julia Coleman, used to say, we must adjust to changing times and still hold to unchanging principles.

Here before me is the Bible used in the inauguration of our first President, in 1789, and I have just taken the oath of office on the Bible my mother gave me a few years ago, opened to a timeless admonition from the ancient prophet Micah:

> He hath showed thee, O' man, what is good; and what doth the
> Lord require of thee, but to do justly, and to love mercy, and to
> walk humbly with thy God.

This inauguration ceremony marks a new beginning, a new dedication within our Government, and a new spirit among us all. A President may sense and proclaim that new spirit, but only a people can provide it.

Two centuries ago our Nation's birth was a milestone in the long quest for freedom, but the bold and brilliant dream which excited the founders of this Nation still awaits its consummation. I have no new dream to set forth today, but rather urge a fresh faith in the old dream.

Ours was the first society openly to define itself in terms of both spirituality and of human liberty. It is that unique self-definition which has given us an exceptional appeal, but it also imposes on us a special obligation, to take on those moral duties which, when assumed, seem invariably to be in our own best interests.

You have given me a great responsibility—to stay close to you, to be worthy of you, and to exemplify what you are. Let us create together a new national spirit of unity and trust. Your strength can compensate for my weakness, and your wisdom can help to minimize my mistakes.

Let us learn together and laugh together and work together and pray together, confident that in the end we will triumph together in the right.

The American dream endures. We must once again have full faith in our country and in one another. I believe America can be better. We can be even stronger than before.

Let our recent mistakes bring a resurgent commitment to the basic principles of our Nation, for we know that if we despise our own government we have no future. We recall in special times when we have stood briefly, but magnificently, united. In those times no prize was beyond our grasp. But we cannot dwell upon remembered glory. We cannot afford to drift. We reject the prospect of failure or mediocrity or an inferior quality of life for any person. Our Government must at the same time be both competent and compassionate.

We have already found a high degree of personal liberty, and we are now struggling to enhance equality of opportunity. Our commitment to human rights must be absolute, our laws fair, our natural beauty preserved; the powerful must not persecute the weak, and human dignity must be enhanced.

We have learned that more is not necessarily better, that even our great Nation has its recognized limits, and that we can neither answer all questions nor solve all problems. We cannot afford to do everything, nor can we afford to lack boldness as we meet the future. So, together, in a spirit of individual sacrifice for the common good, we must simply do our best.

Our Nation can be strong abroad only if it is strong at home. And we know that the best way to enhance freedom in other lands is to demonstrate here that our democratic system is worthy of emulation.

To be true to ourselves, we must be true to others. We will not behave in foreign places so as to violate our rules and standards here at home, for we know that the trust which our Nation earns is essential to our strength.

The world itself is now dominated by a new spirit. Peoples more numerous and more politically aware are craving and now demanding their place in the sun; not just for the benefit of their own physical condition, but for basic human rights.

The passion for freedom is on the rise. Tapping this new spirit, there can be no nobler nor more ambitious task for America to undertake on this day of a new beginning than to help shape a just and peaceful world that is truly humane.

We are a strong nation, and we will maintain strength so sufficient that it need not be proven in combat; a quiet strength based not merely on the size of an arsenal, but on the nobility of ideas.

We will be ever vigilant and never vulnerable, and we will fight our wars against poverty, ignorance, and injustice; for those are the enemies against which our forces can be honorably marshaled.

We are a purely idealistic Nation, but let no one confuse our idealism with weakness.

Because we are free we can never be indifferent to the fate of freedom elsewhere. Our moral sense dictates a clear-cut preference for these societies which share with us an abiding respect for individual human rights. We do not seek to intimidate, but it is clear that a world which others can dominate with impunity would be inhospitable to decency and a threat to the well-being of all people.

The world is still engaged in a massive armaments race designed to ensure continuing equivalent strength among potential adversaries. We pledge perseverance and wisdom in our efforts to limit the world's armaments to those necessary for each nation's own domestic safety. And we will move this year a step toward ultimate goal, the elimination of all nuclear weapons from this Earth. We urge all other people to join us, for success can mean life instead of death.

Within us, the people of the United States, there is evident a serious and purposeful rekindling of confidence. And I join in the hope that when my time as your President has ended, people might say this about our Nation:

- That we had remembered the words of Micah and renewed our search for humility, mercy, and justice;

- That we had torn down the barriers that separated those of different race and region and religion, and where there had been mistrust, built unity, with a respect for diversity;

- That we had found productive work for those able to perform it;

- That we had strengthened the American family, which is the basis of our society;

- That we had ensured respect for the law, and equal treatment under the law, for the weak and the powerful, for the rich and the poor; and

- That we had enabled our people to be proud of their own Government once again.

I would hope that the nations of the world might say that we had built a lasting peace, built not on weapons of war but on international policies which reflect our own most precious values.

These are not just my goals, and they will not be my accomplishments, but the affirmation of our Nation's continuing moral strength and our belief in an undiminished, ever-expanding American dream.

RONALD REAGAN

FIRST INAUGURAL ADDRESS

JANUARY 20, 1981

COMMENTARY

The election of 1980 was a stinging rejection of Jimmy Carter. A January 1980 Gallup Poll found that 78 percent of Americans thought Carter was "a man of high moral principles" but only 29 percent considered him "a person of exceptional abilities." Two-thirds of members of Congress rated Carter's performance as below average. In 1980, the country experienced the second consecutive year of double-digit inflation for the first time since World War I, and, to add to the economic dissatisfaction, the prime interest rate had risen to 21.5 percent, the highest since the Civil War. Mortgage money virtually disappeared. The number of new houses being built sharply declined while older homes went unsold. In the 1976 campaign, Carter had compiled a "misery index" by adding the levels of unemployment and inflation. He used it effectively against his opponent. Four years later, the misery index stood even higher, the inflation rate averaged 12.4 percent, and 7.5 percent of the work force was unemployed. The White House appeared to be in disarray. Carter had dismissed four cabinet members and accepted the resignation of a fifth—several close aides were being investigated for wrongdoing, and the president's brother was charged with receiving funds as an unregistered lobbyist for Libya. In 1976, Carter had declared, "The insiders have had their chance, and they have not delivered. Their time has run out." His Republican opponent in 1980 said essentially the same thing. Dissatisfaction with Carter's handling of both foreign and domestic issues gave the Republicans the opportunity to become the nation's majority party again. But what ultimately undid Carter was his failure to inspire confidence.

Events in Iran caused great political damage to Carter. In January 1979, Islamic fundamentalists overthrew the Shah of Iran. In November, a mob of young Iranians stormed the U.S. Embassy in Tehran and took more than 50 Americans hostage. They pledged to hold them until the Shah was returned to Iran for trial. The Shah had entered the United States for medical treatment shortly after Carter had praised him while approving a multibillion dollar arms sale to this "island of stability." An attempt to rescue the hostages through a military operation (Desert One) failed as eight marines died in the collision of two helicopters in Iran's central desert. For a while, the president's foreign policy troubles strengthened him politically as Americans rallied behind their leader. But as the Iranian situation dragged on, support for Carter waned. The poignant scenes from Tehran of "America Held Hostage" shown on television every night left many Americans feeling angry and frustrated at the diminished prestige and power of their nation. This Iranian spectacle threatened to bring chaos to a region that supplied more than half the world's imported oil. It plunged the Carter administration into a crisis that defied any quick resolution and rapidly eroded popular support for his presidency. In July 1980, Carter's approval rating sank to 21 percent, the lowest recorded for a president since the Gallup Poll initiated this measurement in 1938.

Senator Edward M. Kennedy of Massachusetts challenged Carter for the 1980 Democratic nomination. Though Kennedy did not formally announce his candidacy until November 1979, the expectation that he would run haunted Carter throughout that year. In May 1979, the senator introduced his own competing health care program in Congress. In June, the Americans for Democratic Action started a dump-Carter movement. Following suit, the National Conference of Democratic Mayors assailed Carter on his planned budget cuts for urban areas and labor leader George Meany declared Carter "the most conservative president I have seen in my lifetime." The president, he charged, was attempting to curb inflation by encouraging unemployment. In September, the Democratic Speaker of the House Thomas "Tip" O'Neill told reporters that he didn't think Kennedy "could be denied the nomination if he were to run." In December, the National Organization for Women rebuked Carter by voting not to endorse any candidate in 1980. Early polls showed that Kennedy led Carter by more than 2 to 1 as the choice of Democrats. However, once Kennedy declared his candidacy, his poll ratings plummeted. The senator's primary campaign seemed disorganized and unfocused. He could not adequately articulate why he wanted to be president. Above all, he could not explain an automobile accident in 1969 on the island of Chappaquidick in Massachusetts in which a young woman was killed. The senator also seemed to have a drinking problem. Carter declared that he would not get involved in the primaries because of events in Iran. "At the height of the Civil War," he intoned, "Abraham Lincoln said, 'I have but one task and that is to save the Union.' " Then he added with all due modesty, "Now I must devote my considered efforts to resolving the Iranian crisis." This strategy worked. Carter defeated Kennedy in two-thirds of the primaries. While Carter managed to stave off Kennedy's challenge and barely win his party's renomination, it was an unhappy convention that heard the president's listless call to arms. Carter's campaign aroused little popular enthusiasm as he faced a powerful Republican candidate.

The Republicans entered the 1980 campaign with confidence. The clear choice of the party's rank and file was 69-year-old Ronald Reagan. Like Carter, Reagan had neither political nor administrative experience at the national level—a circumstance that enhanced his outsider appeal. Reagan had begun his political life in the 1930s as a New Deal Democrat. However, the growth of Soviet power after World War II had left him disillusioned with liberalism. By the 1950s, Reagan had become an ardent anticommunist. No doubt Reagan's film career (he made some 50 movies over a 20-year period), helped make him familiar to several generations of Americans. Between his film and political careers, Reagan was a successful salesman. Working for the General Electric Company between 1954 and 1962, he spoke to employees at plants across the country. He also addressed chambers of commerce, trade associations, and civic clubs. In 1964, the year he made his last movie, Reagan delivered a televised address in support of Barry Goldwater. This political debut sufficiently impressed a group of California businessmen who proposed that he run for governor of the state. Although he had never sought nor held public office, Reagan trounced the incumbent Democratic governor by nearly a million votes, the largest majority by which a sitting governor had been defeated in U.S. history. As governor of California for eight years, Reagan became the nation's best-known Republican politician because he associated himself with virtually every conservative cause.

In the Republican primaries, Reagan easily outdistanced a host of other conservative hopefuls. His principal backers considered themselves part of the New Right—a broad, loose coalition of conservative ideologues and fundamentalist Christians. They strongly disapproved of the social and economic excesses of the 1960s and 1970s. Reagan's support also came from neoconservatives. These former liberals were repelled by President Richard Nixon's easing of tensions with the Soviet Union, which was continued by the administrations of

Ford and Carter. They charged that the United States had allowed the Soviets to become a dangerous adversary that now had superiority in both conventional and nuclear arms. This superiority had encouraged the Soviets to engage in reckless adventures such as their support of worldwide terrorism and their 1979 invasion of Afghanistan. Reagan was nominated on the first ballot. He chose George H. W. Bush, former head of the Central Intelligence Agency, as his running mate. Representative John Anderson of Illinois led frustrated Republican liberals into a third party.

Ronald Reagan and Jimmy Carter had very different campaign themes. Reagan successfully exploited domestic distress and international instability. He promised to restore America to greatness. He promised the American people an America like that of his youth, rooted in the small-town, rural values where he claimed to have learned patriotism, self-help, hard work, morality, and belief in God, family, and the flag. On the other hand, Carter repeated that America had to sacrifice in order to survive in a world of scarcity. Reagan favored huge increases in military spending, massive tax cuts, and the end of many federal social programs. He opposed national health insurance and any other new social programs. Carter tried to divert attention from his own record by emphasizing Reagan's right-wing background. He warned that Reagan's election would be a threat to peace. During the second television debate with Carter, which was watched by more than 60 million households, Reagan scored the most decisive point in the campaign. He ended the debate with two brilliant questions: "Ask yourself, are you better off than you were four years ago?" and "Is America as respected throughout the world as it was four years ago?" "The election," said a Carter adviser, "ended up becoming exactly the referendum on unhappiness we had been trying to avoid."

The election results were decisive. Reagan won the popular vote by almost a 10-point margin, 50.7 percent to 41 percent. Anderson received nearly 6 million votes, 6.6 percent. Democratic support declined from 1976 in every state. Reagan carried all the states that Ford had won in 1976, plus 17 others that had previously gone to Carter. Reagan received 489 electoral votes to Carter's 49. Carter lost support from traditional Democratic voters—labor union members, manual workers, and Catholics. While both nonwhites and young adults preferred Carter, their impact was offset by the low turnout among these two groups. In addition, Republicans gained 34 seats in the House of Representatives, their largest gain since 1966. They also increased their strength in the Senate by 12 seats, giving them a majority for the first time since 1954. Jimmy Carter became the first elected incumbent to be defeated for reelection since

1932. And while Reagan's supporters called his election a "landslide" and a "revolution," it should be noted that voter turnout reached a new low and the new president had received a "landslide" of only 26 percent of the total electorate. Nevertheless, conservatives interpreted Reagan's victory as a mandate for their policies. Liberals, perhaps more accurately, argued that the results were a personal rejection of Jimmy Carter for his failure of leadership.

The 1981 inauguration was held for the first time on the west side of the Capitol. Ronald Reagan took the oath of office with his hand on his mother's Bible opened to the seventh chapter, fourteenth verse of Second Chronicles, "If my people . . . shall humble themselves and pray . . . and turn from their wicked ways, then will I . . . forgive their sin, and will heal their land." Next to these words, his mother had written, "A most wonderful verse for the healing of nations." Carter, in the last days of his presidency, had concluded months of negotiations by agreeing to release several billion dollars in Iranian assets that he had frozen in American banks shortly after the seizure of the embassy. As Reagan was being sworn in, the American hostages, after their 444-day ordeal, were released.

Senator Hatfield, Mr. Chief Justice, Mr. President, Vice President Bush, Vice President Mondale, Senator Baker, Speaker O'Neill, Reverend Moomaw, and my fellow citizens:

To a few of us here today, this is a solemn and most momentous occasion; and yet, in the history of our Nation, it is a commonplace occurrence. The orderly transfer of authority as called for in the Constitution routinely takes place as it has for almost two centuries and few of us stop to think how unique we really are. In the eyes of many in the world, this every four year ceremony we accept as normal is nothing less than a miracle.

Mr. President, I want our fellow citizens to know how much you did to carry on this tradition. By your gracious cooperation in the transition process, you have shown a watching world that we are a united people pledged to maintaining a political system which guarantees individual liberty to a greater degree than any other, and I thank you and your people for all your help in maintaining the continuity which is the bulwark of our Republic.

The business of our nation goes forward. These United States are confronted with an economic affliction of great proportions. We suffer from the longest and one of the worst sustained inflations in our national history. It distorts our economic decisions, penalizes thrift, and crushes the struggling young and the fixed income elderly alike. It threatens to shatter the lives of millions of our people.

Idle industries have cast workers into unemployment, human misery and personal indignity. Those who do work are denied a fair return for their labor by a tax system which penalizes successful achievement and keeps us from maintaining full productivity.

But great as our tax burden is, it has not kept pace with public spending. For decades, we have piled deficit upon deficit, mortgaging our future and our children's future for the temporary convenience of the present. To continue this long trend is to guarantee tremendous social, cultural, political, and economic upheavals.

You and I, as individuals, can by borrowing, live beyond our means, but for only a limited period of time. Why, then, should we think that collectively, as a nation, we are not bound by that same limitation?

We must act today in order to preserve tomorrow. And let there be no misunderstanding, we are going to begin to act, beginning today.

The economic ills we suffer have come upon us over several decades. They will not go away in days, weeks, or months, but they will go away. They will go away because we, as Americans, have the capacity now, as we have had in the past, to do whatever needs to be done to preserve this last and greatest bastion of freedom.

In this present crisis, government is not the solution to our problem. Government is the problem!

From time to time, we have been tempted to believe that society has become too complex to be managed by self-rule, that government by an elite group is superior to government for, by, and of the people. But if no one among us is capable of governing himself, then who among us has the capacity to govern someone else? All of us together, in and out of government, must bear the burden. The solutions we seek must be equitable, with no one group singled out to pay a higher price.

We hear much of special interest groups. Our concern must be for a special interest group that has been too long neglected. It knows no sectional boundaries or ethnic and racial divisions, and it crosses political party lines. It is made up of men and women who raise our food, patrol our streets, man our mines and our factories, teach our children, keep our homes, and heal us when we are sick; professionals, industrialists, shopkeepers, clerks, cabbies, and truckdrivers. They are, in short, "We the people," this breed called Americans.

Well, this administration's objective will be a healthy, vigorous, growing economy that provides equal opportunity for all Americans, with no barriers born of bigotry or discrimination. Putting America back to work means putting all Americans back to work. Ending inflation means freeing all Americans from the terror of runaway living costs. All must share in the productive work of this new beginning and all must share in the bounty of a revived economy. With the idealism and fair play which are the core of our system and our strength, we can have a strong and prosperous America at peace with itself and the world.

So, as we begin, let us take inventory. We are a nation that has a government, not the other way around. And this makes us special among the nations of the Earth. Our Government has no power except that granted it by the people. It is time to check and reverse the growth of government which shows signs of having grown beyond the consent of the governed.

It is my intention to curb the size and influence of the Federal establishment and to demand recognition of the distinction between the powers granted to the Federal Government and those reserved to the States or to the people. All of us need to be reminded that the Federal Government did not create the States; the States created the Federal Government.

Now, so there will be no misunderstanding, it is not my intention to do away with government. It is rather, to make it work, work with us, not over us; to stand by our side, not ride on our back. Government can and must provide opportunity, not smother it; foster productivity, not stifle it.

If we look to the answer as to why, for so many years, we achieved so much, prospered as no other people on Earth, it was because here, in this land, we unleashed the energy and individual genius of man to a greater extent than has ever been done before. Freedom and the dignity of the individual have been more available and assured here than in any other place on Earth. The price for this freedom at times has been high, but we have never been unwilling to pay that price.

It is no coincidence that our present troubles parallel and are proportionate to the intervention and intrusion in our lives that result from unnecessary and excessive growth of government. It is time for us to realize that we are too great a nation to limit ourselves to small dreams. We are not, as some would have us believe, loomed to an inevitable decline. I do not believe in a fate that will fall on us no matter what we do. I do believe in a fate that will fall on us if we do nothing. So, with all the creative energy at our command, let us begin an era of national renewal. Let us renew our determination, our courage, and our strength. And let us renew our faith and our hope.

We have every right to dream heroic dreams. Those who say that we are in a time when there are no heroes just don't know where to look. You can see heroes every day going in and out of factory gates. Others, a handful in number, produce enough food to feed all of us and then the world beyond.

You meet heroes across a counter, and they are on both sides of that counter. There are entrepreneurs with faith in themselves and faith in an idea who create new jobs, new wealth and opportunity. They are individuals and families whose taxes support the Government and whose voluntary gifts support church, charity, culture, art, and education. Their patriotism is quiet but deep. Their values sustain our national life.

I have used the words "they" and "their" in speaking of these heroes. I could say "you" and "your" because I am addressing the heroes of whom I speak, "you," the citizens of this blessed land. Your dreams, your hopes, your goals are going to be the dreams, the hopes, and the goals of this administration, so help me God.

We shall reflect the compassion that is so much a part of your makeup. How can we love our country and not love our countrymen, and loving them, reach out a hand when they fall, heal them when they are sick, and provide opportunities to make them self-sufficient so they will be equal in fact and not just in theory?

Can we solve the problems confronting us? Well, the answer is an unequivocal and emphatic yes. To paraphrase Winston Churchill, I did not take the oath I have just taken with the intention of presiding over the dissolution of the world's strongest economy.

In the days ahead I will propose removing the roadblocks that have slowed our economy and reduced productivity. Steps will be taken aimed at restoring the balance between the various levels of government. Progress may be slow, measured in inches and feet not miles, but we will progress. Is it time to reawaken this industrial giant, to get government back within its means, and to lighten our punitive tax burden. And these will be our first priorities, and on these principles, there will be no compromise.

On the eve of our struggle for independence a man who might have been one of the greatest among the Founding Fathers, Dr. Joseph Warren, President of the Massachusetts Congress, said to his fellow Americans:

> Our country is in danger, but not to be despaired of .... On you depend the fortunes of America. You are to decide the important questions upon which rests the happiness and the liberty of millions yet unborn. Act worthy of yourselves.

Well, I believe we, the Americans of today, are ready to act worthy of ourselves, ready to do what must be done to ensure happiness and liberty for ourselves, our children and our children's children.

And as we renew ourselves here in our own land, we will be seen as having greater strength throughout the world. We will again be the exemplar of freedom and a beacon of hope for those who do not now have freedom.

To those neighbors and allies who share our freedom, we will strengthen our historic ties and assure them of our support and firm commitment. We will match loyalty with loyalty. We will strive for mutually beneficial relations. We will not use our friendship to impose on their sovereignty, for or own sovereignty is not for sale.

As for the enemies of freedom, those who are potential adversaries, they will be reminded that peace is the highest aspiration of the American people. We will negotiate for it, sacrifice for it; we will not surrender for it, now or ever.

Our forbearance should never be misunderstood. Our reluctance for conflict should not be misjudged as a failure of will. When action is required to preserve our national security, we will act. We will maintain sufficient strength to prevail if need be, knowing that if we do so we have the best chance of never having to use that strength.

Above all, we must realize that no arsenal, or no weapon in the arsenals of the world, is so formidable as the will and moral courage of free men and women. It is a weapon our adversaries in today's world do not have. It is a weapon that we as Americans do have. Let that be understood by those who practice terrorism and prey upon their neighbors.

I am told that tens of thousands of prayer meetings are being held on this day, and for that I am deeply grateful. We are a nation under God, and I believe God intended for us to be free. It would be fitting and good, I think, if on each Inauguration Day in future years it should be declared a day of prayer.

This is the first time in history that this ceremony has been held, as you have been told, on this West Front of the Capitol. Standing here, one faces a magnificent vista, opening up on this city's special beauty and history. At the end of this open mall are those shrines to the giants on whose shoulders we stand.

Directly in front of me, the monument to a monumental man, George Washington, father of our country. A man of humility who came to greatness reluctantly. He led America out of revolutionary victory into infant nationhood. Off to one side, the stately memorial to Thomas Jefferson. The Declaration of Independence flames with his eloquence.

And then beyond the Reflecting Pool the dignified columns of the Lincoln Memorial. Whoever would understand in his heart the meaning of America will find it in the life of Abraham Lincoln.

Beyond those monuments to heroism is the Potomac River, and on the far shore the sloping hills of Arlington National Cemetery with its row on row of simple white markers bearing crosses or Stars of David. They add up to only a tiny fraction of the price that has been paid for our freedom.

Each one of those markers is a monument to the kinds of hero I spoke of earlier. Their lives ended in places called Belleau Wood, The Argonne, Omaha Beach, Salerno and halfway around the world on Guadalcanal, Tarawa, Pork Chop Hill, the Chosin Reservoir, and in a hundred rice paddies and jungles of a place called Vietnam.

Under one such marker lies a young man, Martin Treptow, who left his job in a small town barber shop in 1917 to go to France with the famed Rainbow Division. There, on the western front, he was killed trying to carry a message between battalions under heavy artillery fire.

We are told that on his body was found a diary. On the flyleaf under the heading, My Pledge, he had written these words:

> America must win this war. Therefore, I will work, I will save, I will sacrifice, I will endure, I will fight cheerfully and do my utmost, as if the issue of the whole struggle depended on me alone.

The crisis we are facing today does not require of us the kind of sacrifice that Martin Treptow and so many thousands of others were called upon to make. It does require, however, our best effort, and our willingness to believe in ourselves and to believe in our capacity to perform great deeds; to believe that together, with God's help, we can and will resolve the problems which now confront us.

And, after all, why shouldn't we believe that? We are Americans. God bless you, and thank you.

──── SECOND INAUGURAL ADDRESS ────

JANUARY 21, 1985

COMMENTARY

The nation seemed prosperous as the 1984 campaign began. Inflation and unemployment remained low and taxes had been reduced. Above all, Ronald Reagan remained popular with the American people. His standing in the Gallup Poll continued the strong upward momentum that began in early 1983, paralleling the economic recovery. In February 1984, Reagan's job performance rating of 55 percent approval represented an unprecedented 20 percentage-point improvement over his 35 percent approval rating recorded in late January 1983. Not since mid-1981, during his "honeymoon" in office, had Reagan received significantly higher job ratings. Reagan's well-publicized "gender gap" still existed. Sixty percent of men compared to 51 percent of women approved of his performance in office. Nevertheless, the fact that a majority of women approved—for the first time since the fall of 1981—was indicative of the general upward trend in the president's popularity. The Republican campaign slogan, "It's Morning in America," reflected the optimistic mood of the country. Reagan seemed unbeatable. At 73, he was already the oldest president in American history. But, the president's advanced age could not be a campaign issue as Reagan's physical vigor and unbroken record of good health made his age more a matter of public admiration rather than concern. This admiration was bolstered by the president's response to an attempt on his life in March 1981. "I forgot to duck," he joked to his wife. And, as he was about to undergo surgery for removal of the bullet, he quipped to the surgeons, "I hope you are all Republicans." The principle question in 1984 was which Democrat would lose to him.

Eight Democrats struggled for their party's nomination through exhaustive and divisive primaries that began on January 20 and ended on June 5. The leading candidate was Walter F. Mondale, who had been vice president in the Jimmy Carter administration. Under the changed rules for the 1984 Democratic convention, members of Congress, governors, mayors, and party officials had a large bloc of guaranteed seats. This gave Mondale an added advantage. Mondale remained a favorite among these party officeholders because they had found him a sympathetic and knowledgeable ally in Washington during the Carter years. Mondale also had kept together an able political staff regarded as the best since John Kennedy's group in 1960. But it was not until the votes in the New Jersey primary, the last to be held, had been counted, that Mondale could claim a majority of the convention delegates. Even then, after some 18 million votes, fewer than 450,000 separated Mondale from his closest rival, Senator Gary Hart of Colorado. More than 1 in 5 voters had chosen the third candidate, the Reverend Jesse Jackson. Jackson became the first black candidate to win substantial support in a bid for the presidential nomination of a major party.

Mondale made a bold and dramatic move. He chose Representative Geraldine A. Ferraro of New York as his running mate. She became the first woman to run for vice president on a major ticket. Mondale believed that this historic choice would help him with women, Catholics, ethnic groups, and in New York, a state essential to the Democrats. Ferraro was a Roman Catholic born to immigrant parents. Married for 24 years and the mother of three children, she had served three terms representing a racially and ethnically diverse congressional district in New York City. But almost immediately after her selection, she had to confront several unfortunate events. The first involved her family finances and tax records, which centered on some questionable real estate activities of her husband. The second was a bitter verbal battle with New York's Archbishop John J. O'Connor over her pro-choice position on the abortion issue. Both of these occurrences hurt the Democratic campaign. However, Mondale's almost unprecedented declaration that if elected, he would raise taxes just about doomed Democratic hopes to recapture the White House.

The Republican convention renominated President Reagan and Vice President George Bush in an unusual joint roll call. The party was confident, optimistic, strong, and united. Reagan, standing before a convention of his party for the last time as a candidate for president, said: "The choices this year are not just between two different personalities or between two political parties. They are between two different visions of the future, two fundamentally different ways of governing—their government of pessimism, fear, and limits . . . or ours of hope, confidence, and growth." After the speech, Ray Charles sang "America the Beautiful." Reagan noted in his diary, "I don't think there was a dry eye in the house." Polls taken as the convention ended showed the Reagan-Bush ticket with a commanding lead. This lead never dwindled.

Television emphasized the differences between Reagan and Mondale, and Reagan's strength as a television campaigner was to prove an enormous asset. The president appeared experienced, relaxed, and amiable. He conveyed to Americans a sense of direction in which he wanted to take the nation. Mondale came across as stiff and uncomfortable. His personality failed to excite or motivate voters. His many political skills, notably those as a debater, were not sufficient when running against Reagan. The president projected a most positive image of a likeable person with many good traits. During a debate with Mondale, when a reporter raised the issue of age, Reagan brought down the house with his reply, "I want you to know that also I will not make age an issue of this campaign. I am not going to exploit for political purposes my opponent's youth and inexperience." Reagan repeated that the federal government was the root of problems, and he promised to "get government off the backs of the people." He repeated the same message endless times using different words and different settings—"We think every day is the Fourth of July. Our opponents think every day is April 15!" He was against government controls, *and he was fiercely opposed to Communism. He considered the Soviet Union an "evil empire" with "aggressive impulses," responsible for causing unrest and revolutions throughout the world. He spoke about his youth and of small-town rural values where he learned patriotism, self-help, hard work, religious faith, family values, and a love for the American flag. With great oratorical skill, he talked about the lives of senior citizens and how their dreams and future hopes could be fulfilled without government restraints and regulations. Reagan's message was simple and consistent. It spoke of broad values rather than of issues, and it succeeded spectacularly. The media referred to Reagan as the "Great Communicator."*

On Election Day, Reagan achieved one of the greatest personal triumphs in U.S. political history. He carried 49 states, losing only Mondale's home state of Minnesota and the District of Columbia. His total of 525 electoral votes surpassed Franklin Roosevelt's modern record of 523 in 1936. His popular vote was of landslide proportion, 58.8 percent to Mondale's 40.6 percent. The economic recovery, plus the president's charm, won him support from large numbers of traditional Democrats, especially Southerners and blue-collar workers. He even won 57 percent of the women's vote. As in every presidential election since 1952, nonwhites voted overwhelmingly Democratic (87 percent). Although the Republican vote was only 13 percent among nonwhites, this figure had been lower in three earlier presidential elections. Reagan hailed the election results as an endorsement of his economic and foreign policies.

Inauguration Day 1985 fell on a Sunday. Reagan took the oath of office, as required by the Constitution, at a private ceremony in the White House. The formal inauguration was scheduled for the following day. But on Sunday afternoon, the inaugural committee came to the White House and urged Reagan to cancel the outdoor ceremony because the windchill factor was predicted to be 20 degrees below zero or worse. Doctors warned that at that temperature, exposed skin would freeze in about 15 seconds. So, on the twenty-first of January, just before noon, Reagan again took the oath of office before about 1,000 people in the Capitol rotunda, and then delivered his second inaugural address.

Senator Mathias, Chief Justice Burger, Vice President Bush, Speaker O'Neill, Senator Dole, Reverend Clergy, members of my family and friends, and my fellow citizens:

This day has been made brighter with the presence here of one who, for a time, has been absent, Senator John Stennis. God bless you and welcome back.

There is, however, one who is not with us today. Representative Gillis Long of Louisiana left us last night. I wonder if we could all join in a moment of silent prayer. (Silence.) Amen.

There are no words adequate to express my thanks for the great honor that you have bestowed on me. I will do my utmost to be deserving of your trust.

This is, as Senator Mathias told us, the 50th time that we the people have celebrated this historic occasion. When the first President, George Washington, placed his hand upon the Bible, he stood less than a single day's journey by horseback from raw, untamed wilderness. There were four million Americans in a union of thirteen States. Today we are sixty times as many in a union of fifty States. We have lighted the world with our inventions, gone to the aid of mankind wherever in the world there was a cry for help, journeyed to the Moon and safely returned. So much has changed. And yet we stand together as we did two centuries ago.

When I took this oath four years ago, I did so in a time of economic stress. Voices were raised saying we had to look to our past for the greatness and glory. But we, the present-day Americans, are not given to looking backward. In this blessed land, there is always a better tomorrow.

Four years ago, I spoke to you of a new beginning and we have accomplished that. But in another sense, our new beginning is a continuation of that beginning created two centuries ago when, for the first time in history, government, the people said, was not our master, it is our servant; its only power that which we the people allow it to have.

That system has never failed us, but, for a time, we failed the system. We asked things of government that government was not equipped to give. We yielded authority to the National Government that properly belonged to States or to local governments or to the people themselves. We allowed taxes and inflation to rob us of our earnings and savings and watched the great industrial machine that had made us the most productive people on Earth slow down and the number of unemployed increase.

By 1980, we knew it was time to renew our faith, to strive with all our strength toward the ultimate in individual freedom consistent with an orderly society.

We believed then and now there are no limits to growth and human progress when men and women are free to follow their dreams.

And we were right to believe that. Tax rates have been reduced, inflation cut dramatically, and more people are employed than ever before in our history.

We are creating a nation once again vibrant, robust, and alive. But there are many mountains yet to climb. We will not rest until every American enjoys the fullness of freedom, dignity, and opportunity as our birthright. It is our birthright as citizens of this great Republic, and we'll meet this challenge.

These will be years when Americans have restored their confidence and tradition of progress; when our values of faith, family, work, and neighborhood were restated for a modern age; when our economy was finally freed from government's grip; when we made sincere efforts at meaningful arms reduction, rebuilding our defenses, our economy, and developing new technologies, and helped preserve peace in a troubled world; when Americans courageously supported the struggle for liberty, self-government, and free enterprise throughout the world, and turned the tide of history away from totalitarian darkness and into the warm sunlight of human freedom.

My fellow citizens, our Nation is poised for greatness. We must do what we know is right and do it with all our might. Let history say of us, these were golden years, when the American Revolution was reborn, when freedom gained new life, when America reached for her best.

Our two-party system has served us well over the years, but never better than in those times of great challenge when we came together not as Democrats or Republicans, but as Americans united in a common cause.

Two of our Founding Fathers, a Boston lawyer named Adams and a Virginia planter named Jefferson, members of that remarkable group who met in Independence Hall and dared to think they could start the world over again, left us an important lesson. They had become political rivals in the Presidential election of 1800. Then years later, when both were retired, and age had softened their anger, they began to speak to each other again through letters. A bond was reestablished between those two who had helped create this government of ours.

In 1826, the 50th anniversary of the Declaration of Independence, they both died. They died on the same day, within a few hours of each other, and that day was the Fourth of July.

In one of those letters exchanged in the sunset of their lives, Jefferson wrote:

> It carries me back to the times when, beset with difficulties and dangers, we were fellow laborers in the same cause, struggling for what is most valuable to man, his right to self government. Laboring always at the same oar, with some wave ever ahead threatening to overwhelm us, and yet passing harmless ... we rode through the storm with heart and hand.

Well, with heart and hand, let us stand as one today. One people under God determined that our future shall be worthy of our past. As we do, we must not repeat the well intentioned errors of our past. We must never again abuse the trust of working men and women, by sending their earnings on a futile chase after the spiraling demands of a bloated Federal Establishment. You elected us in 1980 to end this prescription for disaster, and I don't believe you reelected us in 1984 to reverse course.

At the heart of our efforts is one idea vindicated by twenty-five straight months of economic growth. Freedom and incentives unleash the drive and entrepreneurial genius that are the core of human progress. We have begun to increase the rewards for work, savings, and investment; reduce the increase in the cost and size of government and its interference in people's lives.

We must simplify our tax system, make it more fair, and bring the rates down for all who work and earn. We must think anew and move with a new boldness, so every American who seeks work can find work; so the least among us shall have an equal chance to achieve the greatest things. To be heroes who heal our sick, feed the hungry, protect peace among nations, and leave this world a better place.

The time has come for a new American emancipation. A great national drive to tear down economic barriers and liberate the spirit of enterprise in the most distressed areas of our country. My friends, together we can do this, and do it we must, so help me God. From new freedom will spring new opportunities for growth, a more productive, fulfilled and united people, and a stronger America. An America that will lead the technological revolution, and also open its mind and heart and soul to the treasures of literature, music, and poetry, and the values of faith, courage, and love.

A dynamic economy, with more citizens working and paying taxes, will be our strongest tool to bring down budget deficits. But an almost unbroken fifty years of deficit spending has finally brought us to a time of reckoning. We have come to a turning point, a moment for hard decisions. I have asked the Cabinet and my staff a question, and now I put the same question to all of you. If not us, who? And if not now, when? It must be done by all of us going forward with a program aimed at reaching a balanced budget. We can then begin reducing the national debt.

I will shortly submit a budget to the Congress aimed at freezing government program spending for the next year. Beyond that, we must take further steps to permanently control Government's power to tax and spend. We must act now to protect future generations from Government's desire to spend its citizens' money and tax them into servitude when the bills come due. Let us make it unconstitutional for the Federal Government to spend more than the Federal Government takes in.

We have already started returning to the people and to State and local governments responsibilities better handled by them. Now, there is a place for the Federal Government in matters of social compassion. But our fundamental goals must be to reduce dependency and upgrade the dignity of those who are infirm or disadvantaged. And here a growing economy and support from family and community offer our best chance for a society where compassion is a way of life, where the old and infirm are cared for, the young and, yes, the unborn protected, and the unfortunate looked after and made self-sufficient.

And there is another area where the Federal Government can play a part. As an older American, I remember a time when people of different race, creed, or ethnic origin in our land found hatred and prejudice installed in social custom and, yes, in law. There is no story more heartening in our history than the progress that we have made toward the brotherhood of man that God intended for us. Let us resolve there will be no turning back or hesitation on the road to an America rich in dignity and abundant with opportunity for all our citizens.

Let us resolve that we the people will build an American opportunity society in which all of us, white and black, rich and poor, young and old, will go forward together arm in arm. Again, let us remember that though our heritage is one of blood lines from every corner of the Earth, we are all Americans pledged to carry on this last, best hope of man on Earth.

I have spoken of our domestic goals and the limitations which we should put on our National Government. Now let me turn to a task which is the primary responsibility of National Government, the safety and security of our people.

Today, we utter no prayer more fervently than the ancient prayer for peace on Earth. Yet history has shown that peace will not come, nor will our freedom be preserved, by good will alone. There are those in the world who scorn our vision of human dignity and freedom. One nation, the Soviet Union, has conducted the greatest military buildup in the history of man, building arsenals of awesome offensive weapons.

We have made progress in restoring our defense capability. But much remains to be done. There must be no wavering by us, nor any doubts by others, that America will meet her responsibilities to remain free, secure, and at peace.

There is only one way safely and legitimately to reduce the cost of national security, and that is to reduce the need for it. And this we are trying to do in negotiations with the Soviet Union. We are not just discussing limits on a further increase of nuclear weapons. We seek, instead, to reduce their number. We seek the total elimination one day of nuclear weapons from the face of the Earth.

Now, for decades, we and the Soviets have lived under the threat of mutual assured destruction; if either resorted to the use of nuclear weapons, the other could retaliate and destroy the one who had started it. Is there either logic or morality in believing that if one side threatens to kill tens of millions of our people, our only recourse is to threaten killing tens of millions of theirs?

I have approved a research program to find, if we can, a security shield that would destroy nuclear missiles before they reach their target. It wouldn't kill people, it would destroy weapons. It wouldn't militarize space, it would help demilitarize the arsenals of Earth. It would render nuclear weapons obsolete. We will meet with the Soviets, hoping that we can agree on a way to rid the world of the threat of nuclear destruction.

We strive for peace and security, heartened by the changes all around us. Since the turn of the century, the number of democracies in the world has grown fourfold. Human freedom is on the march, and nowhere more so than our own hemisphere. Freedom is one of the deepest and noblest aspirations of the human spirit. People, worldwide, hunger for the right of self-determination, for those inalienable rights that make for human dignity and progress.

America must remain freedom's staunchest friend, for freedom is our best ally.

And it is the world's only hope, to conquer poverty and preserve peace. Every blow we inflict against poverty will be a blow against its dark allies of oppression and war. Every victory for human freedom will be a victory for world peace.

So we go forward today, a nation still mighty in its youth and powerful in its purpose. With our alliances strengthened, with our economy leading the world to a new age of economic expansion, we look forward to a world rich in possibilities. And all this because we have worked and acted together, not as members of political parties, but as Americans.

My friends, we live in a world that is lit by lightning. So much is changing and will change, but so much endures, and transcends time.

History is a ribbon, always unfurling; history is a journey. And as we continue our journey, we think of those who traveled before us. We stand together again at the steps of this symbol of our democracy, or we would have been standing at the steps if it hadn't gotten so cold. Now we are standing inside this symbol of our democracy. Now we hear again the echoes of our past. A general falls to his knees in the hard snow of Valley Forge; a lonely President paces the darkened halls, and ponders his struggle to preserve the Union; the men of the Alamo call out encouragement to each other; a settler pushes west and sings a song, and the song echoes out forever and fills the unknowing air.

It is the American sound. It is hopeful, big-hearted, idealistic, daring, decent, and fair. That's our heritage; that is our song. We sing it still. For all our problems, our differences, we are together as of old, as we raise our voices to the God who is the Author of this most tender music. And may He continue to hold us close as we fill the world with our sound, sound in unity, affection, and love; one people under God, dedicated to the dream of freedom that He has placed in the human heart, called upon now to pass that dream on to a waiting and hopeful world.

God bless you and may God bless America.

George H. W. Bush

First Inaugural Address

JANUARY 20, 1989

Commentary

The presidential election of 1988 was the first since 1968 without a sitting president in the race. Voter turnout was the lowest since 1924, perhaps reflecting the inability of the candidates to arouse much enthusiasm.

There were signs in the late 1980s that the "Reagan Revolution" was beginning to fade. For all of Reagan's talk about a "safety net" for the nation's poorest citizens, more families lived below the poverty line in 1988 than in 1980. In eight years, the gap between the nation's rich and poor had widened considerably. In October 1987, at the other end of the economic spectrum, the stock market experienced the greatest single-day decline in its history. Although stock prices recovered, the crash eroded confidence in the financial markets. At the same time, "leveraged buyouts," a financial innovation that permitted corporate takeovers backed by huge loans (many in the form of risky "junk bonds"), began to unravel. Some of the nation's largest corporations, unable to carry the enormous debt that they had assumed, began to experience major financial difficulties. In March 1988, a Gallup survey showed that only 40 percent approved of the way Reagan was handling the nation's economic conditions. This was the lowest approval rating since late 1984 when the country was emerging from the severe recession of 1982–1983. In addition, President Reagan's personal popularity deflected attention from a series of scandals that might have destroyed another administration, as more than 100 of his appointees either resigned or were forced out of office by criticism of their ethical or legal conduct.

George H. W. Bush had little serious opposition in winning the Republican Party nomination. Bush's tenure as vice president for eight years helped him to become the early front-runner. An April 1988 Gallup Poll showed that 70 percent of registered voters thought he had the political background and experience for the job of president. Sixty percent considered him honest and ethical, and a majority "would trust his judgment in a crisis." Bush brought more than a quarter-century of experience to the 1988 presidential campaign. He had been a U.S. Navy bomber pilot in World War II, had served in the U.S. House of Representatives for two terms, and had been ambassador to the United Nations, chairman of the Republican National Committee, envoy to China, and director of the Central Intelligence Agency (CIA). He was appealing to Republican Party professionals and to the middle class that had benefited from Reagan's economic policies. However, no vice president had been elected president since Martin Van Buren defeated William Henry Harrison in 1836.

At the Republican convention, Bush was nominated by acclamation. He tried to unite the party by choosing for his running mate J. Danforth (Dan) Quayle, a second-term senator from Indiana with an impeccable conservative voting record. However, the 41-year-old senator seemed to many to be one of the least qualified candidates in recent U.S. political history. Although Bush introduced Quayle as a "man for the future," it was his past that was troublesome. In 1969, associates of his wealthy family had gotten him into the National Guard to avoid active service in Vietnam. He had been admitted to law school because of family connections, and was known for his long hours on the golf course. The question was not Quayle's age but his maturity for such a high office. Republican officials were horrified that the controversy over Quayle was deflecting attention away from Bush. One commentator noted Bush "did a good job of getting out of Ronald Reagan's shadow. Now he has to find a way to get out of Quayle's." To confound the problem, Bush made a statement in his acceptance address at the convention that haunted him for the rest of his political career. After suggesting some new policy initiatives, he made the absolute pledge against increased taxes —"Read my lips: no new taxes!"

Governor Michael Dukakis of Massachusetts won the Democratic presidential nomination on the first ballot by having waged a cautious but effective primary campaign. A graduate of Harvard Law School and the son of Greek immigrants, Dukakis had a record as an excellent administrator. During his three terms as governor, Dukakis presided over an economic boom called the "Massachusetts miracle." His image makers portrayed him as a notorious tightwad. The media said that he bought his suits in an inexpensive store, shopped for house-brand groceries, and criticized his wife for buying too many clothes. Dukakis chose Senator Lloyd Bentsen of Texas as his running mate. However, after the Democratic convention, almost half (48 percent) of all swing voters—those who do not support either candidate strongly—did not know enough about Dukakis to tell whether or not he would make a good chief executive.

Focus groups, spin doctors, handlers, media images, and commercials dominated the campaign. Television sound bites detracted from any serious discussion of issues. Although the Dukakis staff had a well-thought-out strategy in the primaries, they lacked a coherent plan for the presidential race. They underestimated the fierce campaign Bush would wage, which caused Dukakis's negative ratings to increase during the summer and fall campaign. As governor, Dukakis had argued that a bill requiring Massachusetts teachers to lead their students daily in the Pledge of Allegiance was unconstitutional, and he vetoed it. Republican ads used this veto to remind voters of dangerous liberal internationalists who would not defend the United States as vigorously as other Americans. However, the largest number of Republican campaign commercials dealt with the Massachusetts criminal furlough program. The most memorable showed zombie-like prisoners, most of them black or Hispanic, passing through revolving prison doors. The voice-over said that the Dukakis program granted weekend passes to first-degree murderers who were not even eligible for parole—and that many had escaped while on furlough. The most notorious of these escapees was an African American named Willie Horton. A first-degree murderer, Horton had fled to Maryland, where he brutalized a white man and raped his fiancée. The Bush handlers deliberately stirred up racial biases and used Willie Horton as a symbol that Dukakis was soft on crime. Dukakis's cool and intellectual style was no match for Bush, who skillfully connected emotionally with the voters. It was one of the dirtiest campaigns conducted in many years.

Dukakis had begun with a 17-point lead in the early summer. On Election Day, Bush had reversed this to a victory of 53.4 percent to 45.6 percent in the popular vote. Bush carried 40 states and received 426 electoral votes to Dukakis's 111. Bush won because he made liberalism, crime, and patriotism focal issues. Dukakis failed to exploit the budget deficit, Bush's choice of Dan Quayle, and his involvement in the Iran-contra Affair. Voters expressed considerable dissatisfaction with both candidates. While a 62 percent majority of voters were satisfied with the presidential nominees, 37 percent were not. Three voters in 10 said it was very or somewhat likely that they would have cast a vote of "no confidence" for both Bush and Dukakis.

On Inauguration Day 1989, George Bush took the oath of office with his hand on two Bibles held by his wife. One was the Bush family Bible. The other *was the Bible that had been used by George Washington in the nation's first presidential inaugural.*

⁓

Mr. Chief Justice, Mr. President, Vice President Quayle, Senator Mitchell, Speaker Wright, Senator Dole, Congressman Michel, and fellow citizens, neighbors, and friends:

There is a man here who has earned a lasting place in our hearts and in our history. President Reagan, on behalf of our Nation, I thank you for the wonderful things that you have done for America.

I have just repeated word for word the oath taken by George Washington 200 years ago, and the Bible on which I placed my hand is the Bible on which he placed his. It is right that the memory of Washington be with us today, not only because this is our Bicentennial Inauguration, but because Washington remains the Father of our Country. And he would, I think, be gladdened by this day, for today is the concrete expression of a stunning fact, our continuity these 200 years since our government began.

We meet on democracy's front porch, a good place to talk as neighbors and as friends. For this is a day when our nation is made whole, when our differences, for a moment, are suspended.

And my first act as President is a prayer. I ask you to bow your heads:

Heavenly Father, we bow our heads and thank you for your love. Accept our thanks for the peace that yields this day and the shared faith that makes its continuance likely. Make us strong to do your work, willing to heed and hear your will, and write on our hearts these words, "use power to help people." For we are given power not to advance our own purposes, nor to make a great show in the world, nor a name. There is but one just use of power, and it is to serve people. Help us to remember it Lord. Amen.

I come before you and assume the Presidency at a moment rich with promise. We live in a peaceful, prosperous time, but we can make it better. For a new breeze is blowing, and a world refreshed by freedom seems reborn; for in man's heart, if not in fact, the day of the dictator is over. The totalitarian era is passing, its old ideas blown away like leaves from an ancient, lifeless tree. A new breeze is blowing, and a nation refreshed by freedom stands ready to push on. There is new ground to be broken, and new action to be taken. There are times when the future seems thick as a fog; you sit and wait, hoping the mists will lift and reveal the right path. But this is a time when the future seems a door you can walk right through into a room called tomorrow.

Great nations of the world are moving toward democracy through the door to freedom. Men and women of the world move toward free markets through the door to prosperity. The people of the world agitate for free expression and free thought through the door to the moral and intellectual satisfactions that only liberty allows.

We know what works; freedom works. We know what's right; freedom is right. We know how to secure a more just and prosperous life for man on Earth; through free markets, free speech, free elections, and the exercise of free will unhampered by the state.

For the first time in this century, for the first time in perhaps all history, man does not have to invent a system by which to live. We don't have to talk late into the night about which form of government is better. We don't have to wrest justice from the kings. We only have to summon it from within ourselves. We must act on what we know. I take as my guide the hope of a saint: In crucial things, unity; in important things, diversity; in all things, generosity.

America today is a proud, free nation, decent and civil, a place we cannot help but love. We know in our hearts, not loudly and proudly, but as a simple fact, that this country has meaning beyond what we see, and that our strength is a force for good. But have we changed as a nation even in our time? Are we enthralled with material things, less appreciative of the nobility of work and sacrifice?

My friends, we are not the sum of our possessions. They are not the measure of our lives. In our hearts we know what matters. We cannot hope only to leave our children a bigger car, a bigger bank account. We must hope to give them a sense of what it means to be a loyal friend, a loving parent, a citizen who leaves his home, his neighborhood and town better than he found it. What do we want the men and women who work with us to say when we are no longer there? That we were more driven to succeed than anyone around us? Or that we stopped to ask if a sick child had gotten better, and stayed a moment there to trade a word of friendship?

No President, no government, can teach us to remember what is best in what we are. But if the man you have chosen to lead this government can help make a difference; if he can celebrate the quieter, deeper successes that are made not of gold and silk, but of better hearts and finer souls; if he can do these things, then he must.

America is never wholly herself unless she is engaged in high moral principle. We as a people have such a purpose today. It is to make kinder the face of the Nation and gentler the face of the world. My friends, we have work to do. There are the homeless, lost and roaming. There are the children who have nothing, no love, no normalcy. There are those who cannot free themselves of enslavement to whatever addiction, drugs, welfare, the demoralization that rules the slums. There is crime to be conquered, the rough crime of the streets. There are young women to be helped who are about to become mothers of children they can't care for and might not love. They need our care, our guidance, and our education, though we bless them for choosing life.

The old solution, the old way, was to think that public money alone could end these problems. But we have learned that is not so. And in any case, our funds are low. We have a deficit to bring down. We have more will than wallet; but will is what we need. We will make the hard choices, looking at what we have and perhaps allocating it differently, making our decisions based on honest need and prudent safety. And then we will do the wisest thing of all. We will turn to the only resource we have that, in times of need, always grows, the goodness and the courage of the American people.

I am speaking of a new engagement in the lives of others, a new activism, hands-on and involved, that gets the job done. We must bring in the generations, harnessing the unused talent of the elderly and the unfocused energy of the young. For not only leadership is passed from generation to generation, but so is stewardship. And the generation born after the Second World War has come of age.

I have spoken of a thousand points of light, of all the community organizations that are spread like stars throughout the Nation, doing good. We will work hand in hand, encouraging, sometimes leading, sometimes being led, rewarding. We will work on this in the White House, in the Cabinet agencies. I will go to the people and the programs that are the brighter points of light, and I will ask every member of my government to become involved. The old ideas are new again because they are not old, they are timeless: duty, sacrifice, commitment, and a patriotism that finds its expression in taking part and pitching in.

We need a new engagement, too, between the Executive and the Congress. The challenges before us will be thrashed out with the House and the Senate. We must bring the Federal budget into balance. And we must ensure that America stands before the world united, strong, at peace, and fiscally sound. But, of course, things may be difficult. We need compromise; we have had dissension. We need harmony; we have had a chorus of discordant voices.

For Congress too has changed in our time. There has grown a certain divisiveness. We have seen the hard looks and heard the statements in which not each other's ideas are challenged, but each other's motives. And our great parties have too often been far apart and untrusting of each other. It has been this way since Vietnam. That war cleaves us still. But, friends, that war began in earnest a quarter of a century ago; and surely the statute of limitations has been reached. This is a fact, the final lesson of Vietnam is that no great nation can long afford to be sundered by a memory. A new breeze is blowing, and the old bipartisanship must be made new again.

To my friends, and yes I do mean friends, in the loyal opposition, and yes I mean loyal, I put out my hand. I am putting out my hand to you, Mr. Speaker. I am putting out my hand to you, Mr. Majority Leader. For this is the thing: This is the age of the offered hand. We can't turn back clocks, and I don't want to. But when our fathers were young, Mr. Speaker, our differences ended at the water's edge. And we don't wish to turn back time, but when our mothers were young, Mr. Majority Leader, the Congress and the Executive were capable of working together to produce a budget on which this nation could live. Let us negotiate soon and hard. But in the end, let us produce. The American people await action. They didn't send us here to bicker. They ask us to rise above the merely partisan. In crucial things, unity; and this, my friends, is crucial.

To the world, too, we offer new engagement and a renewed vow: We will stay strong to protect the peace. The "offered hand" is a reluctant fist; but once made, strong, and can be used with great effect. There are today Americans who are held against their will in foreign lands, and Americans who are unaccounted for. Assistance can be shown here, and will be long remembered. Good will begets good will. Good faith can be a spiral that endlessly moves on.

Great nations like great men must keep their word. When America says something, America means it, whether a treaty or an agreement or a vow made on marble steps. We will always try to speak clearly, for candor is a compliment, but subtlety, too, is good and has its place. While keeping our alliances and friendships around the world strong, ever strong, we will continue the new closeness with the Soviet Union, consistent both with our security and with progress. One might say that our new relationship in part reflects the triumph of hope and strength over experience. But hope is good, and so are strength and vigilance.

Here today are tens of thousands of our citizens who feel the understandable satisfaction of those who have taken part in democracy and seen their hopes fulfilled. But my thoughts have been turning the past few days to those who would be watching at home to an older fellow who will throw a salute by himself when the flag goes by, and the women who will tell her sons the words of the battle hymns. I don't mean this to be sentimental. I mean that on days like this, we remember that we are all part of a continuum, inescapably connected by the ties that bind.

Our children are watching in schools throughout our great land. And to them I say, thank you for watching democracy's big day. For democracy belongs to us all, and freedom is like a beautiful kite that can go higher and higher with the breeze. And to all I say: No matter what your circumstances or where you are, you are part of this day, you are part of the life of our great nation.

A President is neither prince nor pope, and I don't seek a window on men's souls. In fact, I yearn for a greater tolerance, an easy-goingness about each other's attitudes and way of life.

There are few clear areas in which we as a society must rise up united and express our intolerance. The most obvious now is drugs. And when that first cocaine was smuggled in on a ship, it may as well have been a deadly bacteria, so much has it hurt the body, the soul of our country. And there is much to be done and to be said, but take my word for it: This scourge will stop.

And so, there is much to do; and tomorrow the work begins. I do not mistrust the future; I do not fear what is ahead. For our problems are large, but our heart is larger. Our challenges are great, but our will is greater. And if our flaws are endless, God's love is truly boundless.

Some see leadership as high drama, and the sound of trumpets calling, and sometimes it is that. But I see history as a book with many pages, and each day we fill a page with acts of hopefulness and meaning. The new breeze blows, a page turns, the story unfolds. And so today a chapter begins, a small and stately story of unity, diversity, and generosity shared and written, together.

Thank you. God bless you, and God bless the United States of America.

WILLIAM JEFFERSON CLINTON

FIRST INAUGURAL ADDRESS

JANUARY 20, 1993

COMMENTARY

The 1992 presidential election concentrated more on issues and less on personalities. During the campaign, President George Bush's job approval rating plunged from an historic all-time high of 89 percent in early March 1991 to 29 percent at the end of July 1992. The Democratic candidate was nearly destroyed by scandal, and a billionaire independent waged the strongest third-party challenge since 1912. The candidates found new means to reach voters by using television talk shows, radio call-in programs, and electronic bulletin boards.

The 1991 Gulf War was the most important event of the Bush presidency. On August 2, 1990, Saddam Hussein, the military ruler of Iraq, invaded the neighboring Kingdom of Kuwait, believing that the United States would not respond. However, President Bush feared the war could spread to oil-rich Saudi Arabia, a U.S. ally since the 1940s. He acted decisively. Bush believed that the world's price of oil and the world economy would be endangered. "This will not stand," the president declared. "What is at stake is more than one small country; it is a big idea—a new world order." On January 12, 1991, at the president's request, both houses of Congress voted to authorize the use of force against Iraq, although many Democrats opposed the resolution, arguing that sanctions should be given more time to work. Bush also appealed to the United Nations to resist Iraqi forces. On February 27, 1991, after a month of bombing, 550,000 U.S. and United Nations forces unleashed Operation DESERT STORM. Iraq announced its acceptance of allied terms for a cease-fire and the brief war came to an end. In 100 hours, Kuwait had been liberated and southern Iraq was occupied. According to a Gallup Poll, nearly 80 percent approved of the way Bush handled foreign policy. Most analysts agreed that he was guaranteed renomination and an easy reelection.

In mid-February, before Operation DESERT STORM had begun, the Gallup Poll asked registered Democrats whom they would like to see as their party's nominee for president in 1992. On a list of 13 possible candidates, Bill Clinton ranked twelfth with 2 percent. Two months later, his support had dwindled to one percent. In an extensive Gallup survey conducted in early November 1991, a month after Clinton had officially entered the race, 42 percent of registered Democrats replied that they had never heard of him. Of those who had heard of him, only 6 percent said they would like him as the party's nominee. Exactly one year later, Bill Clinton was elected president of the United States.

William Jefferson Clinton, who chose to go by the more familiar name Bill, was born in the small town of Hope, Arkansas, just two months after his father died in an automobile accident. His mother was a chronic gambler, and his stepfather was an abusive alcoholic. In 1963, Clinton met President John F. Kennedy in the Rose Garden when he was attending the Washington, D.C., national convention of Boys' Nation, a leadership organization for high school students. The Clinton campaign in 1992 made prominent use of pictures showing him shaking hands with Kennedy. Clinton graduated from Georgetown University and won a Rhodes Scholarship for two years of study at Oxford University. In 1974, a year after graduating from Yale Law School, Clinton unsuccessfully ran for a congressional seat. In 1978, at age 32, Clinton became the nation's youngest governor. Defeated in 1980, he was reelected in 1982, and held that office for the next decade. Although his critics within Arkansas were numerous, other governors considered Clinton one of the nation's most effective chief executives.

In October 1991, Clinton entered the race for the Democratic presidential nomination. None of the major Democratic candidates entered the primaries because they did not believe that Bush could be beaten. Clinton quickly moved from little-known candidate to front-runner over former senator Paul Tsongas of Massachusetts, Senator Tom Harkin of Iowa, and former governor Edmund (Jerry) Brown of California. By early April, Clinton had won the nomination. Throughout the primaries, he came under attack for extramarital affairs, for having smoked marijuana, and for charges that he was a draft dodger during the Vietnam War. However, Clinton focused on the economy. Privately, his strategists used the slogan "It's the economy, stupid" to remind themselves of the main campaign issue. Clinton was nominated at the July Democratic con-

*vention and chose as his running mate Senator Albert Gore Jr. of Tennessee, a
fellow moderate Southerner.*

*Patrick (Pat) J. Buchanan, a conservative columnist and television com-
mentator, challenged President Bush in the February New Hampshire primary. Surprisingly, he obtained 37.4 percent of the Republican vote, mainly
by capitalizing on the economic distress New Hampshire citizens were experiencing. Buchanan stressed traditional family values, opposition to the North
American Free Trade Agreement (NAFTA), and support for a Constitutional
amendment outlawing abortion. He remained in the race through the August
convention, receiving 22.8 percent of all votes cast in 35 Republican primaries.
Buchanan gave a strident speech at the convention, proclaiming "a culture
war," and that "we must take back our cities, take back our culture and take
back our country." He told the delegates, "You can't be a Christian, and a Democrat." Buchanan's speech, delivered on television during prime time, left the
impression that the Republican Party was controlled by right-wing ideologues.
Bush and Quayle were renominated on the first ballot.*

*H. Ross Perot, a Texas billionaire with no political experience, became a
major figure in the 1992 presidential election. His campaign began in mid-
September 1991 with a group of well-financed "volunteers." Perot officially
launched his third party on a national televised talk show in February 1992.
The crew-cut, plain-talking Perot captured people's imagination. In an early
June Gallup Poll, Perot held a significant lead among registered voters in test
elections against President Bush and Bill Clinton. Thirty-eight percent of voters named him as the candidate most able to bring about changes the country
needed, while 24 percent named Clinton and 20 percent named Bush. Analysts
at the Gallup Poll observed that Perot supporters did not care where he stood
on issues, as long as they perceived him as an agent of change. There was much
speculation that Perot could carry enough states to force the election to be decided by the U.S. House of Representatives.*

*In January 1990, President Bush had agreed to raise taxes, breaking the
pledge that he had made at the 1988 Republican convention. Under pressure
from congressional Democrats, the president decided to stimulate the economy
by reducing the budget deficit through a payroll tax increase. In June, he requested additional tax increases, ending up with the second largest tax increase
in U.S. history. William Kristol, the conservative writer, noted: "It was not so
much breaking it, but the way he broke it, the almost cavalier way he announced
it. . . . It seemed to reveal, perhaps unfairly, that there was no core belief there.
. . . He doesn't stand for anybody." Bush defended his decision: "I've got to see the*

country go forward, and I've got to take the heat. And I think in the final analysis the American people will understand that." But they did not. The president's decision to raise taxes probably cost him the election.

The three candidates avoided the tradition of facing the disciplined questioners of Sunday morning interview programs. They preferred to discuss politics on early-morning or late-evening talk shows. Bush made 16 appearances on these programs; Perot, 39; and Clinton, 45. Clinton's campaign seemed better organized. He spoke about urban renewal, the right to choose an abortion, job training, gun control, family medical leave, welfare reform, the new information technology, and a comprehensive national health program. In an appeal to younger voters, Clinton put on his sunglasses, got out his saxophone, and played "Heartbreak Hotel" on the Arsenio Hall late-night program. The musical portion of his appearance was brief, but it was repeated endlessly on news programs. Bush seemed harsh, tired, and distracted. During a debate with Clinton and Perot, he checked his watch several times as if he were bored. He spoke about traditional family values, religious faith, and patriotism. He discussed his reasons for stiffer criminal penalties and his opposition to abortion, pornography, and welfare cheats. Above all, though, in a Gallup survey concluded in early November, only 26 percent of those polled, including 35 percent of Republicans, expressed satisfaction with the way things were going in the United States at that time.

Perot did not carry a single state on Election Day. He finished with 18.9 percent of the popular vote, a protest vote expressing dissatisfaction with both major political parties. Perot probably affected the outcome only in Ohio, which might have gone to Bush instead of Clinton had he not been running. President Bush received 37.4 percent of the popular vote, a lower vote than that cast for any Republican since Herbert Hoover in 1932. Bill Clinton won 43 percent, about the same percentage as Richard Nixon in 1968—as in 1968, a majority of voters had voted against the winning candidate. In the electoral college, Clinton received 370 votes to Bush's 168. On a comparative basis, it was a good campaign in which the candidates competed by discussing their specific positions on the major issues confronting the country.

The inaugural ceremony marked the transition of power from 68-year-old George Bush, who had fought in World War II, to 46-year-old Bill Clinton, who was born after the war had ended and whose generation came of age during the civil rights movement and the Vietnam War. Clinton became the third youngest president in U.S. history, after Theodore Roosevelt and John F. Kennedy.

My fellow citizens:

Today we celebrate the mystery of American renewal.

This ceremony is held in the depth of winter. But, by the words we speak and the faces we show the world, we force the spring. A spring reborn in the world's oldest democracy, that brings forth the vision and courage to reinvent America.

When our founders boldly declared America's independence to the world and our purposes to the Almighty, they knew that America, to endure, would have to change. Not change for change's sake, but change to preserve America's ideals; life, liberty, the pursuit of happiness. Though we march to the music of our time, our mission is timeless. Each generation of Americans must define what it means to be an American.

On behalf of our nation, I salute my predecessor, President Bush, for his half-century of service to America. And I thank the millions of men and women whose steadfastness and sacrifice triumphed over Depression, fascism, and Communism.

Today, a generation raised in the shadows of the Cold War assumes new responsibilities in a world warmed by the sunshine of freedom but threatened still by ancient hatreds and new plagues.

Raised in unrivaled prosperity, we inherit an economy that is still the world's strongest, but is weakened by business failures, stagnant wages, increasing inequality, and deep divisions among our people.

When George Washington first took the oath I have just sworn to uphold, news traveled slowly across the land by horseback and across the ocean by boat. Now, the sights and sounds of this ceremony are broadcast instantaneously to billions around the world.

Communications and commerce are global; investment is mobile; technology is almost magical; and ambition for a better life is now universal. We earn our livelihood in peaceful competition with people all across the earth.

Profound and powerful forces are shaking and remaking our world, and the urgent question of our time is whether we can make change our friend and not our enemy.

This new world has already enriched the lives of millions of Americans who are able to compete and win in it. But when most people are working harder for less; when others cannot work at all; when the cost of health care devastates families and threatens to bankrupt many of our enterprises, great and small; when fear of crime robs law-abiding citizens of their freedom; and when millions of poor children cannot even imagine the lives we are calling them to lead, we have not made change our friend.

We know we have to face hard truths and take strong steps. But we have not done so. Instead, we have drifted, and that drifting has eroded our resources, fractured our economy, and shaken our confidence.

Though our challenges are fearsome, so are our strengths. And Americans have ever been a restless, questing, hopeful people. We must bring to our task today the vision and will of those who came before us.

From our revolution, the Civil War, to the Great Depression to the civil rights movement, our people have always mustered the determination to construct from these crises the pillars of our history.

Thomas Jefferson believed that to preserve the very foundations of our nation, we would need dramatic change from time to time. Well, my fellow citizens, this is our time. Let us embrace it.

Our democracy must be not only the envy of the world but the engine of our own renewal. There is nothing wrong with America that cannot be cured by what is right with America.

And so today, we pledge an end to the era of deadlock and drift; a new season of American renewal has begun. To renew America, we must be bold. We must do what no generation has had to do before. We must invest more in our own people, in their jobs, in their future, and at the same time cut our massive debt. And we must do so in a world in which we must compete for every opportunity. It will not be easy; it will require sacrifice. But it can be done, and done fairly, not choosing sacrifice for its own sake, but for our own sake. We must provide for our nation the way a family provides for its children.

Our Founders saw themselves in the light of posterity. We can do no less. Anyone who has ever watched a child's eyes wander into sleep knows what posterity is. Posterity is the world to come; the world for whom we hold our ideals, from whom we have borrowed our planet, and to whom we bear sacred responsibility. We must do what America does best: offer more opportunity to all and demand responsibility from all.

It is time to break the bad habit of expecting something for nothing, from our government or from each other. Let us all take more responsibility, not only for ourselves and our families but for our communities and our country. To renew America, we must revitalize our democracy.

This beautiful capital, like every capital since the dawn of civilization, is often a place of intrigue and calculation. Powerful people maneuver for position and worry endlessly about who is in and who is out, who is up and who is down, forgetting those people whose toil and sweat sends us here and pays our way.

Americans deserve better, and in this city today, there are people who want to do better. And so I say to all of us here, let us resolve to reform our politics, so that power and privilege no longer shout down the voice of the people. Let us put aside personal advantage so that we can feel the pain and see the promise of America. Let us resolve to make our government a place for what Franklin Roosevelt called "bold, persistent experimentation," a government for our tomorrows, not our yesterdays. Let us give this capital back to the people to whom it belongs.

To renew America, we must meet challenges abroad as well as at home. There is no longer division between what is foreign and what is domestic; the world economy, the world environment, the world AIDS crisis, the world arms race; they affect us all.

Today, as an old order passes, the new world is more free but less stable. Communism's collapse has called forth old animosities and new dangers. Clearly America must continue to lead the world we did so much to make.

While America rebuilds at home, we will not shrink from the challenges, nor fail to seize the opportunities, of this new world. Together with our friends and allies, we will work to shape change, lest it engulf us.

When our vital interests are challenged, or the will and conscience of the international community is defied, we will act; with peaceful diplomacy whenever possible, with force when necessary. The brave Americans serving our nation today in the Persian Gulf, in Somalia, and wherever else they stand are testament to our resolve.

But our greatest strength is the power of our ideas, which are still new in many lands. Across the world, we see them embraced, and we rejoice. Our hopes, our hearts, our hands, are with those on every continent who are building democracy and freedom. Their cause is America's cause.

The American people have summoned the change we celebrate today. You have raised your voices in an unmistakable chorus. You have cast your votes in historic numbers. And you have changed the face of Congress, the presidency and the political process itself. Yes, you, my fellow Americans have forced the spring. Now, we must do the work the season demands.

To that work I now turn, with all the authority of my office. I ask the Congress to join with me. But no president, no Congress, no government, can undertake this mission alone. My fellow Americans, you, too, must play your part in our renewal. I challenge a new generation of young Americans to a season of service; to act on your idealism by helping troubled children, keeping company with those in need, reconnecting our torn communities. There is so much to be done; enough indeed for millions of others who are still young in spirit to give of themselves in service, too.

In serving, we recognize a simple but powerful truth, we need each other. And we must care for one another. Today, we do more than celebrate America; we rededicate ourselves to the very idea of America.

An idea born in revolution and renewed through two centuries of challenge. An idea tempered by the knowledge that, but for fate we, the fortunate and the unfortunate, might have been each other. An idea ennobled by the faith that our nation can summon from its myriad diversity the deepest measure of unity. An idea infused with the conviction that America's long heroic journey must go forever upward.

And so, my fellow Americans, at the edge of the 21st century, let us begin with energy and hope, with faith and discipline, and let us work until our work is done. The scripture says, "And let us not be weary in well-doing, for in due season, we shall reap, if we faint not."

From this joyful mountaintop of celebration, we hear a call to service in the valley. We have heard the trumpets. We have changed the guard. And now, each in our way, and with God's help, we must answer the call.

Thank you, and God bless you all.

——— SECOND INAUGURAL ADDRESS ———

JANUARY 20, 1997

COMMENTARY

The economy was again the major issue in the 1996 presidential election. Voters asked themselves which candidate was best for their pocketbook. President Bill Clinton started the campaign ahead of any Republican opponent, and he stayed in front. Clinton, the New Democrat, had become the herald of prosperity, the supporter of a litany of government benefits and, ironically in retrospect, the champion of family values—all with a balanced budget. By July 1996, as the Republican convention assembled to nominate his opponent, 58 percent of those polled by Gallup responded that Clinton provides "*very strong or somewhat strong*" *moral leadership and 64 percent said that he "cares about the needs of people like you." With masterly political skill, Clinton was well positioned to run for reelection both as a protector of the middle class and as a defender of fiscal responsibility—and to become the first Democrat since Franklin D. Roosevelt elected to a second term.*

In July 1996, a record 43 percent of registered voters rated national economic conditions as excellent or good compared to 11 percent prior to the 1992 presidential election. Forty-three percent also thought that economic conditions as a whole were getting better. The unemployment rate had dropped to a six-year low of 5.3 percent in June, and the annual rate of inflation was below 3 percent. Job losses through layoffs and plant closings reached historic lows. By July 1996, the dollar had gained 10 percent in value over 12 months as exports zoomed to record levels. Applications for mortgages soared, and home sales neared a five-year high. Consumer spending was high, particularly for top-line items. The economy grew at a vigorous annual rate of 4.2 percent during the spring. Automobile sales rose sharply, running at an annual rate of 1.5 million new vehicles. Manufacturers added extra shifts to meet the demand. Measured by the Dow-Jones Industrial Average, the stock market rose by almost 75 percent since Clinton's inauguration. While by far, the biggest winners in this unexpected runup had been the richest Americans, middle-income families also benefited. Forty percent of American families own shares, usually through mutual funds and retirement accounts. The value of these holdings had increased a whopping $1.6 trillion! The president proudly pointed to the fact that all of this had been accomplished while reducing the national deficit in each year of his first term.

Less than two years before, in the 1994 midterm election, enough middle-income voters had turned against the Democrats, giving the Republicans control of Congress for the first time since 1956. However, Clinton brilliantly regained his political footing. He championed Social Security and Medicare reforms even when confronted with two government shutdowns. He vetoed Republican measures to cut taxes and curb social programs. He supported environmental protection, as well as consumer health and safety regulations. He enhanced his political standing by shaming congressional Republicans to finally accept an increase in the minimum wage that affected about 10 million of America's lowest paid workers. Shrewdly, Clinton adopted the Republican promise to balance the budget early in the next century, thus inoculating himself against the charge that he was a "tax-and-spend liberal." In fact, he abandoned many liberal themes, such as guaranteed health care, and now stressed "traditional values"—fighting tobacco companies for selling cigarettes to minors, tightening federal drinking water standards, supporting school uniforms, an assault weapons ban, more police on the streets, the death penalty, a victims' rights bill, and V-chips—issues designed to bring wayward Democrats back to the Democratic fold. And by agreeing in late July 1996 to sign a sweeping Republican welfare bill, Clinton defied leaders in his own party and ended a 61-year Democratic promise of federal aid to the nation's poor—but he fulfilled a 1992 campaign pledge to "end welfare as we know it." The New York Times *wrote, "He is a moderate who cannot suppress his liberal impulses, a liberal who cannot escape his moderating instincts. He confounds his friends, who think he has agreed with them, only to find he had not. He confuses his enemies, who think they can work with him only to find they cannot."*

Senator Robert (Bob) Dole of Kansas had become the runaway choice among Republicans for their party's nomination. Although he won every Republican caucus and primary with the exception of New Hampshire, Dole seemed unable to articulate why he wanted to be president and what his party stood for. Dole appeared old and dull, a man of the 1950s and 1960s without a defining message for 1996. His judgment seemed unfocused, choosing the same weekend as a bomb explosion at the Atlanta Olympic Games to urge the removal of the Pennsylvania Avenue barricades to protect the White House from terrorism. His disjointed and rambling speeches, badly stringing one platitude after another, turned off voters (54 percent of registered independents supported Clinton in a mid-July Gallup Poll compared to 36 percent for Dole). He tried to bring the issue of the president's character into the campaign but the voters seemed uninterested. He talked about building a bridge to the past, reminding voters of his record as a World War II hero and his 36 years of service in Congress. In his acceptance speech before a television audience estimated between 25 to 30 million, he seized this prime-time opportunity to present his plan to cut taxes by 15 percent and to balance the federal budget. He depicted the Clinton administration as a "corps of elite who never grew up, never did anything real, never sacrificed, never suffered, and never learned." Dole resigned from the U.S. Senate, where he was majority leader, to devote full time to the campaign.

Third-party or insurgent candidates have contested every twentieth century presidential election. The votes they received ranged from the minuscule to Theodore Roosevelt's 27.4 percent in 1912. In 1992, Ross Perot, running as an independent, had won 18.9 percent of the vote. Almost 20 million Americans showed that either Perot had a very substantial following or that a large number of voters remained unmoved by President Bush or Bill Clinton. In August 1996, Perot, at age 66, announced again, "I want to be your president." In 1992, Perot spent more than $64 million of his own money on his third-party *candidacy. In 1996, rather than repeating this, Perot decided to accept federal campaign funds to run his campaign. In 1992, he had said: "I'm spending my money on this campaign; the two parties are spending your taxpayer money." In 1996, he explained that he wanted to "make sure the American people get involved." Perot ridiculed big government, budget deficits, and trade agreements, like NAFTA, which he said exported American jobs. He denounced the two-party system, promising to "kill that little snake this time." While Clinton supporters dismissed Perot as an unimportant factor in the fall election, Dole took Perot seriously enough to admonish voters to ignore him because the Republican party "is the real Reform Party."*

The campaign consisted of dull speeches, news conferences, and the obligatory televised debates, which attempted to search for issues that truly separated the candidates. Dole made his tax cut the centerpiece of his campaign. Clinton asked big questions but offered few answers. He repeated his talk about a "bridge to the 21st century," and that vague rhetoric seemed to define the campaign. Dole proposed cutting Medicare by $26 billion; Clinton proposed cutting it by $19 billion. Dole spoke against the use of marijuana; Clinton spoke against tobacco. Dole insisted that Clinton was committed to liberalism; the president denied he was a liberal, a denial that caused many Democrats to flinch. It seemed though that a "gender gap" haunted Dole. In every Gallup Poll between mid-January and mid-October 1996, registered women voters' support for Clinton over Dole held steady in the high 50 and the low 60 percentages. This was because of Dole's ambiguous stand on abortion and their perceived Republican bashing of the president's wife, Hillary Rodham Clinton. Women also were bothered by the tone of the Republican "revolutionaries" and by the content of their programs. Historically, women have taken Medicare very seriously and also have been more sympathetic to social spending, especially on education and programs for children.

Voters seemed indifferent—only 24 percent of those questioned said they were following the election "very closely" compared with 42 percent in 1992, with viewership for the first presidential debate down nearly 20 percent from four years ago. Common ephemeral political items—buttons, ribbons, posters, automobile bumper stickers—were minimal. Network coverage of the campaign dropped 40 percent in September from 1992. Large news organizations had interviewed "soccer moms," "angry white males," urban blacks, suburban evangelicals, Reagan Democrats and Clinton Republicans but detected little passion for either candidate. Clinton ignored charges of new scandals—a convicted drug smuggler had attended a White House Christmas party; an April "community outreach" at a Buddhist temple near Los Angeles attended by Vice President Al Gore had turned

into a bizarre Democratic fund-raiser leaving the question of how monks earn-
ing $40 monthly stipends managed $5,000 contributions; the head of Taiwan's
governing Nationalist Party denied he had donated $15 million to the Clinton
reelection fund. Rather, the president stuck to his message as he criss-crossed the
country—and he connected with the cheering crowds, reaching out and them
back to him. In two days alone, he singled out for conversation and heavy doses of
charm a young woman from the Middle East with immigration problems, a girl
with a rare blood disease, a woman distraught over late-term abortions, and a
young father leaning to Dole. The president seemed to inspire and energize him-
self at the same time. It seemed that a bond with the people had emerged.

The 1996 presidential election had very few surprises. The results seemed
almost predictable. Clinton started ahead and stayed there. Some 92 million
voters cast a ballot, roughly 50 percent of those eligible. It was proportionately
the lowest voter turnout since 1924. Clinton won 49.2 percent of the popular
vote to Dole's 40.7 percent and Perot's 8.4 percent. Clinton won with 6.2 per-
centage points more of the popular vote, and nine more electoral votes, than in
1992. Dole carried only the broad band of Great Plains and mountain states
stretching from the Canadian border to Texas, most of the Deep South and In-
diana, a Republican island in the Democratic sea that covered the whole north-
eastern quadrant. For the first time in U.S. history, a Democrat had been elected
to the White House with a Congress controlled by the opposition. Bill Clinton,
at age 50, also became the first Democrat since Franklin Roosevelt, and the third
since the Civil War, to win a second consecutive term. He came very close to a
goal that had obsessed him for four years—winning a majority of the popular
vote. Something that may have been lost in this election and its coverage was the
concept of the president as a paragon. Asked in exit polls if they think Clinton is
"honest," 54 percent responded in the negative.

In near-freezing weather, Chief Justice William Rehnquist administered
the oath of office to President Clinton on Inauguration Day. Mrs. Clinton held
the Bible and Chelsea, the Clintons' daughter, stood at the president's side.

⌒◦⌒

My fellow citizens:

At this last presidential inauguration of the 20th century, let us lift our
eyes toward the challenges that await us in the next century. It is our great
good fortune that time and chance have put us not only at the edge of a new
century, in a new millennium, but on the edge of a bright new prospect in
human affairs—a moment that will define our course, and our character, for
decades to come. We must keep our old democracy forever young. Guided

by the ancient vision of a promised land, let us set our sights upon a land of new promise.

The promise of America was born in the 18th century out of the bold conviction that we are all created equal. It was extended and preserved in the 19th century, when our nation spread across the continent, saved the union, and abolished the awful scourge of slavery.

Then, in turmoil and triumph, that promise exploded onto the world stage to make this the American Century.

And what a century it has been. America became the world's mightiest industrial power; saved the world from tyranny in two world wars and a long cold war; and time and again, reached out across the globe to millions who, like us, longed for the blessings of liberty.

Along the way, Americans produced a great middle class and security in old age; built unrivaled centers of learning and opened public schools to all; split the atom and explored the heavens; invented the computer and the microchip; and deepened the wellspring of justice by making a revolution in civil rights for African Americans and all minorities, and extending the circle of citizenship, opportunity, and dignity to women.

Now, for the third time, a new century is upon us, and another time to choose. We began the 19th century with a choice, to spread our nation from coast to coast. We began the 20th century with a choice, to harness the Industrial Revolution to our values of free enterprise, conservation, and human decency. Those choices made all the difference. At the dawn of the 21st century a free people must now choose to shape the forces of the Information Age and the global society, to unleash the limitless potential of all our people, and, yes, to form a more perfect union.

When last we gathered, our march to this new future seemed less certain than it does today. We vowed then to set a clear course to renew our nation.

In these four years, we have been touched by tragedy, exhilarated by challenge, strengthened by achievement. America stands alone as the world's indispensable nation. Once again, our economy is the strongest on Earth. Once again, we are building stronger families, thriving communities, better educational opportunities, a cleaner environment. Problems that once seemed destined to deepen now bend to our efforts: our streets are safer and record numbers of our fellow citizens have moved from welfare to work.

And once again, we have resolved for our time a great debate over the role of government. Today we can declare: Government is not the problem, and government is not the solution. We—the American people—we are the solution. Our founders understood that well and gave us a democracy strong enough to endure for centuries, flexible enough to face our common challenges and advance our common dreams in each new day.

As times change, so government must change. We need a new government for a new century—humble enough not to try to solve all our problems for us, but strong enough to give us the tools to solve our problems for ourselves; a government that is smaller, lives within its means, and does more with less. Yet where it can stand up for our values and interests in the world, and where it can give Americans the power to make a real difference in their everyday lives, government should do more, not less. The preeminent mission of our new government is to give all Americans an opportunity—not a guarantee, but a real opportunity—to build better lives.

Beyond that, my fellow citizens, the future is up to us. Our founders taught us that the preservation of our liberty and our union depends upon responsible citizenship. And we need a new sense of responsibility for a new century. There is work to do, work that government alone cannot do: teaching children to read; hiring people off welfare rolls; coming out from behind locked doors and shuttered windows to help reclaim our streets from drugs and gangs and crime; taking time out of our own lives to serve others.

Each and every one of us, in our own way, must assume personal responsibility—not only for ourselves and our families, but for our neighbors and our nation. Our greatest responsibility is to embrace a new spirit of community for a new century. For any one of us to succeed, we must succeed as one America.

The challenge of our past remains the challenge of our future—will we be one nation, one people, with one common destiny, or not? Will we all come together, or come apart?

The divide of race has been America's constant curse. And each new wave of immigrants gives new targets to old prejudices. Prejudice and contempt, cloaked in the pretense of religious or political conviction, are no different. These forces have nearly destroyed our nation in the past. They plague us still. They fuel the fanaticism of terror. And they torment the lives of millions in fractured nations all around the world.

These obsessions cripple both those who hate and, of course, those who are hated, robbing both of what they might become. We cannot, we will not, succumb to the dark impulses that lurk in the far regions of the soul everywhere. We shall overcome them. And we shall replace them with the generous spirit of a people who feel at home with one another.

Our rich texture of racial, religious and political diversity will be a Godsend in the 21st century. Great rewards will come to those who can live together, learn together, work together, forge new ties that bind together.

As this new era approaches we can already see its broad outlines. Ten years ago, the Internet was the mystical province of physicists; today, it is a commonplace encyclopedia for millions of schoolchildren. Scientists now are decoding the blueprint of human life. Cures for our most feared illnesses seem close at hand.

The world is no longer divided into two hostile camps. Instead, now we are building bonds with nations that once were our adversaries. Growing connections of commerce and culture give us a chance to lift the fortunes and spirits of people the world over. And for the very first time in all of history, more people on this planet live under democracy than dictatorship.

My fellow Americans, as we look back at this remarkable century, we may ask, can we hope not just to follow, but even to surpass the achievements of the 20th century in America and to avoid the awful bloodshed that stained its legacy? To that question, every American here and every American in our land today must answer a resounding "Yes."

This is the heart of our task. With a new vision of government, a new sense of responsibility, a new spirit of community, we will sustain America's journey. The promise we sought in a new land we will find again in a land of new promise.

In this new land, education will be every citizen's most prized possession. Our schools will have the highest standards in the world, igniting the spark of possibility in the eyes of every girl and every boy. And the doors of higher education will be open to all. The knowledge and power of the Information Age will be within reach not just of the few, but of every classroom, every library, every child. Parents and children will have time not only to work, but to read and play together. And the plans they make at their kitchen table will be those of a better home, a better job, the certain chance to go to college.

Our streets will echo again with the laughter of our children, because no one will try to shoot them or sell them drugs anymore. Everyone who can work, will work, with today's permanent underclass part of tomorrow's growing middle class. New miracles of medicine at last will reach not only those who can claim care now, but the children and hardworking families too long denied.

We will stand mighty for peace and freedom, and maintain a strong defense against terror and destruction. Our children will sleep free from the threat of nuclear, chemical or biological weapons. Ports and airports, farms and factories will thrive with trade and innovation and ideas. And the world's greatest democracy will lead a whole world of democracies.

Our land of new promise will be a nation that meets its obligations—a nation that balances its budget, but never loses the balance of its values. A nation where our grandparents have secure retirement and health care, and their grandchildren know we have made the reforms necessary to sustain those benefits for their time. A nation that fortifies the world's most productive economy even as it protects the great natural bounty of our water, air, and majestic land.

And in this land of new promise, we will have reformed our politics so that the voice of the people will always speak louder than the din of narrow interests—regaining the participation and deserving the trust of all Americans.

Fellow citizens, let us build that America, a nation ever moving forward toward realizing the full potential of all its citizens. Prosperity and power—yes, they are important, and we must maintain them. But let us never forget: The greatest progress we have made, and the greatest progress we have yet to make, is in the human heart. In the end, all the world's wealth and a thousand armies are no match for the strength and decency of the human spirit.

Thirty-four years ago, the man whose life we celebrate today spoke to us down there, at the other end of this Mall, in words that moved the conscience of a nation. Like a prophet of old, he told of his dream that one day America would rise up and treat all its citizens as equals before the law and in the heart. Martin Luther King's dream was the American Dream. His quest is our quest: the ceaseless striving to live out our true creed. Our history has been built on such dreams and labors. And by our dreams and labors we will redeem the promise of America in the 21st century.

To that effort I pledge all my strength and every power of my office. I ask the members of Congress here to join in that pledge. The American people returned to office a President of one party and a Congress of another. Surely, they did not do this to advance the politics of petty bickering and extreme partisanship they plainly deplore. No, they call on us instead to be repairers of the breach, and to move on with America's mission.

America demands and deserves big things from us —and nothing big ever came from being small. Let us remember the timeless wisdom of Cardinal Bernardin, when facing the end of his own life. He said, "It is wrong to waste the precious gift of time, on acrimony and division."

Fellow citizens, we must not waste the precious gift of this time. For all of us are on that same journey of our lives, and our journey, too, will come to an end. But the journey of our America must go on.

And so, my fellow Americans, we must be strong, for there is much to dare. The demands of our time are great and they are different. Let us meet them with faith and courage, with patience and a grateful and happy heart. Let us shape the hope of this day into the noblest chapter in our history. Yes, let us build our bridge. A bridge wide enough and strong enough for every American to cross over to a blessed land of new promise.

May those generations whose faces we cannot yet see, whose names we may never know, say of us here that we led our beloved land into a new century with the American Dream alive for all her children; with the American promise of a more perfect union a reality for all her people; with America's bright flame of freedom spreading throughout all the world.

From the height of this place and the summit of this century, let us go forth. May God strengthen our hands for the good work ahead—and always, always bless our America.

George W. Bush

First Inaugural Address

JANUARY 20, 2001

Commentary

The 2000 presidential election was the most controversial and dramatic since Lincoln's 1860 victory. George Walker Bush, the 54-year-old, two-term governor of Texas, became the fourth person in American history and the first since 1888 to assume the presidency without winning the popular vote. The election of 2000 also bore a striking similarity to that of 1824. In that year, John Quincy Adams, who had fewer popular votes than his opponent Andrew Jackson, became the only other son of a president to win the presidency. In 2000, Bush's opponent, Al Gore, was, like Jackson, a Tennessean. Bush was elected with 271 electoral votes, just one more than the minimum.

Bush won the election after a bruising, 36-day legal battle over the 25 electoral votes of Florida, a state of which Bush's brother Jeb was governor. (The brothers Bush had served simultaneously as governors of states, another first in American history.) The Florida election was decided finally by the nine justices of the U.S. Supreme Court, who split bitterly over the issues. In his first formal statement as president-elect, Bush tried to pull the nation together after its grueling ordeal. He paraphrased the words of Thomas Jefferson, who won the presidency in 1800 after six days of voting and 36 ballots in the House of Representatives. "I will be guided by President Jefferson's sense of purpose," stated Bush, "to stand for principle, to be reasonable in manner, and above all, to do great good for 'the cause of freedom and harmony.'" Bush's excruciatingly close victory also marked the first time since 1955 that the Democratic Party did not control either the White House or one congressional chamber. And in spite of all the statements about healing the nation's political divisions, many Democrats questioned Bush's legitimacy and agreed with outgoing President Clinton's assessment that "our candidate won the election and the only way they [the Republicans] could win the election was to stop the voting in Florida."

Bush succeeded Bill Clinton who left office with the highest average job approval rating of any president in the last 50 years, but with low public ratings of his personal character—a conflicted view of Clinton that emerged during the Monica Lewinsky scandal and ensuing impeachment trial. According to a Gallup Poll conducted January 5–7, 2001, 65 percent of Americans approved of the way Clinton handled his job as president, which was slightly above the average he had received between October and December 2000. In fact, Clinton's average approval rating for his last two years in office was about 61 percent—the highest rating for a final quarter of a presidential tenure in the past half-century. On the other hand, in the January 5–7 survey, just 41 percent of Americans approved of Clinton "as a person" and only 39 percent considered him "honest and trustworthy." Most Americans also expressed mixed feelings about Clinton's record of accomplishments and his place in history. By a substantial margin, 68 percent to 28 percent, Americans expected Clinton to be remembered more for his involvement in personal scandal than for his accomplishments. And, on the last day of his presidency, Clinton admitted to what everyone had long concluded, that he had testified falsely in a sexual harassment lawsuit, which lit a fuse to the impeachment explosion with all its anguish and bitter political combat.

On January 20, 2001, George Walker Bush took the oath of office on the same Bible used at his father's swearing-in, a 1767 King James Version also used when George Washington was inaugurated as the first president in 1789. With the new president on the stage before the West Front of the Capitol were the people who had helped propel him to the presidency: his wife, Laura, who supported him in finding discipline and purpose in his adult life; former president George Bush, who bequeathed him a name and a network of connections; Bill Clinton, whose personal scandals gave Bush a fighting chance against a sitting vice president; and that vice president, Al Gore, who ran what many political analysts thought to be a lackluster campaign. In addition, Chief Justice William Rehnquist, who administered the oath, had voted with the bare majority of the Supreme Court to effectively end Gore's legal contest of the returns from the polls in Florida. That decision determined the outcome of a breathtakingly close election.

As the new president pledged in his inaugural address to unify the nation, arguments persisted about the legitimacy of his victory. Thousands of the *doubtful took to the streets of Washington in angry protest, the first substantial demonstration at an inauguration since Richard Nixon's second in 1973 during the Vietnam War.*

President Clinton, distinguished guests and my fellow citizens:

The peaceful transfer of authority is rare in history, yet common in our country. With a simple oath, we affirm old traditions and make new beginnings.

As I begin, I thank President Clinton for his service to our nation; and I thank Vice President Gore for a contest conducted with spirit and ended with grace.

I am honored and humbled to stand here, where so many of America's leaders have come before me, and so many will follow.

We have a place, all of us, in a long story. A story we continue, but whose end we will not see. It is the story of a new world that became a friend and liberator of the old, a story of a slave-holding society that became a servant of freedom, the story of a power that went into the world to protect but not possess, to defend but not to conquer. It is the American story. A story of flawed and fallible people, united across the generations by grand and enduring ideals. The grandest of these ideals is an unfolding American promise that everyone belongs, that everyone deserves a chance, that no insignificant person was ever born. Americans are called upon to enact this promise in our lives and in our laws; and though our nation has sometimes halted, and sometimes delayed, we must follow no other course.

Through much of the last century, America's faith in freedom and democracy was a rock in a raging sea. Now it is a seed upon the wind, taking root in many nations. Our democratic faith is more than the creed of our country, it is the inborn hope of our humanity, an ideal we carry but do not own, a trust we bear and pass along; and even after nearly 225 years, we have a long way yet to travel.

While many of our citizens prosper, others doubt the promise, even the justice, of our own country. The ambitions of some Americans are limited by failing schools and hidden prejudice and the circumstances of their birth; and sometimes our differences run so deep, it seems we share a continent, but not a country. We do not accept this, and we will not allow it. Our unity, our union, is the serious work of leaders and citizens in every generation; and this is my solemn pledge, "I will work to build a single nation of justice and opportunity." I know this is in our reach because we are guided by a power larger than ourselves who creates us equal in His image and we are confident in principles that unite and lead us onward.

America has never been united by blood or birth or soil. We are bound by ideals that move us beyond our backgrounds, lift us above our interests and teach us what it means to be citizens. Every child must be taught these principles. Every citizen must uphold them; and every immigrant, by embracing these ideals, makes our country more, not less, American.

Today, we affirm a new commitment to live out our nation's promise through civility, courage, compassion and character. America, at its best, matches a commitment to principle with a concern for civility. A civil society demands from each of us good will and respect, fair dealing and forgiveness. Some seem to believe that our politics can afford to be petty because, in a time of peace, the stakes of our debates appear small. But the stakes for America are never small. If our country does not lead the cause of freedom, it will not be led. If we do not turn the hearts of children toward knowledge and character, we will lose their gifts and undermine their idealism. If we permit our economy to drift and decline, the vulnerable will suffer most. We must live up to the calling we share. Civility is not a tactic or a sentiment. It is the determined choice of trust over cynicism, of community over chaos. This commitment, if we keep it, is a way to shared accomplishment.

America, at its best, is also courageous. Our national courage has been clear in times of depression and war, when defending common dangers defined our common good. Now we must choose if the example of our fathers and mothers will inspire us or condemn us. We must show courage in a time of blessing by confronting problems instead of passing them on to future generations.

Together, we will reclaim America's schools, before ignorance and apathy claim more young lives; we will reform Social Security and Medicare, sparing our children from struggles we have the power to prevent; we will reduce taxes, to recover the momentum of our economy and reward the effort and enterprise of working Americans; we will build our defenses beyond challenge, lest weakness invite challenge; and we will confront weapons of mass destruction, so that a new century is spared new horrors.

The enemies of liberty and our country should make no mistake, America remains engaged in the world by history and by choice, shaping a balance of power that favors freedom. We will defend our allies and our interests; we will show purpose without arrogance; we will meet aggression and bad faith with resolve and strength; and to all nations, we will speak for the values that gave our nation birth.

America, at its best, is compassionate. In the quiet of American con-science, we know that deep, persistent poverty is unworthy of our nation's promise. Whatever our views of its cause, we can agree that children at risk are not at fault. Abandonment and abuse are not acts of God, they are fail-ures of love. The proliferation of prisons, however necessary, is no substi-tute for hope and order in our souls. Where there is suffering, there is duty. Americans in need are not strangers, they are citizens, not problems, but priorities, and all of us are diminished when any are hopeless. Government has great responsibilities for public safety and public health, for civil rights and common schools. Yet compassion is the work of a nation, not just a government. Some needs and hurts are so deep they will only respond to a mentor's touch or a pastor's prayer. Church and charity, synagogue and mosque lend our communities their humanity, and they will have an hon-ored place in our plans and in our laws. Many in our country do not know the pain of poverty, but we can listen to those who do. I can pledge our na-tion to a goal, "When we see that wounded traveler on the road to Jericho, we will not pass to the other side."

America, at its best, is a place where personal responsibility is valued and expected. Encouraging responsibility is not a search for scapegoats, it is a call to conscience. Though it requires sacrifice, it brings a deeper fulfillment. We find the fullness of life not only in options, but in commitments. We find that children and community are the commitments that set us free. Our public interest depends on private character, on civic duty and family bonds and basic fairness, on uncounted, unhonored acts of decency which give direc-tion to our freedom. Sometimes in life we are called to do great things. But as a saint of our times has said, every day we are called to do small things with great love. The most important tasks of a democracy are done by everyone. I will live and lead by these principles, "to advance my convictions with civility, to pursue the public interest with courage, to speak for greater justice and compassion, to call for responsibility and try to live it as well." In all of these ways, I will bring the values of our history to the care of our times.

What you do is as important as anything government does. I ask you to seek a common good beyond your comfort; to defend needed reforms against easy attacks; to serve your nation, beginning with your neighbor. I ask you to be citizens. Citizens, not spectators; citizens, not subjects; respon-sible citizens, building communities of service and a nation of character.

Americans are generous and strong and decent, not because we believe in ourselves, but because we hold beliefs beyond ourselves. When this spirit of citizenship is missing, no government program can replace it. When this spirit is present, no wrong can stand against it.

After the Declaration of Independence was signed, Virginia statesman John Page wrote to Thomas Jefferson, "We know the race is not to the swift nor the battle to the strong. Do you not think an angel rides in the whirlwind and directs this storm?" Much time has passed since Jefferson arrived for his inauguration. The years and changes accumulate, but the themes of this day he would know, "our nation's grand story of courage and its simple dream of dignity."

We are not this story's author, who fills time and eternity with His purpose. Yet His purpose is achieved in our duty, and our duty is fulfilled in service to one another. Never tiring, never yielding, never finishing, we renew that purpose today; to make our country more just and generous; to affirm the dignity of our lives and every life.

This work continues. This story goes on. And an angel still rides in the whirlwind and directs this storm.

God bless you all, and God bless America.

──── SECOND INAUGURAL ADDRESS ────

JANUARY 20, 2005

COMMENTARY

George Walker Bush was sworn in on January 20, 2005, for a second term as the forty-third president of the United States. He took the oath of office precisely at noon from critically ill Chief Justice William H. Rehnquist. Bush began his second administration as a leader still facing a host of dramatic challenges brought about by the terrible events of one day in his first term.

On September 11, 2001, eight months into Bush's presidency, 19 al-Qaeda terrorists carried out a series of coordinated attacks against the United States. That morning, the terrorists hijacked four commercial airplanes. Two of the planes were flown deliberately into the twin towers of the World Trade Center in New York City; both towers collapsed. Another plane destroyed part of the Pentagon in Arlington, Virginia. The fourth aircraft, apparently heading toward Washington, D.C., crashed and exploded in a field in rural southwestern Pennsylvania. Nearly 3,000 people, almost all of whom were civilians, were killed in these attacks. It was the worst terrorist incident ever on U.S. soil.

The nation waited intently to see how President Bush would react. After a few days during which the president appeared shaky and seemed uncertain, he began to lead. For most Americans, any lingering doubts about Bush's abilities now vanished. Domestic security and the fight against terrorism became the president's top priority. Acting on his initiative, Congress quickly passed the USA Patriot Act. This law expanded the surveillance powers of domestic law-enforcement agencies in an attempt to tighten internal security and prepare for possible additional attacks against the nation. In 2003, to coordinate this enormous expansion of federal authority, Congress established the Department of Homeland Security, a new, cabinet-level agency.

President Bush accused radical Islamist Osama bin Laden and his al-Qaeda militants of responsibility for the September 11 attacks. Bush also charged the Taliban, the ultraconservative religious group that governed Afghanistan, of harboring bin Laden. When the Taliban refused to extradite bin Laden, the United States and allied military forces attacked Afghanistan on October 7, 2001. Within a month, the Taliban and al-Qaeda leaders were driven from power. Bush's approval rating in the Gallup Poll now stood at 87 percent as the nation rallied behind the president. In those uncertain days that followed the September 11 attacks, Bush received some of the highest performance approval ratings in Gallup's history, including a record high 90 percent in late September.

In early 2002, President Bush began publicly to focus attention on Iraq. On January 29, in his State of the Union address, he declared Iraq to be part of "an axis of evil" that posed "a grave and growing danger" to American security through its possession of "weapons of mass destruction." In October 2002, the Senate and House of Representatives authorized the president to use force if Iraqi dictator Saddam Hussein did not surrender these weapons. On March 18, 2003, after a year of debate in Congress and at the United Nations, President Bush ordered an invasion of Iraq. This decision surely ranks as the most controversial of the president's first term and among the most disputatious presidential decisions in American history.

The Iraqi military was overwhelmed. In less than three weeks, Saddam Hussein's regime was forced from power. On May 1, 2003, Bush declared the end of major combat operations. "In the Battle of Iraq," he stated, "the United States and our allies have prevailed. . . . In this battle, we have fought for the cause of liberty, and for the peace of the world." But the United States never located the "weapons of mass destruction," the principal reason given for the invasion, and those who ordered and authorized the invasion soon came under heavy criticism. This criticism prevailed throughout the remainder of the Bush presidency. To make matters worse, the situation in Iraq rapidly deteriorated, and that country soon seemed to be on the brink of a complicated civil war. On December 14, 2005, President Bush finally admitted: "It is true that much of the intelligence [on Iraq's possession of weapons of mass destruction] turned out to be wrong." Nevertheless, Bush justified his decision to go to war with Iraq, reiterating the necessity to "stay the course" rather than "cut and run."

The main campaign issue in the 2004 presidential election was Bush's response to the September 11, 2001, terrorist attacks. The Democratic Party nominated Senator John Kerry of Massachusetts for president and Senator John Edwards of North Carolina for vice president. The Republicans renominated President Bush and Vice President Richard Cheney by acclamation. Kerry had supported the October 2002 Senate resolution authorizing the president to use force against Saddam Hussein if the Iraqi leader failed to surrender his "weapons of mass destruction." After President Bush ordered the invasion, however, Kerry declared the administration's Iraq policy to be "reckless at best and baseless at worst." This shift harmed Kerry's campaign for the presidency. Bush repeatedly referred to the senator as a "flip-flopper" who changed his position to suit public opinion. In convoluted language, Kerry defended his Senate vote as he attempted to explain that that vote to authorize force was intended as a diplomatic "threat" to Saddam Hussein, not a blank check for war.

To counter Bush's strength among voters on the issue of leadership, especially military leadership, Kerry and his advisers decided to emphasize the senator's service in the Vietnam War. Kerry had received two Purple Hearts for wounds he had suffered and the Silver Star "for conspicuous gallantry." The Gallup Poll suggests, however, that Kerry's strategy failed, as the senator always trailed Bush by large margins on the questions of which candidate could better fight terrorism and which candidate was a strongly decisive leader. The Kerry strategy also may have failed in part because of a series of "Swift Boat" advertisements that attacked Kerry's credibility concerning his Vietnam War record. But Gallup Polls also show that even before the running of the controversial ads, the Democratic National Convention had provided no boost to Kerry—one of the few times in recent elections when a party's convention did not give the party's presidential candidate a "bounce" in the polls.

In an October 22–24, 2004, CNN/USA Today/Gallup Poll, likely voters were given a list of issues and asked to rate how important each would be in their vote for president. At least 85 percent replied that terrorism, the Iraq War, and the economy would be very important. Among these respondents, 46 percent said that terrorism would be extremely important, compared with 41 percent who said this about Iraq and 39 percent who said this about the economy.

The perception that Bush would deal better than Kerry would with terrorism undoubtedly was the decisive reason for the president's reelection.

On Election Day, November 2, 2004, President Bush received 50.7 percent of the more than 122.9 million votes cast to Kerry's 48.3 percent. Bush also prevailed in the electoral vote, 286 to 251, with one vote cast for John Edwards. Bush won reelection with the narrowest percentage of the popular vote for any incumbent president since 1916, in an election that was remarkable for an extremely polarized electorate, unprecedented campaign spending, and an extraordinarily high voter turnout. The basic patterns of the 2004 election were very similar to those of the 2000 presidential election. In only three states did a majority of voters switch their support from one party to another: New Hampshire voted for Bush in 2000 but for Kerry in 2004; New Mexico and Iowa both supported Democrat Al Gore in 2000 but gave their electoral votes to Bush in 2004. This change in outcome in only three states between two consecutive elections is the smallest change since the presidential election of 1888.

As he did in 2001, President Bush took the oath of office in front of the U.S. Capitol. Some 500,000 people traveled to downtown Washington to witness the event. Bush's second inauguration marked the fifty-fifth time that a U.S. president had been sworn in for a four-year term, in unbroken succession since 1789, when George Washington first took the same oath. As in previous inaugural ceremonies, again going back to Washington, after taking the oath, President Bush delivered an inaugural address that outlined the theme of his upcoming four years in office: promoting the advancement of liberty and human freedom throughout the world. Indeed, Bush's inaugural words linking America's ideals with national security echoed those of former presidents Woodrow Wilson, Franklin D. Roosevelt, John F. Kennedy, and Ronald Reagan—presidents who addressed the nation as they confronted two world wars and the Cold War. Now, in the face of the new peril of international terrorism, President Bush boldly restated America's ideals, not only for America, but also for the world.

Vice President Cheney, Mr. Chief Justice, President Carter, President Bush, President Clinton, reverend clergy, distinguished guests, fellow citizens:

On this day, prescribed by law and marked by ceremony, we celebrate the durable wisdom of our Constitution, and recall the deep commitments that unite our country. I am grateful for the honor of this hour, mindful of the consequential times in which we live, and determined to fulfill the oath that I have sworn and you have witnessed.

At this second gathering, our duties are defined not by the words I use, but by the history we have seen together. For a half century, America defended our own freedom by standing watch on distant borders. After the shipwreck of communism came years of relative quiet, years of repose, years of sabbatical—and then there came a day of fire.

We have seen our vulnerability—and we have seen its deepest source. For as long as whole regions of the world simmer in resentment and tyranny—prone to ideologies that feed hatred and excuse murder—violence will gather, and multiply in destructive power, and cross the most defended borders, and raise a mortal threat. There is only one force of history that can break the reign of hatred and resentment, and expose the pretensions of tyrants, and reward the hopes of the decent and tolerant, and that is the force of human freedom.

We are led, by events and common sense, to one conclusion: The survival of liberty in our land increasingly depends on the success of liberty in other lands. The best hope for peace in our world is the expansion of freedom in all the world.

America's vital interests and our deepest beliefs are now one. From the day of our Founding, we have proclaimed that every man and woman on this earth has rights, and dignity, and matchless value, because they bear the image of the Maker of Heaven and earth. Across the generations we have proclaimed the imperative of self-government, because no one is fit to be a master, and no one deserves to be a slave. Advancing these ideals is the mission that created our Nation. It is the honorable achievement of our fathers. Now it is the urgent requirement of our nation's security, and the calling of our time.

So it is the policy of the United States to seek and support the growth of democratic movements and institutions in every nation and culture, with the ultimate goal of ending tyranny in our world.

This is not primarily the task of arms, though we will defend ourselves and our friends by force of arms when necessary. Freedom, by its nature, must be chosen, and defended by citizens, and sustained by the rule of law and the protection of minorities. And when the soul of a nation finally speaks, the institutions that arise may reflect customs and traditions very different from our own. America will not impose our own style of government on the unwilling. Our goal instead is to help others find their own voice, attain their own freedom, and make their own way.

The great objective of ending tyranny is the concentrated work of generations. The difficulty of the task is no excuse for avoiding it. America's

influence is not unlimited, but fortunately for the oppressed, America's influence is considerable, and we will use it confidently in freedom's cause.

My most solemn duty is to protect this nation and its people against further attacks and emerging threats. Some have unwisely chosen to test America's resolve, and have found it firm.

We will persistently clarify the choice before every ruler and every nation: The moral choice between oppression, which is always wrong, and freedom, which is eternally right. America will not pretend that jailed dissidents prefer their chains, or that women welcome humiliation and servitude, or that any human being aspires to live at the mercy of bullies.

We will encourage reform in other governments by making clear that success in our relations will require the decent treatment of their own people. America's belief in human dignity will guide our policies, yet rights must be more than the grudging concessions of dictators; they are secured by free dissent and the participation of the governed. In the long run, there is no justice without freedom, and there can be no human rights without human liberty.

Some, I know, have questioned the global appeal of liberty—though this time in history, four decades defined by the swiftest advance of freedom ever seen, is an odd time for doubt. Americans, of all people, should never be surprised by the power of our ideals. Eventually, the call of freedom comes to every mind and every soul. We do not accept the existence of permanent tyranny because we do not accept the possibility of permanent slavery. Liberty will come to those who love it.

Today, America speaks anew to the peoples of the world:

All who live in tyranny and hopelessness can know: the United States will not ignore your oppression, or excuse your oppressors. When you stand for your liberty, we will stand with you.

Democratic reformers facing repression, prison, or exile can know: America sees you for who you are: the future leaders of your free country.

The rulers of outlaw regimes can know that we still believe as Abraham Lincoln did: "Those who deny freedom to others deserve it not for themselves; and, under the rule of a just God, cannot long retain it."

The leaders of governments with long habits of control need to know: To serve your people you must learn to trust them. Start on this journey of progress and justice, and America will walk at your side.

And all the allies of the United States can know: we honor your friendship, we rely on your counsel, and we depend on your help. Division among free nations is a primary goal of freedom's enemies. The concerted effort of free nations to promote democracy is a prelude to our enemies' defeat.

Today, I also speak anew to my fellow citizens:

From all of you, I have asked patience in the hard task of securing America, which you have granted in good measure. Our country has accepted obligations that are difficult to fulfill, and would be dishonorable to abandon. Yet because we have acted in the great liberating tradition of this nation, tens of millions have achieved their freedom. And as hope kindles hope, millions more will find it. By our efforts, we have lit a fire as well—a fire in the minds of men. It warms those who feel its power, it burns those who fight its progress, and one day this untamed fire of freedom will reach the darkest corners of our world.

A few Americans have accepted the hardest duties in this cause—in the quiet work of intelligence and diplomacy . . . the idealistic work of helping raise up free governments . . . the dangerous and necessary work of fighting our enemies. Some have shown their devotion to our country in deaths that honored their whole lives—and we will always honor their names and their sacrifice.

All Americans have witnessed this idealism, and some for the first time. I ask our youngest citizens to believe the evidence of your eyes. You have seen duty and allegiance in the determined faces of our soldiers. You have seen that life is fragile, and evil is real, and courage triumphs. Make the choice to serve in a cause larger than your wants, larger than yourself—and in your days you will add not just to the wealth of our country, but to its character.

America has need of idealism and courage, because we have essential work at home—the unfinished work of American freedom. In a world moving toward liberty, we are determined to show the meaning and promise of liberty.

In America's ideal of freedom, citizens find the dignity and security of economic independence, instead of laboring on the edge of subsistence. This is the broader definition of liberty that motivated the Homestead Act, the Social Security Act, and the G.I. Bill of Rights. And now we will extend this vision by reforming great institutions to serve the needs of our time. To give every American a stake in the promise and future of our country, we will bring the highest standards to our schools, and build an ownership society. We will widen the ownership of homes and businesses, retirement savings and health insurance—preparing our people for the challenges of life in a free society. By making every citizen an agent of his or her own destiny, we will give our fellow Americans greater freedom from want and fear, and make our society more prosperous and just and equal.

In America's ideal of freedom, the public interest depends on private character—on integrity, and tolerance toward others, and the rule of conscience in our own lives. Self-government relies, in the end, on the governing of the self. That edifice of character is built in families, supported by communities with standards, and sustained in our national life by the truths of Sinai, the Sermon on the Mount, the words of the Koran, and the varied faiths of our people. Americans move forward in every generation by reaffirming all that is good and true that came before—ideals of justice and conduct that are the same yesterday, today, and forever.

In America's ideal of freedom, the exercise of rights is ennobled by service, and mercy, and a heart for the weak. Liberty for all does not mean independence from one another. Our nation relies on men and women who look after a neighbor and surround the lost with love. Americans, at our best, value the life we see in one another, and must always remember that even the unwanted have worth. And our country must abandon all the habits of racism, because we cannot carry the message of freedom and the baggage of bigotry at the same time.

From the perspective of a single day, including this day of dedication, the issues and questions before our country are many. From the viewpoint of centuries, the questions that come to us are narrowed and few. Did our generation advance the cause of freedom? And did our character bring credit to that cause?

These questions that judge us also unite us, because Americans of every party and background, Americans by choice and by birth, are bound to one another in the cause of freedom. We have known divisions, which must be healed to move forward in great purposes—and I will strive in good faith to heal them. Yet those divisions do not define America. We felt the unity and fellowship of our nation when freedom came under attack, and our response came like a single hand over a single heart. And we can feel that same unity and pride whenever America acts for good, and the victims of disaster are given hope, and the unjust encounter justice, and the captives are set free.

We go forward with complete confidence in the eventual triumph of freedom. Not because history runs on the wheels of inevitability; it is human choices that move events. Not because we consider ourselves a chosen nation; God moves and chooses as He wills. We have confidence because freedom is the permanent hope of mankind, the hunger in dark places, the longing of the soul. When our Founders declared a new order of the ages; when soldiers died in wave upon wave for a union based on liberty; when citizens marched in peaceful outrage under the banner "Freedom Now"— they were acting on an ancient hope that is meant to be fulfilled. History has an ebb and flow of justice, but history also has a visible direction, set by liberty and the Author of Liberty.

When the Declaration of Independence was first read in public and the Liberty Bell was sounded in celebration, a witness said, "It rang as if it meant something." In our time it means something still. America, in this young century, proclaims liberty throughout all the world, and to all the inhabitants thereof. Renewed in our strength—tested, but not weary—we are ready for the greatest achievements in the history of freedom.

May God bless you, and may He watch over the United States of America.

BARACK OBAMA

INAUGURAL ADDRESS

JANUARY 20, 2009

COMMENTARY

Barack Hussein Obama was sworn in as the 44th president of the United States on January 20, 2009. It was an exciting and compelling day in American history as the first African American became the nation's chief executive 144 years after the 13th Amendment to the U.S. Constitution abolished slavery and 44 years after the Voting Rights Act outlawed disfranchisement of African Americans.

The power of the moment was captured by an impassioned evangelical invocation delivered by the Rev. Rick Warren—and a moving benediction by Joseph Lowery, an icon of the Civil Rights movement, who quoted from Lift Every Voice and Sing: *"God of our weary years; God of our silent tears." He pleaded for Americans to "make choices on the side of love, not hate, on the side of inclusion not exclusion; tolerance not intolerance." Lowery caused the new president to smile broadly with a recitation asking the Almighty to "help us work for that day when black will not be asked to get back, when brown can stick around, when yellow will be mellow, when the red man can get ahead, man, and when white will embrace what is right." Indeed, it was an emotionally charged day as the new president described himself in his 18-minute inaugural address as "a man whose father less than 60 years ago might not have been served at a local restaurant can now stand before you to take a most sacred oath."*

The new president was surrounded by his extended family, whose ethnic, racial, and religious backgrounds would have shocked past generations of Americans. Obama's 87-year-old Muslim step-grandmother, who had only recently obtained electricity and running water in her metal-roofed shack in

Kenya, came from Africa with a gift of an oxtail fly whisk, a sign of power. The president's father, Barack Sr., who died in 1982, was black. He had converted to Christianity as a young man and attended an exclusive boarding school run by the Anglican Church of Kenya. At age 23, he received a scholarship to study at the University of Hawaii. He married 18-year-old Kansas-born Stanley Ann Dunham, a fellow student who was white. Ann could trace her ancestry back to colonial America. On August 4, 1961, she gave birth to Barack Obama Jr. in Hawaii. Obama's father, who left Hawaii the next year, saw his son but one time more. President Obama has described his mother as "the dominant figure in my formative years. . . . The values she taught me continue to be my touchstone when it comes to how I go about the world of politics."

Presidents, like everyone else, are shaped by the totality of their life experiences. However, President Obama's life contains many firsts for an American president. As a child, Obama attended local elementary schools in Jakarta, Indonesia, where his mother moved after her remarriage. In 1971, Obama returned to Hawaii to live with his maternal grandparents, Madelyn and Stanley Dunham. In his 1995 autobiography, Dreams from My Father: A Story of Race and Inheritance, Obama repeatedly praised their emotional and intellectual support—they enrolled him in Punahou, a private college preparatory school in Honolulu. Obama has written extensively of his struggles to reconcile his multiracial background whereby "my father looked nothing like the people around me—that he was as black as pitch, my mother white as milk. . . . The opportunity that Hawaii offered—to experience a variety of cultures in a climate of mutual respect—became an integral part of my world view, and the basis for the values that I hold most dear."

Obama worked his way through Columbia University with the aid of scholarships and student loans. He then moved to Chicago, where he worked with church groups as a community activist to help rebuild neighborhoods wracked by poverty and devastated by the closure of a local steel plant. He subsequently attended Harvard Law School, where he became the first African-American president of the prestigious Harvard Law Review. This honor received national media attention and led to a publishing contract for a book about race relations in America. The manuscript became Dreams from My Father, a best-selling autobiography. After graduating from Harvard Law School in 1991, Obama returned to Chicago, where he worked with community groups, as a civil rights lawyer, and as a teacher of constitutional law.

Obama was elected to the Illinois Senate in 1996, and reelected in 1998 and 2002. He ran for the U.S. House of Representatives in 2000, but lost. Four years later, however, Obama ran successfully for the U.S. Senate, receiving the largest *victory margin for a statewide race in Illinois history. During his 2004 Senate campaign, Obama delivered the keynote address at the Democratic National Convention in Boston. In an electrifying speech watched by more than 9 million viewers, Obama stated: "There is not a liberal America and a conservative America: there's the United States of America." Ranking among the highpoints of the convention, Obama's speech elevated his stature and made him a rising new star in the Democratic Party.*

On February 10, 2007, Obama announced his candidacy for the Democratic presidential nomination. After a prolonged, vigorous, and close Democratic primary contest with New York senator Hillary Clinton, Obama claimed the Democratic nomination on June 3, 2008, and officially became the party's candidate when the Democratic National Convention nominated him for president on August 28. His main opponent in the general election was Republican candidate John McCain, a longtime senator from Arizona. Obama and McCain fought an extremely competitive race. The two were essentially tied in Gallup Poll matchups during much of the primary election season, from March through May 2008. Obama moved slightly ahead of McCain once he clinched the Democratic nomination in late spring. McCain then succeeded in overtaking Obama after the Republican National Convention in early September. McCain held this lead, according to the Gallup Poll, for 10 days, from September 7 through September 16. But the onset of the Wall Street financial crisis in mid-September, which prompted fears of an economic downturn, helped shift voters back into Obama's column—and this Wall Street crisis appears to have been the turning point in the campaign.

Of the 56 presidential elections in American history, the 2008 contest must rank among the most important, and perhaps the most memorable for this generation. When the campaign began in late 2006, no one could have predicted the remarkable, path-breaking events and turnabouts that would follow, concluding with Obama's election on November 4, 2008. The 2008 presidential election marked many firsts. A biracial man, Obama, and a white woman, Hillary Clinton, competed against each other for the Democratic nomination. Also, Sarah Palin was the first woman to run for vice president on the Republican Party ticket. Obama, 47 years old, became the first African American to win the nomination of a major political party. In contrast, his Republican opponent, John McCain, at age 72, was the oldest person to run for president on a major party ticket. This 25-year age difference was the widest in American history between two presidential nominees. The 2008 election also was the first in which two sitting U.S. senators ran against each other and the first in which neither presidential candidate was born in the continental United States. (Obama was born in Hawaii and McCain in the Panama Canal Zone.)

Obama owed his victory in part to extraordinarily high support from blacks. Obama also won greater support than his Democratic predecessors from highly educated voters. He attracted significant new support from middle-aged voters. In addition, far fewer voters considered themselves Republican in this election than did so in 2004. The resulting more pro-Democratic climate in the country also contributed to Obama's victory. However, certain groups aligned with each party showed predictably high support for that party's candidate. For example, most voters living in households with at least one union member backed Obama, while veterans and gun owners solidly supported McCain. Mc-Cain's principal electoral strengths were with frequent churchgoers, whites, se-niors, Protestants, and men. Obama's support came from their counterparts—non-churchgoers, blacks, younger voters, Catholics, and women. Younger voters turned out in record numbers for Obama—because of both his inspiring ora-tory and message of change, and his mastery of the latest electronic technology to convey his message to them.

The final surprise in this surprising presidential election contest was that there was no surprise on Election Day. After a year in which the major cam-paign issue had been the unpopular Iraq War, the economy became not only the top issue but virtually the only issue that concerned voters from mid-September to early November. President George W. Bush's approval ratings hit new lows, which hurt the Republican Party and candidate McCain. Discontent with eco-nomic conditions hit all-time highs, and in autumn Obama led McCain by nearly 20 points in the Gallup Poll as the candidate best able to deal with the financial crisis. Obama ultimately won fairly easily. He received 52.9 percent of the approximate 131 million votes cast to John McCain's 45.7 percent, and nine states that had voted for George W. Bush in 2004 switched to the Democratic candidate, giving Obama a sizable Electoral College victory, 365 to 173.

Inaugural Day 2009 was historic. Despite freezing cold weather, about 2 million people from every corner of the nation—and from countries overseas—filled the vast expanse between the Capitol and the Washington Monument to bear witness to the racial milestone. Jubilation and profound emotion pre-vailed; reporters noted that tears filled the eyes of an overwhelming number of viewers as they watched the event from 10 jumbo television screens situated on the National Mall. Friends of Obama said that he, too, experienced deep emo-tion, a sense of history—and a dash of disbelief—as he placed his hand on the same burgundy-bound Bible used by Abraham Lincoln in 1861.

The 35-word presidential oath of office appears in the Constitution of the United States. However, Chief Justice John Roberts, who administered the oath, muddled the words. This caused Obama to repeat the solemn promise differ-ently than prescribed in the Constitution. The new president, who retook the oath the following evening, regained his composure, grinned, acknowledged the cheering throngs—and began a somber Inaugural Address to a nation con-vulsed by the worst economic situation in decades. His serious words outlined the severe problems facing a country suddenly confronted with more than 11 million people out of work and trillions of dollars lost in the stock market's tumble. And, as with Franklin D. Roosevelt's inaugural in 1933, there was an optimistic promise: "Today I say to you that the challenges we face are real. They are serious and they are many. They will not be met easily or in a short span of time. But know this, America: They will be met." Obama's formal and austere message seemed a corrective to the celebrative mood of the day.

My fellow citizens:

I stand here today humbled by the task before us, grateful for the trust you have bestowed, mindful of the sacrifices borne by our ancestors.

I thank President Bush for his service to our nation as well as the gener-osity and cooperation he has shown throughout this transition.

Forty-four Americans have now taken the presidential oath. The words have been spoken during rising tides of prosperity and the still waters of peace. Yet, every so often, the oath is taken amidst gathering clouds and rag-ing storms. At these moments, America has carried on not simply because of the skill or vision of those in high office, but because we, the people, have remained faithful to the ideals of our forebears and true to our founding documents.

So it has been; so it must be with this generation of Americans.

That we are in the midst of crisis is now well understood. Our nation is at war against a far-reaching network of violence and hatred. Our economy is badly weakened, a consequence of greed and irresponsibility on the part of some, but also our collective failure to make hard choices and prepare the nation for a new age. Homes have been lost, jobs shed, businesses shut-tered. Our health care is too costly, our schools fail too many—and each day brings further evidence that the ways we use energy strengthen our adversaries and threaten our planet.

These are the indicators of crisis, subject to data and statistics. Less measurable, but no less profound, is a sapping of confidence across our land; a nagging fear that America's decline is inevitable, that the next gen-eration must lower its sights.

Today I say to you that the challenges we face are real. They are serious and they are many. They will not be met easily or in a short span of time. But know this, America: They will be met.

On this day, we gather because we have chosen hope over fear, unity of purpose over conflict and discord. On this day, we come to proclaim an end to the petty grievances and false promises, the recriminations and worn-out dogmas that for far too long have strangled our politics. We remain a young nation. But in the words of Scripture, the time has come to set aside childish things. The time has come to reaffirm our enduring spirit; to choose our better history; to carry forward that precious gift, that noble idea passed on from generation to generation: the God-given promise that all are equal, all are free, and all deserve a chance to pursue their full measure of happiness. In reaffirming the greatness of our nation, we understand that greatness is never a given. It must be earned. Our journey has never been one of shortcuts or settling for less. It has not been the path for the fainthearted, for those who prefer leisure over work or seek only the pleasures of riches and fame. Rather, it has been the risk-takers, the doers, the makers of things—some celebrated, but more often men and women obscure in their labor—who have carried us up the long, rugged path towards prosperity and freedom.

For us, they packed up their few worldly possessions and traveled across oceans in search of a new life. For us, they toiled in sweatshops and settled the West, endured the lash of the whip, and plowed the hard earth. For us, they fought and died in places like Concord and Gettysburg, Normandy and Khe Sahn.

Time and again these men and women struggled and sacrificed and worked till their hands were raw so that we might live a better life. They saw America as bigger than the sum of our individual ambitions, greater than all the differences of birth or wealth or faction.

This is the journey we continue today. We remain the most prosperous, powerful nation on Earth. Our workers are no less productive than when this crisis began. Our minds are no less inventive, our goods and services no less needed than they were last week, or last month, or last year. Our capacity remains undiminished. But our time of standing pat, of protecting narrow interests and putting off unpleasant decisions—that time has surely passed. Starting today, we must pick ourselves up, dust ourselves off, and begin again the work of remaking America.

For everywhere we look, there is work to be done. The state of our economy calls for action, bold and swift. And we will act, not only to create new jobs, but to lay a new foundation for growth. We will build the roads and bridges, the electric grids and digital lines that feed our commerce and bind us together. We will restore science to its rightful place, and wield technology's wonders to raise health care's quality and lower its cost. We will harness the sun and the winds and the soil to fuel our cars and run our factories. And we will transform our schools and colleges and universities to meet the demands of a new age. All this we can do. All this we will do.

Now, there are some who question the scale of our ambitions, who suggest that our system cannot tolerate too many big plans. Their memories are short, for they have forgotten what this country has already done, what free men and women can achieve when imagination is joined to common purpose, and necessity to courage. What the cynics fail to understand is that the ground has shifted beneath them, that the stale political arguments that have consumed us for so long no longer apply.

The question we ask today is not whether our government is too big or too small, but whether it works—whether it helps families find jobs at a decent wage, care they can afford, a retirement that is dignified. Where the answer is yes, we intend to move forward. Where the answer is no, programs will end. And those of us who manage the public's dollars will be held to account, to spend wisely, reform bad habits, and do our business in the light of day, because only then can we restore the vital trust between a people and their government.

Nor is the question before us whether the market is a force for good or ill. Its power to generate wealth and expand freedom is unmatched. But this crisis has reminded us that without a watchful eye, the market can spin out of control. And that a nation cannot prosper long when it favors only the prosperous. The success of our economy has always depended not just on the size of our gross domestic product, but on the reach of our prosperity, on our ability to extend opportunity to every willing heart—not out of charity, but because it is the surest route to our common good.

As for our common defense, we reject as false the choice between our safety and our ideals. Our Founding Fathers, faced with perils that we can scarcely imagine, drafted a charter to assure the rule of law and the rights of man—a charter expanded by the blood of generations. Those ideals still light the world, and we will not give them up for expedience's sake.

And so, to all the other peoples and governments who are watching today, from the grandest capitals to the small village where my father was born, know that America is a friend of each nation and every man, woman, and child who seeks a future of peace and dignity, and that we are ready to lead once more.

Recall that earlier generations faced down fascism and communism not just with missiles and tanks, but with the sturdy alliances and enduring convictions. They understood that our power alone cannot protect us, nor does it entitle us to do as we please. Instead they knew that our power grows through its prudent use; our security emanates from the justness of our cause, the force of our example, the tempering qualities of humility and restraint.

We are the keepers of this legacy. Guided by these principles once more, we can meet those new threats that demand even greater effort, even greater cooperation and understanding between nations. We will begin to responsibly leave Iraq to its people and forge a hard-earned peace in Afghanistan. With old friends and former foes, we will work tirelessly to lessen the nuclear threat, and roll back the specter of a warming planet.

We will not apologize for our way of life, nor will we waver in its defense. And for those who seek to advance their aims by inducing terror and slaughtering innocents, we say to you now that our spirit is stronger and cannot be broken—you cannot outlast us, and we will defeat you.

For we know that our patchwork heritage is a strength, not a weakness. We are a nation of Christians and Muslims, Jews and Hindus, and nonbelievers. We are shaped by every language and culture, drawn from every end of this Earth; and because we have tasted the bitter swill of civil war and segregation, and emerged from that dark chapter stronger and more united, we cannot help but believe that the old hatreds shall someday pass; that the lines of tribe shall soon dissolve; that as the world grows smaller, our common humanity shall reveal itself; and that America must play its role in ushering in a new era of peace.

To the Muslim world, we seek a new way forward, based on mutual interest and mutual respect. To those leaders around the globe who seek to sow conflict, or blame their society's ills on the West, know that your people will judge you on what you can build, not what you destroy.

To those who cling to power through corruption and deceit and the silencing of dissent, know that you are on the wrong side of history, but that we will extend a hand if you are willing to unclench your fist.

To the people of poor nations, we pledge to work alongside you to make your farms flourish and let clean waters flow; to nourish starved bodies and feed hungry minds. And to those nations like ours that enjoy relative plenty, we say we can no longer afford indifference to the suffering outside our borders, nor can we consume the world's resources without regard to effect. For the world has changed, and we must change with it.

As we consider the role that unfolds before us, we remember with humble gratitude those brave Americans who at this very hour patrol far-off deserts and distant mountains. They have something to tell us today, just as the fallen heroes who lie in Arlington whisper through the ages.

We honor them not only because they are the guardians of our liberty, but because they embody the spirit of service—a willingness to find meaning in something greater than themselves.

And yet at this moment, a moment that will define a generation, it is precisely this spirit that must inhabit us all. For as much as government can do, and must do, it is ultimately the faith and determination of the American people upon which this nation relies. It is the kindness to take in a stranger when the levees break, the selflessness of workers who would rather cut their hours than see a friend lose their job, which sees us through our darkest hours. It is the firefighter's courage to storm a stairway filled with smoke, but also a parent's willingness to nurture a child, that finally decides our fate.

Our challenges may be new. The instruments with which we meet them may be new. But those values upon which our success depends—hard work and honesty, courage and fair play, tolerance and curiosity, loyalty and patriotism—these things are old. These things are true. They have been the quiet force of progress throughout our history.

What is demanded, then, is a return to these truths. What is required of us now is a new era of responsibility—a recognition on the part of every American that we have duties to ourselves, our nation, and the world; duties that we do not grudgingly accept, but rather seize gladly, firm in the knowledge that there is nothing so satisfying to the spirit, so defining of our character, than giving our all to a difficult task.

This is the price and the promise of citizenship. This is the source of our confidence—the knowledge that God calls on us to shape an uncertain destiny. This is the meaning of our liberty and our creed, why men and women and children of every race and every faith can join in celebration across this magnificent mall; and why a man whose father less than 60 years ago might not have been served in a local restaurant can now stand before you to take a most sacred oath.

So let us mark this day with remembrance of who we are and how far we have traveled. In the year of America's birth, in the coldest of months, a small band of patriots huddled by dying campfires on the shores of an icy river. The capital was abandoned. The enemy was advancing. The snow was stained with blood. At the moment when the outcome of our revolution was most in doubt, the father of our nation ordered these words to be read to the people: "Let it be told to the future world . . . that in the depth of winter, when nothing but hope and virtue could survive . . . that the city and the country, alarmed at one common danger, came forth to meet [it]."

America: In the face of our common dangers, in this winter of our hardship, let us remember these timeless words. With hope and virtue, let us brave once more the icy currents, and endure what storms may come. Let it be said by our children's children that when we were tested, we refused to let this journey end, that we did not turn back nor did we falter; and with eyes fixed on the horizon and God's grace upon us, we carried forth that great gift of freedom and delivered it safely to future generations.

Thank you. God bless you. And God bless the United States of America.

ARTHUR M. SCHLESINGER JR. (1917–2007) was the author of more than a dozen books, including *The Age of Jackson*; *The Vital Center*; *The Age of Roosevelt* (3 vols.); *A Thousand Days: John F. Kennedy in the White House*; *Robert Kennedy and His Times*; *The Cycles of American History*; and *The Imperial Presidency*. Professor Schlesinger served as Special Assistant to President Kennedy from 1961 to 1963. His numerous awards included the Pulitzer Prize for History, the Pulitzer Prize for Biography, two National Book Awards, the Bancroft Prize, and the American Academy of Arts and Letters Gold Medal for History.

FRED L. ISRAEL is the co-author of *Winning the White House 2008: The Gallup Poll, Public Opinion, and the Presidency*. He has also written *Nevada's Key Pittman* and has edited *The War Diaries of Breckinridge Long* and *Major Peace Treaties of Modern History, 1648–2000* (6 vols.). He holds the Scribe's Award from the American Bar Association for his joint editorship of *The Justices of the United States Supreme Court* (4 vols.). For 25 years, Professor Israel compiled and edited the Gallup Poll into annual reference volumes.